Lecture Notes of the Institute for Computer Sciences, Social Informatics and Telecommunications Engineering

228

Editorial Board

Ozgur Akan
Middle East Technical University, Ankara, Turkey
Paolo Bellavista
University of Bologna, Bologna, Italy
Jiannong Cao
Hong Kong Polytechnic University, Hong Kong, Hong Kong
Geoffrey Coulson
Lancaster University, Lancaster, UK
Falko Dressler
University of Erlangen, Erlangen, Germany
Domenico Ferrari
Università Cattolica Piacenza, Piacenza, Italy
Mario Gerla
UCLA, Los Angeles, USA
Hisashi Kobayashi
Princeton University, Princeton, USA
Sergio Palazzo
University of Catania, Catania, Italy
Sartaj Sahni
University of Florida, Florida, USA
Xuemin Sherman Shen
University of Waterloo, Waterloo, Canada
Mircea Stan
University of Virginia, Charlottesville, USA
Jia Xiaohua
City University of Hong Kong, Kowloon, Hong Kong
Albert Y. Zomaya
University of Sydney, Sydney, Australia

More information about this series at http://www.springer.com/series/8197

Paulo Marques · Ayman Radwan
Shahid Mumtaz · Dominique Noguet
Jonathan Rodriguez · Michael Gundlach (Eds.)

Cognitive Radio Oriented Wireless Networks

12th International Conference, CROWNCOM 2017
Lisbon, Portugal, September 20–21, 2017
Proceedings

 Springer

Editors
Paulo Marques
Instituto de Telecomunicações
Lisbon
Portugal

Dominique Noguet
CEA-LETI
Grenoble
France

Ayman Radwan
Instituto de Telecomunicações
Lisbon
Portugal

Jonathan Rodriguez
Instituto de Telecomunicações
Lisbon
Portugal

Shahid Mumtaz
Instituto de Telecomunicações
Lisbon
Portugal

Michael Gundlach
NOKIA
Munich
Germany

ISSN 1867-8211   ISSN 1867-822X (electronic)
Lecture Notes of the Institute for Computer Sciences, Social Informatics
and Telecommunications Engineering
ISBN 978-3-319-76206-7   ISBN 978-3-319-76207-4 (eBook)
https://doi.org/10.1007/978-3-319-76207-4

Library of Congress Control Number: 2018934321

© ICST Institute for Computer Sciences, Social Informatics and Telecommunications Engineering 2018
This work is subject to copyright. All rights are reserved by the Publisher, whether the whole or part of the material is concerned, specifically the rights of translation, reprinting, reuse of illustrations, recitation, broadcasting, reproduction on microfilms or in any other physical way, and transmission or information storage and retrieval, electronic adaptation, computer software, or by similar or dissimilar methodology now known or hereafter developed.
The use of general descriptive names, registered names, trademarks, service marks, etc. in this publication does not imply, even in the absence of a specific statement, that such names are exempt from the relevant protective laws and regulations and therefore free for general use.
The publisher, the authors and the editors are safe to assume that the advice and information in this book are believed to be true and accurate at the date of publication. Neither the publisher nor the authors or the editors give a warranty, express or implied, with respect to the material contained herein or for any errors or omissions that may have been made. The publisher remains neutral with regard to jurisdictional claims in published maps and institutional affiliations.

Printed on acid-free paper

This Springer imprint is published by the registered company Springer International
Publishing AG part of Springer Nature
The registered company address is: Gewerbestrasse 11, 6330 Cham, Switzerland

Preface

We are delighted to introduce the proceedings of the 12th edition of the European Alliance for Innovation (EAI) International Conference on Cognitive Radio Oriented Wireless Networks (CROWNCOM 2017). This conference has brought together researchers, developers, and practitioners from around the world leveraging and developing new solutions that shape how cognitive radio systems will help deliver the required stringent requirements of future 5G networks. The theme of CROWNCOM 2017 was "Cognitive Radio Systems to Deliver 5G Requirements."

The technical program of CROWNCOM 2017 consisted of 28 full papers, including five invited keynote papers. The conference tracks were: Track 1 – Spectrum Management 1; Track 2 – Network Management; Track 3 – Trials, Testbeds, and Tools; Track 4 – PHY and Sensing; and Track 5 – Spectrum Management 2. Aside from the high-quality technical paper presentations, the technical program also featured five keynote speeches, four tutorial presentations, one plenary session, two demo sessions, and two technical workshops. The five keynote speakers were: Prof. Mischa Dohler (King's College, London), Jaime Afonso (ANACOM and CEPT), Jorge Pereira (European Commission), Keith Nolan (Intel Labs, Europe), and Prof. Maziar Nekovee (University of Sussex). The four tutorials were on "Disruptive Technologies for Flexible Wireless" by Aydin Sezgin and Eduard Jorswieck, "Introduction to SEAMCAT" by Rogério Dionisio, "Increasing Spectrum Efficiency" by Ingrid Moerman, and "Machine Learning for Spectrum Sharing" by Suzan Bayhan and Gürkan Gür.

The two workshops organized were: H2020 FIRE+ Workshop on Radio Access Experimentation and the 5G Spectrum Workshop. The H2020 FIRE+ Workshop brought together five FIRE+ projects on radio access technologies. The presentations addressed the role of experimentally driven research for validating innovative developments on cognitive networks and spectrum-sharing paradigms. The five projects are "ORCA" presented by Ingrid Moerna (IMEC), "eWINE" by Eli De Poorter (IMEC), "FUTEBOL" by Aho Pekka (VTT), "TRIANGLE" by Ricardo Figueiredo (Redzinc), and "MONROE" by Andar Lutu (Simula). The 5G Spectrum Workshop addressed evolving challenges in spectrum access, utilization, allocation, management, as well as validation and experimental results produced so far. The presentations were by Prof. Klaus Moessner (University of Surrey) on the "SPEED5G" project, Dr. Miquel Payaro (CTTC) on "Flex5Gware," Dr. Mythri Hunukumbure (Samsung) on the challenges and opportunities for using mmWave spectrum for mobile communications, and Mr. Scott Blue (Dynamic Spectrum Alliance) on the "Wi-Five G" project.

It was a great pleasure to work with excellent teams. We sincerely appreciate the efforts of the chairs and members of the Steering, Organizing, and Technical Program Committees for their hard work in organizing and supporting the conference, and in completing the peer-review process of technical papers for a high-quality technical program. We are also grateful to the conference coordinator, Monika Szabova (EAI), for her support and to all the authors who submitted their papers to the CROWNCOM 2017 conference and workshops.

We strongly believe that CROWNCOM provides a good forum for all researchers, developers, and practitioners to discuss all aspects of science and technology that are relevant to cognitive networks. We also expect that future CROWNCOM conferences will be as successful and stimulating as this year's event, as indicated by the contributions presented in this volume.

January 2018

Paulo Marques
Ayman Radwan
Shahid Mumtaz
Dominique Noguet
Jonathan Rodriguez
Michael Gundlach

Organization

Steering Committee

Imrich Chlamtac	Create-Net, Italy
Thomas Hou	Virginia Tech, USA
Abdur Rahim Biswas	Create-Net, Italy
Tao Chen	VTT - Technical Research Centre of Finland, Finland
Tinku Rasheed	CREATE-NET, Italy
Athanasios Vasilakos	Kuwait University, Kuwait
Dominique Noguet	CEA-LETI, France

Organizing Committee

General Chair

Paulo Marques   Instituto de Telecomunicações, Portugal

Technical Program Committee Chairs

Dominique Noguet	CEA-LETI, France
Jonathan Rodriguez	Instituto de Telecomunicações, Portugal
Leonardo Goratti	Create-Net, Italy
Shahid Mumtaz	Instituto de Telecomunicações, Portugal
Michael Gundlach	NOKIA, Germany

Publicity and Social Media Chairs

Muttukrishnan Rajarajan	City University of London, UK
Youping Zhao	Beijing Jiaotong University, China

Publication Chair

Ayman Radwan   Instituto de Telecomunicações, Portugal

Panel Chair

Klaus Moessner   University of Surrey, UK

Workshop Chair

Panagiotis Demestichas   University of Pireaus, Greece

Tutorial Chairs

Luiz da Silva	Trinity College Dublin, Ireland
Eduard Jorswieck	TU Dresden, Germany

Sponsorship and Exhibit Chair

Hugo Marques   Instituto de Telecomunicações, Portugal

Demonstration Chairs

Sofie Pollin   KU Leuven, Belgium
Rogério Dionísio   Instituto Politécnico de Castelo Branco, Portugal

Posters and PhD Track Chair

Filipe Pinto   ALTICE LABS, Portugal

Keynote Chair

Pravir Chawdhry   European Commission

Local Chairs

Claudia Barbosa   Instituto de Telecomunicações, Portugal
Joaquim Bastos   Instituto de Telecomunicações, Portugal

Web Chair

Hugo Marques   Instituto de Telecomunicações, Portugal

Conference Coordinator

Monika Szabova   EAI (European Alliance for Innovation)

Technical Program Committee

Hamed Ahmadi   University College Dublin, Ireland
Adnan Aijaz   Toshiba Research European Labs, UK
Ozgur Barış   Akan Koc University, Turkey
Anwer Al-Dulaimi   University of Toronto, Canada
Mackenzie Allen   Virginia Tech, USA
Osama Amin   KAUST, Saudi Arabia
Masayuki Ariyoshi   NEC, Japan
Bernd Bochow   Fraunhofer FOKUS, Germany
Carlos E. Caicedo   Syracuse University, USA
Liu Cui   West Chester University, USA
Antonio De Domenico   CEA-LETI, France
Jean-Philippe Delahaye   DGA-MI, France
Panagiotis Demestichas   University of Piraeus, Greece
Luca De-Nardis   University of Rome La Sapienza, Italy
Marco Di-Felice   University of Bologna, Italy
Rogério Dionisio   Instituto Politecnico de Castelo Branco, Portugal
Jean-Baptiste Doré   CEA-LETI, France
Marc Emmelmann   Fraunhofer FOKUS, Germany

Ozgur Ergul	Koc University, Turkey
Stanislav Filin	National Institute of Information and Communications Technology, Japan
Takeo Fujii	University of Electro-Communications, Japan
Piotr Gajewski	Military University of Technology, Poland
Yue Gao	Queen Mary University of London, UK
Matthieu Gautier	IRISA, France
Andrea Giorgetti	WiLAB, University of Bologna, Italy
Jean-Marie Gorce	INSA, France
David Grace	University of York, UK
Michael Gundlach	Nokia, Germany
Periklis Chatzimisios Alexander	TEI of Thessaloniki, Greece
Pravir Chawdhry	Joint Research Center EC, Italy
Moy Christophe	CentraleSupélec Rennes, France
Florian Kaltenberger	Eurecom, France
Pawel Kaniewski	Military Communications Institute, Poland
Mika Kasslin	Nokia, Finland
Seong-Lyun Kim	Yonsei University, South Korea
Adrian Kliks	Poznan University of Technology, Poland
Heikki Kokkinen	Fairspectrum, Finland
Kimon Kontovasilis	NCSR Demokritos, Greece
Pawel Kryszkiewicz	Poznan University of Technology, Poland
Samson Lasaulce	L2S-CNRS, France
Vincent Le Nir	Royal Military Academia, Belgium
Didier Le Ruyet	CNAM, France
William Lehr	MIT, USA
Janne Lehtomäki	University of Oulu, Finland
Dan Lubar	Relay Services, USA
Irene Macaluso	Trinity College Dublin, Ireland
Paulo Marques	Instituto de Telecomunicações, Portugal
Hugo Marques	Instituto de Telecomunicações, Portugal
Johann Marques – Barja	Trinity College Dublin, Ireland
Petri Mähönen	RWTH Aachen University, Germany
Arturas Medeisis	ITU Representative, Saudi Arabia
Albena Mihovska	Aalborg University, Denmark
Benoit Miscopein	CEA-LETI, France
Ingrid Moerman	UGent/iMinds, Belgium
Altamimi Mohammed	Communications and IT Commission, Saudi Arabia
Markus Mueck	INTEL, Gemany
James Neel	Cognitive Radio Technologies, USA
Dominique Noguet	CEA-LETI, France
Keith Nolan	Intel, Ireland
Rodolfo Oliveira	Universidade Nova de Lisboa, Portugal
Milica Pejanovic-Djurisic	University of Montenegro, Montenegro
Aho Pekka	VTT, Finland

Jordi Pérez-Romero	UPC, Spain
Sofie Polin	KU Leuven, Belgium
Zhijin Qin	Queen Mary University of London, UK
Olav Queseth	Ericsson, Sweden
Igor Radusinovic	University of Montenegro, Montenegro
Ayman Radwan	Instituto de Telecomunicações, Portugal
Mubashir Rehmani	Pierre and Marie Curie University, France
Tanguy Risset	INSA Lyon, France
Jonathan Rodriguez	Instituto de Telecomunicações, Portugal
Henning Sanneck	Nokia Networks, Germany
Shahriar Shahabuddin	University of Oulu, Finland
Isabelle Siaud	b-com, France
Carlos Silva	Universidade Federal do Ceara, Brazil
Adão Silva	Instituto de Telecomunicações, Portugal
Chen Sun	Sony, China
Hongjian Sun	Durham University, UK
Dionysia Triantafyllopoulou	University of Surrey, UK
Theodoros Tsiftsis	Industrial Systems Institute, Greece
Anna Vizziello	University of Pavia, Italy
Gerhard Wunder	Fraunhofer HHI, Germany
Seppo Yrjölä	Nokia, Finland
Jens Zander	KTH, Sweden
Yonghong Zeng	I2R A-STAR, Singapore
Hans-Jürgen Zepernick	Blekinge Institute of Technology, Sweden
Youping Zhao	Beijing Jiaotong University, China

Contents

Invited Papers

Main Track

Network Resource Trading: Locating the Contract Sweet Spot for the Case of Dynamic and Decentralized Non-broker Spectrum Sharing

Robert Schmidt[✉], Arash Toyser, Siddharth Naik, Janis Nötzel,
and Eduard A. Jorswieck

Chair of Communications Theory, Technische Universität Dresden,
01062 Dresden, Germany
{robert.schmidt,arash.toyser,siddharth.naik,janis.notzel,
eduard.jorswieck}@tu-dresden.de, siddharth.naik@frequencytrading.com

Abstract. This paper aims to present a framework for analysing network resource trading between operators. We present the results for the case of orthogonal inter-operator spectrum sharing as a sub-case of the network resource trading between operators.

A two-operator, two-cell scenario has been considered. Operators share bandwidth orthogonally using standard LTE technology, detailed in the paper. An operator can post resources to a local market (neighbouring cells) for trading them with other operators. We were interested in identifying the duration of the resource trading contracts for trading, which would provide throughput gains. Simulations show up to 30% increase of user throughput and a more efficient use of spectrum if we do not consider any monetary cost or value in the model. In a separate idealised scenario, throughput gains of up to 80% are reported.

Keywords: Resource trading · Spectrum sharing · Inter-operator Micro-trading · LTE

1 Introduction

During the last years, there has been a tremendous growth in mobile communications traffic. Alone in the period 2015–2020, mobile traffic is believed to multiply eightfold [3]. Spectrum scarcity is commonly seen as on of the main problems arising from this development. Recent reports [5] substantiate this perspective and explain countermeasures against the "mobile data crunch" that followed the success of data driven mobile services. Among those measures are improvement of spectral efficiency, network densification and increase of available bandwith. Such observations have led to technological developments and deployments like e.g. Long-Term Evolution (LTE) or LTE-Advanced [5,17]. Increasing numbers of network cells and the allocation of higher frequency bands introduce new

© ICST Institute for Computer Sciences, Social Informatics and Telecommunications Engineering 2018
P. Marques et al. (Eds.): CROWNCOM 2017, LNICST 228, pp. 3–14, 2018.
https://doi.org/10.1007/978-3-319-76207-4_1

complications and opportunities since the coverage area of cells operated in these higher bands is reduced [16]. However, these developments and processes involve dealing with significant legal hurdles and require international harmonization. As a consequence of these multiple developments, the concept of spectrum sharing is on the verge of becoming a normality rather than the exception. This perspective is backed up by recent developments such as e.g. the decision of the British regulator Ofcom to allow spectrum sharing in the 3.8 and 4.2 GHz bands [13,14], and has been taken on by GSMA and operators as well [6,12]. The focus of this introduction is the European market, but the trends are identical on the entire globe.

Technically however a lot of the work still has to be done, and it seems due time to address some of the problems coming especially with dynamic spectrum trading in more detail. A number of previous works addressed open problems via extensive simulations. It was shown that high gains can be achieved and spectrum sharing is possible with state of the art technology [9]. Furthermore, fairness [7] and quality of service (QoS) improvements [11] are possible. Many of these simulations are performed with a varying degree of realism. For instance, the assignment of spectrum is often modeled unrealistically or with knowledge about user behavior that can never be matched in reality. We address this short-coming.

In this paper, we consider two operators serving their users in the same geographical area. Adjacent base stations use a market in the vicinity to trade resources. The market has no authority over the base stations. Many local markets might exist, but we omit the question of which base stations trade through which markets which poses its own technical challenges. Here we assume that base station have been already connected to the correct local market. The base stations measure the load that is caused by the users. The core idea is to sell resources when the base station has or predicts low load and buy resources otherwise for a certain duration and a certain price.

In a simulation campaign, we consider a single file download service and measure the time to empty the base station buffer as a load indicator. Using this simple model, we study the effect of the duration of spectrum trades. The duration of the trade is of special interest, as financial considerations and planning play a vital role in the dimensioning of a network. Spectrum sharing is a special case in which all prices of trades are set to zero, e.g. by agreements between operators. We don't consider any prices at this point to remove the effect of the operator's budget or other economical constraints and concentrate on the achievable gains when operators share for short durations. It is also assumed that both parties in the trade are honest and employ the same strategy for the trades. Apart from this technical restriction in the simulations, the approach that we lay out here marks a change from the classical approaches of spectrum sharing [18] towards a micro-trading approach [10]. In some classical approaches, the primary user can interrupt the secondary user which is not possible here. In the micro-trading approach, a central market is used to perform auctions; here, we envisage local markets for fast trades. We believe that even in the same busy hours, the traffic experienced at different base stations is not homogenous and thus short trades in the order of seconds or smaller will increase the data rates of the users.

We are aware that we only skim the surface for a true spectrum sharing architecture. In particular, the technical challenges of the suggested sub-system and its requirements need to be analysed in more detail. This however is out of the scope of this paper. We only show a first assessment of the gain using the proposed model and stress that there is a case for it.

The paper is structured as follows. In Sect. 2, the system definition is outlined and our architecture for a preliminary spectrum sharing implementation as well as an idealized system are introduced. Section 3 describes the heuristic trading algorithm and its parameter choice. Section 4 outlines our system-level simulation approach and Sect. 5 evaluates the performance of the realistic implementation and compares it to the results of the idealized system. Section 6 finally concludes the paper.

2   System Description and Definitions

The system is depicted in Fig. 1. In the following we consider two operators $i \in \{A, B\}$ with each operating one evolved Node B (eNodeB) serving some users UE_{ij}, $j = 1, \ldots, K_i$. The number of available resource blocks (RBs) in the Downlink (DL) is N. Each operator owns a part of the spectrum of n_i RBs, $n_i < N$, $n_i \in \mathbb{N}_+$. A gap of n_g RBs between both spectra is modeled as the guard band, i.e. the operators' operating bands are not necessarily adjacent. The whole spectrum satisfies:

$$n_A + n_B + n_g = N. \tag{1}$$

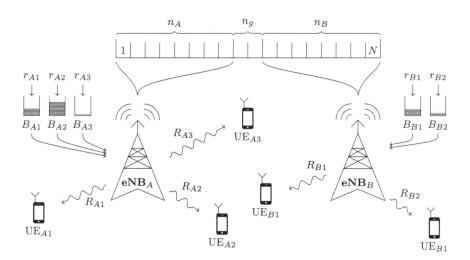

Fig. 1. The system model for the considered spectrum trading scenario.

At each time instant t, each operator serves a number of users $K_i(t) = K_i$ in its cell. For ease of notation and without loss of generality, the parameter t is omitted. The sum of all users in the system is $K = K_A + K_B$.

Data arrives at the eNodeB with a rate r_{ij} from a remote server (not displayed) and fills a buffer with buffer level B_{ij} and of finite size. The network between the eNodeBs and the remote server is assumed to be dimensioned such that it does not present a bottleneck in the simulations. The eNodeBs send this data to the corresponding User Equipment (UEs) with a rate $R_{ij} \ll r_{ij}$, as shown in Fig. 1.

More generally, let $\mathcal{M}_i \subset \mathbb{R}_{++}^{K_i \times M}$ be a set of measurements of one base station with M the number of measurements performed per user. For instance, the rates R_{ij} constitute the set $\mathcal{R}_i \subset \mathbb{R}_+^{K_i} \subset \mathcal{M}_i$ and $B_{ij} \in \mathcal{M}_i$.

We use a finite-buffer traffic model to model the user behaviour. In this model, users only have bursts of data when they access the system. This corresponds better to a real system than a typical full-buffer model, in which users constantly receive and send data. The considered performance metric is the DL throughput per user.

In the following, we only consider the DL. Two implementations for spectrum trading are investigated:

1. a practical spectrum trading implementation
2. a hypothetical implementation merging the operators.

The hypothetical implementation serves as an upper bound for our practical spectrum trading scenario.

In the considered practical implementation, two cells change the bandwidth on which they operate (cf. Fig. 2). Assume operator A to be in the need of additional spectrum. It might get this from operator B provided this one wants to trade its resources. If they exchange n RBs, $n \in \mathbb{N}$, operator A's bandwidth increases to $n'_A = n_A + n$ and B's bandwidth decreases to $n'_B = n_B - n$. This change happens for a previously determined duration t_D. During this time, (1) becomes

$$n_A + n_B + n_g = N = n'_A + n'_B + n_g. \qquad (2)$$

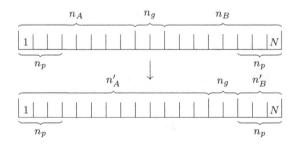

Fig. 2. A practical spectrum trading system: two operators exchange spectrum by increasing or decreasing their bandwidth.

Additionally, in Fig. 2, the extreme case of operator A buying as much spectrum from operator B as possible is shown. The latter gives all resources away except for some protected bands $n'_B = n_p$ which it maintains for QoS reasons.

The trading of resources happens on a market in the vicinity, shown in Fig. 3. An eNodeB tries to buy and sell spectrum according to its needs. Selling of spectrum is done via an "offer".

Definition 1 (Offer). *An offer O is a tuple $(t_s, t_D, n, p_0, p_1, p_2)$ including the start time $t_s \in \mathbb{R}_+$ of a potential spectrum trade, the duration $t_D \in \mathbb{R}_+$, and the number of exchanged resources $n \in \mathbb{N}_+$. p_0 is the posting price on the market, p_1 the consumption price (i.e. when buying) and p_2 the break-clause price. For spectrum sharing, we have $p_0 = p_1 = p_2 = 0$. The expiration time $t_{ex} = t_s + t_D$ is implicit.*

When a base station measures low load, it sends an offer of resources to the market. The functionality of selling and buying is ensured by a subsystem called the "negotiator", present in every base station that participates in the trading of resources.

Definition 2 (Negotiator). *Let $D \in \{-1, 1, 0\}$ be a choice to buy, sell or to not trade spectrum, respectively. Then, for some measurements $\mathcal{M}_i$ and offers $O_1, \ldots, O_L$, the negotiator N_i of a base station of the operator $i \in \{A, B\}$ is a choice function $N_i : (\mathcal{M}_i, O_1, \ldots, O_L) \to D$ that decides whether resources need to be bought or sold on the market.*

Practically, it collects data from the eNodeB (like current data buffer level, DL throughput and so on), evaluates the current offers and decides about the acquisition or sale of resources. Communication is performed directly with the local market, as shown in Fig. 3.

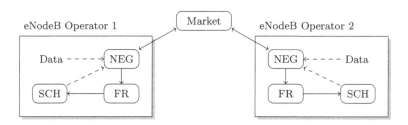

Fig. 3. The general structure of the spectrum trading architecture. NEG is the negotiator, FR the frequency reuse algorithm, and SCH the scheduler.

The market distributes a received offer O to the other negotiator. By applying the negotiator function, a buying decision can be made. In this case, it sends a message back to the market which then acknowledges this trade (if certain constraints like correct timing are met).

Definition 3 (Contract/Trade). *A contract or trade is an offer* O *by a nego-tiator of operator* $i \in \{A, B\}$ *that has been acknowledged by another operators's negotiator* $j \in \{A, B\}, j \neq i$.

At t_s, both eNodeBs change their used spectrum as indicated in the contract. It is assumed that both operators are fair. The sequence of events of a contract is shown in Fig. 4.

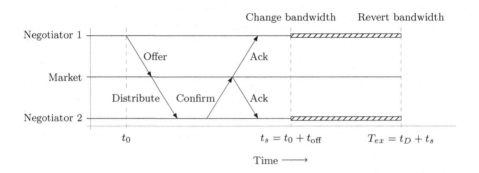

Fig. 4. The timeline of a trade, i.e. one negotiator puts resources on the market which the second accepts.

A negotiator can revoke a previously sent offer. In this case, the first reaction after the initial offer (own revocation or foreign confirmation) is determinant. The market acknowledges every event as well as the expiration of an offer.

Changes in the bandwidth on which to operate are applied via a modified Frequency Reuse (FR) algorithm. This in turn limits the scheduler of the LTE system to some of the available RBs.

Using a hypothetical spectrum sharing scenario (cf. Fig. 5), the maximum gain of spectrum sharing is investigated. Two cells share the spectrum orthogonally, each having the same amount of spectrum ($n_A = n_B$) and no guard bands are modeled ($n_g = 0$). This first scenario constitutes the no spectrum sharing scenario.

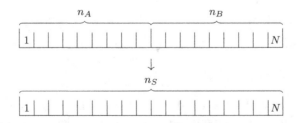

Fig. 5. Spectrum sharing in an ideal system using an single meta-operator (SMO).

The SMO constitutes the hypothetical spectrum sharing counterpart, using bandwidth n_S.

Definition 4 (Single Meta-operator). *Let A, B be two operators with users K_A, K_B and spectrum n_A, n_B. The SMO is the union of the operators, i.e. an operator serving all users $K = K_A + K_B$ on all resources $n_S = n_A + n_B$.*

Both operators A and B merge into one operator with one eNodeB. (1) becomes

$$n_A + n_B = n_S = N. \tag{3}$$

3   Trading Algorithm

The negotiator implements the driving trading algorithm. As already stated in Definition 2, a superset of the (practical) resource allocation can be the input of the choice function. An example of the (practical) resource allocation is the DL cell throughput. Additionally, the (theoretically) available resources can be taken into account. An example is the spectrum that might be bought. Moreover, the negotiator can use further knowledge at the base station, like priorities, buffer levels, historical data on user distribution, traffic demand, and so on.

Upon a decision, the negotiator communicates with the market. This was already shown in Fig. 3.

Our implementation is based on a simple heuristic. We use the buffered data of all users $B_i = B_i(k)$ at discrete time k as well as the current DL cell throughput $\tilde{R}_i = \tilde{R}_i(k)$

$$B_i = \sum_{j=1}^{N_i} B_{ij}, \quad \tilde{R}_i = \sum_{j=1}^{N_i} R_{ij}, \quad i \in \{A, B\}, \quad j = 1, \ldots, N_i \tag{4}$$

as eNodeB measurements $\mathcal{M}_i \supset \{B_{ij}, R_{ij}\}$. The throughput is smoothed using an exponential moving average of the form $R_i(k) = (1 - \alpha)R_i(k - 1) + \alpha\tilde{R}_i(k)$.

Then, it is possible to calculate an estimate of the time it takes to send all buffered data to all users, the Estimated Time to Empty Buffers (ETEB). It is, in seconds:

$$\text{ETEB}_i = \frac{B_i}{R_i}, \quad i \in \{A, B\}. \tag{5}$$

Two thresholds t_{sell} and t_{buy} are used to parameterize the algorithm. If we have a low load such that $\text{ETEB}_i < t_{\text{sell}} < t_{\text{buy}}$, the negotiator offers RBs on the market. If the load is very high, $t_{\text{sell}} < t_{\text{buy}} < \text{ETEB}_i$, the negotiator should try to buy spectrum on the market. If $t_{\text{sell}} \le \text{ETEB}_i \le t_{\text{buy}}$, the negotiator does nothing and revokes possibly sent offers that are still on the market.

The thresholds have been chosen by evaluating the ETEB in a no sharing case. The empirical probability of the load indicator depending on the user arrival process, we fixed it as described in Sect. 4.

The resulting histogram is shown in Fig. 6. Zeroes are suppressed to improve readability. The choice of the thresholds is arbitrary. We opted to "tolerate" the

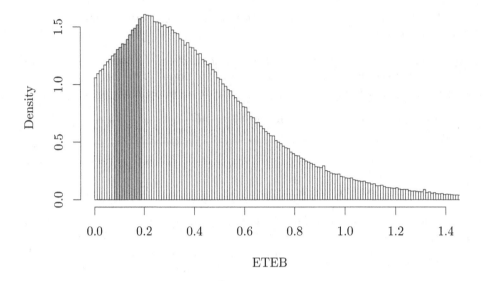

Fig. 6. The histogram of the ETEB of multiple simulation runs.

lower 10% of load during which the negotiator still tries to sell spectrum. For $t_{\text{sell}} < 0.09\,\text{s}$, we measure 10.5%. Another 15% of load above the selling threshold is "tolerated" without selling or buying spectrum (grayed region in Fig. 6). The upper 75% ($t_{\text{buy}} > 0.19\,\text{s}$) are defined as a load that could potentially be remedied by buying spectrum if possible.

The negotiator evaluates these thresholds on a periodic basis and performs the aforementioned actions depending on the outcome of the heuristic.

4   System-Level Simulation Description

For the evaluation of the described system, we used the simulator ns-3 [8] in version 3.26. ns-3 is a modular system-level simulator. It provides modules to simulate all layers from physical to application layer and also includes an LTE module [15]. We extended the simulator to support our architecture as described in Sect. 2 as well as the 3rd Generation Partnership Project (3GPP) FTP model 1, adapted from the publicly available ns-3 License-Assisted Access (LAA) Wi-Fi coexistence module[1].

The parameters of the considered scenario are listed in Table 1.

The scenario consists of two base stations located at the origin of the coordinate system. Ten mobile terminals are attached to each base station, initially uniformly distributed in the circular cell of radius $R = 800\,\text{m}$. They move within the cell according to a Random Waypoint Model that selects the next point by the same uniform distribution and to which they move with $3\,\text{km}\,\text{h}^{-1}$ without halting.

---

[1] The source can be found at http://code.nsnam.org/laa/ns-3-lbt.

Table 1. General system parameters for the practical spectrum sharing case.

Parameter	Value
1st DL sub channel frequency	1805 MHz (EARFCN 1200)
Aggregate channel bandwidth	10 MHz (50 RBs)
Subcarrier bandwidth	15 kHz
Resource block bandwidth	180 kHz
eNOdeB DL transmit power	43 dBm over 50 RBs
Pathloss, in dB	$15.3 + 37.6 \log d$, d in m
Fading	Trace-based typical urban, $3 \, \text{km} \, \text{h}^{-1}$ [2, ETU]
Frame duration	10 ms
TTI (sub-frame duration)	1 ms
Scheduler	Proportional fair scheduler
FR algorithm	Modified hard frequency reuse
Radio link control (RLC) mode	Unacknowledged Mode (UM)
Traffic model	FTP model 1 [1]
User arrival rate λ	$1.5 \, \text{s}^{-1}$
Download file size S	550444 B
Cell radius r_o	800 m
Simulation duration	1100 s
Simulation runs	50 per campaign

Each cell operates on a bandwidth of 5 MHz, divided into 25 RBs. The used traffic model is derived from the 3GPP FTP 1 traffic model from 3GPP TR 36.814 [1]. In [1], files of size 512 kB are sent. In our simulations, we don't use retransmissions except for HARQ. In particular, we use the RLC UM mode and UDP as the transport protocol. Therefore, we chose to send files of size $S = 550\,444$ B and calculate the statistics by only considering files which reach a threshold of received data $S_{\text{rx,min}} = 512\,000$ B.

Furthermore, only the flows which started after 100 s simulated time, belonging to the "steady state", are used for further processing. We argue that after this time, every user has started to download at least one file and the simulation is not in an artificial start-up phase that does not directly stem from the user-arrival process. In fact, we have a Poisson process with intensity $\lambda = \frac{1}{\mathbb{E}[\tau]}$ with τ being the inter-arrival time (the same distribution for all inter-arrival times τ_i, $i = 1, 2, \ldots$, is assumed). Then, the time so that all users started a download can be roughly estimated $T_{all} = n\mathbb{E}[\tau] = \frac{n}{\lambda}$. For the user arrival rate $\lambda = 1.5 \, \text{s}^{-1}$ and 10 users as used in the simulations, the last user can be expected to have started a download after on average 6.66 s. 100 s settling time is thus completely justified.

The user arrival rate λ is calculated as [1, A.2.1.3.4]:

$$\text{offered traffic} = \lambda \cdot S. \tag{6}$$

Considering that the peak rate of an LTE system is around 300 Mbps for a bandwidth of 20 MHz and 4 layers [4], a rate of 18.75 Mbps is the theoretical peak rate in the considered scenario per cell. We choose a user arrival rate of $\lambda = 1.5$ s^{-1} resulting in an offered traffic of approx. 6.6 Mbps. This amounts to a reasonable average load while leaving some free capacity in the system.

The duration of a flow is defined as the time between sending the first packet $t_{1,\text{tx}}$ and receiving the last packet m at time $t_{m,\text{rx}}$. For a user receiving S_{rx} B of data, the DL user throughput, also called the User Perceived Throughput (UPT) [1] is calculated as

$$\text{UPT} = \frac{S_{\text{rx}}}{t_{m,\text{rx}} - t_{1,\text{tx}}}. \tag{7}$$

The time t_{off}, i.e. the duration between posting an offer and its expiration, is fixed to 5 ms, and we neglect any market communication time. The negotiator always proposes the maximum number of resources, i.e. 6 RBs are reserved as protected bands for QoS reasons and the rest is traded. No prices are considered.

5   System-Level Assessment

We are interested in the dependency of the throughput gain as a function of the contract length t_D. Furthermore, we compare the performance of the spectrum sharing implementation to the SMO. The results are shown in Fig. 7.

For the 95%-ile[2], we see clear gains. For the SMO implementation, we measure a gain of 80%, which is in line with previous works.

Depending on the contract duration, various gains are reported. Gains are higher for the shorter contract durations. This comes as no surprise as a base station will be able to get its resources back quickly. However, short contracts have the drawback of a more frequent reselling of resources, putting additional load on the backbone network through increased signaling, an effect which is not modeled here.

A contract duration decrease from 200 to 100 ms offers no significant advantage. In these cases, we find notable gains of 35%. The gains shrinks to the half for 660 ms. With increasing duration, the gains get smaller until eventually becoming negative for long durations. For the duration $t_D = 660$ ms $\approx \frac{1}{\lambda}$, equivalent to the average inter-arrival time, we still have a considerable gain.

For contract durations longer than $t_D = 1320$ ms $\approx \frac{2}{\lambda}$, losses for the 95%-ile start to emerge. For these contract durations, base stations are not able to adapt to changes in the system fast enough.

---

[2] We use this 95%-ile similar to the 95%-ile of a full buffer traffic model, i.e. as a rate that every user achieves that is served by the base station in this cell.

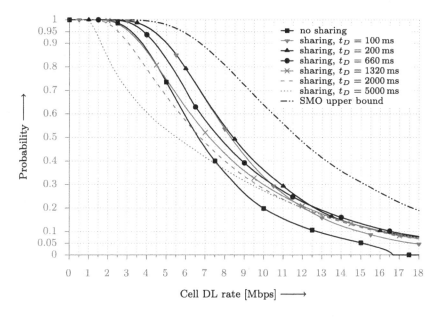

Fig. 7. UPT of a user depending on the duration of a contract t_D.

6   Conclusion

The contribution of this paper is two-fold. We first presented our generalized understanding of resource trading in a mobile communications network under the assumption of two co-primary network operators. Resource trading incorporates the notion of prices. Non-cooperative game theoretic frameworks could thus be used to model also the financial aspects of the different parties. We specialized this notion to a spectrum sharing scenario that makes no assumptions about the user behavior and trades resources on a local market and without common knowledge.

Second, we investigated the gains of this spectrum sharing system in presence of different contract durations. Simulations showed a hypothetical gain in throughput of 80%. Using a simple heuristic, gains of 30% are easily achieved. A trade duration of approximately the average inter-arrival time of the user arrival process shows high gains which incurs lower load in the backhaul network than a more frequent renegotiation.

Further work will concentrate on the following points. First, we want to investigate the QoS improvements of our spectrum sharing implementation. Second, an advanced trading algorithm making use of prediction and game theory is envisaged to improve the performance and incorporate prices.

Acknowledgements. This work was funded by the BMWi and ESF, grant 03EFHSN102 (AT, SN, JN).

We thank the Center for Information Services and High Performance Computing (ZIH) at TU Dresden for generous allocations of computer time.

References

1. 3GPP TR 36.814 Further advancements for E-UTRA physical layer aspects. Technical report, 3rd Generation Partnership Project (2010)
2. 3GPP TS 36.104 Base Station (BS) radio transmission and reception. Technical specification, 3rd Generation Partnership Project (2010)
3. Cisco Visual Networking Index: Global Mobile Data Traffic Forecast Update, 2015–2020. White Paper, Cisco Inc. (2016)
4. Dahlman, E., Parkvall, S., Sköld, J.: 4G LTE/LTE-Advanced for Mobile Broadband. Elsevier, Oxford (2011)
5. GSMA-Mobile Spectrum - Data demand explained. GSM Association (2015)
6. Best practice in mobile spectrum licensing. GSM Association (2016)
7. Guidolin, F., Carpin, M., Badia, L., Zorzi, M.: Fairness evaluation of practical spectrum sharing techniques in LTE networks. In: 2014 IEEE Symposium on Computers and Communications, pp. 1–6. IEEE Press, New York (2014)
8. Henderson, T.R., Lacage, M., Riley, G.F.: Network simulations with the ns-3 simulator. SIGCOMM Demonstr. **14**, 527 (2008)
9. Jorswieck, E.A., Badia, L., Fahldieck, T., Karipidis, E., Luo, J.: Spectrum sharing improves the network efficiency for cellular operators. IEEE Commun. Mag. **52**(3), 129–136 (2014)
10. MacKenzie, R., Briggs, K., Gronsund, P., Lehne, P.H.: Spectrum micro-trading for mobile operators. IEEE Wirel. Commun. **20**(6), 6–13 (2013)
11. Middleton, G., Hooli, K., Tolli, A., Lilleberg, J.: Inter-operator spectrum sharing in a broadband cellular network. In: 2006 IEEE Ninth International Symposium on Spread Spectrum Techniques and Applications, pp. 376–380. IEEE Press, New York (2006)
12. Obiodu, E., Giles, M.: The 5G era: age of boundless connectivity and intelligent automation. GSM Assocation (2017)
13. The future role of spectrum sharing for mobile and wireless data services. Statement, Ofcom (2014)
14. 3.8 GHz to 4.2 GHz band: Opportunities for Innovation. Call for Input, Ofcom (2016)
15. Piro, G., Baldo, N., Miozzo, M.: An LTE module for the ns-3 network simulator. In: Proceedings of the 4th International ICST Conference on Simulation Tools and Techniques, pp. 415–422. ICST, Brussels (2011)
16. Ramsdale, P.A.: The Impact of New Spectrum Management Methods on Mobile Radio Engineering. Spectrum Trading Associates (2004)
17. Sesia, S., Toufik, I., Baker, M. (eds.): LTE – The UMTS Long Term Evolution: From Theory to Practice. Wiley, Hoboken (2009)
18. Tehrani, R.H., Vahid, S., Triantafyllopoulou, D., Lee, H., Moessner, K.: Licensed spectrum sharing schemes for mobile operators: a survey and outlook. IEEE Commun. Surv. Tutor. **18**(4), 2591–2623 (2016)

Meet an Fantastic Sibyl: A Powerful Model in Cognitive Radio Networks

Wei Yang$^{(\boxtimes)}$, Xiaojun Jing, and Hai Huang

School of Information and Communication Engineering,
Beijing University of Posts and Telecommunications, Beijing 100876, China
{yangweibupt, jxiaojun, huanghai}@bupt.edu.cn

Abstract. Dynamic spectrum access is challenging, since an individual secondary user usually just has limited sensing abilities. One key insight is that primary user emergence forecasting among secondary users can help to make the most of the inherent association structure in both time and space, it also enables users to obtain more informed spectrum opportunities. Therefore, primary user presence forecasting is vital to cognitive radio networks (CRNs). With this insight, an auto regressive enhanced primary user emergence reasoning (AR-PUER) model for the occurrence of primary user prediction is derived in this paper. The proposed method combines linear prediction and primary user emergence reasoning. Historical samples are selected to train the AR-PUER model in order to capture the current distinction pattern of primary user. The training samples of the primary user emergence reasoning (PUER) model are combined with the recent samples of auto regressive (AR) model tracking recent parallel. Our scheme does not require the knowledge of the signal or of the noise power. Furthermore, the proposed model in this paper is blind in the detection that it does not require information about the channel. To verify the performance of the proposed model, we apply it to the data during the past two months, and then compare it with other method. The simulation results demonstrate that the AR-PUER model is effective and generates the most accurate forecasting of primary user occasion in several cases. Besides, it also performs much better than the commonly used energy detector, which usually suffers from the noise uncertainty problem.

Keywords: Dynamic spectrum access · Linear prediction
AR-PUER · CRNs

1 Introduction

With the express development of wireless communication system, it posed a tough requirement for the limited radio spectrum resource. On the other hand, in connection with the spectrum report conducted by the Federal Communications Commission (FCC), the majority of the radio spectrum is not in use in reality [1]. Therefore, the perception of CRNs has been proposed as a hopeful technology to deal with the spectrum scarcity as well as the spectrum underutilization problem [2]. The merely consideration is that the secondary users have to vacate the channel within a certain amount of time whenever the primary user becomes active. Thus, the cognitive radio

© ICST Institute for Computer Sciences, Social Informatics and Telecommunications Engineering 2018
P. Marques et al. (Eds.): CROWNCOM 2017, LNICST 228, pp. 15–25, 2018.
https://doi.org/10.1007/978-3-319-76207-4_2

network faces the tricky challenge of detecting the presence of the primary user, particularly in a low signal-to-noise ratio region, since the signal of the primary user might be severely alleviated due to multipath and shadowing before reaching the secondary user. To ensure that there will be no harmful intervention to the primary user, the secondary users need to sporadically detect the presence of the primary user. There are several factors that avoid the spectrum sensing from operating in a reliable manner. One factor is that the strength of the primary users' signals could be very weak when they reach the secondary users. If the secondary user makes a defective decision in detection and establishes transmitting when the primary users are active, its own signal will meddle with the primary users' signals.

The most popular spectrum sensing methods that have been proposed are energy detection, cyclostationary feature detection and matched-filtering detection. Up to now, not much work has been done on blind sensing models. Algorithms based on cyclostationarity have been developed in [3]. However, the performance of these algorithms at a low SNR has not been investigated; it also requires some prior information about the primary users, whereas the proposed model does not. The proposed model performs much better than the commonly used energy detector. Moreover, unlike the energy detector [4] and prior cyclostationary methods, the novel AR-PUER model here is blind and does not require information about the multipath channel distortions that the primary users has undergone on its way to reaching the secondary user.

In this paper, we proposed an auto regressive enhanced primary user emergence reasoning (AR-PUER) model, which does not require the knowledge of the signal or of the noise power. Moreover, the proposed detection algorithm in this paper is blind in the sense that it does not require information about the multipath channel deformations the primary user has undergone on its way to reaching the secondary user.

The rest of this paper is organized as follows. In Sect. 2, the auto regressive enhanced primary user emergence reasoning (AR-PUER) model is presented for the proposed scheme, which includes the detection method, primary user behavior characteristic and AR-PUER treatment process. In Sect. 3, the performance of proposed approach is analyzed, and numerical results are presented. Finally, Sect. 4 briefly concludes this paper.

2 System Model

2.1 Time Correlation Estimate

In order to study the spectrum usage of primary users, the concept of time division is introduced. Time division belongs to time interval that based on a statistical analysis of the primary users' spectrum over a period of time. For some primary users, its time division may be more than one.

With the purpose of make the calculation results closer to the actual use of primary users, the following content will revise the error combined with statistical methods to make the consequence more accurate. To evaluate the disparity between the primary users' spectrum access time and the average time, the concept of time similarity is proposed, which can be defined as

$$\tau(\alpha, \beta) = 1 - \delta(\alpha, \beta) \tag{1}$$

where $\delta(\alpha, \beta) = \frac{|\alpha - \beta|}{\varepsilon}$, $\xi = |\alpha - \beta|$.

In (1), α is the initiation spectrum access time which independent with the statistical time of primary users, β is the average time that primary user access to the spectrum, while ε indicate the time is twenty-four hours. In the meantime, we classify ξ as time freeness that has two kinds of values:

(1) Primary users' own actual time ξ' is known as the code value of time freeness; in the same way, $\tau(\xi')$ is the code value of time similarity.
(2) According to $\xi = |\alpha - \beta|$, we can calculate the observation value of time freeness ξ, while the observation value of time similarity is $\tau(\xi)$ or $\tau(\alpha, \beta)$.

The code value of time similarity can constitute two intervals $(\tau(\xi'), 1)$ and $(0, \tau(\xi'))$, when the observation value $\tau(\alpha, \beta)$ is valid in $(\tau(\xi'), 1)$, accordingly we call $(\tau(\xi'), 1)$ as the valid interval; as a result, $(0, \tau(\xi'))$ is the invalid interval.

Considering the situation that a primary user maybe repeated access to the spectrum, therefore, the primary user exist multiple time similarity, that is to say, there is more than one time similarity located in the valid interval. Consequently, the time similarity of primary user A at $t_1, t_2, \cdots, t_k, \cdots$ can indicated as $\tau_1\left.\begin{array}{c}A\\t_1\end{array}\right., \tau_2\left.\begin{array}{c}A\\t_2\end{array}\right., \ldots, \tau_k\left.\begin{array}{c}A\\t_k\end{array}\right., \cdots$ respectively. Analogously, we see that $\tau_1(\alpha, t_1)\left.\begin{array}{c}A\\t_1\end{array}\right., \tau_2(\alpha, t_2)\left.\begin{array}{c}A\\t_2\end{array}\right., \ldots, \tau_k(\alpha, t_k)\left.\begin{array}{c}A\\t_k\end{array}\right., \ldots$

In the valid interval, the maximum time similarity can characterized as $\tau_{\max}(\alpha, t_i)\left.\begin{array}{c}A\\t_i\end{array}\right.$, while the minimum time similarity can indicated as $\tau_{\min}(\alpha, t_j)\left.\begin{array}{c}A\\t_j\end{array}\right.$. Hence, they can illustrated as $\tau_{\max}\left.\begin{array}{c}A\\t_i\end{array}\right.$ and $\tau_{\min}\left.\begin{array}{c}A\\t_j\end{array}\right.$ for short.

The above time similarity in which interval is valid is mainly determined by the time freeness ξ', because the standard deviation is the best way to evaluate time fluctuations, we can define its standard deviation as the time freeness ξ', which implies

$$\xi' = \sqrt{\frac{1}{N}\sum_{i=1}^{N}(x_i - \bar{x})^2} \tag{2}$$

When ξ' is little, the time similarity τ will be relatively large, and the effective interval will be narrowed accordingly, which reveal the primary users' spectrum access behavior has a strong regularity. On the contrary, when ξ' is large, the time similarity τ will be little at once, and the effective interval will be broaden. This phenomenon expose that the primary users' spectrum access behavior has a weak regularity, which reveal a greater volatility.

2.2   Primary User Behavior Characteristic

At first, we define a fixed number of days (m) as criteria. In order to minimize the interference of human factors, the maximum allowed range of time periods should not exceed the code value of time freeness. The primary users' spectrum access duration begin with D, and end up with $D + m$, which located in the area from line R to $R + n$, with the maximum trigger value during the time period $R + n$.

The access behavior employs natural number coding, that is, for the access behavior which length is n, each of them take an integer value from 1 to m (the maximum value). The access behavior is constructed as follows

R	n	D	m

In the process of operation, we need to determine the evaluation of each primary user. The evaluation can be calculated on the basis of assessment function

$$f_k = \sum_{e \in P} \omega(e) \tag{3}$$

where f_k is the evaluation of primary user k, e is the unit grid, P is the enclosed area with primary users' access behavior, and $\omega(e)$ is the value of unit.

In the progress for the primary users' access behavior characteristic, the procedures are as follows:

(1) Setup the initial number of days as $P(0)$ after initialization;
(2) Evaluate the primary users in accordance with the former assessment function (3), and calculate the evaluation value of primary users in $P(t)$;
(3) Carry on interleaved computation, we can obtain $P(t+1)$ from $P(t)$ after the mean value calculation;
(4) Calculate the end conditions, if $t \leq T$, then $t \to t+1$, and next go to step (2); if $t > T$, then output the primary user with maximum time similarity $\tau_{max} \left| \dfrac{A}{t_i} \right.$ as the optimal solution, and stop the calculation.

2.3   AR-PUER Model

The sensing model in this paper is based on linear prediction and case based reasoning [5, 6], which involves predicting a future value of a stationary discrete-time stochastic process, given a set of past samples of the process.

Considering the time series of received signal vectors as $\{W_1, W_{t-1}, W_{t-2}, \cdots, W_{t-p}\}$. In the auto regressive $AR(p)$ model, samples $\{W_1, W_{t-1}, W_{t-2}, \cdots, W_{t-p}\}$ are used to predict the condition of primary user a_t. In this paper, forward linear prediction will be used. The forward prediction at time t is denoted by a_t and is given by

$$W_t - \varphi_1 W_{t-1} - \varphi_2 W_{t-2} - \cdots - \varphi_p W_{t-p} = a_t, \ \ t = 0, \pm 1, \pm 2, \cdots \tag{4}$$

The retardation factor B is an operator, which have the arithmetic operation $B^k W_t = W_{t-k}, \ \ k \geq 1$. The stipulation of primary user a_t is then defined as

$$(1 - \varphi_1 B - \varphi_2 B^2 - \cdots - \varphi_p B^p) \cdot W_t = a_t \tag{5}$$

When $\Phi(B) = 1 - \varphi_1 B - \varphi_2 B^2 - \cdots - \varphi_p B^p$, the mentioned formula above can illustrated as

$$\Phi(B) \cdot W_t = a_t, \ \ t = 0, \pm 1, \pm 2, \cdots \tag{6}$$

The blind AR-PUER sensing model in this paper combines linear prediction with the primary user emergence reasoning of the received data. Auto regressive model is a widely used technique in numerical analysis and linear algebra [7]. Based on this approach, some signal statistics will be defined, which reveal distinctive features only in the presence of primary users. This discrimination will improve the probability of detection.

In the function $W_t = \Phi^{-1}(B) \cdot a_t$, in which $G(B) = \Phi^{-1}(B) = \sum\limits_{k=0}^{\infty} G_k B^k, |B| < 1$, we see that $W_t = \sum\limits_{k=0}^{\infty} G_k a_{t-k}$ where $G_k, \ \ k = 0, 1, 2 \cdots$ is the Green's function of the $AR(p)$ model. Analogously, in $a_t = \Phi(B) \cdot W_t$ where $I(B) = \Phi(B) = G^{-1}(B) = I_0 - \sum\limits_{k=1}^{\infty} I_k B^k$, $|B| < 1$ ($I_0 = 1$), we can obtain $a_t = W_t - \sum\limits_{k=1}^{\infty} I_k W_{t-k}$. It can be shown from the function that $I_k, \ \ k = 0, 1, 2, \cdots$ is the inverse function for $AR(p)$.

From the stationary sequence $\{W_t\}$, which $W_k, \ \ W_{k-1}, \ \ W_{k-2}, \cdots$ was known, we can have $\hat{W}_j = W_j (j \leq k), \ \hat{a}_{k+l} = 0 (l \geq 1)$. In doing so, some signal statistics forecast formulas based on the auto regressive model will be obtained below.

$$\hat{W}_k(l) = \varphi_1 \hat{W}_k(l - 1) + \varphi_2 \hat{W}_k(l - 2) + \ldots + \varphi_p \hat{W}_k(l - p), l > q \tag{7}$$

$$\hat{W}_k(l) = \sum\limits_{j=1}^{\infty} I_j^{(l)} . W_{k+1-j}, l \geq 1 \tag{8}$$

where
$$\begin{cases} I_j^{(1)} = I_j & j \geq 1 \\ I_j^{(1)} = I_{j+l-1} + \sum\limits_{m=1}^{l-1} I_m I_j^{(l-m)} & j \geq 1, \ \ l \geq 2 \end{cases}$$

Since the primary user emergence reasoning model shares the same training samples and procedures with the auto regressive model, it is possible to combine the training samples selected from both models, and improve the forecasting accuracy with near vectors in both temporal and feature space. Thus we propose an auto regressive

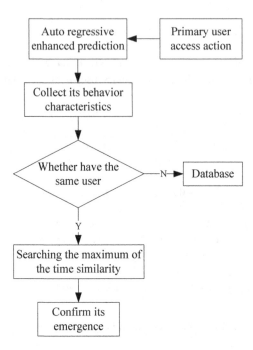

Fig. 1. Auto regressive enhanced primary user emergence reasoning model

enhanced primary user emergence reasoning (AR-PUER) model to enhance the precision of primary user presence without requiring the information about the channel. The spectrum access behavior reasoning model of primary users is shown in Fig. 1.

For the AR-PUER model training with historical data, the procedures of the combined AR and PUER model are as follows:

First of all, searching all the users in the stored access behavior, which have the similar spectrum access time with the real primary user, and then utilize the auto regressive model to enhance the prediction of primary users. Moreover, collect its access behavior characteristics and analysis to determine the primary users which in accordance with the daily access habits according to the time similarity. Once again, chase down its nearest neighbor by means of the above mentioned primary user, and then calculate the time span of them. Furthermore, update the searched user in the light of its access behavior and correction rule. Eventually, make a review and revision, thus evaluate the necessity whether hold it back.

As to the situation that primary users may have a delay during the spectrum access procedure because of some special circumstance, which will result in $\tau(\alpha, \beta)$ is invalid. Accordingly, we introduce the conception of behavior similarity. Frequently, the primary user's construction set is consist of feature set and relation set, which can indicated as $U : U = \{Feature, Relation\}$. Besides, the configuration set U can also include some other user's properties, for example, with the primary user's different access behavior, it may contain the weight coefficient W, that is to say, $U : U = \{Feature, Relation, Weight\}$.

Supposing that *User*1 and *User*2 match all the characteristics, then we have $U_1 = U_2$. If they only have some characteristic values in common, they are partial similarity, and we can utilize *Sim* to express the similarity between them. It can also be defined as the ratio between the matched characteristics with all the features, that is to say $Sim \in [0,1]$. The larger the relation value, the higher the similarity between them. When $Sim = 1$, they are the same user; while different users when $Sim = 0$. The assemblage of any two users can be defined as $V_A = \{a_1, a_2, \cdots, a_n\}$, $V_B = \{b_1, b_2, \cdots, b_n\}$, and then the similarity between them can be expressed as

$$Sim(A, B) = \frac{1}{n} \sum_{i=1}^{n} \sin(a_i, b_i) \qquad (9)$$

If the user's access behavior is not stable, we can set the corresponding weight. Consequently, the expression of behavioral similarity, which include the weight coefficient, can represented as

$$Sim(A, B) \frac{\sum_{i=1}^{n} \sin(a_i, b_i) w_i}{\sum_{i=1}^{n} w_i} \qquad (10)$$

where $\sin(a_i, b_i) = \begin{cases} 1, a_i = b_i \\ 0, a_i \neq b_i \end{cases}$, and α_i stands for the accessed primary user, while β_i express the stored primary user access action. At the moment of $a_i = b_i$, the forecast result is true, moreover, $\sin(a_i, b_i) = 1$; conversely, $\sin(a_i, b_i) = 0$. Simultaneously, we can define the weight coefficient w_i flexibility on the basis of the actual usage condition.

3 Simulations and Analysis

Simulation experiments based on matlab platform are made to check the detection performance in this section. Since the proposed model is a combination of AR model and PUER model, each of these models are also separately utilized. The training window size is mainly set to catch more similar pattern in the historical data. Since the combined AR-PUER model is used for primary user presence forecasting, the training window can be more time-correlated by setting two months of primary user data for training.

The performance of spectrum sensing is characterized by the probability of detection and the probability of false alarm. In the case, the secondary users may cause a severe interference to the primary user. On the contrary, the probability of false alarm means the probability that the secondary user judges primary user to be detected even though the primary user does not occur. Besides, the consumption of radio resource becomes worse because the secondary user changes the currently used channel into another available channel. It has been recognized that there is a tradeoff between the probability of detection and the probability of false alarm according to the sensing threshold [8, 9].

Taking into account the condition that spectrum access of primary users at the weekend and weekday may be different; however, the overall usage of the primary users is similar. Therefore, the experiments only consider the working days, and exploit different numbers to represent various primary users. Subsequently, the simulation is carried out on the trial platform to analyze whether the AR-PUER model is effective. Through the experiment, we can get the statistics data of primary users' presence time and the model successful forecasting number of times. As shown in Fig. 2, where the whole represents the total spectrum access number of primary users, while the success means that the success predictive number for secondary user through the AR-PUER model.

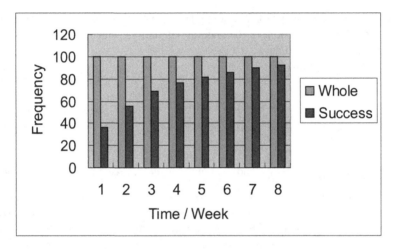

Fig. 2. Service chart of AR-PUER model

For the secondary user, the dynamic spectrum access successful implementation depends largely on the model of AR-PUER detection algorithm and the intelligent degree of the model mainly reflects in how many times it can successfully predict the primary users' emergence. That is to say, the more service time provided by the AR-PUER model is just the number of services that the secondary user would like to get, the higher successful forecasting rate it is. Additionally, the AR-PUER model's intelligence level is also improved and vice versa. The detection performance comparison with energy detector scheme in AWGN channel as shown in Fig. 3.

Primary users in the daily use of the spectrum often occurs in the following situations, such as one day occupy multiple spectrum bands, the same primary user during different time periods of the spectrum is not the same, some spectrum resources even have not been used. Even though there are circumstances exist as above-mentioned, AR-PUER model is still more effective in providing the spectrum access prediction services for secondary users. After analysis and calculation, the success rate of AR-PUER model during the past three months are improved dramatically at the initial time, after that it tends to smooth stably, this can be seen from the data in Fig. 4.

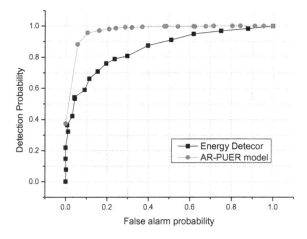

Fig. 3. Comparison with energy detector scheme in AWGN channel

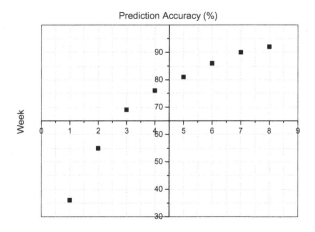

Fig. 4. Prediction trend chart of AR-PUER model

Through the data of first four weeks, it can be seen that the successful rate of the AR-PUER model to forecast the presence of primary users began to rise as time goes by, this reflect that the learning ability of the algorithm increases gradually with time. The following four weeks data show that through a long time of learning, the AR-PUER model can provide stable and high quality service for secondary users, which also demonstrate that the AR-PUER model is effective in the implementation of dynamic spectrum access in secondary users. This process can also be illustrated as a 3D color pie chart in Fig. 5.

The numerical experiment illustrated that the forecasting performance was improved by combining the training samples of the AR and PUER model, and the improvement was repeatable for different primary user data. Accordingly, the proposed

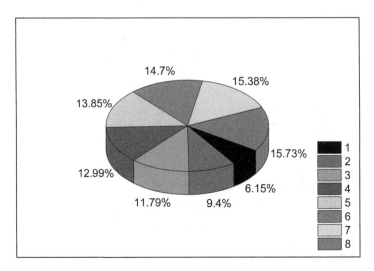

Fig. 5. 3D color pie chart of the prediction outcome

AR-PUER model could improve the probability of detection in the extant radio environment. Summarizing the results of the numerical experiments, the proposed model achieves the best forecasting performance.

4   Conclusion

This paper has introduced a blind auto regressive enhanced primary user emergence reasoning (AR-PUER) model for the cognitive radio. The method is based on linear prediction and case based reasoning. By using a combination of auto regressive prediction and primary user emergence reasoning, time similarity and time freeness are computed in our method. This is useful since it is desirable for a sensing model to operate without requiring the knowledge of the noise statistics. The time similarity is, thus, an indicator of the presence of the primary users in the signal that is received by the secondary user.

The analysis results show that the performance of the proposed model is better than the conventional manners for the detection of primary users. Besides, the simulation outcomes demonstrate that the AR-PUER model is effective and generates the most accurate forecasting of primary users occurrence in several cases.

Acknowledgement. This work was supported in part by the National Natural Science Foundation of China under Grant Nos. 61143008, 61471066, National High Technology Research and Development Program of China under Grant No. 2011AA01A204, and the Fundamental Research Funds for the Central Universities.

References

1. Kolodzy, P.: Spectrum policy task force. Fed. Commun. Comm. Technol. Rep. Docket **40**(4), 147–158 (2002)
2. Jajszczyk, A.: Cognitive Wireless Communication Networks (Hossian, E., Bhargava, V.) [Book Review]. IEEE Communications Magazine, p. 18, November 2008
3. Gardner, W.A.: Signal interception: performance advantages of cyclicfeature detectors. IEEE Trans. Commun. **40**(1), 149–159 (1992)
4. Sonnenschien, A., Fishman, P.M.: Radiometric detection of spread-spectrum signals in noise of uncertain power. IEEE Trans. Aerosp. Electron. Syst. **28**(3), 654–660 (1992)
5. Juell, P., Paulson, P.: Using reinforcement learning for similarity assessment in case-based systems. IEEE Intell. Syst. **18**(4), 60–67 (2003)
6. Jeng, B.C., Liang, T.P.: Fuzzy indexing and retrieval in case-based systems. Expert Syst. Appl. **88**(1), 135–142 (1995)
7. Golub, G.H., Van Loan, C.F.: Matrix Computations. Johns Hopkins University Press, Baltimore (1983)
8. Digham, F.F., Alouini, M.-S., Simon, M.K.: On the energy detection of unknown signals over fading channels. IEEE Transactions on Commun. **55**(1), 21–24 (2007)
9. Liang, Y.-C., Zeng, Y., Peh, E., Hoang, A.T.: Sensing-throughput tradeoff for cognitive radio networks. In: IEEE International Conference on Communications, pp. 5330–5335, June 2007

REM-Based Indoor Wireless Network Deployment - An Experimental Study

Adrian Kliks$^{(\boxtimes)}$ and Łukasz Kułacz

Faculty of Electronics and Telecommunications,
Poznan University of Technology, Poznan, Poland
{adrian.kliks,lukasz.kulacz}@put.poznan.pl

Abstract. In this paper we discuss the results of the conducted experiment, where dedicated databases have been used for management of deployment of indoor small-cells. As the transmission has been realized in the TV band, the ultimate goal of the study was initialize new data transmission in a spectrum sharing mode while protecting the DVB-T signal. Every time when the cognitive user wanted to initiate new transmission, it asked the database for permission and for a set of parameters defining transmit opportunities. The experiment has been carried out with two sets of USRP N210 devices.

Keywords: Vertical spectrum sharing · Radio environment maps
Experiments and trials

1 Introduction

The intensive research on cognitive radio technology has been conducted for almost two decades, starting from 1999 and 2000 when Mitola III published his key concepts on environment-aware radios [1,2]. As the idea of dynamic and more intelligent spectrum access seemed to be a good solution towards better spectrum utilization in next wireless communication networks, numerous research centers and laboratories have concentrated on specific aspects of the so-called cognitive cycle. Even, new visions on the functionality delivered by the cognitive radios have been proposed (see e.g. [3]), as it has been revealed that the pure cognitive radio that relies on the spectrum sensing will not be reliable enough in practical realizations. As a consequence, the application of advanced, database oriented spectrum management systems have been proposed as an alternative to this problem [4,5]. These databases are often called geolocation databases (GLDB) or radio-environment maps (REMs).

Two approaches are of practical interest today, the licensed shared access (LSA) concept [6], which is mainly considered in Europe, and which assumes the presence of the incumbent license owner, who decided to share its spectrum with other users. The second widely accepted solution is the one proposed in US and called Citizens Broadband Radio Service (CBRS) with Spectrum Access System (SAS) [7], where three tiers of users are considered, and the devices assigned to

© ICST Institute for Computer Sciences, Social Informatics and Telecommunications Engineering 2018
P. Marques et al. (Eds.): CROWNCOM 2017, LNICST 228, pp. 26–36, 2018.
https://doi.org/10.1007/978-3-319-76207-4_3

the lowest tier operate in pure cognitive manner [8,9]. Let us highlight the recent updates on CBRS interfaces released in June and July 2017 by WInnForum [10,11].

During the last years great achievement have been made in the context of utilization of vacant TV channels (known as TV White Spaces,TWVS) for wireless communications. Numerous trials and pilots have been realized all over the world, showing the applicability of this transmission scheme to various use-cases. The good summary and lists of these trials can be find in [12,13]. In our paper we present the results from the conducted experiment, where we have utilized the REM database for management of the cognitive indoor small-cell wireless network operating in TV band. The database has been prepared based on the measurement campaigns carried out in Poznan, Poland, where the power of the all detectable received DVB-T signals has been measured in certain locations inside and in close vicinity of the building. Based on these measurements, kriging algorithm has been applied to calculate the approximated values of the received power in any place inside the building. Once such a reception map has been created, it is used for calculation of the maximum allowable transmit power of the new wireless transmitter operating in a selected TV channel, as shown in [14,15]. As comparing to these past works, the key novelty of this paper is that such remote database, available via internet connection, has been applied for real-time management of the deployment of new white-space wireless transceivers. Two active white-space connection have been established in an arbitrarily selected laboratory in Poznan, Poland, following the decisions made by the REM-manager.

The rest of the paper is organized as follows. First, we briefly revise the database structure and its assumed role in spectrum management. Next, we discuss the setup for the considered experiment, and present the achieved results in last chapter. Finally, we draw some conclusions on applicability of REM databases.

2   REM Database Description

Numerous researches conducted in recent years have proved that application of sole spectrum sensing as a tool for detection of the presence of the primary user signal is not sufficient enough for practical implementation. The reliability of single-node spectrum sensing, especially in low signal-to-noise ratio regime, is either too low or too complicated or it takes too much time to acquire enough samples for stable decision. In that context, Radio Environment Map (REM) is a tool frequently envisaged to be one of the technical enablers for practical deployment of secondary systems operating in the legacy bands. However, in order to guarantee the required quality of service of both systems (but mainly to protect the legacy system from harmful influence originated in secondary systems), the map has to be properly designed, utilizing detailed knowledge about the parameters of the incumbent system that has to be protected. Depending on application, various types of maps can be created and stored for better management of new white-space systems. These include, e.g., coverage maps, signal-to-interference-and-noise (SINR) ratio, maps of allowed maximum transmit power, trajectory maps etc. In all mentioned cases, however, it is not possible to measure any value with infinitesimally small granularity, thus various spatial approximation methods have to be applied. In our experiment we have implemented a kriging algorithm that takes into account the presence of indoor and outdoor walls, as defined in [15,16]. Once such a spatially approximated map is created it can be used for calculation of the maximum allowable transmit power of the secondary user on each possible point inside building. Thus, the process of creation of a REM database and the whole procedure introduced and discussed in [14,15], and applied in our experiment can be summarized in a nutshell as follows:

1. If the map of interest relies on any measured value (such as power of the received signal), the dedicated measurement campaign should be conducted;
2. Once the measurements of a certain metric are finished, the spatial approximation algorithm, such as kriging, has to be applied to calculate the values of the considered metric in any prospective location of interest;
3. Calculated map has to be stored with required granularity and precision which define a tradeoff between the accuracy of the map and storage size;
4. Stored maps (in our case distribution of the observed signal power of any detectable DVB-T signal) can be applied for various purposes; in the experiment carried out for this paper we have used the SINR map for calculation of the maximally allowed Equivalent Isotropical Radiated Power (EIRP) value for any location in the considered building; this maximum EIRP value is computed in such a way that the new wireless link does not infer too much interference to the legacy, DVB-T system; in order to assess the interference observed by the primary user, the propagation model defined in [15,16] has been implemented.

3   Experiment Setup

As it has been already mentioned, the ultimate goal of the conducted experiment was to increase the spectrum utilization by establishing new indoor white-space wireless links in TV band such that the DVB-T signal is not distorted. The experiment has been carried out in the ground floor in the premises of Faculty of Electronics and Telecommunications at Poznan University of Technology, Poland, in last day of April 2017. The white-space transmitter was implemented in GNU Radio environment that steered the connected USRP N210 board equipped with the WBX board. Some of the functions have been delivered by National Instruments in form of dedicated blocks in GNU Radio Companion, however the new blocks (e.g., those for database querying) have been implemented in C. For data transmission we have selected freely available *Big Buck Bunny* media sequence, which was streamed via UDP port, coded and modulated with GMSK modulation scheme. Such a selection gives us a possibility to analyze the influence of potential interfering signals observed by the white space receiver, thus we do not apply any coding or advanced modulation schemes. In other words, we can observe, how the potential interference coming from primary system and other simultaneous secondary systems influences the white space receiver, and vice-versa - how the out-of-band transmission of simple modulation scheme impacts the primary system[1]. If allowed, the GMSK signal was delivered to the USRP block and broadcasted over the air inside the building using omnidirectional antenna.

Analogous approach has been applied to the white-space receiver, whose connection diagram is shown in form of a screen-shot in Fig. 1. Beside the blocks similar to those applied at the transmitter (such as GMSK demodulator, decoder), one may observed the presence of the parallel chain of blocks used for maintaining the connectivity with remote database. Moreover, it can be noticed that the software spectrum analyzer has been also applied, which shows the power spectral density (PSD) of the received GMSK signal. Finally the VLC player is visible that visualizes the decoded stream collected at UDP port.

Please note that the whole communication was steered by the remote database, implemented on dedicated laptop with Matlab installed on it. This REM server was accessible via Ethernet connection and was responsible for granting access to the white-spaces depending on the given location. In order to guarantee connectivity between the remote REM server and the white-space devices, each computer emulating such white space device, was equipped with dedicated WLAN-dongle. Such a solution was necessary as the only way to provide communication between USRP and personal computer is via Ethernet cable, so two simultaneous network connections were needed. The experimental scenario has been illustrated in two consecutive figures, Figs. 2 and 3.

In a broader scope the experiment consisted of two key phases: first step was to establish the first white-space connection with the use of REM databases and observe the spectrum inside the room by means of the R&S FLS6 spectrum analyzer; in the second step, another white-space link was established in the same room such that neither the DVB-T signal nor the existing white-space transmission was distorted. Each key phase consisted of a sequence of smaller steps:

1. first, the new white-space transmitter sends a query to the remote database (via WLAN connection) with request for new transmission grant;
2. second, after receiving the request, the database calculates the allowed maximum transmit power and sends this message back to the transmitter; at the same time the database stores the parameters of the new prospective link (including center frequency etc.); this information will be then later delivered to the white-space receiver;
3. third, the white-space receiver periodically checks the database for any new entry indicating that new transmissions to it; the reception parameters may be adjusted if needed according to the stored parameters.

---

[1] Please notice, however, that the selection of the transmission scheme is not critical in our experiment, and one can easily exchange the GMSK modulation scheme with the one widely considered for white space transmission, such as multicarrier schemes (OFDM) from IEEE 802.11af, or its filtered version (FBMC) from IEEE 1900.7 standard.

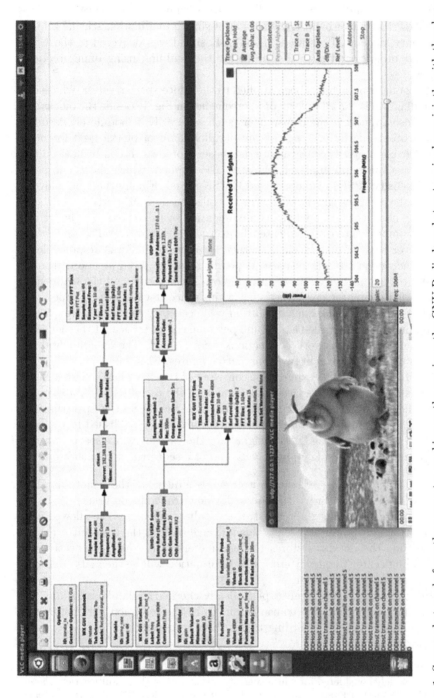

Fig. 1. Screen-shot made from the computer working as the receiver; the GNU Radio based structure is shown jointly with the observed power spectral density of received signal and the decoded film played on vlc media player

Fig. 2. Photograph of the first white-space transceiver (left side computer with USRP board put on it) and REM database (right computer connected with Internet via Ethernet cable); the left-side computer communicates with database using WLAN-dongles stick into it

Fig. 3. Photograph of the second white-space transceiver (the one with USRP board laying on it); the computer communicates with database using WLAN-dongles

4   Achieved Results

The procedure described in the previous section has been applied in the real-time experiment. In the first phase, the new white-space device asked for new transmit grants, and once it has received them it started data transmission. Next, second white-space device tries to get positive response for the spectrum access requests. In both cases, centralized remote REM database controlled the whole process. As the messages stored in a log file of the remote database present the consecutive steps of the experiment, we present the key messages of this log file below:

- No new requests //*database awaits new request from new transceivers*
- No new requests
- ...
- New request with coordinates A = {20, 276, 468, 5, 0} //Coordinates inside the building
- Allowed transmit power *result* = −8.9391 dBm
- No new requests
- Adding new user A = {20, 276, 468, 5, 3}
- No new requests
- No new requests
- ...
- No new requests
- New request with coordinates A = {21, 310, 407, 6, 0}
- Allowed transmit power *result* = −47.8770 dBm
- No new requests
- Adding new user A = {21, 310, 407, 6, 3}
- No new requests

One may observe that the database provides a periodic update on the status of the whole REM-based spectrum management system. If the new request is provided, it calculates the maximum transmit power in dBm for a provided location, as discussed in Sect. 2 (please see the last bullet in the list). Unfortunately, in the conducted experiment the duration of the server response was long and would not be practically applicable in practice. The response of the database for the spectrum inquiry was of the range of tens of seconds. Such a long server reply is due to the fact that we applied very high accuracy of the applied algorithm - the space granularity (raster) applied for calculation of potential interference induced to the primary system by prospective TVWS transmitter was set to 1 dm, resulting in 10^6 calculation points.

In Fig. 4 the PSD of the observed signal after the first key-phase (once the first white-space link has been established) is shown where the center frequency of the white-space link was set to 507 MHz, relatively close to the observable DVB-T signal spectrum with the center frequency of 522 MHz. We did not observed any noticeable noise increase in the TV band.

In Fig. 5 we show again the PSD of the observed signals, but for a case when two white-space links have been established. The second link operates on the center frequency equal to 514 MHz. One may observe that the allowed transmit power was lower as compared to the previous case, as the database needs to protect now two systems, both DVB-T one and the existing white-space transmission. Again we did not observed visually any changes in the DVB-T spectrum. Also in both white-space links the reception of the transmitted video

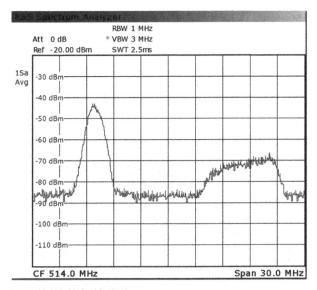

Fig. 4. Power spectral density observed inside the room after the first white-space link has been established

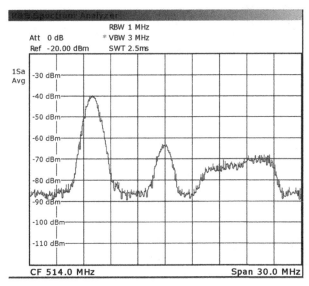

Fig. 5. Power spectral density observed inside the room after the second white-space link has been established

streaming was possible. It means that the out-of-band interference was rather low and negligible. In consequence, such a simultaneous spectrum usage as shown in Fig. 5 is possible.

Finally, once the first white-space transmitter has been granted by the REM based system, the latter has to create a new or update the existing table with the spatial distribution map of the observed signal to noise ratio - see Fig. 6.

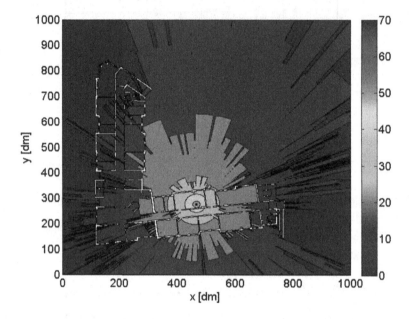

Fig. 6. Spatial distribution of the observed signal to noise ratio when one white-space device is active

5   Conclusions

In this work, we have presented the achieved results of the conducted experiment, where two whites-space links have been established and managed by means of dedicated remote REM database. It may be concluded that it is technically possible to practically deploy real-time indoor cognitive radio systems in parallel to the existing legacy systems. The remote REM based system manages the whole deployment process, in particular it calculates the maximum acceptable EIRP values for any new user and adds this user to the dedicated database. However, the process of calculating new allowed values of EIRP was in our case very slow (in terms of tens of seconds), what makes the application of such a system challenging. This problem is indeed a subject for further analysis and investigation, as the access to database has to be very fast and reliable. In general, however, the experiment has proved that it is justified to consider low range white-space transmission that relies on REM based management system.

Acknowledgments. The presented work has been funded by the National Science Centre in Poland within the SONATA project based on decision no. DEC-2015/17/D/ST7/04078.

References

1. Mitola, J.: Cognitive Radio: An Integrated Agent Architecture for Software Defined Radio, Ph.D. thesis, KTH Royal Institute of Technology (2000)
2. Mitola, J.: Cognitive radio architecture evolution. Proc. IEEE **97**(4), 626–641 (2009). https://doi.org/10.1109/JPROC.2009.2013012
3. Haykin, S., Thomson, D.J., Reed, J.H.: Spectrum sensing for cognitive radio. Proc. IEEE **97**(5), 849–877 (2009)
4. Yilmaz, H.B., Tugcu, T., Alagoz, F., Bayhan, S.: Radio environment map as enabler for practical cognitive radio networks. IEEE Commun. Mag. **51**(12), 162–169 (2013)
5. Perez-Romero, J., Zalonis, A., Boukhatem, L., Kliks, A., Koutlia, K., Dimitriou, N., Kurda, R.: On the use of radio environment maps for interference management in heterogeneous networks. IEEE Commun. Mag. **53**(8), 184–191 (2015)
6. Mustonen, M., et al.: An evolution toward cognitive cellular systems: licensed shared access for network optimization. IEEE Commun. Mag. **53**(5), 68–74 (2015)
7. Federal Communications Commission, FCC14-49: Amendment of the Commissions Rules with Regard to Commercial Operations in the 3550–3650 MHz Band, GN Docket No. 12–354, FURTHER NOTICE OF PROPOSED RULEMAKING, 23 April 2014
8. Federal Communications Commission, FCC14-47: Amendment of the Commissions Rules with Regard to Commercial Operations in the 3550–3650 MHz Band, GN Docket No. 12–354, FURTHER NOTICE OF PROPOSED RULE-MAKING", 17 April 2015. https://apps.fcc.gov/edocs_public/attachmatch/FCC-15-47A1_Rcd.pdf
9. Federal Communications Commission: Broadband Division, "3650-3700 MHz Radio Service", 27 April 2017. https://www.fcc.gov/wireless/bureau-divisions/broadband-division/3650-3700-mhz-radio-service
10. WInnForum: WINNF-TS-0016 Spectrum Access System (SAS) - Citizens Broadband Radio Service Device (CBSD) Interface Technical Specification, 18 July 2017. https://workspace.winnforum.org/higherlogic/ws/public/document?document_id=4275
11. WInnForum: WINNF-16-S-0016 V2.0.0 Spectrum Access System (SAS) - Citizens Broadband Radio Service Device (CBSD) Interface Technical Specification, 14 June 2017. https://workspace.winnforum.org/higherlogic/ws/public/document?document_id=4275
12. Dynamic Spectrum Alliance: Worldwide Commercial Deployments, Pilots, and Trials. http://dynamicspectrumalliance.org/pilots/. Accessed 8 August 2017
13. COHERENT Project Deliverable D4.1: Report on enhanced LSA, intra-operator spectrum sharing and micro-area spectrum sharing, Section 2.5.2, published June 8, 2016. http://www.ict-coherent.eu/coherent/wp-content/uploads/2015/10/COHERENT_D4_1_v1.pdf
14. Kułacz, Ł., Kliks, A., Kryszkiewicz, P.: Wykorzystanie baz danych srodowiska radiowego REM do zarzadzania przydzialem zasobow widmowych. In: Krajowa Konferencja Radiokomunikacji, Radiofonii i Telewizji, Poznan, Poland, 21–23 June 2017

15. Kliks, A., Kryszkiewicz, P., Kułacz, Ł.: Measurement-based coverage maps for indoor REMs operating in TV band. In: Proceedings of 12th IEEE International Symposium on Broadband Multimedia Systems and Broadcasting 2017, Cagliari, Italy, 7–9 June 2017
16. Konak, A.: Estimating path loss in wireless local area networks using ordinary kriging. In: Conference Paper in Proceedings - Winter Simulation Conference, January 2011. https://doi.org/10.1109/WSC.2010.5678983

Autonomous Spectrum Assignment
of White Space Devices

Chaitali Diwan$^{(\boxtimes)}$, Srinath Srinivasa, and Bala Murali Krishna

International Institute of Information Technology, Bangalore, India
{chaitali.diwan,balamurali.krishna}@iiitb.org, sri@iiitb.ac.in

Abstract. White-space spectrum has temporal and spatial variations, and fragmentation, making the spectrum assignment for devices in this space challenging. In this paper, we propose an autonomous agent model for spectrum assignment of white space devices at a given location. Each white space device (WSD) acts autonomously out of self-interest, choosing a strategy from its bag of strategies. It obtains a payoff based on its choice and choices made by all other WSDs. Based on the payoffs received by different strategies, WSDs evolve their strategic profile over time. This has the effect of demographic changes in the population which is published as demographic profile by the Master. WSDs are expected to choose a strategy with a probability distribution based on this, for optimising network utilisation. In evaluation runs, network utilisation levels in such an approach are found to be high, and approaching optimal values computed in a centralised fashion.

Keywords: White spaces · Dynamic spectrum access
Multi-agent systems · Evolutionary game theory
White space database · Optimising spectrum utilisation

1   Introduction

White space refers to licensed radio spectrum that is not being utilised by the licensee. Across the world, white space contributes to a lot of available spectrum that is wasted. Recent research has enabled the use of this spectrum for broadband internet access using a paradigm called dynamic spectrum access. In this model, the primary owner and the licensee, (typically terrestrial TV) would retain primacy over the spectrum, while letting the secondary users or white space devices (WSD) utilise this spectrum whenever a primary user is not using it. WSDs have to ensure that none of their transmissions interfere with the primary users. The most efficient way to ensure this is to use *geo-location databases* which has now become a standard way for operating in white spaces in most of the countries. Geo-location white space spectrum database (WSDB) is an authoritative source that publishes the spectral and temporal availability of the free channels in a given location. It implements the rules of authority and uses the stored information of the licensed primary users, secondary users, terrain

© ICST Institute for Computer Sciences, Social Informatics and Telecommunications Engineering 2018
P. Marques et al. (Eds.): CROWNCOM 2017, LNICST 228, pp. 37–48, 2018.
https://doi.org/10.1007/978-3-319-76207-4_4

information, tower specific parameters, interference, etc. It also considers re-use of a channel and enforces social and environmental norms, such as allowing only low power transmissions near a contour or a national border.

White space devices can be of different types with varying characteristics, and with the proliferation of Internet of Things (IoT), the diversity in WSDs is very high, making it a challenge to manage their use of the free spectrum as well as their interaction with the WSDB. For this reason, WSDs are broadly categorised into two types: *Master WSD* and *secondary WSDs*. In any given WSD deployment, the Master WSD communicates directly with the WSDB, while secondary WSDs always communicate with WSDB through the Master WSD [1,2]. (We refer to secondary WSD as "WSD" and Master WSD as "Master" through out the paper.) A new deployment is started by the Master registering itself with the WSDB, and subsequently, secondary WSDs registering with the Master. Whenever a WSD wants to operate in the white space spectrum, it sends a request to the Master which in-turn forwards the request to the WSDB, and obtains the list of available frequency ranges along with the maximum transmission power, start and end time of spectrum availability for each of the spectrum frequency ranges. It notifies the WSDB when it uses a channel. When a primary user needs the spectrum, WSD must cease to operate in that frequency range.

In the above protocol, the main challenge is that of dynamic spectrum assignment to cater to the disparate needs of the different WSDs. One way to approach this problem is for the Master to perform all the allocations. However, the Master is also usually a low power device, and cannot afford the costly computations needed for optimally allocating spectrum in a dynamic environment. In addition, in a centralised decision-making model, the rest of the system will need to cease operations until the Master completes its decision-making and performs channel allocations.

To address this problem, we propose an autonomous-agent model for spectrum assignment of white space devices at a given location. In this model, each WSD acts autonomously out of self-interest, to allocate spectrum for itself. Based on its choice and the choices made by all other WSDs, it obtains a payoff. The payoff acts as a feedback function for the WSD to refine its strategy for making its choice. Such a system is trained on a given workload profile, until such time that the distribution of strategies (also called the "demographic profile") stabilises across the population.

In a deployed system, the role of the Master is limited to profiling the load based on the traffic data and the desired demographic profile based on the training. The Master publishes both these data in order to enable WSDs to alter the probability with which they choose a given strategy.

1.1 Related Work

Initial efforts towards spectrum allocation in white space networks were based on variants of graph colouring algorithms, some examples include [3–5]. These algorithms considered fixed topology or topology with infrequent updates. Spectrum assignment problem considered in [6] also assumes fixed spectrum availability.

Cao and Zheng in [7], Nie and Comaniciu in [8] and Suris *et al.* in [9] studied the spectrum assignment problem in white space network as cooperative game which is useful in scenarios where a single service provider deploys large number of wireless devices and enforces collaboration agreements among them.

Centralised approaches to spectrum allocation have been investigated in [10–13]. Although they have very high spectrum utilisation, they are not very suitable for dynamic networks characterised by large amounts of flux in the number of WSDs, their spectrum needs and traffic, thereby increasing the complexity of the algorithm.

Chen and Huang in [14] designed an evolutionary algorithm to iteratively select the least congested channel among a set of available channels. Anandkumar *et al.* in [15], and Liu and Zhao in [16] used distributed multi-armed bandit learning algorithms for spectrum allocation. However, these models consider both primary and secondary users to be slotted. Li in [17] and Xu *et al.* in [22] use game theoretic solutions for distributed channel selections, but they consider the system model to be static.

Spectrum assignment of white space devices studied in [18–20] have also been modelled as non-cooperative games, but they require complete network information for making the spectrum assignments. Chen and Huang in [21] proposed a distributed learning algorithm for channel selection based on channel data rate, but the solution assumes a fixed channel selection profile of users.

Wicke *et al.* in [23] proposed an approach to competitive multi-agent task allocation in a different setting inspired by bounty hunters. However, in this model, the tasks that agents compete for, are not exclusive and an agent can take another unfinished task by a previous agent and obtain a higher payoff.

In this paper, we propose a model that has a distributed decision making by autonomous agents which co-ordinate with each other using a central shared memory located at the Master. This ensures an efficient method of spectrum management with high spectrum utilisation. Our model considers the network structure to be dynamic as is the case in white spaces and doesn't need complete network information for the operation. With the exception of a centralised model in [13], none of the above papers focus primarily on the white space spectrum characteristics like duration of usage, maximum allowed transmission power and white space devices properties like the frequency range, spectrum demand, transmission capacity, etc. for spectrum assignment. By taking these properties into account, our model provides more value to the white space devices and helps to increase overall network utility and social welfare.

Unlike most of the spectrum assignment models which have a fixed algorithm for spectrum assignment, our model provides different algorithms to choose a channel in the form of strategies. This makes it a rich and flexible model and any new algorithms can be easily integrated with the model by expanding the strategy set of the white space devices.

Each white space network may change overtime and have different network characteristics and constraints at different times. Our model is flexible and adaptable to this due to it being autonomous and self evolving. When the model is deployed on different networks, each network will have a different demographic profile of strategies and different dominant strategies according to the network dynamics. Thus, our model can be trained for different environments and demand patterns and allow it to seamlessly adapt its strategy distribution with changes in load patterns. The demographic profile and demand pattern published by the Master also helps the new WSD entering the system to automatically have the wisdom of the network.

2   System Model

We consider the spectrum assignment model of white space network, at a given location and associated with a single Master, as a multi-agent system where each WSD acts as an autonomous agent. Formally, we define the system as follows:

$$S = (C, A, \psi). \tag{1}$$

Here, C is a set of channels licensed to some primary users, that have allowed WSDs to operate. Each channel $c_i \in C$ is said to be in one of the three different states:

$$state(c_i) = \begin{cases} 0, & \text{if free} \\ 1, & \text{if occupied by primary user} \\ 2, & \text{if occupied by secondary user or WSD.} \end{cases} \tag{2}$$

$A = \{m, W\}$ is a set of autonomous agents where m is the Master WSD, and W is a set of secondary WSDs. The term ψ refers to a set of "strategies" that the system is endowed with. All WSDs have a copy of the set of strategies listed in ψ. Each strategy $\psi_i \in \psi$ denotes a heuristic with which, a WSD makes a choice regarding its requirements.

Demand and Offer. Each WSD has its own set of requirements and constraints, regarding the spectrum. We call this as the "Demand" from the WSD and represent it as a vector: $D = (r_{fr}, r_{Tx}, r_{nc}, r_d)$. Here r_{fr} is the operating frequency range, r_{Tx} is the maximum transmission power of WSD, r_{nc} and r_d are the required bandwidth and duration respectively.

Whenever a WSD wants to communicate in a white space spectrum, it requests the Master for a list of free spectrum fragments. Master obtains information from the geo-location database and forwards it as a set of "Offers" $R = \{O_1, O_2, \ldots, O_k\}$ to the WSD. Each offer $O_j \in R$ is a vector of the form $O_j = (o_{fr}, o_{Tx}, o_{nc}, o_d)$, such that each element of the offer vector *covers* the corresponding element in the demand vector.

While every offer made by the Master is a possible allocation for the WSDs requirements, not all offers bring the same value. Choosing some offers may result in wasted time or bandwidth, while choosing some other offer may have repercussions on choices available to other WSDs.

A WSD does not have the information or resources to compute the impact of its decision on others. It chooses an offer based on local considerations and this choice is defined by the current strategy chosen by the WSD.

Strategy and Fitness. As mentioned earlier, each WSD is endowed with a set ψ of strategies. Initially, a WSD chooses a strategy $\psi_i \in \psi$ uniformly at random. For each of the offers received by the WSD, it computes a gain along several dimensions, namely: feasibility, transmission power, bandwidth, duration and continuity of use. The gains are then tempered differently based on the current strategy, to compute the overall fitness of an offer given the demand.

The feasibility of an offer is a binary variable used to filter away incorrect offers if any. This is computed as follows:

$$f_f = \begin{cases} 1, & \text{if } r_{fr} \text{ is within } o_{fr} \text{ and } o_{nc} \geq r_{nc} \\ 0, & \text{otherwise.} \end{cases} \tag{3}$$

The gains with respect to bandwidth, power and duration requirements are computed as follows:

$$f_n = 1 - \frac{|o_{nc} - r_{nc}|}{max(o_{nc}, r_{nc})} \tag{4}$$

$$f_t = 1 - \frac{|o_{Tx} - r_{Tx}|}{max(o_{Tx}, r_{Tx})} \tag{5}$$

$$f_d = 1 - \frac{|o_d - r_d|}{max(o_d, r_d)}. \tag{6}$$

If a given channel in the offer has been used in the previous transmission of the WSD, it is also said to constitute a gain as it reduces the need to re-calibrate the transmission on a different channel. This is formally represented by a value f_h for a given offer O_j which is set to 1 if the same channel offered by O_j was used in the previous transmission as well, or 0 otherwise.

$$f_h = \begin{cases} 1, & \text{if same channel was used in the previous request} \\ 0, & \text{otherwise.} \end{cases} \tag{7}$$

A strategy tempers the importance of each of the above gains in different ways, and is represented by a four dimensional simplex $\psi_i = (i_n, i_d, i_t, i_h)$ such that $i_n + i_d + i_t + i_h = 1$.

The fitness of a given offer O_j according to the current strategy ψ_i is given by:

$$F(\psi_i, D, O_j) = f_f \Big(i_n f_n + i_d f_d + i_t f_t + i_h f_h \Big). \tag{8}$$

Once the fitness value is calculated for every offer by comparing it against the demand of the WSD, the offer that has the maximum fitness value is chosen.

$$\max_{\forall O_j \in R} \Big(F(\psi_i, D, O_j) \Big). \tag{9}$$

A Representative Bag of Strategies. In our work, the system is endowed with a set of strategies that are explained here. Different strategies compute the fitness of the offer calculated using Eq. (8) in different ways by setting the four dimensional simplex $\psi_i = (i_n, i_d, i_t, i_h)$ of importance scores according to the strategy. The strategy set ψ can be extended by adding more strategies tailored to suit the network requirements or WSD specific strategy.

Longest duration: WSD chooses an offer that has the longest duration o_d. For this strategy, the importance score i_d is very high, whereas i_n, i_t and i_h are low.

Highest allowed transmission power: WSD chooses offer that has the highest permissible transmission power o_{Tx}. Hence, the importance score of i_t is very high and rest of the importance scores are low.

Frequently used: WSD chooses an offer which is frequently used, the importance score of i_h is a high value and rest of the importance scores are low.

Most recently used: WSD chooses an offer that is most recently used. This strategy means WSD wants to continue using the channel it is already using, hence the importance score of i_h is very high (close to 1) and rest of the importance scores are very low (close to 0).

First fit: WSD chooses the first feasible offer. The importance scores for i_d, i_n, i_t are thus assigned 0 and i_h is assigned 1.

Least-biased match: WSD chooses a channel(s) which is close to its operating parameters and to its requirements. This strategy may seem to be best for the total network utilisation, and is also called the "Best match" strategy. The importance scores i_d, i_n, i_t are given equal value, $i_d = i_n = i_t = 1/3$ and $i_h = 0$.

Channel Allocation. WSDs allocate channels for themselves based on the fitness of an offer computed according to the current strategy. They then stake claim on this channel by issuing an atomic TEST&SET operation on the WSDB (via the Master).

TEST&SET tests the state of a channel and allocates it, if the channel is free. This is done in one atomic step to prevent race conditions. If the TEST&SET succeeds, the WSD proceeds to use the channel that it staked claim to. If the operation fails, then the WSD tries to allocate itself to the next best offer based on the fitness value computed.

The actual payoff obtained by a WSD for a given strategy is defined as the fitness value of the offer, which results in a successful allocation of the channel. The payoff obtained at the ith attempt is denoted by ϕ_i. The payoff is set to 0 for every failed attempt.

Demographic Profile. "Demographic profile" is the means by which the WSDs interact with each other. WSDs take advantage of the white space network's infrastructure requirement of communicating with the WSDB via the Master, and piggy back the information about their payoffs to the Master. The

Master uses this information to create the demographic profile, which is the probability distribution of the success of the strategies. Master thus acts as a broker or facilitator among the WSDs without any decision making capabilities. In the absence of such a broker, there would be a need for lot of message exchanges between WSDs which would increase communication complexity.

The initial choice of a strategy by a WSD is made using a uniformly random function. However, over time, as payoffs accumulate in a differentiated fashion across strategies, the system allows for WSDs to change their strategy using an evolutionary rationale.

Following is the calculation used to find the success of a strategy. For each WSD w_k, success of its currently adopted strategy ψ_i is calculated by computing the ratio of sum of positive payoff each WSD gets in comparison with the total number of attempts t_k the WSD makes to get the channel.

$$success(\psi_i, w_k) = \frac{\sum_{i=0}^{t_k} \phi_i}{t_k}. \tag{10}$$

Let $wsds(\psi_i)$ denote the set of all WSDs which have chosen strategy ψ_i. The *demographic dividend* for strategy ψ_i is given by:

$$dividend(\psi_i) = \sum_{\forall w_k \in wsds(\psi_i)} success(\psi_i, w_k). \tag{11}$$

Finally, the *demographic profile* across the system is computed by assigning new probabilities to the strategies using the strategy success calculated above.

$$P(\psi_i) = \frac{dividend(\psi_i)}{\sum_{\forall \psi_i \in \psi} dividend(\psi_i)}. \tag{12}$$

The demographic profile is published by the Master and is continuously updated.

WSD uses a strategy it selected for a certain time period t_p called an *epoch*. At the end of each epoch, the WSD uses the demographic profile published by the Master and optionally changes its strategy. This is controlled by a tuning parameter $\beta \in [0, 1]$, where with a probability β, the WSD continues with its current strategy and with a probability $(1 - \beta)$, it chooses a new strategy, with a random distribution based on the demographic profile.

WSD sets the tuning parameter β based on the history of its payoff. If a WSD is continuously getting higher payoff from the current strategy, it may incrementally increase the value of β. For example, a mobile WSD may set β close to 1 for a strategy that chooses a channel with maximum transmission power, which would allow the WSD to operate seamlessly on the same channel (under the same Master) even if it moves far away from the Master.

WSD may also use a strategy temporarily, like in case of a primary user unexpectedly wanting to transmit on a spectrum which a WSD is already transmitting on. WSD being a secondary device, gives up the spectrum it is currently using and quickly acquires a new channel using a strategy like the "First fit" strategy (picking up feasible offer encountered) which doesn't need much processing. Even though WSD uses a different strategy in such a case, it doesn't shift to this strategy.

System Equilibrium and Training. As WSDs change their strategies, the global demographic profile changes too. We say that the system has reached the state of equilibrium (or, in a state of evolutionary best-response) when the maximum change in the probability for any strategy, falls below a threshold ϵ.

A given deployment of WSDs is "trained" under different "demand profiles" using a simulation framework, until the demographic profile is learned for that demand profile.

We consider three different demand profiles - Peak, Lean and Bursty which vary in the number of WSDs making requests and spectrum demands of the WSD. In Peak Demand Profile (PDP), there are many active WSDs and most WSDs make greater demands on the spectrum. In Lean Demand Profile (LDP), number of WSDs requesting the spectrum is less and most of the WSDs would make low or moderate demands on the spectrum. In Bursty Demand Profile (BDP), WSDs becoming active and demand requirement is random. For each of the demand profiles, a separate demographic profile is published for the consumption of WSD and also each WSD may follow a different strategy for each of the demand profiles.

The Master node can determine the current demand profile based on the traffic that is being routed through it. Based on the training, it also determines the suitable demographic profile for such a demand profile. The Master publishes both these data in the shared memory during deployment.

If the WSD moves from one Master to other, it has to connect with the new Master, however, it will be able to quickly adapt to the new network and choose a strategy and channel using the demographic profile of the new Master.

3   Evaluation

We conducted experimental simulation to quantify the performance of our model using an open-source simulation package $OMNET++$. For our experiments, we used the data from the study conducted by one of our partners IIM-Ahmedabad, India [24], on internet usage data in rural India. We also used the data from Google spectrum database[1].

We considered 20 free channels in our experiments. We modelled the three different demand profiles as follows: In PDP, WSDs becoming active is modelled as a Poisson distribution with a value of $\lambda \geq 15$ active WSDs/hour, in LDP, it is modelled as a Poisson distribution with a value of $\lambda \leq 8$ active WSDs/hour and in BDP, it is modelled as a Gaussian distribution. Primary users being active was also modelled according to the data mentioned above.

---

[1] http://www.google.com/get/spectrumdatabase/.

Demand Cards. WSD's spectrum requirements are simulated in the form of *Demand Cards* which are representative of the combinations of the usage parameters of the WSD. Each demand profile is associated with a deck of *Demand Cards* with different probabilities assigned to them. A WSD chooses a card from the current deck uniformly at random, to simulate its demand.

Table 1. Demand Cards

Card	No of channels	Duration	Transmission power
Card 1	1	1–3 h	23 dBM
Card 2	2	3–5 h	26 dBM
Card 3	2	3–5 h	36 dBM
Card 4	4	5–8 h	30 dBM
Card 5	3	>8 h	36 dBM

Table 1 shows few of the demand cards that we used for our simulations (Out of 60+ demand cards created with this data). These demand cards were created based on the study on internet usage data in rural India, which included data on average number of hours spent per day by the user in accessing internet, internet usage patterns on different days, type of applications or services used, type of content used (video, audio streaming, web conferencing etc.) and their usage percentage.

For different demand profiles, different cards are chosen by the WSDs. During PDP, WSD chooses cards like 4 and 5, that make higher demands on spectrum with higher probability, than other cards. During LDP, WSD chooses cards like 1 having less spectrum demands with higher probability, and 2 and 3 with moderate probability. During BDP, WSD chooses any of the cards from the deck with equal probability. Similarly, we created demand cards of different combinations of the above parameters for the data obtained from Google spectrum database and used them in our simulations.

Evaluation Results. We evaluated the efficiency of our model by comparing the spectrum allocation of the white space network done by our autonomous spectrum assignment model with the spectrum allocation done by a centralised model. We considered centralised model of spectrum allocation as the benchmark, since it represents the ideal allocation for all the WSDs due to its global knowledge and the ability to freeze network operations while performing the allocation.

Figure 1a shows the mean spectrum utilisation for both the models for PDP. We can see that the utilisation for autonomous model is comparable to that of the utilisation for the centralised model. We found similar results for LDP and BDP demand profiles. Figure 1b, c and d show graphs of probability of usage of each strategy at different time intervals for PDP, LDP and BDP demand profiles

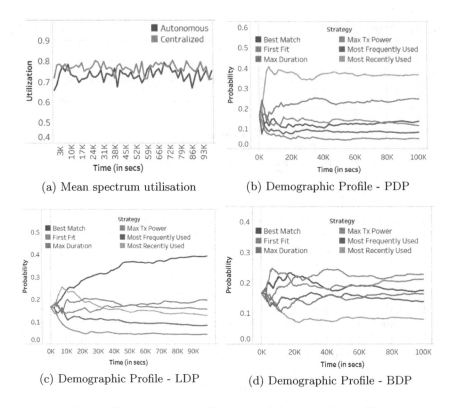

(a) Mean spectrum utilisation

(b) Demographic Profile - PDP

(c) Demographic Profile - LDP

(d) Demographic Profile - BDP

Fig. 1. Mean spectrum utilisation and demographic profiles

respectively. At each time instance, the probability values of all the strategies constitute the demographic profile at that instance. We can see that one of the strategies emerges with high probability in all the three demand profiles. For example, in PDP (Fig. 1b), "Most recently used" strategy has higher probability than other strategies, followed by "Maximum duration". We can also see that the demographic profile stabilises after sometime and the probabilities of strategies do not change beyond a threshold ϵ (0.01 in this case).

We ran simulations for different combinations of WSDs and different values of network characteristics. In all the cases, we observed that the strategies stabilise overtime and the system reaches a state of equilibrium. This also indicates that none of the WSDs are starving. We can conclude this because, if the WSDs were in a state of starvation, they would have changed their strategies in order to get better payoff and hence the demographic profile would not have stabilised. To further confirm the fairness of our model, we compared the mean of average payoffs of all the WSDs in our model with the centralised model and found them to be close.

Our algorithms that form various strategies are efficient and the fitness function which finds an optimal channel from all the available feasible channel(s) runs in linear time.

4   Conclusions

In this paper, an autonomous-agent model for spectrum assignment of white space devices is presented. The self-evolving and autonomous white space devices allocate spectrum to themselves in a way that maximises their utility, while also maximising the overall spectrum utility of the network. The developed solution of autonomous spectrum assignment can be deployed and self-trained for any geographical area with different internet usage patterns and network topology for optimum network utilisation. It is also flexible to adapt its strategy distribution with changes in load patterns or network dynamics. The model not only provides different algorithms to choose a channel in the form of strategies, but can also be customised and enriched with new algorithms. In our future work, we plan to expand the strategy set for the white space devices. We also propose the WSDs to have heterogeneous strategy set according to their idiosyncrasies, as against the current WSDs which have the same set of strategies. We also plan to include topological parameters like path loss and terrain information into our model for optimising network utilisation.

Acknowledgements. This work is partially supported by EU-India REACH Project under Grant ICI+/2014/342-896. The project aims to develop advanced technical solutions for providing high-speed broadband internet access in rural India in the unlicensed white space spectrum.

References

1. Zhu, L., Chen, V., Malyar, J., Das, S., McCann, P.: Protocol to access white-space (PAWS) databases (2015)
2. Murty, R., Chandra, R., Moscibroda, T., Bahl, P.: Senseless: a database-driven white spaces network. IEEE Trans. Mob. Comput. **11**(2), 189–203 (2012)
3. Li, C., Liu, W., Li, J., Liu, Q., Li, C.: Aggregation based spectrum allocation in cognitive radio networks. In: 2013 IEEE/CIC International Conference on Communications in China-Workshops (CIC/ICCC), pp. 50–54. IEEE (2013)
4. Halldórsson, M.M., Halpern, J.Y., Li, L.E., Mirrokni, V.S.: On spectrum sharing games. In: Proceedings of the Twenty-Third Annual ACM Symposium on Principles of Distributed Computing, pp. 107–114. ACM (2004)
5. Cao, L., Zheng, H.: Distributed spectrum allocation via local bargaining. In: SECON, pp. 475–486 (2005)
6. Chen, D., Zhang, Q., Jia, W.: Aggregation aware spectrum assignment in cognitive ad-hoc networks. In: 3rd International Conference on Cognitive Radio Oriented Wireless Networks and Communications, CrownCom 2008, pp. 1–6. IEEE (2008)
7. Cao, L., Zheng, H.: Distributed rule-regulated spectrum sharing. IEEE J. Sel. Areas Commun. **26**(1), 130–145 (2008)

8. Nie, N., Comaniciu, C.: Adaptive channel allocation spectrum etiquette for cognitive radio networks. Mob. Netw. Appl. **11**(6), 779–797 (2006)
9. Suris, J.E., DaSilva, L.A., Han, Z., MacKenzie, A.B.: Cooperative game theory for distributed spectrum sharing. In: IEEE International Conference on Communications, ICC 2007, pp. 5282–5287. IEEE (2007)
10. Bourdena, A., Kormentzas, G., Pallis, E., Mastorakis, G.: A centralised broker-based CR network architecture for TVWS exploitation under the rtssm policy. In: 2012 IEEE International Conference on Communications (ICC), pp. 5685–5689. IEEE (2012)
11. Bourdena, A., Kormentzas, G., Skianis, C., Pallis, E., Mastorakis, G.: Real-time TVWS trading based on a centralized CR network architecture. In: 2011 IEEE GLOBECOM Workshops (GC Workshop), pp. 964–969. IEEE (2011)
12. Pei, Y., Ma, Y., Peh, E.C.Y., Oh, S.W., Tao, M.-H.: Dynamic spectrum assignment for white space devices with dynamic and heterogeneous bandwidth requirements. In: 2015 IEEE Wireless Communications and Networking Conference (WCNC), pp. 36–40. IEEE (2015)
13. Kash, I.A., Murty, R., Parkes, D.C.: Enabling spectrum sharing in secondary market auctions. IEEE Trans. Mob. Comput. **13**(3), 556–568 (2014)
14. Chen, X., Huang, J.: Evolutionarily stable open spectrum access in a many-users regime. In: 2011 IEEE Global Telecommunications Conference (GLOBECOM 2011), pp. 1–5. IEEE (2011)
15. Anandkumar, A., Michael, N., Tang, A.: Opportunistic spectrum access with multiple users: learning under competition. In: 2010 Proceedings IEEE INFOCOM, pp. 1–9. IEEE (2010)
16. Liu, K., Zhao, Q.: Decentralized multi-armed bandit with multiple distributed players. In: Information Theory and Applications Workshop (ITA), pp. 1–10. IEEE (2010)
17. Li, H.: Multi-agent q-learning of channel selection in multi-user cognitive radio systems: a two by two case. In: IEEE International Conference on Systems, Man and Cybernetics, SMC 2009, pp. 1893–1898. IEEE (2009)
18. Felegyhazi, M., Čagalj, M., Hubaux, J.-P.: Efficient MAC in cognitive radio systems: a game-theoretic approach. IEEE Trans. Wireless Commun. **8**(4), 1984–1995 (2009)
19. Niyato, D., Hossain, E.: Competitive spectrum sharing in cognitive radio networks: a dynamic game approach. IEEE Trans. Wireless Commun. **7**(7), 2651–2660 (2008)
20. Han, Z., Pandana, C., Liu, K.: Distributive opportunistic spectrum access for cognitive radio using correlated equilibrium and no-regret learning. In: IEEE Wireless Communications and Networking Conference, WCNC 2007, pp. 11–15. IEEE (2007)
21. Chen, X., Huang, J.: Spatial spectrum access game: nash equilibria and distributed learning. In: Proceedings of the Thirteenth ACM International Symposium on Mobile Ad Hoc Networking and Computing, pp. 205–214. ACM (2012)
22. Xu, Y., Wang, J., Wu, Q., Anpalagan, A., Yao, Y.-D.: Opportunistic spectrum access in cognitive radio networks: global optimization using local interaction games. IEEE J. Sel. Top. Sig. Process. **6**(2), 180–194 (2012)
23. Wicke, D., Freelan, D., Luke, S.: Bounty hunters and multiagent task allocation. In: Proceedings of the 2015 International Conference on Autonomous Agents and Multiagent Systems, pp. 387–394. International Foundation for Autonomous Agents and Multiagent Systems (2015)
24. Jain, R.: REACH Internal Technical Report - Internet usage data in rural India. IIM Ahmedabad, India (2017)

Machine Learning-Aided Radio Scenario Recognition for Cognitive Radio Networks in Millimeter-Wave Bands

Jingyun Wang[1], Youping Zhao[1(✉)], Xin Guo[2], and Chen Sun[2]

[1] School of Electronic and Information Engineering,
Beijing Jiaotong University, Beijing, China
yozhao@bjtu.edu.cn
[2] Sony China Research Laboratory, Sony (China) Ltd., Beijing, China
{Xin.Guo,Chen.Sun}@sony.com

Abstract. Radio scenario recognition is critically important to acquire comprehensive situation awareness for cognitive radio networks in the millimeter-wave bands, especially for dense small cell environment. In this paper, a generic framework of machine learning-aided radio scenario recognition scheme is proposed to acquire the environmental awareness. Particularly, an advanced back propagation neural network-based AdaBoost classification algorithm is developed to recognize various radio scenarios, in which different channel conditions such as line-of-sight (LOS), non-line-of-sight (NLOS), and obstructed line-of-sight (OLOS) are encountered by the desired signal or co-channel interference. Moreover, the advanced AdaBoost algorithm takes the offline training performance into account during the decision fusion. Simulation results show that machine learning can be exploited to recognize the complicated radio scenarios reliably and promptly.

Keywords: BP-AdaBoost · Channel condition recognition
Cognitive radio networks · Machine learning · Radio scenario recognition

1 Introduction

In light of the emerging fifth generation (5G) mobile communication systems, massive MIMO, ultra-dense networks (UDN) and millimeter-wave communications are among the most promising technologies. To deal with the challenging interference management issues of ultra-dense small cell networks operating in the millimeter-wave bands, cognitive radio (CR) technologies can to be employed [1]. CR has been investigated intensively as an effective approach to dynamically adapting to the changes of environment and quality of service (QoS) of users. In cognitive radio networks, observation, reconfiguration and learning abilities are commonly expected [1]. Comprehensive

This work is supported in part by Sony China Research Laboratory, Sony (China) Ltd. Prof. Zhao's work is also supported in part by Beijing Natural Science Foundation (4172046).

© ICST Institute for Computer Sciences, Social Informatics and Telecommunications Engineering 2018
P. Marques et al. (Eds.): CROWNCOM 2017, LNICST 228, pp. 49–62, 2018.
https://doi.org/10.1007/978-3-319-76207-4_5

situation awareness, especially, the radio scenario recognition, is the prerequisite to acquiring or enhancing the learning ability of CR. A radio scenario can be characterized by a broad range of features in context of network topology, locations and configurations of base stations (BS) and user equipment (UE), radio propagation condition, spectrum usage, and source of interference, just to name a few. Moreover, in order to meet with the varying QoS requirements of UEs in the dense small cell environment, comprehensive situation awareness is required as the power of both desired signal and co-channel interference could be dynamically changing. For future ultra-dense small cell networks operating in the millimeter-wave bands, the ability of radio scenario recognition and interference management becomes even more important in order to identify the actual source of co-channel interference and the channel condition for the desired signal as well as the co-channel interference. Only with accurate and prompt radio scenario awareness, the QoS of users can be better ensured by making appropriate adaptations or reconfigurations of radio parameters. Mobility support and QoS support for millimeter-wave wireless networks are the major motivations for this work. How to realize comprehensive radio scenario recognition for ultra-dense networks in the millimeter-wave bands is the main issue investigated in this paper.

As we know, machine learning is an effective approach to voice or image recognition. Some research on machine learning-based scenario recognition focuses on robotics or image processing by employing probabilistic models, convolutional neural networks or multi-layered neural networks [2–4]. For the radio environmental awareness, radio scenario recognition may include various aspects such as spectrum occupation, signal classification, and radio channel condition recognition [5–9]. For example, a spectrum prediction algorithm based on artificial neural networks is proposed in [5]; spectral coherence and artificial neural networks are further employed to classify the modulation types of signals [6]. With regard to the channel condition, some researchers analyze the statistical characteristics of the received signal [7], while some researchers apply machine learning algorithms to none-LOS (NLOS) identification for ultra-wide band (UWB) systems [8, 9]. For example, a NLOS identification algorithm based on least square support vector machine (LSSVM) is presented in [8]. However, in order to improve the positioning accuracy, most of the existing work on radio channel condition recognition mainly considers the classification of line-of-sight (LOS) and none-LOS (NLOS) for the desired signal only. Communications in the millimeter-wave bands need to consider more environmental factors such as obstruction due to foliage. Scenarios with the obstructed LOS (OLOS), which are caused by moving or fixed objects (e.g., pedestrians, trees), are usually ignored for communications in low-frequency bands (e.g., sub-6 GHz band). Moreover, in order to improve the classification ability, boosting algorithms have been adopted to develop a strong classifier by combining multiple "weak" classifiers or base classifiers [10]. The weak classifier can be based on back propagation neural network (BP-NN) or support vector machine (SVM). AdaBoost algorithm is a kind of boosting algorithms. The AdaBoost algorithm enables high accuracy of classification with simple structure, which is suitable for the nonlinear classification problems of radio scenario recognition. In addition, radio environmental map (REM) which stores multi-dimensional radio scenario parameters has been proposed for CRs [11]. REM can serve as the "navigator" for the CRs by offering very comprehensive radio scenario information.

This article proposes a generic machine learning-aided radio scenario recognition scheme for dense small cell networks operating in the millimeter-wave bands. An advanced back propagation neural network based AdaBoost (BP-AdaBoost) algorithm is developed, which takes the offline training performance into account during the decision fusion. To the best of our knowledge, it is the first attempt to employ the AdaBoost algorithm for radio scenario recognition. Furthermore, three kinds of channel conditions (namely, LOS, NLOS, and OLOS) are taken into account for both the desired signal and the co-channel interference. Simulation results demonstrate the effectiveness and the advantages of the proposed algorithm.

The rest of this paper is organized as follows. In Sect. 2, the framework of machine learning-aided radio scenario recognition scheme is proposed. Main modules of radio scenario recognition are discussed in details. In Sect. 3, the advanced BP-AdaBoost algorithm is analyzed. In Sect. 4, the simulation results are presented to show the key performances. Summary is given in the last section together with discussions on future work.

2   Framework of Radio Scenario Recognition

Figure 1 shows the framework of the proposed radio scenario recognition scheme, which mainly consists of the following four key modules.

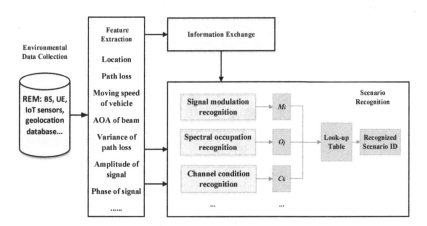

Fig. 1. Framework of the proposed radio scenario recognition scheme.

(i) **Environmental data collection** module: this module collects environmental data from multiple sources such as BS, UE, geolocation database, various environmental sensors, e.g., rain fall meter, Internet of things (IoT) sensors and the REM [11, 14].

(ii) **Feature extraction** module: this module extracts the useful features such as the path loss and its statistics, angle-of-arrival (AoA) of the desired signal and interference. Furthermore, instantaneous amplitude, phase and frequency of the signal can be employed for modulation classification or recognition.

(iii) **Information exchange** module: this module exchanges the system information among different entities such as BS, UE, and spectrum coordinator to make informed decisions, e.g., to classify the source of co-channel interference (either intra-cell interference or inter-cell interference).

(iv) **Scenario recognition** module: this module conducts the classification tasks relevant to scenario recognition, such as channel condition recognition, signal modulation recognition, spectral occupation recognition, and so on. The radio scenario type (i.e., the scenario ID in Fig. 1) can be determined by retrieving a look-up table, which maps the results of various recognition tasks such as channel condition, signal modulation, and spectral occupation. Each recognized scenario ID represents a unique radio scenario of interest.

This article takes the channel condition recognition as an example in the following subsections. To obtain comprehensive channel condition recognition in the millimeter-wave bands, not only LOS/NLOS but also OLOS are considered for both the desired signal and the co-channel interference. Figure 2 shows four typical radio scenarios with different channel conditions, just for illustration. Among these scenarios, Fig. 2(a) and (b) illustrate two scenarios with intra-cell co-channel interference, whereas Fig. 2(c) and (d) illustrate two scenarios with inter-cell co-channel interference. Particularly, in Fig. 2(a), the desired signal for UE_1 has LOS path. However, the desired signal for UE_1 is blocked by buildings and is in NLOS condition in Fig. 2(b). In Fig. 2(c), UE_1 experiences the inter-cell co-channel interference with LOS path, whereas it experiences the inter-cell interference with OLOS path in Fig. 2(d).

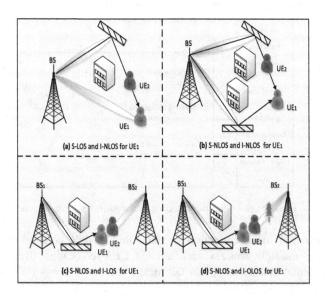

Fig. 2. Various radio scenarios of channel condition in millimeter wave bands. Note: in this figure, "S-LOS" represents the desired signal in LOS condition whereas "I-NLOS" represents the co-channel interference in NLOS condition.

2.1   Feature Extraction

To recognize the complicated radio scenario, the following parameters or features can be used for information exchange and channel condition classification.

(1) Location of UEs and BSs;
(2) AOA of the desired signal or interference;
(3) Path loss of the desired signal or the statistics of the path loss (such as variance of path loss);
(4) Root mean square delay spread;
(5) Probability distribution function of the received desired signal or interference.

As mentioned above, these features are mainly employed for information exchange and channel condition recognition. Obviously, which features are extracted and exploited can directly affect the ability and performance of radio scenario recognition. When the current features cannot meet the performance requirements, it indicates more features or deeper features from the raw data need to be extracted. For example, higher-order statistics (e.g., variance of path loss) is one of the deeper features employed in this paper. Similarly, the key idea of deep learning (e.g., convolutional neural networks and deep belief networks) is to design a feature extractor which transforms the raw data into a suitable internal representation [12]. The performance of radio scenario recognition can be enhanced by exploiting the additional deeper features.

2.2   Information Exchange

Interference exchange module is a critically important module in the proposed radio scenario recognition framework, especially for dense small cell networks. With exchanged information from neighboring cells, the source of interference and the type of co-channel interference can be determined effectively. The flow chart of information exchange between network entities such as UE, serving BS and spectrum coordinator (SC) is elaborated in Fig. 3. The key procedures are discussed as follows.

(1) UE transfers "information-1" to the serving BS (①). Note: "information-1" in Fig. 3 refers to the UE location information, received power, AOA, etc.
(2) According to the extracted features, the serving BS checks whether co-channel interference exist or not (by evaluating the interference-to-noise ratio of UE). If co-channel interference exists, the BS further checks whether the co-channel interference is from the serving cell itself (②–③).
(3) If it is determined that the co-channel interference is from the neighboring cell, the serving SC will find out which BS is the source of co-channel inter-cell interference first, and then report to the serving BS (④–⑤). Note: "information-2" in Fig. 3 includes the information about the source of interference.
(4) Based on the collected data and the exchanged information, the serving BS recognizes the type of interference (⑥).

With the help of the information exchange module, the various channel conditions of the desired signal as well as the various types of co-channel interference are taken into account in the scenario recognition module.

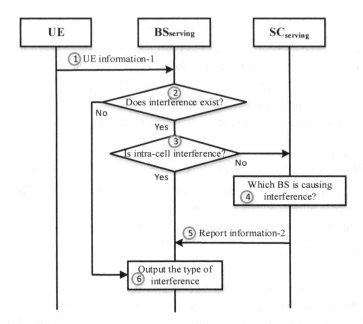

Fig. 3. Information exchange for co-channel interference recognition. Note: "information-1" refers to the UE location information, received power, AOA, etc.; "information-2" refers to the source of interference.

3 Advanced BP-AdaBoost Algorithm

In this section, the proposed advanced BP-AdaBoost algorithm for the radio scenario recognition module is discussed in two subsections. In the first subsection, the traditional BP-AdaBoost algorithm is discussed, which is a matured approach to simple classification problems with two different classes. The most convenient way is to apply the AdaBoost algorithm to multi-class problems directly. In the second subsection, the proposed advanced BP-AdaBoost algorithm can be used to address more complicated classification problems with multiple classes through decision fusion. Channel condition (e.g., LOS, NLOS, and OLOS) classification is an example application of the radio scenario recognition.

3.1 BP-AdaBoost Algorithm

Back propagation neural network (BP-NN) is well-known for its pattern recognition or classification capability. In this paper, BP-NN is employed as the "weak classifier" or "sub-classifier" of the AdaBoost algorithm. The BP-AdaBoost algorithm employs a number of BP neural networks in a cascade structure.

The BP-AdaBoost algorithm is carried out according to the following steps, as shown in Fig. 4.

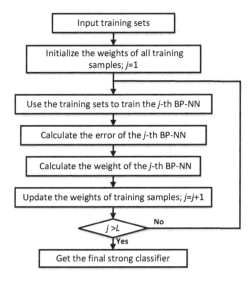

Fig. 4. Block diagram of the BP-AdaBoost algorithm

(1) Input the training sets: (x_i, y_i), $i = 1, 2, \ldots, K$; x can be a matrix populated with the selected features; $y_i = 1$ or -1, where "1" and "−1" represent the two types of scenarios to be recognized, respectively.

(2) Initialize the weights of all training sets, and set $j = 1$.

$$D_j(i) = \frac{1}{k}. \tag{1}$$

(3) Use the training subset (x_i, y_i) for training the j-th BP-NN and then get the output $g_j(i)$ of the BP-NN sub-classifier in the training step.

(4) Calculate the error (ε) of the j-th BP-NN as defined by (2).

$$\varepsilon = \sum_{i=1}^{K} D_j(i) \left(\frac{|g_j(i) - y_j(i)|}{2} \right). \tag{2}$$

(5) Calculate the weight (α_j) of the j-th BP-NN as expressed by (3).

$$\alpha_j = \frac{1}{2} \ln \left(\frac{1 - \varepsilon}{\varepsilon} \right). \tag{3}$$

(6) Update the weights of training samples by (4) and (5).

$$D_{j+1}(i) = D_j(i) \exp(-\alpha_j g_j y_j). \tag{4}$$

$$D_{j+1}(i) = \frac{D_{j+1}(i)}{B_j}. \tag{5}$$

where B_j is a normalization factor to ensure that the sum of the weights is equal to 1. B_j is defined by (6).

$$B_j = \sum_{i=1}^{K} D_{j+1}(i). \tag{6}$$

(7) Increase j by 1, i.e., $j = j + 1$. If $j > L$ (where L is the total number of BP neural networks employed by the BP-AdaBoost algorithm), get the final strong classifier $Y(x)$ as defined by (7). Otherwise, repeat Step-3.

$$Y(x) = sign\left[\sum_{j=1}^{L} \alpha_j g_j\right]. \tag{7}$$

Note that, as indicated by (7) in the last step of the BP-AdaBoost algorithm, the output of the strong classifier only has two types of output, i.e., either 1 or −1. The BP-AdaBoost algorithm used in the article can be replaced by any other classifiers which can distinguish two classes (e.g., Bayes classifier, LSSVM, etc.).

3.2   Advanced BP-AdaBoost Algorithm

Figure 5 shows the block diagram of the proposed advanced BP-AdaBoost classification algorithm, which employs a number of BP-AdaBoost sub-classifiers in parallel. To make more reliable radio scenario recognition, both the offline training performance for each scenario and the online classification results from each sub-classifier are taken into account during the decision fusion.

Supposing there are M ($M \geq 3$) different types of radio scenarios to be recognized, N sub-classifiers need to be employed and N is defined by (8).

$$N = C_M^2. \tag{8}$$

where C_M^2 is the total combinatorial number for taking any two types of scenarios out of M different scenarios.

Accordingly, N input data sets are collected and each input data set consists of the training or testing data corresponding to two different types of scenarios, as shown in the top box of Fig. 5. Note that each input data set may include a number of features. The detailed procedure of the advanced BP-AdaBoost algorithm is discussed as follows.

(1) The first step is to initialize the input data sets. The data sets include training sets and testing sets tagged by M different types of scenarios. For instance, "data set-i" consists of training data and testing data sets corresponding to "scenario-i".

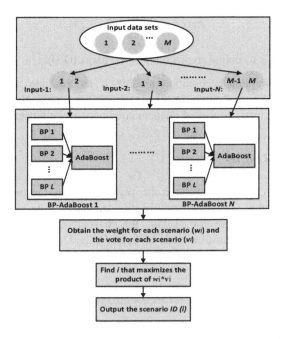

Fig. 5. Block diagram of the advanced BP-AdaBoost classification algorithm

(2) The second step is to train and test the BP-AdaBoost neural networks. The input set-*j* corresponds to the input of *j*-th BP-AdaBoost sub-classifiers, which can identify two different types of scenarios.

(3) The third step is to calculate the vote of *N* BP-AdaBoost classifiers for each scenario and the weight for each scenario. For instance, the vote (v_i) represents the total number of votes for the *i*-th scenario by *N* sub-classifiers; The weight (w_i) represents the average correct recognition rate for the *i*-th scenario in the training stage. In the testing stage, *j*-th sub-classifier outputs the recognized "scenario ID", say, *i*. In some sense, the weight (w_i) shows the offline training performance for the *i*-th scenario, as defined by (9).

$$w_i = \frac{\sum_{j=1}^{N} R(i,j)}{M - 1}. \tag{9}$$

where, $R(i, j)$ is the correct recognition rate corresponding to the *i*-th scenario for the *j*-th BP-AdaBoost sub-classifier.

(4) The fourth step is to make decision fusion for each scenario through a weighted voting. The product of weight (w_i) and vote (v_i) for each scenario is calculated and then find out the scenario ID (*i*) which corresponds to the maximal product, as expressed by (10).

$$\max_i w_i v_i \quad i = 1, 2, \ldots, M. \tag{10}$$

(5) The final step is to output the recognized scenario ID (i).

The channel condition recognition module is an example application of the advanced BP-AdaBoost algorithm. In this example, to recognize the LOS, NLOS, or OLOS scenario, the total number of channel conditions to be recognized is 3.

4 Simulation Results

Simulations are conducted to evaluate the performance of the proposed advanced BP-AdaBoost algorithm. The simulation results demonstrate the effectiveness of the advanced BP-AdaBoost algorithm. Taking the channel condition recognition as an example, the simulated scenarios include LOS, NLOS and OLOS. The system settings and key parameters assumed in the simulations are listed in Table 1.

Table 1. System parameters used in the simulation

Parameters	Value
Operating frequency	28 GHz
Number of hidden layer	1
Number of hidden layer nodes	6
Number of iterations in BP neural network	5
Learning rate of BP neural network	0.1
Learning goal of BP neural network (i.e., recognition error rate)	0.0004
Number of BP neural networks in AdaBoost (L)	10
Number of scenarios to be recognized (M)	3
Number of training sets or samples (K)	10000
Number of testing sets or samples	1000
Path loss exponent of OLOS/NLOS/LOS (α)	2.5/3.4/2.1
Shadow factor of OLOS/NLOS/LOS (σ in dB)	5.5/9.7/3.6

Moreover, the simulation is carried out by using the following millimeter-wave path loss model [13], as defined by (11).

$$PL[dB](d) = 20 \times \log_{10}\left(\frac{4\pi d_0}{\lambda}\right) + 10\alpha \log_{10}\left(\frac{d}{d_0}\right) + X_\sigma. \tag{11}$$

where d_0 is the given reference free space distance ($d_0 = 1$ m); λ is the wavelength of the carrier frequency (28 GHz); d is the distance between the transmitter and the receiver in meters ($d \geq d_0$); X_σ is a random variable following the zero mean Gaussian distribution of $N(0, \sigma^2)$; α is the path loss exponent and σ is the shadow factor.

Figure 6 shows the performance comparison of the advanced BP-AdaBoost algorithm when using single feature vs. two features. Note that in Fig. 6, "Single feature" represents the "path loss" only whereas "Two features" refers to "path loss" and "variance of path loss". Figure 6 shows the correct recognition rate trained by two features is higher than that when trained by single feature, especially for the OLOS recognition. In addition, for all three types of channel conditions, the correct recognition rates are over 99% when using two features. The simulation results indicate that an internal representation of raw features (e.g., the variance of path loss) can improve the performance of classifier significantly and reveal the potential benefits of exploiting the deeper features.

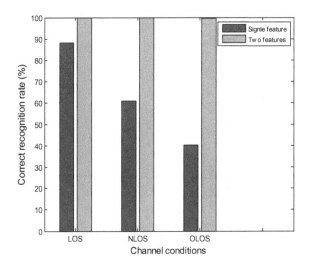

Fig. 6. Performance of the advanced BP-AdaBoost in terms of correct recognition rate

Furthermore, we compare the performance of the advanced BP-AdBoost algorithm with the traditional LSSVM algorithm in terms of correct recognition rate and operation time, as shown in Table 2 and Fig. 7. The correct recognition rate for LOS and NLOS are obtained with the same training and testing sets. The algorithm with two features has good ability to identify different types of channel conditions, which is shown in Table 2.

Table 2. Comparison of correct recognition rate

Methods	Correct recognition rate			
	LOS		NLOS	
	Two features	Single feature	Two features	Single feature
Advanced BP-AdaBoost algorithm	99.9%	88.3%	100%	60.9%
LSSVM [8]	99.8%	74.4%	100%	60.3%

Figure 7 shows the comparison of operation time (i.e., the computer running time) with different number of training samples (K = 6000 and 7000, respectively). Note that the simulation is conducted with a laptop computer (CPU: intel core i7 quard core, 2 GHz clock rate, and 4 GB RAM). With the increase of training samples, the operation time of the proposed Advanced BP-AdaBoost algorithm increases slightly whereas the LSSVM classifier requires much longer operation time. This simulation result shows that the proposed algorithm can ensure the effectiveness of scenario recognition and has faster training speed than the LSSVM algorithm. This simulation result also indicates the computational complexity of the proposed algorithm is much lower than the LSSVM.

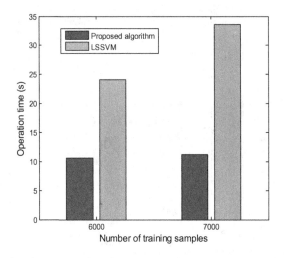

Fig. 7. Operation time comparison between the advanced BP-AdaBoost and LSSVM.

In sum, the simulation results demonstrate that the radio scenario recognition based on our proposed advanced BP-AdaBoost algorithm has significant performance advantages in terms of correct recognition rate and computational complexity. The advantages of the proposed scheme will become even more pronounced when dealing with more complicated scenarios such as scenarios with multiple interferers. Specifically, with the help of comprehensive environmental data obtained from multiple sources, it is highly possible to recognize the channel condition of each interferer separately by taking advantage of the narrow beamwidth of millimeter-wave antennas.

5   Summary

To obtain comprehensive and prompt radio scenario cognition for cognitive dense small cell networks operating in the millimeter-wave bands, a generic framework of machine learning-aided radio scenario recognition scheme is proposed in this paper. Particularly, taking the channel condition recognition as an example application, an advanced BP-AdaBoost algorithm is developed to identify the LOS, NLOS or OLOS channel conditions for both the desired signal and the various types of co-channel interference. Decision fusion is employed in the advanced BP-Adaboost algorithm, which takes the offline training performance into account. The correct recognition rate and operation time of the advanced BP-AdaBoost algorithm are evaluated and compared against the traditional LSSVM algorithm through simulations, which demonstrates the significant advantages of the proposed algorithm. Simulation results also indicate additional features or deeper features can help to improve the performance of the radio scenario recognition.

The scenario classifier simulated in this paper takes a simplistic view of the types of "scenarios", seeking predominantly to classify the signal path of interest and a single interference path as LOS, NLOS, or OLOS. For future work, we may consider more complicated scenarios with multiple interferers. The complexity of the proposed advanced BP-AdaBoost algorithm can be further analyzed and optimized. In addition, the operation time of the advanced BP-AdaBoost classifier might be further reduced by adopting parallel programming with multi-core CPU or graphics processing unit (GPU). Moreover, the internal functions of the AdaBoost algorithm can be further studied to export multiple classes directly. Last but not least, thorough performance evaluation with real-world measurement data is another important task of future work.

References

1. He, A., et al.: A survey of artificial intelligence for cognitive radios. IEEE Trans. Veh. Technol. **59**(4), 1578–1592 (2010)
2. Zhao, H., Liu, Y., Zhu, X., Zhao, Y., Zha, H.: Scene understanding in a large dynamic environment through a laser-based sensing. In: IEEE International Conference on Robotics and Automation (ICRA), pp. 127–133 (2010)
3. Liao, Y., Kodagoda, S., Wang, Y., Shi, L., Liu, Y.: Understand scene categories by objects: a semantic regularized scene classifier using convolutional neural networks. In: IEEE International Conference on Robotics and Automation (ICRA), pp. 2318–2325 (2016)
4. Harb, M., Abielmona, R., Naji, K., Petriu, E.: Neural networks for environmental recognition and navigation of a mobile robot. In: IEEE Conference on Instrumentation and Measurement Technology, pp. 1123–1128 (2008)
5. Tumuluru, V.K., Wang, P., Niyato, D.: A neural network based spectrum prediction scheme for cognitive radio. In: IEEE International Conference Communications (ICC), pp. 1–5, May 2010
6. Fehske, A., Gaeddert, J., Reed, J.H.: A new approach to signal classification using spectral correlation and neural networks. In: First IEEE International Symposium on New Frontiers in Dynamic Spectrum Access Networks, pp. 144–150 (2005)
7. Kegen, Y., Dutkiewica, E.: NLOS identification and mitigation for mobile tracking. IEEE Trans. Aerosp. Electron. Syst. **49**(3), 1438–1452 (2013)
8. Li, W., Zhang, T., Zhang, Q.: Experimental researches on an UWB NLOS identification method based on machine learning. In: 2013 IEEE International Conference on Communication Technology (ICCT), pp. 473–477 (2013)
9. Xiao, Z., Wen, H., Markham, A.: Non-line-of-sight identification and mitigation using received signal strength. IEEE Trans. Wireless Commun. **14**(3), 1689–1702 (2015)

10. Freund, Y., Schapire, R.E.: A desicion-theoretic generalization of on-line learning and an application to boosting. In: Vitányi, P. (ed.) EuroCOLT 1995. LNCS, vol. 904, pp. 23–37. Springer, Heidelberg (1995). https://doi.org/10.1007/3-540-59119-2_166
11. Yilmaz, H.B., Tugcu, T., Alagöz, F., Bayhan, S.: Radio environment map as enabler for practical cognitive radio networks. IEEE Commun. Mag. **51**(12), 162–169 (2013)
12. Lechun, Y., Bengio, Y., Hinton, G.: Deep learning. Nature **521**(7553), 436–444 (2015)
13. Sulyman, A.I., Nassar, A.T., Samimi, M.K., MacCartney, G.R., Rappaport, T.S., Alsanie, A.: Radio propagation path loss models for 5G cellular networks in the 28 GHz and 38 GHz millimeter-wave bands. IEEE Commun. Mag. **52**(9), 78–86 (2014)
14. Zhao, Y., Le, B., Reed, J.H.: Network support – the radio environment map. In: Fette, B. (ed.) Cognitive Radio Technology, pp. 325–366. Elsevier (2009)

Dynamic Base Station Sleep Control via Submodular Optimization for Green mmWave Networks

Akihiro Egami, Takayuki Nishio$^{(\boxtimes)}$ ⓘ, Masahiro Morikura ⓘ, and Koji Yamamoto ⓘ

Graduate School of Informatics, Kyoto University, Yoshida-honmachi, Sakyo-ku, Kyoto 606-8501, Japan
`nishio@i.kyoto-u.ac.jp`

Abstract. This paper proposes a dynamic millimeter-wave (mmWave) base station (BS) sleep control scheme for green mmWave networks. The typical coverage radius of mmWave BS is short due to high propagation and shadowing loss, thus large number of BSs are required to be deployed densely. A network consisting of many BSs consumes large energy. Sleep and activation control is a promising technique to reduce energy consumption. However, to select a set of BSs to sleep from large number of BSs to maximize total throughput under on condition that the total energy consumption of the network is limited is a NP-hard problem and it requires huge computation time. This paper formulates sleep control based on submodular optimization which can be solved quickly by using a greedy algorithm and the performance in the worst case is guaranteed to be $(1 - e^{-1})$-approximation. We design a utility function defined as total expected rate for mmWave access networks in consideration of the characteristics of mmWave communication, and prove that it is submodular and monotone. The sleep and activation control of mmWave BSs is formulated as a combinatorial optimization problem to maximize a monotone submodular function under the constraint that the number of BSs to be activated is limited due to energy constraints. Simulation results confirmed that the proposed scheme obtains a BS set achieving higher throughput than random selection and the scheme is polynomial time algorithm.

Keywords: mmWave · Sleep control · Submodular optimization

1 Introduction

The rapidly increasing mobile traffic in mobile access networks, such as cellular networks and wireless local area networks (WLANs), is leading to bandwidth shortages. The millimeter wave (mmWave) band is generally considered a key enabler of both high-speed and high-capacity wireless access for next generation (5G) cellular networks and WLANs [1,2]. Networks operating at this band have

© ICST Institute for Computer Sciences, Social Informatics and Telecommunications Engineering 2018
P. Marques et al. (Eds.): CROWNCOM 2017, LNICST 228, pp. 63–74, 2018.
https://doi.org/10.1007/978-3-319-76207-4_6

the ability to provide high-speed and high-capacity wireless Internet access [3,4] because its wide bandwidth enables multi-gigabit per second data transmission rates. However, the coverage of a mmWave base station (BS) is much smaller than that of a conventional BS that uses microwave because of its higher signal propagation loss. Furthermore, the received signal strengths of mmWave communication can be severely degraded when pedestrians block the line-of-sight (LOS) paths [5]. This phenomenon is known as the human blockage problem. In order to provide LOS paths to several users, the dense deployment of a large number of mmWave BSs have to be densely deployed.

However, dense deployment of mmWave BSs consumes a large amount of energy. Energy consumption is also an open issue in microwave communication systems that employ small-cell architectures. To reduce energy consumption, a dynamic BS sleep control scheme is proposed [6,7]. This scheme allows both the redundant BSs to sleep and the other BSs to be activated. The BS activation problem that selects the optimal set of BSs to activate is typically formulated as a combinatorial optimization problem or a non-linear optimization problem, and such problems are typically nondeterministic polynomial time (NP)-hard. Thus, it takes very long time to solve the problem especially when the number of BSs is large. Therefore, an algorithm is needed that can obtain either an optimal or a suboptimal solution in a practical computation time is needed.

Abbasi and Ghaderi [8] proposed a dynamic BS sleep control system for cellular networks via submodular optimization. Submodular optimization is considered in the literature related to combinatorial optimization problems, which are typically NP-hard problem. For submodular optimization, some algorithms that provide good approximations have been proposed [9,10]. In [8], BS sleep control was formulated as a submodular optimization problem and was solved using a heuristic algorithm based on a greedy algorithm that provides $(1 - e^{-1})$-approximation. However, both the radio propagation characteristic and system design of the microwave communications are quite different from those of our target, namely mmWave communications. For example, serious human blockage does not occur in conventional microwave communications. Dynamic handover schemes have been proposed to solve the human blockage problem [11]. The specific BSs that are active affect the dynamic handover gain, which therefore needs to be considered when selecting which BSs should sleep.

This paper proposes a dynamic BS sleep control scheme via submodular optimization for mmWave communication systems with dynamic BS handovers. We design a utility function by considering both the propagation characteristics of mmWaves and the handover gain, and we prove that the utility function is both submodular and monotone. The BS sleep control system is formulated as a combinatorial optimization problem for maximizing a monotone and submodular function under a knapsack constraint, in which the number of active BSs is limited by energy constraints. Our numerical results confirm both that we can quickly obtain satisfactory approximation solutions for the optimization problem using a greedy algorithm and that the proposed sleep control scheme increases the total throughputs of mmWave networks.

2   System Model

Both the BSs and the user terminals (UTs) are deployed in a two-dimensional area. When m BSs and n UTs are deployed, the sets of the BSs and the UTs are represented as $M = \{1, 2, 3, \ldots, m\}$ and $U = \{1, 2, 3, \ldots, n\}$, respectively. In order to reduce energy consumptions, some BSs are activated while the others sleep. We represent a set of active BSs as a subset of the power set $S \in 2^M$. We assume that the total energy consumed by the network is limited. The energy constraint given by

$$\sum_{j \in S} c_j \leq c_{\text{th}}, \tag{1}$$

where c_j represents the energy consumed by BS j and c_{th} represents the limitation on network energy consumption. The limitation of energy consumption limits the maximum number of activated BSs S.

We assume that m BSs are deployed in a hexagonal arrangement where the coverage of adjacent BSs overlap each other so as eliminate coverage holes. Figure 1 shows an example of the deployment of the BSs and the available PHY rate for LOS communication to UTs located in the area. The BSs use directional antennas that have beamforming in all directions. Thus, a BS covers a circular area, which is called a cell. Each user's PHY rate of each UT located in the cell is determined by their received signal strength indicator (RSSI) according to the IEEE 802.11ad standard [12]. Table 1 shows the correspondences between PHY rates and RSSIs. We represent the received signal strength and PHY rate of a communication between UT i and BS j as p_{ij} and $r(p_{ij})$ respectively. UTs in the cell edge eventually use minimum PHY rate for LOS communications.

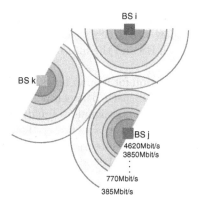

Fig. 1. The deployment of BSs and available rate.

We classify a set of UTs covered by BS j into two subsets of UTs; $R_j, R'_j \subseteq U$. Figure 2 shows an example of R_j, R'_j. UTs in R_j and that in R'_j are covered by only BS j and by multiple BSs including BS j, respectively. For the sake of

Table 1. PHY rates corresponding to RSSIs

PHY rate (Mbit/s)	RSSI (dBm)
385	−68
770	−66
⋮	⋮
3850	−54
4620	−53

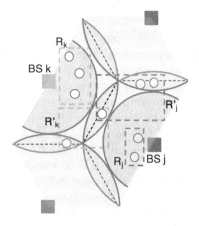

Fig. 2. Subsets of UTs and their locations.

simplicity, this paper assumes that an operator of the system knows R_j and R'_j accurately since UTs can know which BSs cover them from control frames such as beacon transmitted by each BS and the information can be feedbacked to the operator.

Next we mention an assumption for human blockage. As mentioned in Sect. 1, when a pedestrian blocks an LOS path between a BS and a UT, the received signal strength decreases sharply. The signal attenuation A is modeled as Gaussian distribution with $\mu = 13.4$ and $\sigma = 2.0$ [13]. Thus, PHY rate for NLOS communication becomes $r(p_{ij} - A)$. Moreover, we assume that LOS path blockages occur stochastically, where a link between BS j and UT i is blocked with a certain probability P_{ij} [14].

We explain assumptions for UTs in R'_j. As we mentioned above, since only UTs in the cell edge could be covered by multiple BSs and UTs in the cell edge use minimum PHY rate, UTs in R'_j use minimum PHY rate represented as $r_{\min}$. Since human blockage degrades RSSI 13.4 dB averagely, UTs in R'_j could not communicate with BS j in most case when their links are blocked. Thus, for the sake of simplicity, PHY rate for UTs in R'_j becomes zero when their links are blocked. Furthermore, we assume that a proactive BS handover scheme [15] is activated for UTs covered by multiple BSs. When a LOS path between a UT in R'_j and BS j is blocked, the UT communicating with a BS is transferred to another BS. Thus, the UTs in R'_j can communicate at $r_{\min}$ unless all the links with activated BSs are blocked. When the BSs in set S are activated, the probabilities that all LOS paths for UT i are blocked and that at least one of them is not blocked are, respectively, represented as

$$P_i^{\text{NLOS}}(S) = \prod_{j \in S} P_{ij}^{\mathbb{1}_{R'_j}(i)}, \tag{2}$$

$$P_i^{\text{LOS}}(S) = 1 - \prod_{j \in S} P_{ij}^{\mathbb{1}_{R'_j}(i)}, \tag{3}$$

where $\mathbb{1}_X(y)$ is an indication function that is 1 if X includes y and 0 otherwise.

We assume file download as an application for mmWave access networks. Since mmWave communication could achieve higher throughput than Internet and data server often limit the maximum transmission rate to reduce server load, we assume that the maximum throughput of the download is limited to several tens Mbit/s at the server side.

3   Submodular Optimization for mmWave BS Sleep Control

3.1   Problem Formulation

We consider a BS sleep control problem under the energy constraint (1). We propose a utility function given by

$$G(S) = \sum_{i \in U} \mathbb{E}[r_i], \tag{4}$$

where $\mathbb{E}[r_i]$ is the expected PHY rate of UT i, which is a function of S. $\mathbb{E}[r_i]$ is given as follows:

$$\mathbb{E}[r_i] = \sum_{j \in S} \{(1 - P_{ij})r(p_{ij}) + P_{ij}r(p_{ij} - A)\} \mathbb{1}_{R_j}(i) + r_{\min}\left(1 - \prod_{j \in S} P_{ij}^{\mathbb{1}_{R'_j}(i)}\right). \tag{5}$$

The first and second terms represent average PHY rates for UT i when the UT is covered by a BS and when the UT is covered by multiple BSs. As mentioned in Sect. 2, UTs covered by multiple BSs use minimum PHY rate $r_{\min}$, the rate becomes zero when their links are blocked, and the BS handover could be operated when blockage. Unless all the links are blocked, UTs can communicate with $r_{\min}$, the probability of which is (3).

Maximizing the proposed function increases the average throughput of mmWave communication. Since the capacity of mmWave communication is much larger than those of both conventional WLANs and cellular networks, connecting several users to a BS is preferable so that the capacity of mmWave communication is fully utilized. This is why we employ a summation for the function.

A constraint is the limitation of energy consumption shown in (1). Thus, from (1) and (4), the mmWave BS sleep control problem is formulated as follows:

$$\underset{S}{\text{maximize}} \quad G(S),$$

$$\text{subject to} \quad \sum_{j \in S} c_j \leq c_{\text{th}}, \tag{6}$$

We prove that the objective function increases monotonically and is a submodular function. Before this proof, we introduce both a lemma and a definition, as follows:

Lemma 1. *Let X and Y be sets with $X \cap Y = \emptyset$. Then,*

$$\prod_{j \in X \cup Y} P_{ij}^{\mathbb{1}_{R'_j}(i)} = \prod_{j \in X} P_{ij}^{\mathbb{1}_{R'_j}(i)} \prod_{j \in Y} P_{ij}^{\mathbb{1}_{R'_j}(i)}. \tag{7}$$

Proof. Let $X = \{x_1, x_2, \cdots, x_n\}$ and $Y = \{y_1, y_2, \cdots, y_m | y_i \neq x_j$ for any i and $j\}$, thus $X \cup Y = \{x_1, x_2, \cdots, x_n, y_1, y_2, \cdots, y_m\}$. Therefore,

$$\prod_{j \in X \cup Y} P_{ij}^{\mathbb{1}_{R'_j}(i)} = P_{i,x_1}^{\mathbb{1}_{R'_{x_1}}(i)} \cdots P_{i,x_n}^{\mathbb{1}_{R'_{x_n}}(i)} P_{i,y_1}^{\mathbb{1}_{R'_{y_1}}(i)} P_{i,y_m}^{\mathbb{1}_{R'_{y_m}}(i)}$$

$$= \prod_{j \in X} P_{ij}^{\mathbb{1}_{R'_j}(i)} \prod_{j \in Y} P_{ij}^{\mathbb{1}_{R'_j}(i)}. \tag{8}$$

$\square$

Definition 1. *If $f(S') \leq f(S)$ stands for every $S, S' \in 2^M$ with $S' \subseteq S$, $f(\cdot)$ is a monotone function.*

Theorem 1. *$G(S)$ is a monotone function.*

Proof. Let $S, S' \in 2^M$ and $S' \subseteq S$

$$G(S) - G(S')$$

$$= \sum_{i \in U} \left\{ \sum_{j \in S} [(1 - P_{ij})r(p_{ij}) + P_{ij}r(p_{ij} - A)] \mathbb{1}_{R_j}(i) + r_{\min} \left(1 - \prod_{j \in S} P_{ij}^{\mathbb{1}_{R'_j}(i)} \right) \right\}$$

$$- \sum_{i \in U} \left\{ \sum_{j \in S'} [(1 - P_{ij})r(p_{ij}) + P_{ij}r(p_{ij} - A)] \mathbb{1}_{R_j}(i) + r_{\min} \left(1 - \prod_{j \in S'} P_{ij}^{\mathbb{1}_{R'_j}(i)} \right) \right\}$$

$$= \sum_{i \in U} \left\{ \sum_{j \in S \setminus S'} [(1 - P_{ij})r(p_{ij}) + P_{ij}r(p_{ij} - A)] \mathbb{1}_{R_j}(i) \right.$$

$$\left. + r_{\min} \prod_{j \in S'} P_{ij}^{\mathbb{1}_{R'_j}(i)} - r_{\min} \prod_{j \in S} P_{ij}^{\mathbb{1}_{R'_j}(i)} \right\}. \tag{9}$$

Then, Lemma 1 gives

$$(9) = \sum_{i \in U} \left\{ \sum_{j \in S \setminus S'} [(1 - P_{ij})r(p_{ij}) + P_{ij}r(p_{ij} - A)] \mathbb{1}_{R_j}(i) \right.$$

$$\left. + r_{\min} \left[\prod_{j \in S'} P_{ij}^{\mathbb{1}_{R'_j}(i)} (1 - \prod_{j \in S \setminus S'} P_{ij}^{\mathbb{1}_{R'_j}(i)}) \right] \right\}. \tag{10}$$

From $P_{ij} \leq 1, 0 \leq r(\cdot)$ and $0 < r_{\min}$, (10) ≥ 0. Thus, $G(S') \leq G(S)$.   □

Now, we prove that the objective function $G(S)$ is a submodular function.

Definition 2. *If, for every $S, S' \in 2^M$ with $S' \subseteq S$, and $x \in 2^M \setminus S$, $f(S \cup x) - f(S) \leq f(S' \cup x) - f(S')$ holds, $f(S)$ is a submodular function.*

Theorem 2. *$G(S)$ is a submodular function.*

Proof. Lemma 1 gives

$$G(S' \cup x) - G(S') - \{G(S \cup x) - G(S)\}$$

$$= \sum_{i \in U} \left\{ \sum_{j \in x} [(1 - P_{ij})r(p_{ij}) + P_{ij}r(p_{ij} - A)] \mathbb{1}_{R_j}(i) \right.$$

$$\left. + r_{\min} \left[\prod_{j \in S'} P_{ij}^{\mathbb{1}_{R'_j}(i)} \left(1 - \prod_{j \in x} P_{ij}^{\mathbb{1}_{R'_j}(i)}\right) \right] \right\}$$

$$- \sum_{i \in U} \left\{ \sum_{j \in x} [(1 - P_{ij})r(p_{ij}) + P_{ij}r(p_{ij} - A)] \mathbb{1}_{R_j}(i) \right. \tag{11}$$

$$\left. + r_{\min} \left[\prod_{j \in S} P_{ij}^{\mathbb{1}_{R'_j}(i)} \left(1 - \prod_{j \in x} P_{ij}^{\mathbb{1}_{R'_j}(i)}\right) \right] \right\}$$

$$= \sum_{i \in U} \left[r_{\min} \prod_{j \in S'} P_{ij}^{\mathbb{1}_{R'_j}(i)} \left(1 - \prod_{j \in S \setminus S'} P_{ij}^{\mathbb{1}_{R'_j}(i)}\right) \left(1 - \prod_{j \in x} P_{ij}^{\mathbb{1}_{R'_j}(i)}\right) \right].$$

From $P_{ij} \leq 1$ and $0 < r_{\min}$, (11) ≥ 0. Thus, $G(S \cup x) - G(S) \leq G(S' \cup x) - G(S')$.   □

3.2   Algorithms to Solve the Problem

The above-mentioned problem is NP-hard. We employ a greedy algorithm to obtain a solution, which is proved to provide a good approximate solution for submodular optimization. A simple greedy algorithm starts with the empty set

S_0 and, during iteration k, the element maximizing the discrete derivative is added as long as a following constraint is satisfied.

$$S_k = S_{k-1} \cup \{\arg \max_x f(S_{k-1} \cup x) - f(S_{k-1})\}, \tag{12}$$

where $f(\cdot)$ is a monotone and submodular function. Nemhauser et al. [16] proved that a simple greedy algorithm provides a $(1 - e^{-1})$-approximation for a special case of the problem in which the same $c_j = c$ for all $j \in M$. In our problem, when all BSs consume the same amount of energy, we can employ the greedy algorithm to solve the problem and the solution is guaranteed to provide a $(1 - e^{-1})$-approximation.

Sviridenko [9] proposed a modified greedy algorithm for problems involving nonnegative integer weights. In iteration k, the modified algorithm selects an element based on the following update rule:

$$S_k = S_{k-1} \cup \{\arg \max_x \frac{f(S_{k-1} \cup x) - f(S_{k-1})}{c_x}\}. \tag{13}$$

Sviridenko proved that the algorithm provides a $(1 - e^{-1})$-approximation. We could employ this algorithm to solve our problem in a case where each BS consume different amount of energy.

4   Numerical Evaluation

4.1   Simulation Scenario

Figure 3(a) and (b) show examples of the BSs and UTs deployment. We assumed both that n UTs were located in a $300\,\mathrm{m}^2$ area and that they followed two types of distribution.

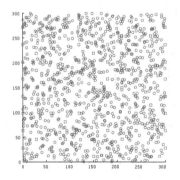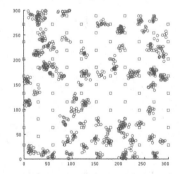

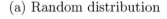

(a) Random distribution   (b) Cluster distribution

Fig. 3. Distribution of both BSs (red squares) and UTs (blue circles). (Color figure online)

Random distribution. UTs were located randomly.

Cluster distribution. We assumed that the users in an exhibition hall used a mmWave WLAN. The UTs were distributed based on Matern cluster process, as users might typically be found in such a venue when gathering around displays. In the Matern cluster process, the UTs were deployed for clustering and the locations of the cluster centers were determined according to a Poisson process with an intensity of λ_0. Cluster points were located within a disc of radius R around the centers of the clusters, and the UTs were distributed according to a Poisson process with an intensity of λ_1.

The transmit power and antenna gain for all BSs were set to 20 dBm and 16 dBi, respectively, and the attenuation constant was set to 2. $P_{i,j}$ was set to 0.2 for every value of i and j. The energy cost of activated BS c_j was set to the same value c_{BS} for every BS j. The maximum number of activated BSs was limited to $m_{act} = c_{th}/c_{BS}$, and the constraint (1) was represented as $|S| \leq m_{act}$.

As mentioned in Sect. 3.1, increasing the sum of the expected PHY rate leads to an increase in the average throughput for mmWave communication. We evaluated the throughput of each activated BS based on the number of packets transmitted successfully while considering both the traffic model and human blockage model. We assumed file download as an application for mmWave access networks, and we assumed that each user accounted for 30 Mbit/s user datagram protocol downlink traffic. We assumed that each user downloaded the file (100 MB) and waited 10 s before starting to download the next one.

We assumed both that the occurrence of human blockage followed the Poisson process and that its interval followed the exponential distribution. t_b and t_{nb} represent the duration of human blockage and its interval, respectively, and A represents attenuation. We simplified Ref. [13] for a binary model and then determined the values of both t_b and A. t_b [s] and A [dB] are according to Weibull distribution ($\lambda = 0.59, k = 6.32$) and Gaussian distribution ($\mu = 13.4, \sigma = 2.0$), respectively. We set the value of t_{nb} such that the ratio of the duration of human blockage duration to the total time was $P_{ij}(= 0.2)$. t_{nb} [s] is according to Exponential distribution ($\lambda = 0.46$).

We evaluated the computational time to solve the sleep control problem, the utility function, defined as the total expected PHY rate, and the total throughput of the activated BSs assuming both file download and human blockage. We compared the proposed scheme with a random selection scheme and a naive scheme. The random selection scheme selected m_{act} BSs randomly. The naive scheme calculated the utilities of all sets of m_{act} BSs and selected the BS set that maximized the utility function.

4.2 Numerical Result

Figure 4 shows computation time of each algorithm as a function of m_{act}. A MacBook Air (13-inch, Mid 2013) was used. The naive scheme with $m_{act} = 3$ required approximately 134 min to obtain its results, which is too long for

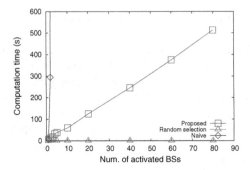

Fig. 4. Computation time vs. m_{act} for $n = 1000$ and $m = 93$.

dynamic sleep control. The time required by the proposed scheme was much shorter than that required by the naive scheme. The computational time for the proposed scheme increased linearly as m_{act} increased. This is because the proposed scheme employing the greedy algorithm calculated the utility function $O(mm_{act})$ times. The random selection scheme selected a set without calculating the utility function. Hence, its complexity was $O(1)$. The naive scheme calculated the utility function $O(\binom{m}{m_{act}})$ times.

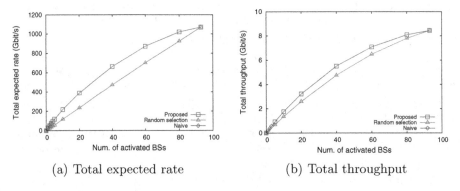

(a) Total expected rate   (b) Total throughput

Fig. 5. Total expected rate and total throughput vs. m_{act} for $n = 1000$ and $m = 93$, and randomly distributed UTs.

Random distribution. Figure 5(a) and (b) show the total expected rate and the total throughput as functions of m_{act}, respectively, for when the UTs were distributed randomly. Because the naive scheme took too long to obtain results, we omit them when $m_{act} \geq 4$. As m_{act} increased, both the total expected rate and total throughput increased because the numbers of UTs covered by the activated BSs increased. The proposed scheme achieved an approximately 40.0% higher total expected rate as well as an approximately 15.8% higher total throughput than the random selection scheme did for $m_{act} = 40$.

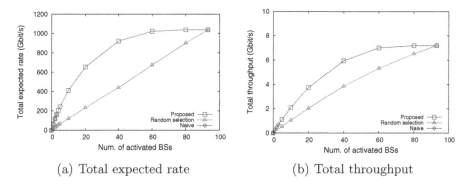

(a) Total expected rate   (b) Total throughput

Fig. 6. Total expected rate and total throughput vs. m_{act} for $\lambda_0 = 100/300^2$, $R = 10\,\mathrm{m}$, $\lambda_1 = 900/100\pi R^2$ and $m = 93$, and UTs distributed according to the Matern cluster process.

Cluster distribution. Figure 6(a) and (b) show the total expected rate and the total throughput as functions of m_{act}, respectively, for when the UTs were distributed according to the Matern cluster process. The proposed scheme achieved an approximately 109.3% higher total expected rate as well as an approximately 54.0% higher total throughput than the random selection scheme did for $m_{\mathrm{act}} = 40$. The gain of the proposed scheme was higher than for the case in which UTs were located randomly. Since the UTs were clustered, the number of UTs in each BS varied. Thus, the proposed scheme has the ability to select BSs that increases the throughput, while the random selection scheme might select a BS that has few UTs. As shown in the evaluations, the proposed scheme can obtain a set of BSs to achieve a high throughput with a practical computation time.

5   Conclusion

This paper proposed a dynamic BS sleep control scheme for green mmWave networks. The proposed scheme employed a utility function consisting of both the PHY rate and the probability of LOS path blockage between a BS and a UT. We proved that the proposed utility function both increases monotonically and is submodular. The BS sleep control system is formulated as a submodular optimization problem of maximizing a monotone, submodular function under the knapsack constraint, in which the number of activated BSs was limited due to energy constraints, where a greedy algorithm provided a $(1-e^{-1})$-approximation for the worst case. The numerical results confirmed both that the proposed scheme could quickly obtain a good approximation for the solution and that maximizing the proposed the objective function increased the average throughput of mmWave communications.

Acknowledgement. This work was supported in part by JSPS KAKENHI Grant Number 17H03266.

References

1. Rappaport, T.S., Sun, S., Mayzus, R., Zhao, H., Azar, Y., Wang, K., Wong, G.N., Schulz, J.K., Samimi, M., Gutierrez, F.: Millimeter wave mobile communications for 5G cellular: it will work!. IEEE Access **1**, 335–349 (2013)
2. Dehos, C., González, J.L., De Domenico, A., Kténas, D., Dussopt, L.: Millimeter-wave access and backhauling: the solution to the exponential data traffic increase in 5G mobile communications systems? IEEE Commun. Mag. **52**(9), 88–95 (2014)
3. Yong, S.K., Chong, C.C.: An overview of multigigabit wireless through millimeter wave technology: potentials and technical challenges. EURASIP J. Wirel. Commun. Netw. **2007**(1), 1–10 (2006)
4. Guo, N., Qiu, R.C., Mo, S.S., Takahashi, K.: 60-GHz millimeter-wave radio: principle, technology, and new results. EURASIP J. Wirel. Commun. Netw. **2007**(1), 48 (2007)
5. Giannetti, F., Luise, M., Reggiannini, R.: Mobile and personal communications in the 60 GHz band: a survey. Wirel. Pers. Commun. **10**(2), 207–243 (1999)
6. Zhou, S., Gong, J., Yang, Z., Niu, Z., Yang, P.: Green mobile access network with dynamic base station energy saving. In: Proceedings of the ACM MobiCom, Beijing, China, vol. 9, no. 262, pp. 10–12, September 2009
7. Oh, E., Krishnamachari, B., Liu, X., Niu, Z.: Toward dynamic energy-efficient operation of cellular network infrastructure. IEEE Commun. Mag. **49**(6), 56–61 (2011)
8. Abbasi, A., Ghaderi, M.: Energy cost reduction in cellular networks through dynamic base station activation. In: Proceedings of the IEEE SECON, Singapore, pp. 363–371 (2014)
9. Sviridenko, M.: A note on maximizing a submodular set function subject to a knapsack constraint. Oper. Res. Lett. **32**(1), 41–43 (2004)
10. Krause, A., Guestrin, C.: Submodularity and its applications in optimized information gathering. ACM Trans. Intell. Syst. Technol. **2**(4), 32 (2011)
11. Oguma, Y., Nishio, T., Yamamoto, K., Morikura, M.: Proactive handover based on human blockage prediction using RGB-D cameras for mmwave communications. IEICE Trans. Commun. **99**(8), 1734–1744 (2016)
12. IEEE Std 802.11ad: Wireless LAN medium access control (MAC) and physical layer (PHY) specifications Amendment 3: Enhancements for Very High Throughput in the 60 GHz Band (2014)
13. Maltsev, A., Erceg, V., Perahia, E., Hansen, C., Maslennikov, R., Lomayev, A., Sevastyanov, A., Khoryaev, A.: Channel models for 60 GHz WLAN systems, Document IEEE 802.11-09/0334r8, May 2010
14. Bai, T., Vaze, R., Heath, R.W.: Analysis of blockage effects on urban cellular networks. IEEE Trans. Wirel. Commun. **13**(9), 5070–5083 (2014)
15. Oguma, Y., Arai, R., Nishio, T., Yamamoto, K., Morikura, M.: Proactive base station selection based on human blockage prediction using RGB-D cameras for mmwave communications. In: Proceedings of IEEE Globecom, San Diego, CA, pp. 1–6, December 2015
16. Nemhauser, G.L., Wolsey, L.A., Fisher, M.L.: An analysis of approximations for maximizing submodular set functions - I. Math. Prog. **14**(1), 265–294 (1978)

Implementation of a Pseudonym-Based Signature Scheme with Bilinear Pairings on Android

Leonardo Oliveira$^{(\boxtimes)}$ (iD), Victor Sucasas, Georgios Mantas,
and Jonathan Rodriguez

Instituto de Telecomunicações, Aveiro, Portugal
leonardooliveira@ua.pt

Abstract. Privacy preservation is of paramount importance in the emerging smart city scenario, where numerous and diverse online services will be accessed by users through their mobile or wearable devices. In this scenario, service providers or eavesdroppers can track users' activities, location, and interactions with other users, which may discourage citizens from accessing smart city services. Pseudonym-based systems have been proposed as an efficient solution to provide identity confidentiality, and more concretely pseudonym-based signature schemes have been suggested as an effective means to authenticate entities and messages privately. In this paper we describe our implementation of a pseudonym-based signature scheme, based on bilinear-pairings. Concretely, our implementation consists of an Android application that enables users to authenticate messages under self-generated pseudonyms, while still enabling anonymity revocation by a trusted third party in case of misbehavior. The paper presents a description of the implementation, performance results, and it also describes the use cases for which it was designed.

Keywords: Privacy-preserving · Mobile applications
Bilinear pairings

1 Introduction

Privacy-preserving solutions are required to address the users' privacy concerns and foster a rapid penetration of smart city applications in the real world. Providing anonymous and secure communication between mobile applications and the Smart City infrastructure is cornerstone in this scenario, and current technology faces the problem that traditional Public Key Management systems do not provide privacy. Moreover, the current digital anonymous credential systems in the state-of-the-art are too complex to be applied in wearable or mobile devices due to its computation delay and communication overhead.

Previous research efforts have pointed out several privacy issues that demand novel solutions [1]. For example, Public Key Infrastructure is not suitable for

© ICST Institute for Computer Sciences, Social Informatics and Telecommunications Engineering 2018
P. Marques et al. (Eds.): CROWNCOM 2017, LNICST 228, pp. 75–87, 2018.
https://doi.org/10.1007/978-3-319-76207-4_7

privacy preservation, and new Key Management Systems should be implemented [2]. In this framework, pseudonym-based systems have been suggested as promising research direction, since pseudonyms can be used to hide the users' real identity [3], and still can enable revocation mechanisms in case of misbehavior. Pseudonyms are issued by a certification authority and they can be used to sign messages, thus providing authentication and integrity [4,5]. Also, pseudonyms can be renewed on demand to avoid linkability of different data transactions, which could eventually allow eavesdroppers to infer the users identities. This pseudonym renewal requires a permanent contact with the Certification Authority, except systems that provide pseudonym self-generation, such as the work in [6], which has been followed by other works such as [7–9]. This paper describes the implementation of the system described in [7], which was originally designed for a Vehicular Network, and it has been now adapted into a mobile application.

The rest of the paper is structured as follows: Sect. 2 describes the system model, the system functionality, and some use case scenarios envisaged for this system; Sect. 3 provides a brief description of the cryptosystem; Sect. 4 provides the implementation details; Sect. 5 shows a performance evaluation; and finally, Sect. 6 concludes this paper.

2   System Model

The system is composed of a set of smartphones (clients) running a mobile app that enables privacy-preserving authentication between each other. Namely, clients can send signed messages in an anonymous manner, i.e., the receiver can trust the sender of the message but it is not feasible to figure out the identity of the original sender (except if traffic analysis techniques are applied at the network level, which is out of the scope of this work and it should be addressed by appropriate countermeasures). These clients can sign the transmitted messages with their self-generated pseudonyms, which cannot be linked to the users real identities. Moreover, different pseudonyms from the same user can also not be linked to each other. Hence, all pseudonyms shared in the network will be statistically indistinguishable.

A message is any type of information that is being shared between the clients. The system also enables the transmissions of null messages, where the proposed message authentication application is used with the sole purpose of authenticating the client and not to convey any message in particular. Section 2.2 provides a real scenario exemplifying the type of messages that could be exchanged.

Apart from clients, the system is also composed of a certification authority (CA) and verifiers. The CA is in charge of generating public parameters required for the cryptosystem implemented in the proposed system, and the generation of credentials for legitimate users. The CA is also in charge of revoking users credentials in case of misbehavior. The verifier is any entity receiving and validating a signed message, for this validation the verifier is not required to have a valid credential, only the public parameters generated and distributed by the CA are sufficient to validate messages.

2.1 System Functionalities

The system provides mechanisms to: (i) enable the CA to provide certificates to trusted clients, so only legitimate clients can successfully send signed messages; and (ii) enables clients to use the certificates to generate pseudonyms on demand and sign messages with such pseudonyms; (iii) enables verifiers to validate signed messages from legitimate clients and discard messages from dishonest clients that are not provided with valid certificates. The proposed system assures the privacy of each sender (client), since the verifiers cannot link the pseudonyms to the users real identities or to other pseudonyms of the same client. Figure 1 illustrates the interaction between the system's entities, that will be described below.

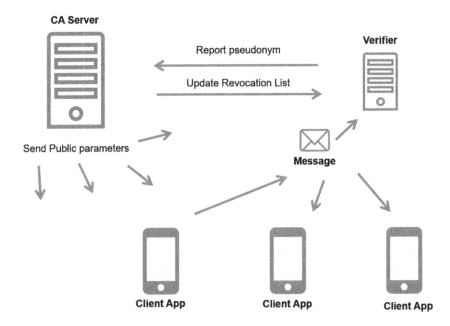

Fig. 1. The interactions between the entities in the system. Any client can act as a verifier.

The system also enables conditional privacy, i.e., it allows the trusted authority (the CA) to identify the origin of a message in exceptional situations. This can occur when a client is malfunctioning or misbehaving, which could lead to the transmission of signed messages with misleading information. In such a case, the CA can track the pseudonym used by the sender of these messages to the users real identity. Moreover, the CA can include the future pseudonyms of the blacklisted misuser in a Revocation List (RL), enabling other users to ignore future messages from the same sender.

Before being capable of sending messages, a client needs to be certified. This happens in a registration process that starts in a Certified Authority (CA). The CA holds all the information of the clients that belong to the system, including, of course, their real identity. For each registered client, the CA can issue credentials. Those credentials can be used by clients to authenticate themselves or authenticate transmitted messages towards a verifier.

When receiving a message, the verifier validates its authenticity. The verification can be done by other clients or verifying entities deprived of credentials. A message is valid if it comes from a valid client, which only happens with clients that use a credential issued from the CA. Nonetheless, the verifier still cannot know the origin of message, he can just perform the verification algorithm needed to validate it. The verification algorithm can be performed by any entity holding the public parameters generated by the CA.

The system is time-based and requires loose synchronization between entities. Namely, clients can renew all the pseudonyms updating a public parameter that can be self-generated. In the verification process, a time restriction public key must also be renewed and distributed by the CA to all potential verifiers. Hence, the system is divided in time slots, in which the CA and the users update a restriction key and the pseudonyms respectively. The revocation list must also be renewed and distributed by the CA with all blacklist pseudonyms.

2.2   Use-Case Scenarios

The proposed system can be used in any use case scenario requiring privacy-preserving authentication. The proposed system however has been designed and will be tested in a real environment in a crowdsourcing application, where users collect information about the surrounding environment and transmit this information to a back end server. Namely, users of the developed app running the client side of the system will send messages with information like air pollution, noise level and their landmarks. The information will be gathered by sensor integrated in the mobile devices or externalized and connected to the users smartphones through Bluetooth. These messages, after being signed with a pseudonym, will be sent to a data aggregator, i.e., a smart-city server, where they would be validated while preserving the senders privacy. Thus, this server would act as a verifier of the transmitted information. The stored information will perform data analysis to generate statistical information about air and noise quality of different locations. The data aggregator (verifier) will also be in charge of detecting misbehavior (e.g., users transmitting misleading or adulterated data) and eventually contact the CA to report the affected pseudonyms, hence triggering the anonymity revocation mechanism in the CA. After that, all pseudonyms from blacklist clients would be revoked and the client would be ignored in the future results. It is worth commenting that a number of research works have already proposed effective means to detect data outliers that could be used in the proposed use case scenario.

The proposed system is also suitable for a scenario where several clients need to authenticate themselves to get access to a given service, while preserving their privacy. In that case, they would send empty messages, where the only important part would be the signature itself, that could be validated by the service provider. The service provider, playing the role of verifier, would grant access to authorized clients without the knowledge of their real identities. Cases of misbehavior, like the usage of the same pseudonym several times in a short space of time, could trigger anonymity revocation.

3   Pseudonym-Based Signature Scheme

Although we would like to refer interested readers to the works [6] and [7] for more details on the pseudonym based signature scheme and the conditional privacy-preserving system respectively, in this section we describe briefly the mathematical operations included in our implementation. The system is divided in the following logical blocks: (i) parameter generation; (ii) credential generation;·(iii) pseudonym generation; (iv) message signing; and (v) signature verification.

For the public parameter generation, the CA performs the following steps, and publishes the tuple $(G_1, G_2, P, H_1, H_2, H_3, P, W)$ and the time variant tuple (Q_i, W_i). The time variant values must be computed again in each time slot. The value s is the CA secret key.

1. The CA selects two cyclic groups of prime order p, G_1 and G_2, in which the discrete logarithm problem is hard and with an efficient bilinear map e such that $e : G_1 \times G_1 \rightarrow G_2$.
2. The CA also picks two cryptographic hash functions $H_1, H_2 : \{0,1\}^* \rightarrow G_1$ and $H_3 : \{0,1\}^* \rightarrow Z_p$ (where Z_p is the multiplicative group).
3. The CA selects P as generator of G_1.
4. The CA computes a time variant public key $Q_i = H_1(T(time))$.
5. The CA selects a secret $s \in_R Z_p$.
6. The CA obtains $W = sP$ and a restriction key $W_i = sQ_i$.

To generate a credential for a client, the CA performs:

1. The CA selects randomly $\mu \in Z_p$.
2. The CA computes the secret value as $Su = P\frac{1}{(s+\mu)}$.
3. The CA sends the user the credential (μ, Su).

It is worth commenting that in the implemented system, every user receives 10 credentials where the μ values are obtained with a hash chain $\mu_i = H_3^i(\mu)$ for $i = \{0, \ldots, 10\}$.

Then, each user/client can self-generate pseudonyms using these credentials:

1. The client computes $Q_i = H_1(T(time))$.
2. The client computes a pseudonym for each of the 10 credentials by computing $Pseu_j = \mu_j Q_i$ for $i = \{1, \ldots, 10\}$.

Clients provided with a valid credential can sign a message m using their self-generated pseudonyms:

1. The client selects $\alpha, r, r' \in_R Z_p$.
2. The client computes $T = \alpha Su$, $R_{G_1} = rQ_i$ and $R = e(Q_i, P)^{r'}$.
3. The client computes $c = H_2(M||T||R_{G_1}||R||Pseu_j||T(time))$, where the operator $||$ represents concatenation.
4. The client computes $s_1 = \alpha c + r'$ and $s_2 = \mu_j c + r$.

The signature of m with the pseudonym $Pseu_j$ is the tuple $\sigma = (T, c, s_1, s_2)$. Which can be verified by any entity having the public parameters by performing the following steps:

1. The verifier obtains $Q_i = H_1(T(time))$.
2. The verifier computes $R'_{G_1} = s_2 Q_i - cPseu_j$ and $R' = e(Q_i, P)^{s_1}/e(Pseu_j + W_i, T)^c$.
3. The verifier computes $c' = H_2(M||T||R'_{G_1}||R'||Pseu_j||T(time))$.
4. The verifier considers the signature valid if $c' = c$ holds.

These steps have been implemented into the described system in the different entities defined in the system model. Due to space constraints we do not detail here preliminary mathematical definitions or proofs of security. More details can be found in the works [6,7].

4 Implementation Details

Our implementation of the system is based in Java. This enables to compilation and deployment in different contexts. In the proposed scenario, it is deployed in a mobile app, running in Android, where the client side of the system is placed.

In what concerts to the algorithmic part of the system, we used Java Pairing-Based Cryptography Library (JPBC) [10], a Java library that allowed us to implement all the cryptographic calculations related to bilinear maps. This library can run out of the box on Android 2.1+, which was verified in our implementation. The system is mainly split into the entities described in the system model: The CA, the Verifier and the Client (The clients can also act as verifiers when receiving signed messages). The following subsections describe the implementation details of the different mechanisms of the proposed system:

4.1 Public Parameter Generation

The Public Parameters are all the necessary cryptographic parameters used to perform several calculations in different steps of the system. These parameters are available publicly and distributed by the CA. It gives access to the cyclic groups G1 and G2, the multiplicative group of prime order p, Zp, the generator P, the permanent public key W, time restriction public key Wi, the current time slot, the time variant parameter and the hash functions H1, H2 and H3.

This class is wrapped by other classes, and it is never directly manipulated in the interface of the implementation. In fact, this layer of the package developed is the lower one. All the mathematical part is abstracted in the three main entities described below. The CA Server, the Verifier and the Client are the outer layers of the system, representing the main logical entities.

For a rationale of the implementation, the lines below describe the enclosed modules, represented in the Fig. 2.

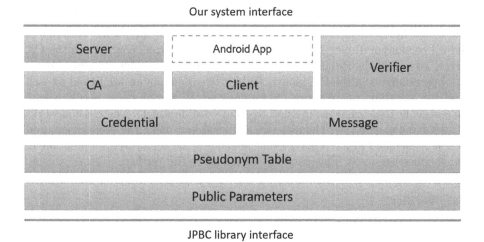

Fig. 2. The layered interconnection between the components, from the JPBC library to our system interface.

4.2   CA Server

The CA Server is the central part of the system. It contains an instance of the CA, that handles all the confidential information of the system required to issue credentials and revoke anonymity. Once again, the server abstracts all the interactions with the CA instance. When it starts running, it is available to answer to requests of Public Parameters, Credentials - by the clients - and exclusion of pseudonyms - by verifiers. The CA instance, when created, generates the original copy of the Public Parameters, described above. Also, the number of time slots and the number of pseudonyms by time slot are defined here. The CA can generate a Credential for each Client. The CA class can generate as many credentials as the server needs. Each Credential is later used by the Client to generate its pseudonyms. Despite of this, the server also must have a list of all the pseudonyms to enable anonymity revocation if needed. Because of this, the pseudonyms are also generated in the server side using a copy of the credentials issued by the CA. The server uses another class to handle this, called

Pseudonym Table. The Pseudonym Table provides a systematic manner to store lists of pseudonyms by time slot. In theory, it is a table of N pseudonyms by T time slots.

The class provides an interface to automatically manipulate those pseudonyms, including its generation. When the server - or also the verifier and client - needs to generate a list of pseudonyms, it provides the correspondent credential and time slot.

4.3 Client

The Client holds its information, so it has a Credential, the Public Parameters and a Pseudonym Table. The first time the client runs, he connects to the CA server, asking for the Public Parameters and a credential. After, he generates its set of pseudonyms in the Pseudonym Table. The pseudonyms are linked to each time slot and they can be generated on demand. When the client needs to send a message, he uses a specific method to do it, sendMessage(). The method works using some dependencies: the message is first signed using the pseudonym, and after it is included inside a packet that also holds the signature, the pseudonym and the message itself. This packet is then sent to the verifier.

4.4 Verifier

The Verifier, when initializing, has to get the Public Parameters from the CA Server and an updated version of the pseudonym blacklist (also called revocation list) - the list of blocked pseudonyms. This blacklist is refreshed at least when there is a new time slot. With that completed, the Verifier is ready to validate received messages. When it receives a validation of a message, first it checks the blacklist to verify if the pseudonym is not banned. If it is, it returns that the message is invalid. If not, it performs the calculations to check the validity of the message. According to the calculations, it returns whether the message is valid or not. If, for some reason, the verifier detects a suspicious activity for a given pseudonym, for instance, being used too many times in a small interval of time, it can report it to the server.

Figure 3 shows the implementation's class diagram, generated with ObjectAid UML Explorer, in the Eclipse IDE.

In this analysis, it is missing some implementation details of the client side. It is done in a mobile app, running on Android 4.4+. The android app uses the Client class of the package. For demonstration purposes, the developed app allows the client to connect to the server, receiving the credential and public parameters, and manually synchronize the time slots and generate pseudonyms. The pseudonyms can be selected manually to send messages. If for some reason the time slot is outdated, all the attempts to send messages will fail, so the synchronization must be accomplished.

In Fig. 4, we represent the pseudonyms in the application side. A pseudonym is a point in an elliptic curve. To be exact, in our implementation, each

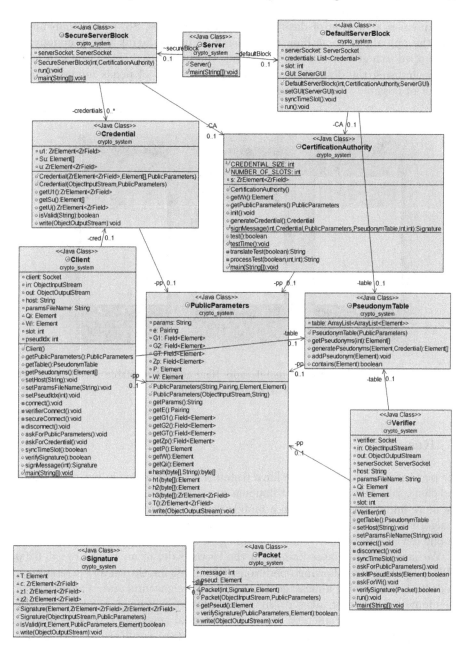

Fig. 3. System's class diagram, generated with ObjectAid UML Explorer, a tool available in the Eclipse IDE.

pseudonym is a portion of data described in 128 bytes. So, rather than numbers, the app shows something more visual and meaningful. The pseudonyms are mapped to a grid of colours, where they can be selected. The client can send a message using the desired pseudonym. The quantity of pixels represents the amount of possible variations that pseudonyms can have.

Fig. 4. Some screenshots to the mobile app. The client's available pseudonyms are represented on the top, and the actions are logged below.

5   Results

For performance evaluation, we have tested the performance in both the server and client side. Opposed to what happens in the server side, the clients resources are more limited since it runs in a mobile device. Due to the strong component of algorithmic computations performed in this cryptosystem, computations on a mobile device can be more time consuming.

We measured the lapsed times in the server side, in an Intel Core i5-6200 CPU, executing the following operations: (i) initializing the server; (ii) issuing a credential; (iii) signing a message; (iv) verifying a signature; and v) generating a pseudonym. The server takes 207 ms to initialize, which involves generating the private and public parameters. For each credential generation, it takes 373 ms. The signature generation takes 60 ms, the signature verification takes 94 ms. Generating a pseudonym takes 50 ms. For a scenario of 1 million users, with 10 pseudonyms per time slot, it would take more than 8 min to precompute all the pseudonyms. This pseudonym precomputation is advisable to speed up the anonymity revocation mechanism since the time of searching for a pseudonym in a list is negligible. For example, searching over 500.000 pseudonyms takes less than 2 ms.

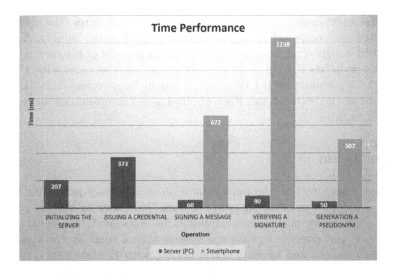

Fig. 5. Time performance in both the server and client side

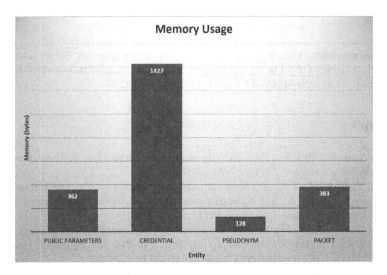

Fig. 6. Memory usage in both the server and client side

These time measurements were also performed in a smartphone (Samsung Galaxy S6), running a Exynos 7420 Octa CPU. The computations in the client side are: (i) signing a message; (ii) verifying a signature; and (iii) generating a pseudonym. In general, it resulted in around 10× more time spent when compared to server side. The full results are presented in Fig. 5.

In terms of memory, the size of each component is negligible. Despite of this, it is worth analysing the amount of data transmitted between entities. The public parameters have 362 bytes. A credential has 1427 bytes (the credentials implemented are composed by 10 secret values in G2 and 1 in G1). A packet composed by a signed message has 383 bytes plus the size of the message itself. Each pseudonym has 128 bytes. In the server side, for a scenario with 1 million users, with 10 pseudonyms per time slot, it would be necessary 1.28 GBytes to precompute all the pseudonyms. Figure 6 illustrates the proportion between the size of such entities.

6   Conclusion

In this paper we describe the implementation of a privacy-preserving system based on a pseudonym-based signature scheme that relies on bilinear pairings. Despite of the heavy algorithmic computations associated to bilinear pairing operations, it was possible to obtain a system with a small footprint in terms of time performance and memory consumption, with the integration of JPBC library, running on Java. The same results were also promising when obtained in the client side (implemented in an Android smartphone), proving that bilinear pairings can be efficiently implemented on mobile devices for some specific use cases.

Acknowledgement. This work is supported by the European Structural Investment Funds, through CENTRO 2020 [Project Nr. 017785 (CENTRO-01-0247-FEDER-017785)] and EU-H2020-MSCA-ITN-2016 SECRET-722424.

References

1. Li, M., Lou, W., Ren, K.: Data security and privacy in wireless body area networks. IEEE Wirel. Commun. **17**(1), 51–58 (2010)
2. Wasef, A., Lu, R., Lin, X., Shen, X.: Complementing public key infrastructure to secure vehicular ad hoc networks [security and privacy in emerging wireless networks]. IEEE Wirel. Commun. **17**(5), 22–28 (2010)
3. Boneh, D., Franklin, M.: Identity-based encryption from the Weil pairing. In: Kilian, J. (ed.) CRYPTO 2001. LNCS, vol. 2139, pp. 213–229. Springer, Heidelberg (2001). https://doi.org/10.1007/3-540-44647-8_13
4. Huang, J.-L., Yeh, L.-Y., Chien, H.-Y.: ABAKA: an anonymous batch authenticated and key agreement scheme for value added services in vehicular ad hoc networks. IEEE Trans. Veh. Technol. **60**(1), 248–262 (2011)
5. Lu, R., Lin, X., Shi, Z., Shen, X.S.: A lightweight conditional privacy-preservation protocol for vehicular traffic-monitoring systems. IEEE Intell. Syst. **28**(3), 62–65 (2013)
6. Zhang, Y., Chen, J.-L.: A delegation solution for universal identity management in SOA. IEEE Trans. Serv. Comput. **4**(1), 70–81 (2011)
7. Sucasas, V., Mantas, G., Saghezchi, F.B., Radwan, A., Rodriguez, J.: An autonomous privacy-preserving authentication scheme for intelligent transportation systems. Comput. Secur. **60**, 193–205 (2016)

8. Sucasas, V., Mantas, G., Radwan, A., Rodriguez, J.: An OAuth2-based protocol with strong user privacy preservation for smart city mobile e-Health apps. In: IEEE ICC (2016)
9. Sucasas, V., Mantas, G., Radwan, A., Rodriguez, J.: A lightweight privacy-preserving OAuth2-based protocol for smart city mobile apps. In: GLOBECOM Workshops (2016)
10. De Caro, A., Iovino, V. jPBC: Java pairing based cryptography. In: Proceedings of the 16th IEEE Symposium on Computers and Communications, ISCC (2011)

Cognitive Radio Policy-Based Adaptive Blind Rendezvous Protocols for Disaster Response

Saim Ghafoor$^{(\boxtimes)}$ (iD), Cormac J. Sreenan, and Kenneth N. Brown (iD)

Department of Computer Science, University College Cork, Cork, Ireland
saim.ghafoor@insight-centre.org, {cjs,k.brown}@cs.ucc.ie

Abstract. In disaster scenarios, with damaged network infrastructure, cognitive radio (CR) can be used to provide temporary network access in the first few hours. Since spectrum occupancy will be unknown, the radios must rely on spectrum sensing and opportunistic access. An initial goal is to establish rendezvous between CR nodes to set up the network. The unknown primary radio (PR) activity and CR node topology makes this a challenging task. Existing blind rendezvous strategies provide guarantees on time to rendezvous, but assume channels with no PR activity and no external interferers. To handle this problem of blind multi-node rendezvous in the presence of primary users, we propose an Extended Modular Clock Algorithm which abandons the guarantee on time to rendezvous, an information exchange mechanism for the multi-node problem, and various cognitive radio operating policies. We show that the adapted protocols can achieve up to 80% improvement in the expected time to rendezvous and reduce the harmful interference caused to the primary radio.

Keywords: Adaptive radio · Blind rendezvous
Cognitive radio network · Cognitive radio operating policy
Disaster response network · Primary radio activity

1 Introduction

In many disaster scenarios, communication networks are vital for ensuring efficient and effective first response; however, the disaster may have caused significant damage to the existing infrastructure. Cognitive Radio (CR) can provide an effective solution for creating an initial disaster response network until a more permanent network is re-established [1]. The CR can sense what links exist to the remaining infrastructure, sense what spectrum is available, and exploit the spectrum opportunistically while avoiding primary radio activity. Given the nature of the disaster, with unknown PR activity and spectrum spatial diversity, each CR node must sense the spectrum independently rather than using spectrum databases, and must rendezvous with each other in available channels. This creates the challenging problem of efficiently achieving rendezvous in an unknown environment with unknown primary radio activity.

© ICST Institute for Computer Sciences, Social Informatics and Telecommunications Engineering 2018
P. Marques et al. (Eds.): CROWNCOM 2017, LNICST 228, pp. 88–99, 2018.
https://doi.org/10.1007/978-3-319-76207-4_8

For two CR nodes, we define rendezvous as the completion of a handshake mechanism between the radios on a single channel. This assumes that the two radios are within transmission range of each other, that they coincide on the channel for a sufficient time period, and that the channel has no detectable primary radio activity or excessive interference for the radios over that time period. When there is no predefined schedule for visiting channels, and no common control channel, this is known as the blind rendezvous problem. There are some sophisticated blind rendezvous protocols, including Modular Clock Algorithm (MCA) [2], Modified MCA (MMCA) [2] and Jump-Stay [3]. These provide guarantees on the time to rendezvous, but they assume a set of channels on which there is no primary radio activity or external interference. Unpredictable arrivals of primary radios on these channels invalidates the guarantee, and may result in the CR nodes causing unacceptable interference to the primary radio. We make two contributions to address this problem. First, we propose an Extended Modular Clock Algorithm (EMCA) which abandons the guarantee, but has a shorter cycle time, and is intended to reduce the average time to rendezvous. Secondly, we explore different operating policies for the CR nodes to handle the behaviour of the primary users, with the aim of reducing harmful interference without adversely affecting time to rendezvous. In addition, we propose an information exchange mechanism for the multi-node problem, to further reduce the time to rendezvous.

We conduct an empirical investigation of these protocols in simulation. We generate randomised but realistic PR activity patterns, and consider the rendezvous problem for different numbers of unsynchronised CR nodes. We measure the average time to rendezvous and the amount of harmful interference experienced by the primary radios. We demonstrate that EMCA with appropriate operating policies can achieve up to 80% improvement in the average time to rendezvous compared to the existing blind rendezvous protocols. We demonstrate that policies which temporarily blacklist channels with detected PR activity are able to reduce incidents of harmful interference caused to the primary users.

To summarise our contributions,

1. we propose an Extended Modular Clock Algorithm (EMCA) to provide better expected time to rendezvous for unknown environments with PR activity;
2. we propose CR operating policies which adapt to PR activities to reduce harmful interference on PR systems, specifically Normal, Reactive with and without timeslot truncation, and Proactive, which attempts to learn and avoid PR activity;
3. we propose a neighbor exchange mechanism to expedite the rendezvous process for multiple CR nodes; and
4. we demonstrate the effectiveness of EMCA and the operating policies on simulated primary radio activity patterns.

2   Related Work

Blind rendezvous strategies (e.g. [2–7]) have gained much attention in CR Adhoc Networks. The modular clock algorithm (MCA) [2] is a blind rendezvous protocol which guarantees rendezvous for radios with identical channel sets. Each radio cycles through its channel set of size m for up to $2P$ slots, where P is the smallest prime $\geq m$, before restarting with a new hopping rate. MMCA [2] caters for different channel sets, with limit $2P^2$. Asynchronous timeslots are shown to be beneficial in reducing TTR in MCA [8]. Jump-Stay (JS) [3] and Extended JS [4], with limits $3P$ and $4P$, is similar to MCA/MMCA, but alternates rounds between hopping and staying on the same channel. All of these protocols assume that the channels are free from primary radio activity. If a primary user appears, the protocols either interfere, or lose their guarantee of rendezvous. To help avoid harmful interference, IEEE 802.22 specifies operating policies for CR deployment and operation [9] for broadband services using TV White Spaces (TVWS). There appear to be no studies analysing rendezvous performance based on PR activity patterns and practical operating policies.

3   System Preliminaries

System Model: We consider an LxL network area, with N nodes. Each node, due to spatial diversity can only access m channels from G randomly, where $G = \{1, 2, 3, \ldots, n\}$. Therefore, common channels among nodes may vary. We assume a connected topology, where all nodes are within range of each other. Each CR is equipped with a single wireless interface. We further assume a time slotted system where timeslot (TS) duration is fixed and known to all users. We assume that nodes are not synchronised with each other. We assume that a CR initially performs sensing for channel accessibility and excludes channels occupied by e.g. emergency services or other prioritised users. Later, it can perform fast sensing for PR detection [9]. For PR detection, we assume an energy detection model and, for identification, a technique such as cyclostationary signatures can be used [10]. We assume that PR traffic is evenly distributed in the space, however our proposed algorithm doesn't depends on the evenly distributed PR traffic.

Primary User Activity Model and Patterns: The performance of cognitive network highly depends on PR activity patterns. PR activity models are widely used to represent a spectrum usage pattern and measurements for performance evaluation [11,12]. We use a popular continuous time alternating ON/OFF Markov Renewal Process to model PR activity [11,13,14]. In this model, the duration of ON/OFF states of a channel i are denoted as T_{ON}^i and T_{OFF}^i. The renewal period $Z_i(t)$ will occur when one ON/OFF period is complete, where, $Z_i(t) = T_{ON}^i + T_{OFF}^i$. We have used the formulation mentioned in [13–15], where the channels ON/OFF periods are both exponentially distributed with p.d.f., $f_X(t) = \lambda_X \times e^{-\lambda_X(t)}$ for ON state and $f_Y(t) = \lambda_Y \times e^{-\lambda_Y(t)}$ for OFF state. The duration of time in which channel i is in the ON state i.e. U^i, is given as:

$$U^i = \frac{E[T_{ON}^i]}{E[T_{ON}^i] + E[T_{OFF}^i]} = \frac{\lambda_Y}{\lambda_X + \lambda_Y} \tag{1}$$

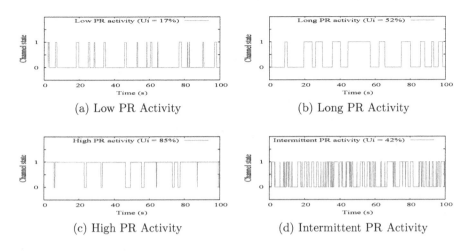

Fig. 1. Different PR activity patterns.

Algorithm 1. Function EMCA

Input: t (counter to change r_i), i (node id), T (timeslot), m_i.
Output: c (selected channel by node i).

1: calculate p_i, the prime number greater than
   or equal to m_i
2: **if** $T_i < 1$ **then**
3:     choose initial $j_i^t = rand[0, m_i)$
4:     choose r_i from $[0, p_i)$ randomly
5: **end if**
6: **if** $t \geq p_i$ **then**
7:     choose r_i from $[0, p_i)$ randomly
8:     $t_i = 0$

9: **end if**
10: $j_i^t = (j_i^t + r_i) \bmod p_i$
11: **if** $j_i^t < m_i$ **then**
12:     $c = c_{i,j_i^t}$
13: **else**
14:     $c = c_{i,rand([0,m_i))}$
15: **end if**
    return c;

---

where $E[T_{ON}] = 1/\lambda_{ON}$ and $E[T_{OFF}] = 1/\lambda_{OFF}$ are the means of exponential distributions, and λ_X and λ_Y are the exponential distribution rate parameters. The probability of channel i being in the ON or OFF state at time t can be calculated as below, where $P_{ON}(t) + P_{OFF}(t) = 1$. To illustrate, PR activity patterns are shown in Fig. 1.

$$P_{ON}(t) = \frac{\lambda_Y}{\lambda_X + \lambda_Y} - \frac{\lambda_Y}{\lambda_X + \lambda_Y} e^{-(\lambda_X + \lambda_Y)t} \qquad (2)$$

$$P_{OFF}(t) = \frac{\lambda_X}{\lambda_X + \lambda_Y} + \frac{\lambda_Y}{\lambda_X + \lambda_Y} e^{-(\lambda_X + \lambda_Y)t} \qquad (3)$$

4 Extended Modular Clock Algorithm (EMCA) with Neighbor Information Exchange Mechanism

EMCA (Algorithm 1) is based on the Modular Arithmetic approach of MCA [2], adapted to account for the effect of PR activity. In EMCA, r is the rate/step

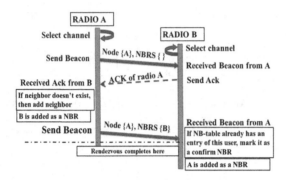

Fig. 2. Neighbor information passing mechanism.

value by which CRs hop the available channel set (ACS), m is the total number of channels, and P is the smallest prime number larger or equal to m. EMCA initializes by choosing an initial index and a rate value randomly. The rate value will remain same for a rendezvous cycle of P timeslots. If rendezvous does not occur within P, then r will be re-selected. At each iteration, the next index value will be calculated using $mod(P)$. In EMCA, the rendezvous cycle is short (P TS) and unavailable channels are remapped randomly from ACS to avoid biased selection of channels early in the order. In MCA [2] and MMCA [2], the iteration limits are $2P$ and $2P^2$, to ensure rendezvous if different rates are selected, even if the sequence starts are not synchronised. Since we cannot guarantee rendezvous even if two radios are on the same channel in the same slot, because of unknown PR activity, we reduce this limit to allow a search of all channels, but a faster rate re-selection, in the hope of speeding up the time to rendezvous.

For a successful rendezvous, two nodes must complete a handshake process. We propose a beaconing mechanism in which nodes embed into the beacon a list of neighboring nodes they have overheard. As shown in Fig. 2, if two nodes find their own ID in each other's beacons, then we assume rendezvous can be completed. For example, when Node B receives a beacon from A it will send an ACK. A now knows that B has received its beacon, and adds B to its neighbour list. If B receives A's next beacon, it will discover its own ID in the list. It knows that A has received its ACK, and can add A to its neighbour list.

5   Cognitive Radio Operating Policies

A CR must be able to identify and vacate channels occupied by a primary user, and avoid those channels for some specified time. These restrictions are described in [9] as channel availability check (CAC) and channel non-occupancy period (CNP). CAC is the time during which a channel should be checked for the presence of a PR. CNP is the period during which a CR should avoid transmission on a channel which is already detected as occupied. For TV white spaces (TVWS) [9], which have long activity patterns, the CAC time is by default 30 s,

Algorithm 2. EMCA for Normal Operating Policy

Input: m_i (total number of channels), i (node id).

```
 1: t_i = 0                              13:        if channel c is occupied then
 2: T_i = 0                              14:           Add c in BLC_i
 3: while not rendezvous with all nodes do  15:        condition = true
 4:    c = EMCA(i, t_i, T_i, m_i)        16:        else
 5:    condition = false                 17:           Attempt rendezvous on c
 6:    beacon = 0                        18:        end if
 7:    if channel c is in BLC list then  19:     end while
 8:        Do nothing                    20:  end if
 9:    else if channel c is occupied then 21:  wait for timeslot to end
10:        Add c in BLC_i                22:  t_i = t_i + 1
11:    else                             23:  T_i = T_i + 1
12:        while beacon ≠ 5 & condition ≠  24: end while
       true do
```

and CNP is a minimum of 10 min. In order to respect the specification, we have proposed different CR operating policies, which work with the rendezvous strategies and are adaptable in response to PR activity. The intention is to reduce harmful interference. Specifically, each channel will be checked for PR activity at the time of selection and before each beacon transmission, and will be blacklisted (BL) if found to be occupied; BL channels will be kept in a black-listed channel list (BLC) and will not be used for transmission or PR detection until its CNP expires. The proposed policies are described below, together with a simple "Listen before Talk" policy for comparison.

Listen Before Talk (LBT) or No Policy: In LBT, a channel will be checked before every transmission, and will not be used if PR activity is detected. However, such channels are not blacklisted, and rendezvous attempts will continue at the next scheduled beacon transmission.

Normal Operating Policy (Norm): At the start of a timeslot, the selected channel will be checked for PR activity. If PR is detected, the whole timeslot will be abandoned; otherwise, the beacon transmission phase will start with LBT. If before any beacon transmission a PR is detected the radio will not transmit for the rest of the timeslot. If PR activity is detected, the channel will be moved to BLC, and remain there until its CNP expires. At the start of the next timeslot, a new channel will be selected. The policy is shown in Algorithm 2.

Reactive Operating Policy: The Normal policy wastes time by staying silent on the current channel. To avoid this, the Reactive policy immediately continues hopping through the channels using its existing channel selection algorithm. CR operating limitations are as before, where LBT is followed with CAC/CNP checks. There are two variations, depending on whether or not the timeslot is truncated on PR activity detection. Maintaining the timeslot structure keeps any time synchronisation between nodes, while starting a new timeslot means that a node will reach the P limit faster (in real time), and so if needed can change its rate more quickly.

Algorithm 3. EMCA for Reactive Operating Policy

Input: m_i (total number of channels), i (node id).

```
1:  t_i = 0                                          29:              Add c in BLC_i
2:  T_i = 0                                          30:          else
3:  while not rendezvous with all nodes do          31:              channel c is unoccupied
4:      c = EMCA(i, t_i, T_i, m_i)                   32:              channel_unoccupied = true
5:      channel_unoccupied = false                   33:              selected_channel = c
6:      channel_occupied = false                     34:          end if
7:      beacon_sent = 0                              35:      end while
8:      channel_select = 0                           36:      else
9:      procedure CHANNEL SELECTION                  37:          channel c is idle
10:         if c is in BLC_i then                    38:          selected_channel = c
11:             while channel_select ≠ m_i &         39:      end if
        channel_unoccupied ≠ true do                 40:      end procedure
12:                 c = EMCA(i, t_i, T_i, m_i)       41:      procedure BEACON TRANSMISSION
13:                 if c is in BLC_i then            42:          while beacon_sent ≠ 5 do &
14:                     Do nothing                   channel_occupied ≠ true
15:                 else if c is occupied then       43:              if selected_channel is occupied
16:                     Add c in BLC_i               then
17:                 else                             44:                  Add c in BLC_i
18:                     channel c is unoccupied      45:                  channel_occupied = true
19:                     channel_unoccupied = true    46:              else
20:                     selected_channel = c         47:                  selected_channel is unoccupied
21:                 end if                           48:                  Attempt    rendezvous    on
22:             end while                            selected_channel
23:         else if c is occupied then               49:              end if
24:             while channel_select ≠ m_i &         50:          end while
        channel_unoccupied ≠ true do                 51:      end procedure
25:                 c = EMCA(i, t_i, T_i, m_i)       52:      wait for timeslot to end
26:                 if c is in BLC_i then            53:      t_i = t_i + 1
27:                     Do nothing                   54:      T_i = T_i + 1
28:                 else if c is occupied then       55: end while
```

Without Timeslot Truncation (RwoT): The node will search for a free channel until one is found or all channels are examined. If no free channel is found, the node will remain quiet until the end of the timeslot. A new rate and index will be selected when node completes a full round (Algorithm 3).

With Timeslot Truncation (RwT): Each time a node selects a new channel, the timeslot number will also increase. Algorithm 3 is also applicable for RwT, but where the TS increment occurs with every channel selection.

Proactive Operating Policy (Pro): The Proactive policy attempts to learn the behaviour of the primary users, going beyond the use of the blacklist. For each channel, it maintains a channel weight C_w^i, which approximates the channel's probability of being unoccupied (or OFF), as shown in Eq. 4. Channel state matching is defined as positive successful match (PSM) (Estimated State (ES) = 0, Observed State (OS) = 0), negative successful match (NSM) (ES = 1, OS = 1), false alarm (FA) (ES = 1, OS = 0) and miss detection (MD) (ES = 0, OS = 1). MD occurs when a node declares an occupied channel as unoccupied and FA occurs when node declares an unoccupied channel as occupied. Using the C_w^i values, each node then maintains a sorted Weighted Channels list (WCL).

$$C_w^i(weight) = \frac{(P_{PSM} + P_{FA})}{(P_{PSM} + P_{NSM} + P_{FA} + P_{MD})} \tag{4}$$

Algorithm 4. EMCA for Proactive Operating Policy

Input: m_i (total number of channels), i (node id).

1: $t_i = 0$
2: $T_i = 0$
3: **while** not rendezvous with all nodes **do**
4:     $c = EMCA(i, t_i, T_i, m_i)$
5:     update channel weight
6:     $channel_{unoccupied}$ = false
7:     $channel_{occupied}$ = false
8:     $beacon_{sent} = 0$
9:     $channel_{select} = 0$
10:     **procedure** CHANNEL SELECTION
11:         **if** c is in BLC_i **then**
12:             **while** $channel_{select} \neq m_i$ & $channel_{unoccupied} \neq true$ **do**
13:                 select channel from WCL_i
14:                 update channel weight
15:                 **if** c is in BLC_i **then**
16:                     Do nothing
17:                 **else if** c is occupied **then**
18:                     Add c in BLC_i
19:                 **else**
20:                     channel c is unoccupied
21:                     $channel_{unoccupied}$ = true
22:                     $selected_{channel}$ = c
23:                 **end if**
24:             **end while**
25:         **else if** c is occupied **then**
26:             **while** $channel_{select} \neq m_i$ & $channel_{unoccupied} \neq true$ **do**
27:                 select channel from WCL_i
28:                 update channel weight
29:                 **if** c is in BLC_i **then**
30:                     Do nothing
31:                 **else if** c is occupied **then**
32:                     Add c in BLC_i
33:                 **else**
34:                     channel c is unoccupied
35:                     $channel_{unoccupied}$ = true
36:                     $selected_{channel}$ = c
37:                 **end if**
38:             **end while**
39:         **else**
40:             channel c is idle
41:             $selected_{channel}$ = c
42:         **end if**
43:     **end procedure**
44:     **procedure** BEACON TRANSMISSION
45:         Similar as in other policies
46:     **end procedure**
47:     wait for timeslot to end
48:     $t_i = t_i + 1$
49:     $T_i = T_i + 1$
50: **end while**

The policy starts by selecting a channel in each timeslot as normal. However, if channel is occupied then WCL will be used to pick another channel in proportion to the weights in WCL. The intention is to augment an existing channel selection algorithm by temporarily returning to channels most likely to be free, rather than staying silent during a slot when PR activity is detected (Algorithm 4).

6 Performance Evaluation

We evaluate the channel selection algorithm and operating policies in simulation, in order to be able to account for the effect of asynchronous cognitive radio nodes, and uncertain primary user activity. We measure both the time to rendezvous and the amount of harmful interference caused to the primary users, and we compare EMCA to MMCA, JS and to a random channel selection. In each case, we apply the different operating policies uniformly to each rendezvous protocol.

Simulation Setup: Our evaluation uses the well known network simulator NS-2, with extensions to the Cognitive Radio Cognitive Network framework [16], notably for PR activity and channel prediction at the MAC layer, and rendezvous strategies and policies at the network layer. The number of CR nodes used are 2 and 10, where each node can access only 7 out of 10 possible channels, selected randomly. Each node starts within a window of one time slot and at a random time. The CNP time is used as 3xTS. Each TS is divided into five equal parts, where beacon transmissions are scheduled randomly within first half of every part, so that each node will have sufficient time for beaconing/listening.

Table 1. Rate parameter values for channel states used in simulation

PR activity	Simulation parameters	Channel ids									
		1	2	3	4	5	6	7	8	9	10
High	λ_X	0.25	0.3	0.25	0.23	0.22	0.25	0.22	0.23	0.32	0.21
	λ_Y	0.93	1	1.03	1.45	1.10	0.64	1.41	1.59	0.64	1.45
	U_i	0.79	0.77	0.8	0.86	0.84	0.72	0.87	0.87	0.66	0.87
Mix	λ_X	10000	1.03	0.22	0.22	1.33	10000	1.28	0.23	0.25	1.79
	λ_Y	0	0.3	0.31	1.2	1.2	0	0.28	0.49	0.93	1.3
	U_i	0	0.23	0.58	0.85	0.47	0	0.18	0.68	0.79	0.42

The Tx range is 250 m for CRs, and network area is $1000 \times 1000 \, \text{m}^2$. PR activity patterns are generated using rate parameters λ_X and λ_Y, as shown in Table 1. For Zero PR activity, rate values are used as $\lambda_X = 10000$ and $\lambda_Y = 0$. We consider Zero, High and Mixed PR activity patterns, where in mixed PR activity each channel follows a different traffic pattern, as shown in Fig. 1. For space reasons, we omit Low and Long PR patterns, whose results lie between Zero and High. The metrics used for evaluation are (i) Average TTR (ATTR), which is the time from when the first node starts to the time when last node receive its beacon confirmation and (ii) Harmful Interference (HI), which is the average number of times when interference is caused by a CR towards PR.

Performance of EMCA with CR Operating Policies: To evaluate the performance of EMCA over different CR operating policies, we vary PR activities with different traffic patterns shown in Fig. 1. We run 100 simulations for each case and take the average of all simulations. Each simulation runs until each node finds every other node in the network. We show the average time to rendezvous for each rendezvous algorithm and operating policy, for each traffic pattern, in Fig. 3 (for 2 nodes) and Fig. 4 (for 10 nodes).

For the zero PR case (Figs. 3a and 4a), EMCA achieves the lowest time to rendezvous, and Random is only marginally slower. As expected, MMCA and JS are significantly slower, because their rendezvous guarantee requires longer cycles before changing the rate. For these zero PR experiments, the operating policies do not apply and so do not affect TTR.

When we introduce PR activity (Figs. 3 and 4(b) and (c)), EMCA and Random still outperform the other two algorithms, which suffer from the longer cycle times even though the rendezvous guarantee no longer applies. EMCA is still the fastest algorithm, with the improvement over JS and MMCA ranging up to one order of magnitude depending on the operating policy. Random is still only marginally worse than EMCA. The impact of the different operating policies is now clearer. The Normal policy is slower than the others, and its TTR increases with higher PR activity, as any detected PR activity causes the nodes to stop transmitting. The reactive and proactive policies show that this time can be used more effectively. RwT shows up to 80% improvement over the Normal policy

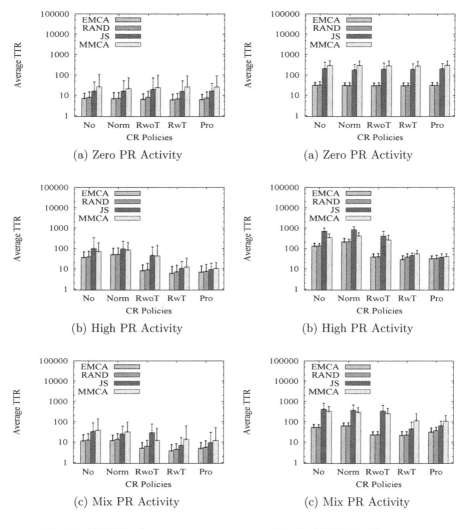

Fig. 3. ATTR for 2 nodes

Fig. 4. ATTR for 10 nodes

(Fig. 3b), with Proactive only slightly slower. The Proactive policy also brings the TTR for JS and MMCA down to close to the level of EMCA and Random.

In Figs. 5 and 6, we show the average number of incidents of harmful interference (i.e. when CR transmissions coincide with PR activity) in the same experiments as for Figs. 3 and 4. There is obviously no harmful interference in the zero PR case, and so the graphs are omitted. For the High and Mix PR cases, we again see the benefits of the Reactive and Proactive policies. At some points, the harmful interference is observed as zero even with PR activity for EMCA. In the two node experiments, harmful interference is relatively low, with less than one incident expected per full rendezvous cycle dropping to between 1% and 2% chance of any incident for the reactive and proactive policies. In the

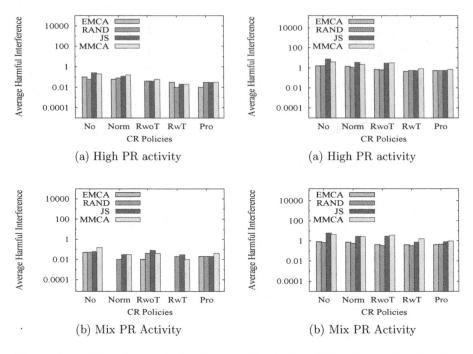

(a) High PR activity

(a) High PR activity

(b) Mix PR Activity

(b) Mix PR Activity

Fig. 5. Harmful interference for 2 nodes   **Fig. 6.** Harmful interference for 10 nodes

10 node cases, harmful interference is higher, particularly for JS and MMCA because of their higher TTRs, but dropping to below one expected instance per rendezvous cycle for the reactive and proactive policies. Proactive and Reactive, though, are marginally better. Considering both time to rendezvous and harmful interference, the results show that EMCA with the Proactive policy is the preferred configuration.

7   Conclusion

It is widely acknowledged that the flexibility of cognitive radio networks makes them especially suitable for operation in unknown environments, such as disaster response. Blind rendezvous is essential in such situations, but existing techniques make assumptions about primary radio activity and the radio environment. In order to overcome these restrictive assumptions, this paper presented an Extended Modular Clock blind rendezvous protocol, which is an adaptive protocol and can minimize the network setup delay in a disaster situation. Experiments with a variety of primary radio traffic models show up to 80% improvement in the key metric time to rendezvous. Reductions in the effect of harmful interference in comparison with existing rendezvous strategies is also observed empirically. Furthermore, three different operating policies are presented to improve adaptation to primary radio activities. The best policy is

Proactive, which prefers to return to channels with lower previous PR activity. It offers an order of magnitude improvement in time to rendezvous over the basic LBT policy, and improves the performance for all of the studied rendezvous algorithms. This study can help regulatory/standard-bodies and service providers for CR deployment in urban and mission critical areas over different spectrum bands. Future work will focus on developing a more sophisticated learning scheme for Proactive, and on multihop blind rendezvous.

Acknowledgement. This publication has emanated from research conducted with the financial support of Science Foundation Ireland (SFI) under the CTVR (SFI 10/CE/I1853), CONNECT (13/RC/2077) and INSIGHT (SFI/12/RC/2289) grants.

References

1. Ghafoor, S., Sutton, P.D., Sreenan, C.J., Brown, K.N.: Cognitive radio for disaster response networks: survey, potential, and challenges. IEEE Wirel. Commun. **21**(5), 70–80 (2014)
2. Theis, N.C., Thomas, R.W., DaSilva, L.A.: Rendezvous for cognitive radios. IEEE Trans. Mob. Comput. **10**(2), 216–227 (2011)
3. Liu, H., Lin, Z., Chu, X., Leung, Y.W.: Jump-stay rendezvous algorithm for CRNs. IEEE Tran. Parallel Distrib. Syst. **23**(10), 1867–1881 (2012)
4. Lin, Z., Liu, H., Chu, X., Leung, Y.W.: Enhanced jump-stay rendezvous algorithm for cognitive radio networks. IEEE Commun. Lett. **17**(9), 1742–1745 (2013)
5. Zhang, Y., Yu, G., Li, Q., Wang, H., Zhu, X., Wang, B.: Channel-hopping-based communication rendezvous in CRNs. IEEE Trans. Netw. **22**(3), 889–902 (2014)
6. Chao, C.M., Fu, H.Y., Zhang, L.R.: A fast rendezvous-guarantee channel hopping protocol for CRNs. IEEE Trans. Veh. Technol. **64**(12), 5804–5816 (2015)
7. Pu, H., Gu, Z., Lin, X., Hua, Q.S., Jin, H.: Dynamic rendezvous algorithms for cognitive radio networks. In: IEEE International Conference on Communications (ICC), pp. 1–6 (2016)
8. Robertson, A., Tran, L., Molnar, J., Fu, E.H.F.: Experimental comparison of blind rendezvous algorithms for tactical networks. In: IEEE WoWMoM, pp. 1–6 (2012)
9. IEEE 802.22.2: Part 22.2: Installation and Deployment of CR Systems (2012)
10. Sutton, P.D., Nolan, K.E., Doyle, L.E.: Cyclostationary signatures in practical cognitive radio applications. J. Sel. Areas Commun. **26**(1), 13–24 (2008)
11. Saleem, Y., Rehmani, M.H.: Primary radio user activity models for cognitive radio networks - a survey. J. Netw. Comput. Appl. **43**, 1–16 (2014)
12. Saleem, Y., Yau, K.A., Mohamad, H., Ramli, N., Rehmani, M.H.: SMART- a SpectruM-Aware clusteR-based rouTing scheme for distributed cognitive radio networks. Elsevier Comput. Netw. **91**, 196–224 (2015)
13. Kim, H., Shin, K.: Efficient discovery of spectrum opportunities with MAC-layer sensing in cognitive radio networks. IEEE Trans. Mob. Comput. **7**(5), 533–545 (2008)
14. Kim, H., Shin, K.: Fast discovery of spectrum opportunities in cognitive radio networks. In: IEEE DySPAN 2008 (2008)
15. Min, A.W., Shin, K.G.: Exploiting multi-channel diversity in spectrum-agile network. In: Proceedings of the INFOCOM (2008)
16. http://faculty.uml.edu/Tricia_Chigan/Research/CRCN_Simulator.htm

Application of the CBRS Model for Wireless Systems Coexistence in 3.6–3.8 GHz Band

Adrian Kliks[1]([envelope])[iD], Paweł Kryszkiewicz[1], Łukasz Kułacz[1], Karol Kowalik[2],
Michał Kołodziejski[2], Heikki Kokkinen[3], Jaakko Ojaniemi[3], and Arto Kivinen[3]

[1] Faculty of Electronics and Telecommunications,
Poznan University of Technology, Poznan, Poland
{adrian.kliks,pawel.kryszkiewicz,lukasz.kulacz}@put.poznan.pl
[2] INEA, Poznan, Poland
{karol.kowalik,michal.kolodziejski}@inea.com.pl
[3] Fairspectrum, Helsinki, Finland
{heikki.kokkinen,jaakko.ojaniemi,arto.kivinen}@fairspectrum.com

Abstract. In this paper we discuss the results of the experiment conducted in Poznan, Poland, where the performance of CBRS spectrum sharing model in 3.6–3.8 GHz band has been verified. Three-tier model has been tested, where the highest priority has been assigned to the fixed WiMAX users, whose transmit parameters cannot be modified. Second tier of users was constituted by the peer-to-peer microwave line, whereas the third tier of lowest priority covered the low-power cognitive small-cells. The whole system has been managed by the dedicated remote database located in Finland. Experiments have been carried out in the laboratory, where mainly the functionality of the management of the third tier user has been tested, while protecting the users assigned to two higher tiers.

Keywords: Vertical spectrum sharing · CBRS · Trials

1 Introduction

The concept of cognitive radio technology has recently celebrated it maturity, as it has been first proposed in 1999 by Mitola [1,2]. During these two decades of intensive research work (see e.g., [3]), it has been revealed that the pure cognitive radio that relies on the spectrum sensing will not be reliable enough in practical applications. The application of advanced, database oriented spectrum management systems have been proposed to solve this problem [4,5]. Two key concepts are of practical interest today. Licensed shared access (LSA) concept [6] is mainly considered in Europe, and it assumes the presence of the incumbent license owner, who decided to share its spectrum with other users. In the alternative approach, proposed in US and called Citizens Broadband Radio Service (CBRS) with Spectrum Access System (SAS) [7], three tiers of users are

© ICST Institute for Computer Sciences, Social Informatics and Telecommunications Engineering 2018
P. Marques et al. (Eds.): CROWNCOM 2017, LNICST 228, pp. 100–111, 2018.
https://doi.org/10.1007/978-3-319-76207-4_9

considered. While the first two tiers are similar to the LSA concept, the lowest tier of users operates in a best-effort manner, so they are allowed to transmit as long as they do not cause harmful interference to the other users from higher tiers (these type of users are called General Authorized Access, GAA, users). Latest updates on the CBRS architecture and application can be find in [8,9]. It is also worth noticing that the recent updates on CBRS interfaces have been released in June and July 2017 by WInnForum [10,11].

In our paper we consider the application of the second approach, as this is the case tailored to the 3.5 GHz band and assumes the presence of three types of users. Such a model seems to be well-suited to the business case considered for practical application by the network operator INEA, who delivers services in Greater Poland area in Poland. WiMAX deployment at INEA has started in 2010 and so far it provided fast and affordable connectivity for Internet and telephony services to almost 6000 households across the 30,000 km^2 region. Currently the WiMAX technology is considered to be *dead*, but INEA's WiMAX network still operates and occupies radio spectrum resources. Therefore INEA would like to utilize allocated spectrum in a more efficient way by sharing it with other radio systems.

In particular, INEA would like to evaluate vertical spectrum sharing model, i.e., the coexistence of the existing WiMAX 802.16e working in the 3.5 GHz band together with the microwave radio-links serving corporate users. It was observed that corporate users require more capacity during the day time and residential users served by WiMAX require more capacity outside office hours. The residential and corporate users are collocated on the same geographical area and the two radio systems are active simultaneously. However, both radio systems can be configured with various channel bandwidth. Therefore, LSA system can direct the two radio system to modify their channel bandwidth (allowing also some overlapping) and transmit power in order to shift capacity but at the same time maintaining limited interference levels. It is assumed that each radio system maintains a small amount of capacity at all times.

Moreover, it has been decided to use a next tier of users (as GAA users in SAS) in order to verify if it is feasible to utilize the frequency resources in a more efficient way. These third tier users are realized by the means of Universal Software Radio Peripheral (USRP), which needs to obtain permission for transmission opportunity in a given geographical and frequency location from an LSA controller. USRP will start some data transmission in such a way that the primary users will not be affected.

Thus the goal of this sharing scheme is to utilize the daily traffic patterns of the WiMAX clients and offer the unused fragments of band to the corporate clients via radio-links while verifying additional spectrum access opportunities using USRP.

2 Proposed Vertical Spectrum Sharing Model for 3.6–3.8 GHz

2.1 Multi-tier Spectrum Sharing - Scenario Definition

In our exercise we consider a multi-tier spectrum sharing model based mainly on the CBRS solution discussed above. The ultimate goal is to utilize the spectrum in 3.6–3.8 GHz band in a more efficient way. Currently, this fragment of spectrum is mainly associated with WiMAX transmission, where high power WiMAX base station covers wide geographical area (of a few kilometers radius) and deliver services to fixed customer-premises equipment (CPE). However, as the development of WiMAX system has lost its momentum in favor of LTE/LTE-A systems, it is widely treated as *dead*. However, due to the legal commitments, this network cannot be simply turned off, and still it provides some revenues (although decreasing) to the network operator. From that perspectives, we consider to reuse the spectrum in efficient way, mainly to deliver point-to-point transmission via microwave link. The WiMAX users will constitute the highest priority users (first tier), whereas the microwave links will be treated as incumbents which do not interfere to the WiMAX system. However, in our multi-tier experiment we also consider the presence of third tier of users, which we call general authorized access (following the CBRS nomenclature). In such approach, the GAA subsystem will operate in the same frequency band as WiMAX and microwave link do, but their priority will be the lowest from these three. It means that by assumption the GAA transmission cannot distort neither WiMAX nor microwave link. The considered scenario is shown in Fig. 1, where a fragment of the area covered by WiMAX base station is presented.

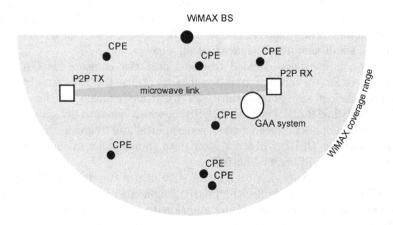

Fig. 1. Considered scenario for multi-tier spectrum sharing

The coexistence of such three types of networks will be probably not possible if these networks will be fully autonomous. Thus, we consider the presence of dedicated database-oriented management system, which will be used to coordinate and control the three networks. The graphical representation of the concept is shown in Fig. 2. One can observe, both WiMAX and microwave link communicate with the database-focused management system via Simple Network Management Protocol (SNMP), where all the steering and control instructions will be sent via management information base messages (MIBs) by addressing appropriate object identifier (OID). At the same time GAA subsystem communicates with the database by application of the pure CBRS protocol.

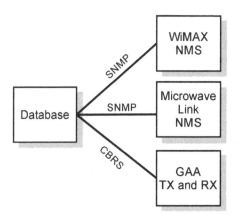

Fig. 2. Database management system for considered scenario

2.2   Database Structure and Functionality

In the Spectrum Management System, SNMP client communicates with WiMAX and Microwave (MW) Link Network Managements systems through a Virtual Private Network client. SNMP client stores the status data in Structured Query Language (SQL) Database (DB). Clocked Control uses SNMP client to change the center frequency and channel bandwidth of WiMAX and MW devices based on the daytime. Citizens Broadband Radio Service (CBRS) Spectrum Access System (SAS) [7–9] serves the spectrum resource request coming from General Authorized Access (GAA) Citizens Broadband radio Service Devices (CBSD) using SAS-CBSD protocol specified by Wireless Innovation Forum [10–12]. SAS server reads protocol information from SQL DB and stores protocol information there. Spectrum Inquiry, Grant, and Heartbeat requests in SAS Server invoke DB Engine. DB Engine queries the measurement data from WiMAX and MW links with SNMP client. In the considered setup WiMAX reports Carrier to Interference and Noise Ratio (CINR) in both downlink and uplink. For the microwave link estimated potential throughput is reported. DB Engine evaluates the interference risk to WiMAX and MW links caused by requesting CBSD. The evaluation is based on an assumed propagation model. Modeling is enhanced with WiMAX and MW link measurement information (Fig. 3).

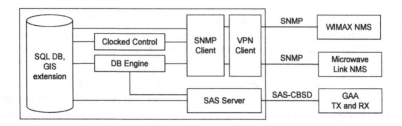

Fig. 3. Structure of spectrum management system database

The detailed version of the logic applied in the database for controlling third-tier of users is shown in Fig. 4.

2.3 GAA Subsystem Functionality

At the same time the GAA subsystem, i.e., USRP device in our case, applies the following algorithm for accessing the spectrum:

1. *Step 1.* First, the GAA transmitter sends the registration request (following the implemented CBRS protocol), where it asks for registration in the whole system. As a response it receives a dedicated device identification number. The coordinates of the devices are also delivered to the system.
2. *Step 2.* After registration, the GAA subsystem inquires the database for a set of parameters defining its transmit opportunities (like maximum EIRP value) for a list of selected subbands, e.g., it may ask for these sets of parameters for three 2 MHz wide frequency subbands with center frequency of 3.64 GHz, 3.70 GHz and 3.75 GHz. As a response the GAA subsystem receives the limits of the allowed parameters.
3. *Step 3.* The GAA transmitter sends the request for granting transmission by the database, where the proposed transmit parameters are defined. The database either grants the transmission with the proposed parameters (see Step 5 then), or blocks the request (see Step 4).
4. *Step 4.* If the GAA device does not receive a positive grant response, it may either modify the transmit parameters (e.g., proposed transmit power) in the considered frequency band or switch to other band of interest. In both cases the new grant request is sent to the database with new set of parameters.
5. *Step 5.* The device will start transmission (please note that until now there was no wireless activity in the GAA subsystem, as the communication with remote database was guaranteed via external control channel). After agreed transmission time, the device will analyze the so-called heartbeat response, where the database inform, if the transmission can be continued (then repeat Step 5) or the transmission has to be stopped (then the algorithm goes back to Step 3).
6. *Step 6.* Once the device has no data to sent it will deregister from the system, releasing the device identification number.

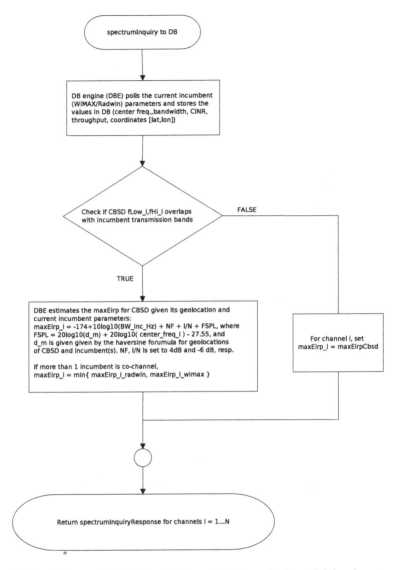

Fig. 4. Algorithm applied at the database side for controlling GAA subsystems

The algorithm presented above is fully adaptive and tries to maximize the rate of the GAA link in the transmission regime defined by the database. The detailed version of the implemented logic in the GAA subsystem is algorithmically presented in Fig. 5

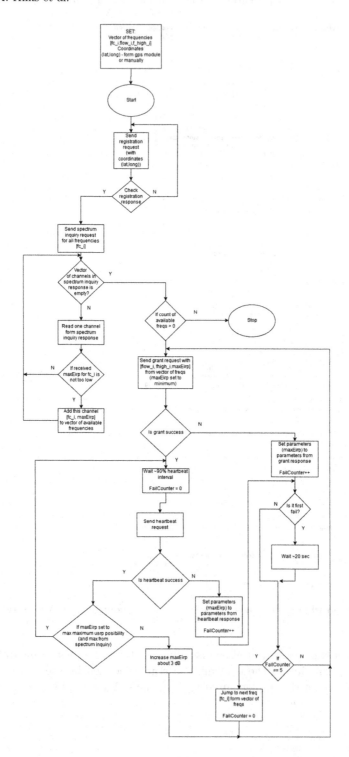

Fig. 5. Algorithm applied at the GAA side for dynamic spectrum access

3   Experiment Results

The whole experiment has been conducted in the INEA laboratory, where both WiMAX test base station with associated CPE has been deployed simultaneously with the point-to-point microwave link and underlying Software Defined Radio (SDR)-based, best effort transmitter (GAA system).

3.1   WiMAX and Microwave Link Setup

Regarding WiMAX the 802.16e-2005 base station (Cambium Networks PMP320) has been selected as the representative of existing operating network in Poznan. Please note that capacity in a WiMAX network is not fixed. Each customer-premises equipment (CPE) operates with spectral efficiency that changes in time and is influenced by three parameters: modulation, forward error correction (FEC) coding and MIMO mode. The network capacity of a given base station depends on the number of CPEs and their spectral efficiency. The WiMAX link worked in 2×2 MIMO mode on a center frequency set to 3.664 GHz with 10 MHz channel bandwidth. The transmit power of the base station may (following the specifications) change in the range from -40 to 27.5 dBm. The applied modulation and coding scheme assumed the 64-point quadrature amplitude modulation with code rate set to $\frac{5}{6}$. The directional antennas had 16 dBi gain. During the simulations only control data have been transmitted. The microwave link manufactured by RADWIN operated at 3.674 GHz center frequency and occupied 10 MHz bandwidth. The applied antennas had 19.5 dBi gain, and allowed for 2×2 MIMO transmission. As can be observed, these two systems did not interfere to each other, as they are separated in frequency domain. Before we start deploying third tier users (GAA subsystems), we have observed both transmitted signal using Rogde & Schwartz spectrum analyzer FSL6. The measured power spectral density (PSD) and spectrogram for center frequency set to 3.669 GHz and resolution bandwidth equal to 30 kHz, are shown in Fig. 6.

3.2   GAA Subsystem

In parallel to the two legacy systems, i.e., first-tier WiMAX link and second-tier microwave link, we deploy the GAA subsystem. Our ultimate goal is to increase the spectrum efficiency (by application of such advanced spectrum sharing scheme) while guaranteeing the performance of two protected systems. The GAA system is constituted by the USRP N210 platform equipped with the CBX daughter-board operating in the frequency range 1.2 GHz to 6 GHz with a maximal bandwidth of 40 MHz. The USRP board has received transmit stream from GnuRadio software that has been connected to the database and followed the algorithm described in the previous section. The database has processed the requests send by the GAA transmitters applying two performance constraints with regard to the WiMAX and microwave links, i.e., the GAA transmission may be started (or continued) as long as the observed carrier to interference and noise (CINR) ratio in the WiMAX link was above 20 dB, and as long as the microwave

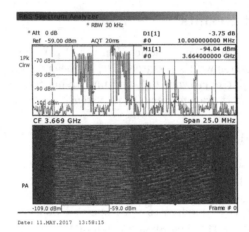

Fig. 6. Power spectral density of WiMAX and radioline links

link was active (the quality of the link was high enough to transmit any data - potential throughput reported by devices higher than 0). The selection of these constraints was caused by the limited list of parameters that can be read by the remote database via SNMP protocol.

3.3   Use Case 1 - One Active GAA Subsystem

In the first experiment, only one USRP transmitter queries the database for new transmission opportunities for five subbands, each 2 MHz width, with center frequencies as follows: 3.657 GHz (below the WiMAX band), 3.664 GHz (as the WiMAX center frequency), 3.669 GHz (exactly between the WiMAX and microwave links), 3.674 GHz (as the microwave center frequency) and 3.682 GHz (above the microwave band). The following set of messages send to the database (denoted as *USRP* in the log below) and responses (denoted as *Server*) has been received:

- *USRP* - manual - position: (52.4075, 16.7853) //registration message
- *Server* - Registration completed
- *USRP* - Spectrum Inquiry //inquiry with the list of 5 center frequencies
- *Server* - SI response, freq: 3.657e+09, max eirp: 25.6 //response with the max EIRP value for the certain center frequency
- *Server* - SI response, freq: 3.664e+09, max eirp: −45.3978
- *Server* - SI response, freq: 3.669e+09, max eirp: −30.9539
- *Server* - SI response, freq: 3.674e+09, max eirp: −30.9539
- *Server* - SI response, freq: 3.82e+09, max eirp: 25.6
- *USRP* - Available freq: 3.657e+09, max gain: 31.5 //list of available frequencies and maximum permitted gain to the USRP power amplifier
- *USRP* - Available freq: 3.82e+09, max gain: 31.5

- *Server* - Access granted - gain $= 0$, freq $= 3.657\mathrm{e}{+}09$ //received grant for first frequency and setup of the heartbeat time
- *Server* - Heartbeat set to 60 s.
- *USRP* - Heartbeat remaining time: 47 s.
- *USRP* - ...
- *USRP* - Heartbeat remaining time: 5 s.
- *USRP* - Heartbeat remaining time: 0 s.
- *Server* - Heartbeat OK! //after 60 s, we can continue transmission, so the USRP tries to get higher power; it increases the transmit power twice, and it got grant again
- *USRP* - Try more...
- *Server* - Access granted - gain $= 3$, freq $= 3.657\mathrm{e}{+}09$
- *Server* - Heartbeat set to 60 s.
- *USRP* - ...

One may observe that only for the two border frequencies the database provided positive values of maximum EIRP value, as only these two frequencies do not overlap with the first and second tier of users. Clearly, in the CBRS model the GAA system may operate simultaneously with the same frequency band as other legacy systems as long as it does not interfere too much. In our case, however, the location of the GAA transmitter (provided in the first, registration message) was so close to the WiMAX receiver, so that the maximum EIRP calculated by the database was below the transmit possibilities of the GAA transmitter. Once the USRP device receives the response to the inquiry and grant requests, it starts transmission on the first available frequency (GMSK modulation, 2 MHz bandwidth). The observed averaged PSD in such a case is illustrated in Fig. 7, where one may observe the spectrum of three simultaneously transmitted signals. Please note that during the experiment the performance parameters were permanently monitored by the remote database (i.e., CINR for WiMAX and

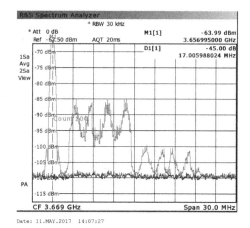

Fig. 7. Averaged power spectral density observed in the first use case

potential throughput for microwave link), but these were also displayed locally. Once the USRP devices started its wireless activity, the performance of both systems was not violated.

3.4   Use Case 2 - Two Active GAA Subsystems

As an extension of the first use case, we decided to verify the behavior of the system when second GAA subsystem is deployed in the same area. Thus, after the first USRP transmitter initiated its wireless transmission, second GAA transmitter send the registration, spectrum inquiry and grant request. When the same set of center frequencies have been selected, both GAA transmitters have transmitted their signals on the same frequency band (i.e., 3.657 GHz), as the database does not have any mechanism for protection of GAA users. Thus, in the second phase we have modified the list of frequencies of interest, and one of the GAA subsystem was not interested in transmitting any data using center frequency of 3.657 GHz. In consequence, both USRP devices were allowed to transmit, however this time first USRP transmitted at the lower frequency (3.657 GHz), whereas the second USRP uses the highest center frequency (3.684 GHz). This situation is observed in Fig. 8. The observed performance of WiMAX and radioline was not deteriorated.

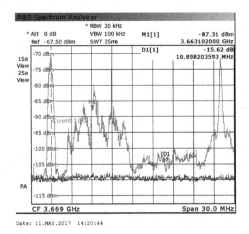

Fig. 8. Averaged power spectral density observed in the second use case

4   Conclusions

This work shows an example of a practical utilization of 3 tier spectrum sharing system in 3.6–3.8 GHz band. The results highlight that a remote database, being able to receive QoS information from incumbent systems allows GAA system to transmit, increasing spectral efficiency. The experiments prove that while the standardized CBRS protocol structure is relatively simple, much effort is to be put in designing algorithms for both database and GAA device.

Acknowledgments. The work has been funded by the EU H2020 project COHERENT (contract no. 671639).

References

1. Mitola, J., Cognitive radio: an integrated agent architecture for software defined radio, Ph.D. thesis, KTH Royal Institute of Technology (2000)
2. Mitola, J.: Cognitive radio architecture evolution. Proc. IEEE **97**(4), 626–641 (2009)
3. Haykin, S., Thomson, D.J., Reed, J.H.: Spectrum sensing for cognitive radio. Proc. IEEE **97**(5), 849–877 (2009)
4. Yilmaz, H.B., Tugcu, T., Alagoz, F., Bayhan, S.: Radio environment map as enabler for practical cognitive radio networks. IEEE Commun. Mag. **51**(12), 162–169 (2013)
5. Perez-Romero, J., Zalonis, A., Boukhatem, L., Kliks, A., Koutlia, K., Dimitriou, N., Kurda, R.: On the use of radio environment maps for interference management in heterogeneous networks. Commun. Mag. IEEE **53**(8), 184–191 (2015)
6. Mustonen, M., et al.: An evolution toward cognitive cellular systems: licensed shared access for network optimization. IEEE Commun. Mag. **53**(5), 68–74 (2015)
7. Federal Communications Commission, FCC14-49: Amendment of the Commissions Rules with Regard to Commercial Operations in the 3550–3650 MHz Band, GN Docket No. 12-354, Further Notice of Proposed Rulemaking. Accessed 23 Apr 2014
8. Federal Communications Commission, FCC14-47: Amendment of the Commissions Rules with Regard to Commercial Operations in the 3550–3650 MHz Band, GN Docket No. 12-354, Further Notice of Proposed Rulemaking. https://apps.fcc.gov/edocs_public/attachmatch/FCC-15-47A1_Rcd.pdf. Accessed 17 Apr 2015
9. Federal Communications Commission: Broadband Division, 3650–3700 MHz Radio Service. https://www.fcc.gov/wireless/bureau-divisions/broadband-division/3650-3700-mhz-radio-service. Accessed 27 Apr 2017
10. WInnForum, WINNF-TS-0016: Spectrum Access System (SAS) - Citizens Broadband Radio Service Device (CBSD) Interface Technical Specification, 18 July 2017. https://workspace.winnforum.org/higherlogic/ws/public/document?document_id=4275
11. WInnForum, WINNF-16-S-0016 V2.0.0: Spectrum Access System (SAS) - Citizens Broadband Radio Service Device (CBSD) Interface Technical Specification, 14 June 2017. https://workspace.winnforum.org/higherlogic/ws/public/document?document_id=4275
12. WInnForum, WINNF-17-SSC-0001: Spectrum Sharing Committee Policy and Procedure: CBRS Air Interface and Measurement Registration, 18 April 2017

Spectrum Occupancy Classification Using SVM-Radial Basis Function

Mitul Panchal$^{(\boxtimes)}$, D. K. Patel, and Sanjay Chaudhary

School of Engineering and Applied Science,
Ahmedabad University, Ahmedabad, Gujarat, India
mitul.panchal@iet.ahduni.edu.in,
{dhaval.patel,sanjay.chaudhary}@ahduni.edu.in

Abstract. With recent development in wireless communication, efficient spectrum utilization is major area of concern. Spectrum measurement studies conducted by wireless communication researchers reveals that the utilization of spectrum is relatively low. In this context, we analyzed big spectrum data for actual spectrum occupancy in spectrum band using different machine learning techniques. Both supervised [Naive Bayes classifier (NBC), K-NN, Decision Tree (DT), Support Vector Machine with Radial Basis Function (SVM-RBF)] and unsupervised algorithms [Neural Network] are applied to find the best classification algorithm for spectrum data. Obtained results shows that combination of SVM-RBF is the best classifier for spectrum database with highest classification accuracy appropriately for distinguishing the class vector in the busy and idle state. We made analysis-based on empirical SVM-RBF model to identify actual duty cycle on the particular band across four mid-size location at Ahmedabad Gujarat.

Keywords: Big data · Spectrum occupancy
Spectrum measurement · Communication · Machine learning
Classification

1 Introduction

The rapid growth of connected devices around the world has drastically increased the demand of wireless spectrum. Every wireless service needs a certain amount of spectrum for transmission of data. Although, Spectrum is a limited resource and expensive too, so we need to enhance current wireless spectrum capacity using the existing spectrum information. Monitoring explicitly, the current spectrum system has not been utilized perfectly. Therefore, it's very important to understand current trends of spectrum bands and to identify occupied or unoccupied slots with specific time interval on the spectrum band which would help to improve the current wireless system in a more advanced way and benefits to the opportunistic spectrum access policy. Big spectrum data is new resource for future wireless communication and it contains detailed information about the

© ICST Institute for Computer Sciences, Social Informatics and Telecommunications Engineering 2018
P. Marques et al. (Eds.): CROWNCOM 2017, LNICST 228, pp. 112–127, 2018.
https://doi.org/10.1007/978-3-319-76207-4_10

spectrum behaviour and utilization. We use this big spectrum data for extracting some meaningful information using statistical methods which helps us to improve the spectrum sensing framework and recognize the requirement of spectrum band.

The term Big data describes the large volume of data both structured and unstructured [1]. Big data can be analyzed for insights that lead to a better decision and strategic business moves. Big spectrum data in [2], is a new resource for wireless communication to leverage the significance of spectrum and improve the spectrum allocation and enhance the capacity beyond the current scenario. Spectrum band holds two types of users, namely, the primary users (PUs) which have a licence for that band and other one is secondary users (SUs) which are non-licensed users. Various spectrum measurement campaigns are conducted for acquiring a wide range of the spectrum band. In [3–5] many spectrum measurements campaigns are performed to identify and understand occupancy statistics. Also in [6], the occupancy statistics were utilized in Singapore and identified those channel that has low or no active utilization. In [7], authors had covered frequency range between 804 MHz to 2750 MHz in urban Auckland, New Zealand. This analysis indicates that on average the actual spectral usage of the band is only about 6.2%. Furthermore, in [8], occupancy statistics were carried out in the band of 30 MHz to 3000 MHz in Dublin, Ireland. The results illustrates that the average spectrum usage during the measurement period was just 13.6%. In [9], an extensive measurement campaign conducted in Aachen Germany, compared indoor and outdoor results. They determined a very high spectrum occupancy in the indoor scenario in the band from 20 MHz up to 3 GHz. Considerably less occupancy was measured in the outdoor scenario. Similar work has also been conducted in [10], where measurement campaigns were made in the urban and rural area at Atlanta. In this measurement, they had done experiments in frequency range of 400 MHz to 7.2 GHz and spectrum occupancy was 6.5% where spectrum vacancy was 77.6% of the amount of white space in 5.4 GHz at urban area whereas 0.8% usage spectrum in rural area and 96.8% spectrum vacant in 6.6 GHz white space. In [11], the use of spectrum occupancy information is made to predict the channel status in the consequent time slot so that optimal spectrum sensing order can be achieved.

The proposed approach improves the throughput of the system while meeting quality of service. On other hand, machine learning technique is known for the most promising solutions in statistics. Machine learning algorithms are often heuristics, meaning they do not require prior or prerequisite assumptions of data. Hence, our objective is to investigate spectrum occupancy using ML algorithms and to acquire comprehensive knowledge about spectrum database. Foremost motivation is that machine learning has a different kind of strategies to find out the useful inference on data. The main contribution here is to formulate the model for prediction of spectrum usage class whether it is idle or busy channel using machine learning classification algorithms and prove that it's best fit method for spectrum database (Table 1).

Table 1. Measurement device details

Equipment	Specifications (MHz)	Remarks
RF Explorer	15–2700 and 4850–6100	Enhance capabilities
Nagoys telescopic NA-773	15–2700	HAM bands
Whip dipole antenna	2400–2500	High quality 2 dBi
Rubber duck antenna	5400–5900	Coverage 2.4 GHz band

The rest of paper is organized as follows: Sect. 2 focuses on measurement setup and methodology. Section 3, shows measurement scenario considered for this work. Spectrum occupancy characteristics are discussed in Sect. 4. Section 5, discusses different current methods for occupancy. The machine learning approach is discussed in Sect. 6. Results are compared in Sect. 6. Finally, Sect. 7 concludes the paper and discusses the future work.

2   Measurement Setup and Data

For our measurement setup, the equipment RF Explorer hand-held device in [12], is used for the spectrum acquisition. The range of RF Explorer is 15 to 6000 MHz. It's basically powerful hand-held hardware device which captures the spectrum data in real-time and also provides connectivity with a local laptop which has installed RF Explorer Windows software. This software provides a real-time visualization of data, trace export facilities and frequency monitoring. Figure 1 illustrates live GSM-900 data being captured on RF Explorer windows software.

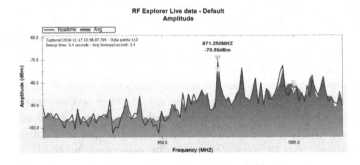

Fig. 1. RF explorer live receiving GSM-900 frequency

The measurement setup plays the key role for obtaining spectrum occupancy result because the percentage of accuracy result entirely depends on many levels of data accuracy. It's an essential part of every spectrum measurement setup. Here, measurement setup is carried out covering 820 to 960 MHz frequency which lies in GSM-900 frequency band in ahmedabad, Gujarat. For analysis purpose, we have selected two GSM channel which lies in between 880–915 MHz (uplink) and 920–935 MHz (downlink), providing 124 RF channels with a bandwidth of 200 kHz. As mentioned in [13], there are some basic parameters that should clearly be specified like frequency name (GSM-900), location (four location of ahmedabad), direction (Omni-directional), polarization (Rx antenna is vertically polarized) and time variation (sampling rate 200 KHz and measurement duration 2 h).

3 Measurement Scenario

In this paper, we present the statistical analysis of spectrum occupancy in four most populated areas in Ahmedabad namely Nehrunagar, Navarangpura, Shivranjini and Vastrapur. Here considering only GSM-900 spectrum band and determining occupancy level in that band. The acquired data-set contains two main parameters one is power spectrum density (PSD) and another one is time variation (millisecond) which is continuously changing according to frequency power level in a spectrum band. The detail routes of spectrum data acquisition are shown in Fig. 2. At the other extreme, the minimum and maximum power level suggest the most frequent use of the signal. This difference would be separated by using thresholding algorithm. The approach of deriving spectrum occupancy is dependent on different parameters and methods; whereas the recent literature survey on spectrum occupancy measurement in [14] has proved that most frequent methodology for the spectrum occupancy measurement has Average Duty Cycle method, Markov Chain and Linear Regression. In the following section, we apply all the above methods for finding an occupancy statistics empirically with help of above data acquisition method (Fig. 3). The duty cycle can be calculated by following.

Fig. 2. A 44 location in Ahmedabad where spectrum measurement were collected

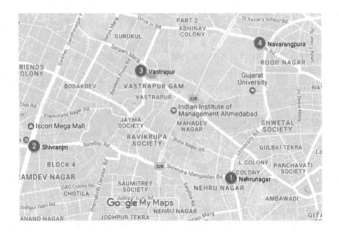

Fig. 3. A map of the four location in ahmedabad where spectrum measurement were collected

$$Duty\ Cycle = \frac{Signal\ Occupation\ period\,(n)}{Total\ observation\ period\,(m)} \times 100\%$$

where n represents time slot t, m denotes a total number of the time slot. Here received signal level is above the threshold.

4 Spectrum Occupancy Characteristics

In this model, all the parameters are used in terms of power level (dBm), because power spectrum density (PSD) corresponding to signal is different at all level or varies at all the times (Fig. 5). Thus, we have collected data from four areas Nehrunagar, Navarangpura, Vastrapur and Shivranjini. We measured common GSM-900 signal in all the locations and there are different utilization patterns acquired. Figure 4 represents the average power spectrum density in each location, moreover every location has different threshold value, but the range remains between −70 to −80 dBm. For threshold, we have taken average value

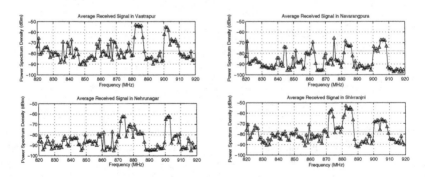

Fig. 4. Average power spectrum density at four location

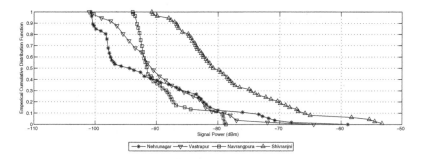

Fig. 5. Empirical cumulative distribution function showing spectrum occupancy

as threshold (λ) using Eq. 1, where $\tau_{(i)}$ is signal power and N is number of sample. In [7], these result helps us to identify the quantitative analysis. Figure 4, provides the overall trend of GSM signal occupancy irrespective of cities, time, sites and frequency and all the data points which were collected across the center frequency of 892.85 MHz. This cumulative distribution function shows the spectrum occupancy trends to each of the four location. It illustrates that Shivranjini is top most area where spectrum occupancy level is higher then Nehrunagar, Vastrapur and Navarangpura respectively. Using Empirical cumulative distribution it estimates the probability of each power spectrum density level in that location. Empirical CDF is a consistent estimate of the true CDF of any given value using Eq. 3. The empirical function $\hat{F}_n(t)$ gives weight of $\frac{1}{N}$ for each point of CDF, therefore it's also called step function. In below case, I is identical to X value, then weight of each value that is given to CDF is increased by $I + 1$. For every identical value of X, the given space of t is as follows

$$\lambda = \frac{1}{N} \sum_{i=1}^{N} \tau_{(i)} \tag{1}$$

$$I = \begin{cases} 0 & X_i \nleq t \\ 1 & X_i \neq X_{i+1} \Leftrightarrow Xi \leq t \\ I_{X_i \leq t} + I_{X_{i+1} \leq t} & X_i = X_{i+1} \Leftrightarrow X_i, X_{i+1} \leq t \end{cases} \tag{2}$$

$$\hat{F}_n(t) = \frac{1}{n} \sum_{i=1}^{n} I_{X_i \leq t} \tag{3}$$

5   Methods for Spectrum Occupancy

In [15], different spectrum measurement campaigns have different goals varying from general analysis of spectrum utilization to specific individual wireless technologies. Furthermore, this section includes discussion on several important methodological aspects to be considered while evaluating spectrum occupancy.

Due to the differences in the signal modulation involved as well as the differences in the bandwidths utilized by each channel, energy spectral densities correspond to signals transmitted for different wireless services can be expected to be different.

This section gives the overview of all three methods which are used in this paper for deriving occupancy. Spectrum data is continuously generated through the device with a specific time interval. Linear correlation method finds the relationship between the parameter and finds the best fit variable which gives the relation between an independent variable and dependent variable [16]. This method gives a correlation metrics so using this we can model that and find the distribution of data.

Another method is duty cycle measurement which helps to find a specific load on particular frequency band at a particular time. The time interval is a most important role in duty cycle as it determines the average usage of frequency. The duty cycle methods are the most frequent methods for spectrum occupancy in [17]. Continuous Time Semi-Markov Chain (CTSMC) model, which is especially used to find patterns in real time database and classify the state in the database like idle or busy state. In [18], DTMC model is widely used in DSA/CR to describe the binary occupancy patterns in a channel in a time domain.

5.1   Linear Correlation Method

The normal linear model equation given in [19]:

$$y_i = \beta_1 x_{1i} + \beta_2 x_{2i} + \ldots + \beta_n x_n \tag{4}$$

$$+ b_1 z_{1i} + b_2 z_{2i} + \ldots + b_n z_{ni} + \epsilon_i \tag{5}$$

$$y = X\beta + \varepsilon \tag{6}$$

$$b_i \sim N(0, \sigma D) \tag{7}$$

$$\epsilon_{ij} \sim N(0, \sigma \Lambda) \tag{8}$$

where

1. $y = [y_1, y_2 \ldots, y_n]^T$
2. X is the model matrix
3. $\beta = [\beta_1, \beta_2, \ldots, \beta_n]^T$ is the vector of regression coefficients
4. $\varepsilon = [\varepsilon_1, \varepsilon_2 \ldots, \varepsilon_n]^T$ is the vector of errors
5. N_n represents the n-variable multivariate normal distribution.
6. Λ and D are variance component

y_i is explains the relationship between one or more independent variables, called regressor variables, and a dependent variable, called the response variable (X). The parameters of the model are called the regression coefficients, specified as $\beta_1, \beta_2, \beta_3 \ldots, \beta_n$ and the error variance, defined as σ^2. The above model has one random-effect term, the error term ε_i given by

$$\varepsilon_i \sim N(0, \sigma^2)$$

5.2   Average Duty Cycle Method

Duty cycle [DC] model described in [18], where Ψ_t is able to describe its time evolution with sufficient level of accuracy. Notice that the DC in [20], is directly related to the instantaneous load or traffic load level supported by the channel. Although, traffic load would be experienced in a radio channel is frequently the result of an important number of random factors and aspects such as the number of incoming and outgoing users, the resource management policies employed in the system. The shape of Ψ_t, in this case, can be approximated by the summation of bell-shaped exponential terms centred at time instants t_m, with amplitudes A_m and widths σ_m given by:

$$\Psi_t \approx \Psi_{min} + \sum_{m=0}^{M=1} A_m e^{-(\frac{t-T_m}{\sigma_m})^2}, 0 \leq t \leq T \tag{9}$$

where $\Psi_{min} = min\{\Psi(t)\}$, T is the time interval over which $\Psi(t)$ is periodic (i.e. one day). The analysis of empirical data indicates that $\Psi(t)$ can accurately be described by means of M = 3 terms with τ_1 and τ_2 corresponding to busy hours and $\tau_0 = \tau_2 - T$. Notice that A determines the average value of $\Psi(t)$ in the time interval [0, T]. In [21], the occupancy level of various spectrum bands is quantified throughout this work in terms of the duty cycle.

5.3   Continuous Time Semi-Markov Chain Model

In [18], temporal spectrum occupancy pattern of a primary radio channel can adequately be modelled by means of a two-state Markov chain since it may be either busy or idle at a certain time instant. Let's denote $S = \{s_0, s_1\}$ the space state for a primary radio channel, with the s_0 state indicating that the channel is idle and the s_1 state indicating that the channel is busy. The behavior of a Markov chain can statistically be described with a set of transition probabilities among states. In the simulation of the Discrete Time Markov Chains (DTMC) channel occupancy model, the duration's of the sojourn times T were determined:

$$T_i = N_i * T_s \tag{10}$$

$$P = \begin{bmatrix} p_{00} & p_{01} \\ p_{10} & p_{11} \end{bmatrix} \tag{11}$$

The behavior of a markov chain can statistically be described as in [22] with a set of transition probabilities among states. If the state space S is finite with n states, the transition probability distribution can be described with a n × n square matrix.

$$P(t_k, t_l) = [p_{ij}(t_k, t_l)]_{n \times n} \tag{12}$$

To reproduce certain DC, indicated as Ψ in early, the transition probabilities of Eq. 11, that need to be satisfy some particular relations, determined as follows.

The n-element normalized row vector $\pi = [\pi_i]_{1 \times n} = [\pi_0, \pi_1, \ldots, \pi_{n-1}]$, called the stationary distribution of the system, has elements representing the probability that the system is in each of its states in the long term, i.e. $\pi_i = P(S = s_i)$. For the occupancy model, where n = 2, the elements of π are given by [22].

Notice π_1 that represents the probability that the channel is in the busy state in the long term and it can thus be related to the channel's DC (i.e., $\Psi = \pi_1$).

$$\pi_0 = \frac{p_{10}}{p_{01} + p_{10}} \tag{13}$$

$$\pi_1 = \frac{p_{01}}{p_{01} + p_{10}} \tag{14}$$

There are many more approaches for spectrum occupancy model in [23] but here we applied Linear Mixed Effect Model on data. As mentioned earlier that, our data contains different site location, time, different power level, sweep frequency parameter which are captured by RF Explorer. One advantage of this model is, that it also works empirically with continuous data. A brief overview of Linear Mixed effect model is shown below.

5.4   Linear Mixed Effect Model for Spectrum Occupancy

The main advantage of linear mixed effect model are flexible, for instance enabling the modelling of altering slopes and intercepts. Linear regression has taken multiple input parameter which could be added in different dimensions e.g. space, frequency, time. For spectrum occupancy measurement, below Linear Mixed Effect Model is follows:

$$\begin{aligned} \text{Occ.Perc}_{ij} = \beta_0 + \beta_1 \text{Nav}_{ij} + \beta_2 \text{Neh}_{ij} + \beta_3 \text{Vast}_{ij} \\ + \beta_4 \text{Shiv}_{ij} + \epsilon_{ij} \end{aligned} \tag{15}$$

Linear mixed effect model takes all the parameter simultaneously. Consequently, all various location data matrix could be added in time and determine real-time spectrum occupancy. One significant benefit is that we can estimate spectrum occupancy in time domain as well as frequency domain and also build the prediction model. Here, we have calculated an occupancy rate for the different site. Table 2 shows the intercept of that model which is 0.72032 and applying linear mixed effect regression model (Eq. 15) for each location, we could determine occupancy rate in percentage. We could clearly see the spectrum occupancy in Navrangpura 0.72%, similarly for Nehrunagar 0.78% and so on. Table 3 illustrates result compression of spectrum occupancy rate using above three methods.

Figure 6 describes the residual plot versus fitted value. It is scattered plot of residual value on the y-axis and fitted value on the x-axis (estimated value). This plot is used to detect non-linearity, unequal error variances and outliers. The residual "bounces randomly" around 0 line. This suggests the assumption that the relationship is linear is reasonable. The residual roughly forms a "horizontal band" around 0 line. It also suggests that the variance of the error terms are equal. There have no one residual stands out from the basic random pattern

Table 2. Statistical parameter of linear mixed effect model

	Estimate	Std. error	tstate	DF	pValue
(Intercept)	0.72032	0.70323	1.0243	107	<0.05
Nehrunagar	−0.00046449	0.0028857	−0.16097	107	<0.05
Navrangpura	−0.00022675	0.0060755	−0.037322	107	<0.05
Vastrapur	0.0019761	0.0044519	0.44388	107	<0.05
University	0.0015222	0.003544	0.4295	107	<0.05

Table 3. Occupancy compression

Methods	Occ. rate	Std. error	Location
Liner mixed effect model	14.4%	0.7032	SEAS
Average Duty Cycle	40.3%	0.4801	SEAS
Discrete time Markov model	19.7%	0.6508	SEAS

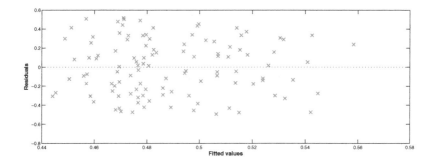

Fig. 6. Plot of residuals vs. fitted values

on residual, it means there are no outliers available. Here variance of residual increases with increasing fitted response which is knows as heteroscedasticity. This figure illustrates that there is some heteroscedasticity available.

$$Residual = Observed - Predicated$$

Consequently in Fig. 7, the corresponding is normal probability plot of the residual. This normal probability looks alike when residual is normally distributed and there is no outlier. It means this relationship is approximately linear with exception of few data point. We could proceed with the assumption that the error terms are normally distributed upon removing some outliers from data set and clearly see the points making diagonal line roughly straight. It means that 95% of residual is approximately fitted. Therefore, this data set follows the standard normal distribution.

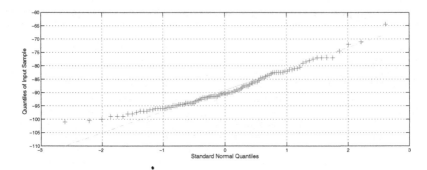

Fig. 7. Q-Q Plot of sample data versus standard normal

6   Statistical Analysis Using Radial Basis Function

Nowadays Machine Learning techniques are most important and fundamental things for big data analysis and statistics. Therefore, many researchers and academicians have acquired an interest in machine learning. There are two main parts in ML, supervised and unsupervised algorithms. These algorithms are most important for classification, clustering and prediction of future trends. Consequently, here we have use Machine learning algorithms to find an occupancy on spectrum data. In [11], machine learning techniques are used to identify occupancy in spectrum data and derive best-fit algorithms for spectrum data classification. Also, there are so many classification algorithms available such as Support Vector Machine, K-NN, Neural Network, Generalized Linear Model Decision Tree, Tree Bagger, Naive Bayes and so on. All these algorithms are used for classification purpose in a different areas. In this article proposed, SVM + FFT algorithm is used with which we obtained very good accuracy. But one major drawback is that it requires much computational time to train a large amount of spectrum data. So, moving a step ahead, we proposed SVM as it is advanced and requires less computational time. Also we explored the Support Vector Machine when using Radial Basis Function with scaling factor of 2, which derives classification result. We propose SVM-RBF model for calculating classification and its accuracy in MATLAB.

The work below depicts, how Redial Basis Function (RBF) with SVM combinations performs. For binary classification, given training data (x_i, y_i) for i = 1.......N, with $x_i \in \mathbb{R}^d$ and $y_i \in \{0, 1\}$ learn classifier such that

$$f(x_i) \begin{cases} \geq \lambda & y_i = 1 \\ < \lambda & y_i = 0 \end{cases} \tag{16}$$

where λ value derived from Eq. 1 and $y_i f(x_i) \geq \lambda$ is busy state and $y_i f(x_i) < \lambda$ is idle state. The linear SVM classifier consists in defining function

$$f(x) = \sum_i (x_i^T, x) + b \tag{17}$$

which finds optimum hyper-plane and x^T weight vector which is normal to hyper-plane and b is bias value for weight vector. For non-linear, second solution is SVM with kernel function where kernel is a function that simulates the projection of initial data in a feature space with higher dimension $\Phi : K^n \rightarrow H$. In this new space data is considered linearly separable. By applying this, dot product and replacing value (x_i^T, x) in Eq. 18.

$$K(\mathbf{x}, \mathbf{x}') = \exp\left(-\frac{\|\mathbf{x} - \mathbf{x}'\|^2}{2\sigma^2}\right)$$ (18)

The new SVM-RBF function to classify the training data is:

$$f(x) = \sum_{i=0}^{N} y_i\, \alpha_i K(\mathbf{x}_i, \mathbf{x}') + b$$ (19)

where α_i Lagrange multiplier to solve problem easily.

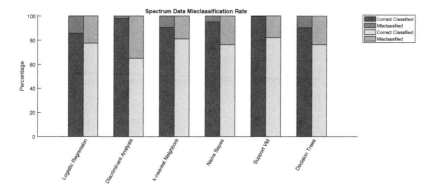

Fig. 8. Miss-classification rate of different classifier

Figure 8 illustrates classification accuracy of different algorithms. This figure represents training and testing set classification rate where violet and red colors indicate the training set correctly classified and miss-classified same as in testing set light pink and light blue indicates correctly classified and miss-classified rate in spectrum data. The updated SVM classifier (Eq. 19) algorithm use σ with value 2, where σ is scaling factor, whose value can change according to training set value. The confusion matrix describes the performance of different classification model on a set of test data for which the true value is known. The confusing matrix itself is relatively simple to understand, but the related terminology can be confusing. In order to understand, this figure explains different binary classifier's confusion. There are two possible predicated class, idle or busy. If it is predict idle it means signal is ideal, else signal is busy. The different binary classifier algorithms like Neural Network, Logistics regression K-NN, Decision Tree,

Naive Bayes and SVM-RBF are applied and test statistics is derived. In SVM-RBF, the classifier made a total of 972 predictions, for which classifier predicated 830 times idle and 142 times busy. In reality, they are 841 ideal and 131 busy samples. Overall, classifier correct classification rate is $TP + TN/$Total is 87.5%, so miss-classification rate is 12.5% and precision rate (correct prediction rate error) is 0.93%. This accuracy rate is very much higher compared to other classifier which indicates that SVM-RBF is the best classifier for Spectrum data. All the statistical accuracy-related result for algorithm is displayed in Table 4.

Table 4. Comparison of classification algorithm error

Classifier	Precision rate (predication rate)	Miss-classification error	Accuracy
Decision tree	0.85%	23.6%	76.4%
GLM	0.16%	23.4%	76.6%
Naive byes	0.42%	22.7%	77.3%
K-NN	0.84%	17.6%	87.5%
SVM-RBF	0.93%	12.5%	87.5%

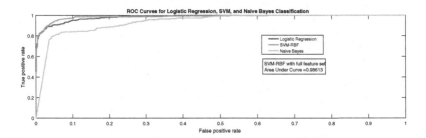

Fig. 9. ROC plot illustrate three discrete classifier

After classification of accuracy from the SVM-RBF we made receiving operating characteristics curve for cross verification, which is presented in Fig. 9. It's plot of true positive rate against false positive rate for different possible outcomes of a diagnostic test. It shows the trade-off between sensitivity and specificity. The closer the curve follows the left-hand border and top border of the ROC space, the more accurate test. The Fig. 9, illustrates three classifier algorithms performance. Using SVM-RBF function, the bounded line is to closer to 1 respectively logistic and naive Bayes classifier are decreased to lower bound. The area under the curve in SVM-RBF is 98.5% which means classification accuracy is very much higher than other algorithms.

Above spectrum analysis conducted with a supervised algorithm is based on a Support Vector Machine classifier. The algorithm analyses a set of positive and negative class based on a frequency of occurrence in each class, estimating probabilities that value has positive and/or negative significance. Based on the probability of each value occurrence, channel or frequency probability is computed by calculating the product of that probabilities. This process requires pre-classification in two classes, Idle and busy data-set, specific to a supervised learning process, with which is calculated the occurrence of channel state in class. Obtained classification method also compared to simple SVM algorithm for the validity and efficiency of the SVM + RBF algorithm and it has outperformed to simple SVM algorithm. Table 5 illustrates the comparison result of the algorithms and it shows miss-classification rate and total classification loss are very low compared to SVM algorithms. In statistical classification, a confusion matrix is also known as an error matrix. It's specific table layout that generates a visualization of the performance of classification algorithm, typically in the supervised algorithm. Each column of the matrix represents the predicted class while each row represents the actual class. Confusion matrix has demonstrated in Table 6. To estimate the clustering results, accuracy, specificity, specificity, precision, recall, and F-measure were calculated over pairs of points. For a specific pair of points that share at least one cluster in the overlying clustering results, these measures try to estimate whether the prediction of this pair as being in the same cluster was correct with respect to the underlying true categories in the data. Precision is calculated as the fraction of pairs correctly put in the same cluster, recall is the fraction of actual pairs that were identified, and F-measure is the harmonic mean of precision and recall. Table 7 presented the statistical parameters for the efficiency of both the algorithms on spectrum data classification which is derived from the confusion matrix. In this study, for having an accurate assessment of the classification of two methods, it will be evaluated on the effectiveness, using same data set on which spectrum analytic is applied on frequency.

Table 5. Compression of SVM and SVM-RBF algorithms

Classifier	Sample size	Time (s)	Miss classification rate (MCR)	Loss
SVM	973	0.589	0.1182	13%
SVM-RBF	973	0.272	0.0946	7%

Table 6. Confusion matrix of SVM + RBF for efficiency

N = 973	Predicated: Idle	Predicated: Busy	
Actual Idle	TN = 238	FP = 75	313
Actual Busy	FN = 30	TP = 630	660
	268	705	

Table 7. Efficiency of algorithms

Algorithm	Accuracy	Sensitivity	Specificity	Precision	Recall	F-measure
SVM	0.8673	0.7692	0.9136	0.8081	0.7692	0.7882
SVM + RBF	0.8920	0.7596	0.9545	0.8876	0.7596	0.8187

7 Conclusion

This paper presents spectrum occupancy in GSM-900 band. We captured spectrum data of four different locations in Ahmedabad city. We analyzed traditional methods for spectrum occupancy and residual plot shown a good indicator of the occupancy but that methods are less accurate and required more computational time for the process of the spectrum data. Hence, machine learning comes in to the picture for the promising solution with less computational time and proposed a new method which derives the best accuracy an efficient way. By implementing SVM-RBF classifier algorithm, we determined that the SVM-RBF is the best fit for big spectrum data classification as it requires less computational time for training a data and demonstrates a good classification accuracy. This method could also be extended for different bands like ISM, Microwave, Satellites-Radar band and UHF-VHF band for opportunistic spectrum access.

Acknowledgment. We thank anonymous reviewers and our team members for the continuative support. This work was supported by Gujarat Council on Science and Technology, Department of Science & Technology, Government of Gujarat under the grant GUJCOST/MRP/2015-16/2659. The authors also thank Ahmedabad University for Infrastructure support.

References

1. Ding, G., Wu, Q., Wang, J., Yao, Y.-D.: Big spectrum data: the new resource for cognitive wireless networking. arXiv preprint arXiv:1404.6508 (2014)
2. Sasirekha, G., Dasari, S.R.: Big spectrum data analysis in DSA enabled LTE-A networks: a system architecture. In: 2016 IEEE 6th International Conference on Advanced Computing (IACC), pp. 655–660. IEEE (2016)
3. MacDonald, J.T.: A survey of spectrum utilization in Chicago. Illinois Institute of Technology, Technical report (2007)
4. Yucek, T., Arslan, H.: A survey of spectrum sensing algorithms for cognitive radio applications. IEEE Commun. Surv. Tutor. **11**(1), 116–130 (2009)
5. Patil, K., Prasad, R., Skouby, K.: A survey of worldwide spectrum occupancy measurement campaigns for cognitive radio. In: 2011 International Conference on Devices and Communications (ICDeCom), pp. 1–5. IEEE (2011)
6. Islam, M.H., Koh, C.L., Oh, S.W., Qing, X., Lai, Y.Y., Wang, C., Liang, Y.-C., Toh, B.E., Chin, F., Tan, G.L., et al.: Spectrum survey in Singapore: occupancy measurements and analyses. In: 2008 3rd International Conference on Cognitive Radio Oriented Wireless Networks and Communications, CrownCom 2008, pp. 1–7. IEEE (2008)

7. Chiang, R.I., Rowe, G.B., Sowerby, K.W.: A quantitative analysis of spectral occupancy measurements for cognitive radio. In: IEEE 65th Vehicular Technology Conference-VTC2007-Spring, pp. 3016–3020. IEEE (2007)

8. Tugba Erpek, K.S., Jones, D.: Spectrum occupancy measurements, shared spectrum company reports, shared spectrum company, January 2004–August 2005. http://www.sharedspectrum.com/wp-content/uploads/Ireland_Spectrum_Occupancy_Measurements_v2.pdf

9. Wellens, M., Wu, J., Mahonen, P.: Evaluation of spectrum occupancy in indoor and outdoor scenario in the context of cognitive radio. In: Cognitive Radio Oriented Wireless Networks and Communications, pp. 420–427. IEEE (2007)

10. Petrin, A., Steffes, P.G.: Analysis and comparison of spectrum measurements performed in urban and rural areas to determine the total amount of spectrum usage. In: Proceedings of the International Symposium on Advanced Radio Technologies (ISART 2005), pp. 9–12 (2005)

11. Azmat, F., Chen, Y., Stocks, N.: Analysis of spectrum occupancy using machine learning algorithms. IEEE Trans. Veh. Technol. **65**(9), 6853–6860 (2016)

12. Explorer, R.: Handheld hardware. http://www.wimo.com/rf-explorer-spectrum-analyser-signal-generator_e.html

13. Matheson, R.J.: Strategies for spectrum usage measurements. In: IEEE 1988 International Symposium on Electromagnetic Compatibility, Symposium Record, pp. 235–241. IEEE (1988)

14. Chen, Y., Oh, H.-S.: A survey of measurement-based spectrum occupancy modeling for cognitive radios. IEEE Commun. Surv. Tutor. **18**(1), 848–859 (2014)

15. López-Benítez, M., Casadevall, F.: Statistical prediction of spectrum occupancy perception in dynamic spectrum access networks. In: 2011 IEEE International Conference on Communications (ICC), pp. 1–6. IEEE (2011)

16. Pagadarai, S., Wyglinski, A.M.: Measuring and modeling spectrum occupancy: a massachusetts perspective. In: Proceedings of the International Symposium on Advanced Radio Technologies (2010)

17. López-Benítez, M., Casadevall, F.: Methodological aspects of spectrum occupancy evaluation in the context of cognitive radio. Eur. Trans. Telecommun. **21**(8), 680–693 (2010)

18. López-Benítez, M., Casadevall, F.: Discrete-time spectrum occupancy model based on Markov chain and duty cycle models. In: 2011 IEEE Symposium on New Frontiers in Dynamic Spectrum Access Networks (DySPAN), pp. 90–99. IEEE (2011)

19. Pagadarai, S., Wyglinski, A.: A linear mixed-effects model of wireless spectrum occupancy. EURASIP J. Wirel. Commun. Netw. **2010**(1), 1 (2010)

20. López-Benítez, M., Casadevall, F.: Spatial duty cycle model for cognitive radio. In: 21st Annual IEEE International Symposium on Personal, Indoor and Mobile Radio Communications, pp. 1631–1636. IEEE (2010)

21. López-Benítez, M., Casadevall, F.: Spectrum occupancy in realistic scenarios and duty cycle model for cognitive radio. Adv. Electron. Telecommun. Special Issue on Radio Commun. Ser. Recent Adv. Future Trends Wirel. Commun. **1**(1), 1–9 (2010)

22. Ibe, O.: Markov processes for stochastic modeling. Elsevier, Boston (2013)

23. López-Benítez, M., Casadevall, F.: Spectrum usage models for the analysis, design and simulation of cognitive radio networks. In: Venkataraman, H., Muntean, G.M. (eds.) Cognitive Radio and its Application for Next Generation Cellular and Wireless Networks. LNEE, vol. 116, pp. 27–73. Springer, Heidelberg (2012). https://doi.org/10.1007/978-94-007-1827-2_2

Analysis of Blockchain Use Cases in the Citizens Broadband Radio Service Spectrum Sharing Concept

Seppo Yrjölä[(✉)]

Nokia Innovation Steering, Oulu, Finland
seppo.yrjola@nokia.com

Abstract. The Blockchain (BC) technology has received religious attention in the financial and internet domains, and recently interest has spread to adjacent sectors like communications. This paper seeks to identify the impact of the BC technology in novel spectrum sharing concepts using the Citizens Broadband Radio Service (CBRS) concept as an example. The results indicate that the BC core characteristics can be utilized in several use cases addressing current CBRS implementation considerations. The CBRS concept could particularly benefit of BCs in building trust, consensus and lowering the transaction cost. In BC deployments, confidentiality should be taken into consideration through hybrid and private BC options. Furthermore, the cognitive radio spectrum sharing – BC combination paves the way for new business models and distributed services.

Keywords: Blockchain · Citizens Broadband Radio Service · Cognitive radio
Mobile broadband · Spectrum sharing · 5G

1 Introduction

The number of mobile broadband (MBB) subscribers, connected 'things' and the amount of data used per user is set to grow significantly leading to increasing spectrum demand [1]. The US President's Council of Advanced Science & Technology (PCAST) report [2] emphasized the need for novel thinking within wireless industry to meet the growing spectrum crisis in spectrum allocation, utilization and management. The essential role of cognitive radio and spectrum sharing were underlined to find a balance between the different services with their different spectrum requirements and system dynamics. At the same time, Blockchain (BC) technology has received significant attention as a potential answer to the most vexing trust and data security challenges related to transactions, contracting, and funds exchange in the Internet across various domains [3]: from original bitcoins [4] and finance [5], to real estate [6], health [7], energy [8], and government [9]. In telecommunications, to date early BC studies has focused mainly on the context of Internet of Things (IoT) [10].

So far, only a subset of the cognitive radio (CR) [11] and spectrum sharing concepts researched in technology and regulation has reached market acceptance, the license exempt access with intelligent user terminals and spectrum sensing [12], Dynamic Spectrum Sharing (DSA) non-collaborative concept with radar detection

© ICST Institute for Computer Sciences, Social Informatics and Telecommunications Engineering 2018
P. Marques et al. (Eds.): CROWNCOM 2017, LNICST 228, pp. 128–139, 2018.
https://doi.org/10.1007/978-3-319-76207-4_11

function of Dynamic Frequency Selection (DFS) [13], or the unlicensed TV White Space (TVWS) [14, 15] as examples. Based on the decade of profound CR and in particular TVWS concept studies, a couple of novel licensing based sharing models have recently emerged, and are under regulation and standardization, the Licensed Shared Access (LSA) [16] from Europe and the Citizens Broadband Radio Service (CBRS) from the US [17]. Related to these prominent spectrum sharing concepts, particularly for the CBRS, there is not prior research regarding their business and technology enabler analysis. Market success criteria for dynamic spectrum access technologies in general has been studied in [18], and the feasibility and attractiveness of the CBRS spectrum sharing concepts applying business model theory framework has been addressed in [19]. In [20], different CBRS stakeholder groups' considerations are summarized and general Spectrum Access System (SAS) requirements discussed. Moreover, the applicability and validation of the Internet and MBB technology enablers has received very little attention as focus to date has been on more general and future oriented CR techniques [21]. In the literature, to the best knowledge of the author, no research to date has analyzed the application of the BC technology and its underlying characteristics to the spectrum sharing concepts. This paper investigates:

1. What kind of blockchain characteristics support spectrum sharing concepts and the CBRS framework?
2. What are the potential use cases?

The rest of the paper is organized as follows. First, the CBRS framework and the BC technology are shortly introduced in Sects. 2 and 3. Section 4 links CBRS deployment considerations with the BC technology characteristics into potential use cases, and analyze their applicability. Conclusions are drawn in Sect. 5.

2 Citizens Broadband Radio Service Concept

The Federal Communications Commission (FCC) released Report and Order and Second Further Notice of Proposed Rulemaking to establish rules for shared use of the 3550–3650 MHz band in April 2015 [17]. Followed by intense discussion and consultation with the industry [22], the FCC released second Report and Order and Order on Reconsideration [23], and finalizes the rules [24] governing the CBRS in the 3550–3700 MHz band in 2016. The framework defines a contiguous 150 MHz block that the FCC calls *Citizens Broadband Radio Service*. The 3550–3650 MHz spectrum is currently allocated for use by the US Department of Defense (DoD) radar systems and Fixed Satellite Services (FSS) while the 3650–3700 MHz spectrum incumbents are the FSS and the grandfathered commercial Wireless Broadband Services (WBS). The FCC prefigures the CBRS as an "innovation band" where they can assign spectrum to commercial MBB systems like the Third Generation Partnership Project (3GPP) Long Term Evolution (LTE) on a shared basis with incumbent users.

The sharing framework consists of three tiers: *Incumbent Access* (IA), *Priority Access* (PA) and *General Authorized Access* (GAA). The FCC licenses for the PA layer users will be assigned via competitive bidding, and allowed to operate up to a total of 70 MHz of the 3550–3650 MHz spectrum segment enjoying interference protection from the GAA operations. A *PA License* (PAL) licensee's non-renewable authorization is for a 10 MHz channel in a single census tract for three years, with the ability to aggregate up to six years up-front. One licensee may hold up to 40 MHz of PALs in any given census tract at any given time. In addition to MNO and WBS users the PAL layer may cover utilities, IoT verticals and governmental users. The specific channels of auctioned PALs are assigned, re-assigned, and terminated by the *Spectrum Access System*. The PALs will be opened for the third GAA tier users, when unused and further automatically terminated and may not be renewed at the end of the term. The '*use*' status of PALs in the CBRS 'use it or share it' approach is determined using two engineering approaches [23]. First, licensees should report the coverage area of the set of *CBRS devices* (CBSDs) based on actual network deployments called the *PAL protection area* (PPAs). Second, to maximize an objective PPA, the SAS maintains a list of CBSDs belonging to the PPA and do not authorize other CBSDs on the same channel in geographic areas and at maximum power levels that will cause aggregate interference within a PPA [23].

The FCC revisited the CBRS rules [24] in 2016, and introduced the *light-touch leasing process* to enable secondary markets for the spectrum use rights held by PA licensees. Under the framework, no FCC oversight is required for partitioning and disaggregation, and PA licensees are free to lease any portion of their spectrum or license outside of their PPA. The PPA can be self-reported by PAL owner or calculated by the SAS. The PAL channel can be re-allocated beyond the PPA, but within the census tract. Furthermore, the FCC will permit stand-alone or SAS managed *spectrum exchanges* and let market forces determine the role of the SAS value added services.

The opportunistic GAA operates under a *licensed-by-rule* framework and has no interference protection from other CBRS users, while it must protect incumbents and PALs. This dynamic third layer with the minimum availability of 80 MHz aims to facilitate the rapid deployment of compliant small cell devices while minimizing administrative costs and burdens on the public, licensees, and the FCC. Furthermore, the GAA is planned to spur innovation as a flexible and scalable low-cost entry point for a wide choice of services and new entrants, e.g., small and local businesses, utilities, healthcare, public safety and smart cities. For established Mobile Network Operators (MNOs) and PAL licensees, the GAA offers, e.g., PAL offload during IA interruption, Wireless local access network (Wi-Fi) type capacity offload, backhauling and WBS.

The CBSDs are fixed base stations (BS), or networks of such, and can only operate under the authority and management of a centralized SAS, which could be multiple as shown in Fig. 1. Both the PAL and the GAA users are obligated to use only the certified FCC approved CBSDs, which must register with the SAS with information required by the rules, e.g., operator ID, device identification and parameters, and location information. In a typical MNO deployment scenario, the CBSD network is a managed network comprising of the *Domain Proxy* (DP) and Network Management System (NMS) functionality. The DP may be a bidirectional information routing engine or a more intelligent mediation function enabling flexible self-control and interference optimizations in such a network. In addition, DP enables combining, e.g., the small cells of a shopping mall or sports venue to a virtual BS entity, or provides a translational capability to interface legacy radio equipment with a SAS.

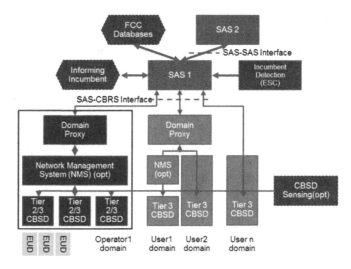

Fig. 1. CBRS functional architecture.

In addition to spectrum assignment, the SAS controls the interference environment, and enforces protection criteria and exclusion zones to protect higher priority users, and dynamically determines and enforces CBSDs maximum power levels in space and time [23]. In the recent FCC rules [24], the FCC requires all SASs to have consistent models for interference calculations. Furthermore, the SAS takes care of registration, authentication and identification of user information, SAS-SAS message exchange, and performs other functions as set forth in the FCC rules [20]. All the CBSDs and End User Devices (EUDs) must be capable of two-way communications across the entire 3.5 GHz band and discontinuing operation or changing frequencies at the direction of the SAS. In order to meet the mission critical requirements of the DoD IAs, the FCC adopted rules to require *Environmental Sensing Capabilities* (ESC) in and adjacent to the CBRS band to detect incumbent radar activity in coastal areas and near inland military bases. The confidentiality of the sensitive military incumbent information will be ensured through strict operational security (OPSEC) requirements and corresponding certification for the ESC elements and operator authorization [25]. Once IA activity is detected, the ESC communicates that information to a SAS for processing, and if needed, a SAS orders commercial users to vacate an interfering channel within 300 s in frequency, location, or time [23].

The CBRS market introduction is planned to start with the opportunistic GAA layer and incumbent protection utilizing static *exclusion zones* (EZ) only to provide a low-cost entry point into the band. In the second phase, the ESC system enables the rest of the country, particularly major coastal areas to become available, as the EZs will be converted into *protection zones* (PZ). ESC deployments near the EZs can consist of commercially operated sensor networks, or CBSD infrastructure based sensing or their combination. Prospective SAS administrator with ESC or stand-alone ESC operators must have their systems approved through the same process as SAS administrators.

The *FCC databases* are in authority to input the FCC information, e.g., registered or licensed commercial users, EZ areas requiring ESC into SAS. Additionally, the functional architecture depicted in Fig. 1 includes the *Informing Incumbent* option enabling the federal IA to directly inform the SAS ahead of plans concerning changes in the spectrum usage [26].

The Spectrum Sharing Committee (SSC) of the Wireless Innovation Forum (WInnF) [27] consisting of governmental, MBB, wireless, Internet and defense ecosystems representatives has finalized operational and functional requirements protocols for data and communications across the various open interfaces within the system [27] to enable early trial implementations of interoperable systems. The White House aims to expand wireless innovation in spectrum sharing further through identifying an additional federal owned spectrum for future commercial sharing, subject to the success of sharing at 3.5 GHz [28].

3 Blockchain Technology

In 2008, Nakamoto [4] outlined a new bitcoin protocol for a P2P electronic cash system using cryptocurrency, i.e., a digital or virtual currency that uses cryptography for security. This protocol introduced a set of rules in the form of decentralized, distributed processes that ensured the integrity of data exchanged among numerous non-trusting participants without going through a trusted central intermediary. Blockchain can be defined as a digital ledger designed to keep a transparent, accessible, verifiable and auditable distributed record of data sets tagged from different pieces of information belonging to different participants. Furthermore, BC networks can identify multi-entity conflicts, and forks and resolve them automatically to converge to a single, accepted view of events [29]. Figure 2 illustrates the typical steps in creating a BC [30] conforming the following general principles [3, 31]:

- Cryptography and hashing values validate data recorded on the BC and uniquely identify parties in a transaction. Blocks are encrypted in cascade, where the hash of the previous block will be used in the encryption of the current block.
- Each data item in a BC will have a timestamp, and confirmed ownership.
- Decentralized, distributed ledgers provide exact copies of transactions, which are shared by many parties in a P2P network.
- The choice of mining node, which broadcasts collected and validated block back to the network, depends on the consensus mechanism used.
- If the ledger of a BC tracks an asset, the ledger can be used to issue digital currency and perform financial transactions in that currency.
- BC publicly record digital transaction, though not with all the details. E.g., in many cryptocurrency ledgers and transaction platforms blocks are encrypted but transactions remain open.
- Private permissioned network option enables controlled, regulated environment with higher throughput compared to public type.

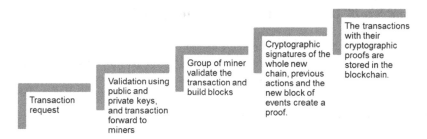

Fig. 2. Illustrative blockchain process.

Blockchains have been outlined in [3, 31] to offer reduced transaction costs, improve security, open up new business opportunities, and transform existing value chains and business models. Particularly, the BC technology enables automatization and acceleration of business-to-business smart contracts and needed workflows implemented as a robust, distributed P2P system that is tolerant of node failures. A Smart contract is a computer code that is stored on a BC and runs in every node of the peer-to-peer network providing digitally signed, computable agreement between two or more parties [32]. It codifies and controls negotiation principles required in contracting like consensus, provenance, immutability and finality.

In parallel to research activities, established IT vendors and numerous startups are exploring BC opportunities across industries [30]. Recently, the Linux foundation announced the Hyperledger project [33], a collaborative effort to advance BC technology by identifying and addressing important features for a cross-industry open source 'enterprise grade' standard for distributed ledgers. Furthermore, Ethereum [34] has shown a proof of concept of the BC programming and smart contract platform.

Potential deployment considerations found in research and early trials, particularly in the financial sector, include throughput, scalability and latency in large public BCs, legal enforceability, transactional confidentiality particularly in the public BCs, consensus mechanism determination & complexity, and integration with legacy systems and workflows [10]. In a fully transparent public permissionless BC, every node independently verify and process all the transaction with full visibility into database's current state, modification requested by a transaction, and a digital signature proving the origin. Furthermore, several discussed BC features were originally introduced in order to avoid regulatory restriction and enforcement. Regarding vulnerability and security concerns, BC technology has already been subject to one of the most aggressive environment by way of the Bitcoin cryptocurrency. In addition to technical consideration, particularly in the smart contract use cases the true issues were found in human centric legal and regulatory environment and processes [35]. The BC governance is a critical factor in the mitigation of the above-discussed issues. Hybrid and private BC options enable controlled consensus model environment with higher throughput and scalability compared to public type. Furthermore, white list of permitted miners with all blocks signed digitally by their miner of origin combined with distributed non-incentivized consensus scheme will significantly lower transaction costs.

4   Analysis of Blockchain Use Cases in CBRS

This section summarizes current implementation considerations with the CBRS concept, defines core characteristics of the BC, and develops potential use cases. The applicability of use cases are analyzed and assessed against BC core characterizes.

4.1   CBRS Implementation Considerations

Building on the definition of the CBRS and the BC, the following layers and interfaces in the functional CBRS architecture, depicted in Fig. 1, were identified as potential early adoption areas of the BC:

- Incumbent access system - that need to be protected while offering excess spectrum for sharing;
- National regulatory authority - conditions, rules and incentives for sharing;
- Spectrum Access System - database that stores the rules and availability of spectrum, spectrum assignment & interference control and spectrum broker;
- Environmental Sensing Capability - to detect incumbent activity while ensuring confidentiality;
- CBSD access networks - to utilize the PAL and the GAA spectrum, including optional DP and NMS;
- SAS - SAS communication - to exchange inter-SAS data records known to one SAS and communicated to another SAS;
- ESC - SAS interface - communicates information about the presence of a signal from a federal incumbent user system to one or more approved SASs.

In the early spectrum sharing research [12, 19–21] the following considerations and issues from technology, regulation, and business perspectives have been raised:

How to avoid lengthy and costly contractual agreements in a relatively short-term spectrum transaction while meeting regulatory reporting, tracking, and transparency requirements? In addition to the availability, liquidity and predictability of the shared spectrum it is essential to enable acceptably low incentifying 'pay as you grow' *transaction costs* for local small cell operators [18, 20].

How to ensure *integrity* of systems, network and shared cross-industry data? Particular consideration should be given to *OPSEC*, mission critical sensitive military incumbent data, and the operator's *business sensitive* network data.

How to deploy inter-organizational near real time data and spectrum *asset exchange* between non-trusting *co-opetitive* stakeholders?

How to fully utilize sharing concept enabled unbundling of spectrum, infrastructure and services in *business model innovations*, e.g., through platform enabled as-a-Service business models for SAS and ESC and administrators, communication service providers, and technology vendors.

How to cope with growing data volumes and *complexity* while ensuring *scalability*? Dynamic channel assignment and co-existence management (CXM) of CBSDs becomes complicated due to a large number of small networks and standalone CBSDs in the same local geographical area, utilizing different radio technologies.

4.2   BC Core Characteristics

The applicability of the use cases can be analyzed against the following BC core characteristics discussed in Sect. 3 that differentiates it from the traditional relational database solutions:

1. Shared database write access with multiple writers;
2. Absence of trust between multiple writers;
3. Disintermediation;
4. Interaction and dependence between transactions (Fig. 3).

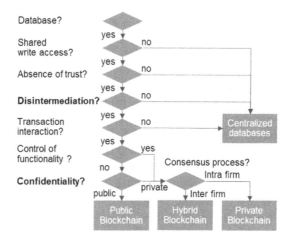

Fig. 3. Blockchain core characteristics and logic used in use case assessment.

Furthermore, *control of functionality, consensus process & validators*, and *confidentiality* factors will be used in analyzing the applicability of the public, hybrid or private BC options. In summary, considering trade-off in which disintermediation is gained at the cost of confidentiality.

4.3   Use Case Analysis

Based on the introduced BC characterization and early learning from the financial sector, BC use cases can be categorized in the following classes [36]:

- In *lightweight transaction*, one or more scarce assets are transacted and exchanged between limited numbers of participants utilizing a BC shared ledger marketplace.
- *Provenance tracking* tracks the origin and movement of high value items and assets across a supply chain utilizing virtual "certificates of authenticity".
- In *inter-organizational recordkeeping*, BC acts as an authoritative final "transaction log" mechanism for collectively recording and notarizing any type of data of high importance or financial meaning.
- In *multiparty integration*, multiple parties write data to a collectively managed record in order to overcome friction while proving redundancy.

Lightweight transaction - Lower transaction cost and friction with resiliency and automatic reconciliation in real time can provide benefits in PAL spectrum Secondary Market Leasing Agreement (SMLA) *marketplace*, and ESC *sensor data as-a-Service* type of use cases [27]. Furthermore, BC could be used by the regulatory BC agent to inspect and record the data, and stop transaction if needed. In the future, deployments in dense urban areas and IoT verticals with similar types of needs for sharing could benefit of a common micro transaction marketplace. Additionally, inter-operator *roaming* connecting CBRS network users seamlessly to a 'coverage' networks can benefit of hybrid BCs with permissioned and public components eliminating third-party clearinghouses through smart contracts. The *neutral host* use case utilizes necessary resources in a specific geographic area, e.g., a building, campus or a public space like a sports stadium; manages these resources subject to agreements with resource owners and clients; and provides connectivity for clients to make use of the platform(s) to provide services to their end customers. Rules and agreements between the various asset providing networks can be codes as smart contracts.

Provenance tracking - CBRS applications can include common FCC ruled SAS interference calculation *models*, propagation models, elevation models and other associated geographic data, *product* (ESC, SAS, CBSD) centric system tests and certification, and integrity checking (e.g., supply chain tracking for OPSEC) for regulatory certification and periodic review and modification. In general, BC can be used to provide *Identity-as-a-Service* eSIM solution to machines in IoT environments.

Inter-organizational recordkeeping - *Audit trail* of critical communication with time stamps and proof of origin can be used in the FCC database, inter-SAS and ESC-SAS *data exchanges*, CBSD interference measurement data reporting. ESC performance monitoring and fault detection data [27], and for the *official registry* for government licensed assets and certified network elements, e.g., CBSDs. FCC OPSEC mitigation rules [24] on information gathering and retention withdraws ESC data from the potential BC use case list.

In *multiparty integration* - In the CBRS concept, elements and organization need a shared view of the reality, not originating from a single source. The *inter-SAS communication* (ISC) Essential Data [24] that shall be exchanged near real time symmetrically between all pairs of SASs consists of ESC sensor characteristics, CBSD physical installation parameters, CBSD coexistence parameters, information on all active CBSD grants, PPA records, and SAS-SAS coordination event records. In the future, collaboration can be extended to *co-existence management* (CXM) clearinghouse databases for exchange of co-existence related information, and inter-operator horizontal sharing. SASs with overlapping areas or operation must be capable of maintaining a consistent representation of the spectrum environment in order to maintain aggregated interference protection limits, avoid conflicting channel & spectrum grants, and to coordinate operations of all CBSDs in the CBRS band. Furthermore, CB smart contracts can be leveraged in inter-SAS data use agreements (Table 1).

Table 1. Summary of use cases and blockchain applicability analysis.

Use case	Shared write	Absence of trust	Disintermediation	Interaction	Confidentiality
SAS-SAS data exchange	+	+	+	+	Hybrid
SAS marketplace	+	+	+	+	Hybrid
Sensing as a service	+	+	+	+	Hybrid
Element tracking	+	+	+	+	Hybrid
Neutral hosting	+	+	+	+	Hybrid
Operator roaming	+	+	+	+	Hybrid
CBSD measurements	+	−	±	−	Private
FCC database	−	−	−	−	Private
ESC sensing	+	+	−	−	Private

5 Conclusion

In this paper, we have developed and analyzed blockchain use cases for the novel spectrum sharing concept. This study discussed the implementation considerations of the CBRS spectrum sharing concept, and how the BC technology can be applied as a potential solution. We argue that the BC technology has potential to significantly reduce transaction costs in the CBRS through automatization of business-to-business complex multi-step workflows in contracting, brokering and data exchange. It codifies and controls negotiation principles required in contracting like consensus, provenance, immutability and finality. Furthermore, flexibility and scalability introduced into regulation and spectrum management lower the entry barrier and enable new entrants to access local spectrum based on their specific business needs. The BC contribute to transition from administrative to market-based spectrum management. Results of our analysis show that the automatization with cryptographic verifiability increase and build trust between key stakeholders and devices, which is essential trigger for any sharing concept. We believe that the integration of BCs in the spectrum management and control processes have potential to transform traditional MBB ecosystem, bring in new players and impact future system designs. Increased system dynamics in spectrum sharing will introduce a need for near real time network management capabilities that could benefit of IoT type P2P BC transactions of data, assets or services. Technology harmonization and integration with legacy in ecosystems will be essential to ensure economies of scale and fast time to market. Hybrid and private BC options will help in meeting the confidentiality requirements.

This paper serves as a starting point for analyzing the applicability of the BC technology and its key characteristics around the CBRS. Future work is needed to dwell deeper into studying and validating the core characteristics of the BC for the key stakeholders and their particular use case requirements in the CBRS context. Potential deployment considerations in the CBRS context calls for focused research in the areas of legal enforceability, transactional confidentiality, and consensus mechanism determination. The successful deployment of the BC technologies has potential to significantly improve the efficiency of the dynamic spectrum sharing concepts, influence the regulatory and management approaches of spectrum and create new business opportunities. This calls for a collaborative effort from the government, industry and academia to build and validate dynamic capabilities and technology enablers needed.

Acknowledgments. This work has been done in the microOperator (μO) and the Microoperator concept for boosting local service delivery in 5G (uO5G) research projects within the 5G programs of Tekes - the Finnish Funding Agency for Technology and Innovation. The author would like to acknowledge the project consortium members: Aalto University, University of Oulu, Elisa, Eltel Networks, Fairspectrum, University Properties of Finland, Verkotan, Finnish Ministry of Transport and Communications, Finnish Communications Regulatory Authority and Tekes.

References

1. ITU-R: Final Acts WRC-15. World Radiocommunication Conference, Radio Communication Sector of the International Telecommunication Union, Geneva (2015)
2. The White House: Realizing the Full Potential of Government-Held Spectrum to Spur Economic Growth. President's Council of Advisors on Science and Technology (PCAST) Report (2012)
3. Tapscott, D., Tapscott, A.: Blockchain Revolution: How the Technology Behind Bitcoin is Changing Money, Business and the World. Portfolio Penguin, London (2016)
4. Nakamoto, S.: Bitcoin: A Peer-to-Peer Electronic Cash System (2008)
5. Kelly, J., Williams, A.: Forty Big Banks Test Blockchain-Based Bond Trading System (2016). http://www.nytimes.com/reuters/2016/03/02/business/02reuters-bankingblockchain-bonds.html
6. Oparah, D.: 3 Ways that the Blockchain will Change the Real Estate Market (2016). http://techcrunch.com/2016/02/06/3-ways-that-blockchain-will-change-the-real-estate-market/
7. Kar, I.: Estonian Citizens will soon have the World's most Hack-Proof Health-Care Records (2016). http://qz.com/628889/this-eastern-european-country-ismoving-its-health-recordsto-the-blockchain/
8. Lacey, S.: The Energy Blockchain: How Bitcoin Could be a Catalyst for the Distributed Grid (2016). http://www.greentechmedia.com/articles/read/the-energy-blockchain-could-bitcoin-be-a-catalyst-forthe-distributed-grid
9. Walport, M.: Distributed ledger technology: beyond block chain. U.K. Government Office for Science, London, U.K., Technical report (2016)
10. Christidis, K., Devetsikiotis, M.: Blockchains and smart contracts for the internet of things. IEEE Access **4**, 2292–2303 (2016)
11. Mitola, J., Maguire, G.: Cognitive radio: making software radios more personal. IEEE Pers. Commun. **6**(4), 13–18 (1999)
12. Cabric, D., Mishra, S., Brodersen, R.: Implementation issues in spectrum sensing for cognitive radios. In: Proceedings of the 38th Asilomar Conference on Signals, Systems and Computers. Pacific Grove, pp. 772–776 (2004)
13. FCC: 03-287 the Commission's Rules to Permit Unlicensed National Information Infrastructure Devices in the 5 GHz Band. Federal Communications Commission (2004)
14. FCC: White Spaces. http://www.fcc.gov/topic/white-space

15. Ofcom: TV White Spaces Pilot. http://stakeholders.ofcom.org.uk/spectrum/tv-white-spaces/white-spaces-pilot/
16. ECC: Licensed Shared Access (LSA). ECC report 205 (2014)
17. FCC: Report and Order and Second FNPRM to Advance Availability of 3550–3700 MHz Band for Wireless Broadband (2015)
18. Chapin, J., Lehr, W.: Cognitive radios for dynamic spectrum access - the path to market success for dynamic spectrum access technology. IEEE Commun. Mag. 45(5), 96–103 (2007)
19. Yrjölä, S., Matinmikko, M., Ahokangas, P.: Evaluation of recent spectrum sharing concepts from business model scalability point of view. In: IEEE International Symposium on Dynamic Spectrum Access Networks (DYSPAN), pp. 241–250 (2015)
20. Sohul, M., Yao, M., Yang, T., Reed, J.: Spectrum access system for the citizen broadband radio service. IEEE Commun. Mag. 53(7), 18–25 (2015)
21. Patil, V.M., Patil, S.R.: A survey on spectrum sensing algorithms for cognitive radio. In: Proceedings of the 2016 International Conference on Advances in Human Machine Interaction, pp. 1–5 (2016)
22. WINNF Spectrum Sharing Committee. http://www.wirelessinnovation.org/spectrum-sharing-committee
23. FCC: 16-55: The Second Report and Order and Order on Reconsideration Finalizing Rules for Innovative Citizens Broadband Radio Service in the 3.5 GHz Band (3550–3700 MHz) (2016). https://apps.fcc.gov/edocs_public/attachmatch/FCC-16-55A1.pdf
24. OFR: Electronic Code of Federal Regulations, Title 47: Telecommunication, Part 96 - Citizens Broadband Radio Service. The Office of the Federal Register (OFR) and the Government Publishing Office. http://www.ecfr.gov/cgi-bin/text-idx?node=pt47.5.96&rgn=div5
25. NTIA: Using On-Shore Detected Radar Signal Power for Interference Protection of Off-Shore Radar Receivers. Technical report 16-521. The US Department of Commerce, National Telecommunications and Information Administration (2016)
26. WInnF: SAS Functional Architecture. Spectrum Sharing Committee of the Wireless Innovation Forum (2016). http://groups.winnforum.org/d/do/8512
27. WInnF: WINNF-15-S-0112-V1.0.0 CBRS Operational and Functional Requirements. Spectrum Sharing Committee (SSC) of the Wireless Innovation Forum (2016)
28. FCC: sharing recommendations. Federal Communications Commission Technical Advisory Council Advanced Sharing and Enabling Wireless Technologies (EWT) WG (2016). https://transition.fcc.gov/bureaus/oet/tac/tacdocs/meeting92314/TACMeetingSummary9-23-14.pdf
29. Antonopoulos, A.M.: Mastering Bitcoin: Unlocking Digital Cryptocurrencies, 1st edn. O'Reilly Media, Inc, Sebastopol (2014)
30. Dicks, D., Sherrington, S.: Blockchains & its Impact on the Telecom Industry, Heavy Reading Reports (2016)
31. Tsai, W., Blower, R., Zhu, Y., Yu, L.: A system view of financial blockchains. In: IEEE Symposium on Service-Oriented System Engineering (SOSE), pp. 450–457 (2016)
32. Szabo, N.: Smart contracts: building blocks for digital markets. Extropy, no. 16 (1996)
33. Hyperledger Project, Linux Foundation (2016). https://www.hyperledger.org/
34. Ethereum, White Paper (2016). https://github.com/ethereum/wiki/wiki/White-Paper
35. Lauslahti, K., Mattila, J., Seppälä, T.: Smart Contracts – How will Blockchain Technology Affect Contractual Practices? ETLA Report no. 57 (2016). https://www.etla.fi/julkaisut/alykas-sopimus-miten-blockchainmuuttaa-sopimuskaytantoja/
36. Greenspan, G.: Four genuine blockchain use cases (2016). https://www.linkedin.com/pulse/four-genuine-blockchain-use-casesgideon-greenspan

Lessons Learned from Long-Term and Imperfect Sensing in 2.4 GHz Unlicensed Band

Jacek Dzikowski$^{(\boxtimes)}$ and Cynthia Hood

Illinois Institute of Technology, 10 West 35th Street, Chicago, IL 60616, USA
dzikjac@hawk.iit.edu, hood@iit.edu

Abstract. Accuracy of spectrum sensing affects the decision making operation of cognitive radio. In order to achieve meaningful results, in related experimental and simulation work, realistic wireless environment representation is a necessity. Existing spectrum occupancy models range from simple additive white Gaussian noise to elaborate, based on large scale wireless spectrum measurements, but universal models are not available. Creating such a model for unlicensed bands would be particularly difficult, if not impossible, because of its unpredictability and inherent dynamics. On the other hand, our experience shows that using real-life, relatively low-resolution, data collected using inexpensive spectrum analyzer provides insight consistent with observations made with more sophisticated setups, preserves more nuances than simple models, and could be a viable alternative to spectrum occupancy modeling.

Keywords: Cognitive radio · Wireless environment model · WiSpy
Long-term measurement

1 Introduction

Spectrum sensing is a fundamental element of cognitive radio operation and it is very sensitive to the "garbage in, garbage out" principle. In other words, having a good representation of wireless environment is key to meaningful cognitive radio experiment. For that purpose, researchers frequently need to resort to using synthetic environments for that purpose, usually in the form of spectrum occupancy models. However, models have their limitations and "do not necessarily reflect real-world scenarios in most of the cases" [1]. And while the model catalog has became fairly extensive over the years, many of them are only applicable to a specific spatio-temporal situations. Also, it is uncertain "whether a general, if not universal, model exists that can unify most existing models" [2].

One of the directions communication networks (including cognitive radio) are heading towards is heterogeneity, where long- and short-range activities need to co-exist. Many measurement campaigns, with equipment frequently placed on the rooftops of high-rise buildings [3], may be incapable of capturing certain short-range radio activities, especially at the street level or indoors, and fail to capture potentially important subtleties. At the same time still need more insight and understanding of

© ICST Institute for Computer Sciences, Social Informatics and Telecommunications Engineering 2018
P. Marques et al. (Eds.): CROWNCOM 2017, LNICST 228, pp. 140–150, 2018.
https://doi.org/10.1007/978-3-319-76207-4_12

complex wireless environments and the more nuances we capture the better representations of wireless environment we can create.

All the above arguments ring particularly true when one considers unlicensed bands, which are particularly challenging from the perspective of cognitive radio development. Diversity of technologies involved (both long- and short-range), and inapplicability of primary/secondary user scenario in many cases, increase complexity. So does mobility.

In order to better understand the nature and spatio-temporal dynamics of unlicensed band environment a more comprehensive, dedicated and multi-point measurement campaign would be more useful. However, as survey [2] shows, unlicensed bands (i.e. 2.4 GHz and 5 GHz) are usually only a part of much wider spectrum being monitored and less frequently considered on its own. Equipment, know-how, and logistical complications can make such large-scale, multi-point measurements cost-prohibitive.

If measurement quality requirements were to be relaxed, an affordable and easy-to-use spectrum analyzer such as WiSpy [4] could potentially offer a viable solution to that problem. This work presents an overview of findings based on relatively long-term 2.4 GHz band measurements performed using this device. One of the goals was to discover what kind of information can be extracted from data collected with limited precision. Another one was to use statistics of collected data to build a simple AWGN (additive white Gaussian noise) model and evaluate its deficiencies in comparison to the real-life traces.

This work is divided into following sections. Section 2 introduces related work and Sect. 3 provides necessarily preliminaries. Followed by Sect. 4, where our findings are presented and Sect. 5 where we state our conclusions.

2   Related Work

WiSpy users used to submit their own spectrum environment recordings to the Metageek (WiSpy creators) website, but these were usually very short-term, meant to illustrate particular local findings. We are not aware of other work based on long-term WiSpy measurements. On the other hand, environmental studies dedicated exclusively to 2.4 GHz band exists, such as [5], and others are a part of wide-band project (as the ongoing one at IIT [3]). Chen [2] provides an extensive survey of such campaigns and studies.

Still, Lopez-Benitez [6] argues that obtaining "reliable and accurate real-time information on spectrum occupancy" by cognitive radios needs to be addressed more. In his work he outlines current challenges and points out practical limitations. Performance under imperfect sensing performance is a particularly important aspect which our work can help address. Other aspects would be: finite sensing period and limited number of observations. Studies on effects of quality of sensed information on performance are also important to other areas, such as radio environment map construction [7] or cognitive radio network modeling and simulation. In fact, development of our agent-based simulation framework [8] sparked the initial interest in spectrum occupancy models.

We discovered that spectrum models range from fairly simple, such as AWGN, to complex, multi-parameter ones and are used to provide either as representations of the environment or for prediction purposes. In his survey, Chen [2] distinguishes between parameter (power, occupancy, duty cycle) statistics models, parameter cumulative distribution and probability density functions, Markov chain and linear regression models. In this work, only AWGN model is employed.

3 Preliminaries

Data collection setup comprised of a Windows PC (running Chanalyzer 2.1 software) and WiSpy 2.4× spectrum analyzer. WiSpy 2.4× [4] is a portable USB (v1.1 or better) spectrum analyzer operating in 2.4 GHz band. Chanalyzer [4] is a spectrum monitoring software designed to work with WiSpy devices. Version 2.1, which was used for data collection, is discontinued, but still available for download at [9] (Table 1).

Table 1. WiSpy 2.4× technical specifications.

Parameter	Value(s)
Frequency range	2.400 to 2.495 GHz
Amplitude resolution	0.5 dBm
Resolution bandwidth	(2.4 GHz) 58.036 to 812.500 kHz
Sweep time	(2.4 GHz) 507 ms

Time-frequency measurements were conducted indoors at the Illinois Institute of Technology for approximately three months (Dataset A, see Table 2 for details). Due to time and computing power constraints some experiments were conducted using a smaller dataset B, a subset of dataset A.

Table 2. Dataset details.

Parameter	Value(s)
Start time	A and B: Tue, 19 Jan 2010 12:52:56 GMT
End time	A: Thu, 22 Apr 2010 17:51:34 GMT
	B: Mon, 25 Jan 2010 08:12:15 GMT
Measured quantity	Power [dBm]
Size	A: 256 frequencies × 22 757 357 data points
	B: 256 frequencies × 1 415 486 data points
Frequency range	2.400 to 2.495 GHz
Resolution bandwidth	373.26 kHz

For each frequency/real-life data trace we created an AWGN synthetic trace, where signal is modeled using normal distribution with real-data mean and variance of a given frequency with addition of zero-mean noise.

4   Observations and Results

4.1   Overview (Dataset B)

Figure 1 shows a min/mean/max signal power as a function of frequency plot based on data from dataset B. Activity on WiFi channels 1, 6 and 11 appears to be the most prominent on the mean power plot, with visible, characteristic profile.

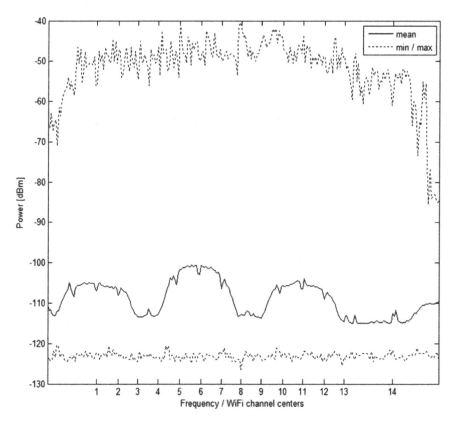

Fig. 1. Basic statistics of wireless environment (based on dataset B).

4.2   Temporal Trends (Dataset A)

Figure 2 shows time series plots for one week of measurements of WiFi channels 1, 6, 11 (center frequencies) utilization. Temporal patterns are evident: more transmission in

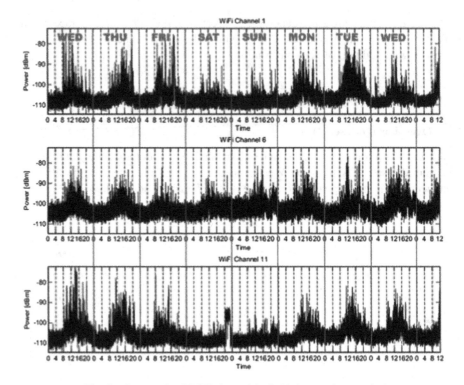

Fig. 2. One week of WiFi channel 1, 6, 11 (center frequencies).

the afternoons and on weekdays, and lower activity on weekends - in this case following typical campus network usage by IIT community.

Next plot (Fig. 3) shows daily relative frequency of signal power value occurrence (ratio of number of times when particular value was observed to total number of observations; based on three months of measurements) for WiFi channel 6 for different days of week. Extracted patterns suggest that examined spectrum frequency range is utilized in a similar way on every day of the week.

In similar fashion, but at a different time scale, Fig. 4 shows hourly relative frequency of signal power value for the same channel for Mondays (other days of the week have comparable characteristics). Higher afternoon activity as seen on Fig. 2 is again evident.

It is worth mentioning that information shown on Fig. 4 could be considered as a simple internal cognitive radio model of daily spectrum utilization for a given channel that can be easily generated from datasets like the ones used in this study.

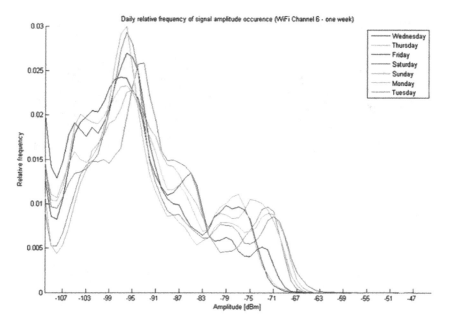

Fig. 3. Daily relative frequencies of signal power occurrence on WiFi channel 6 center frequency.

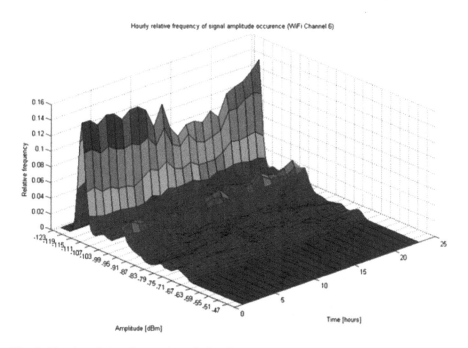

Fig. 4. Hourly relative frequencies of signal power occurrence on WiFi channel 6 center frequency - Mondays.

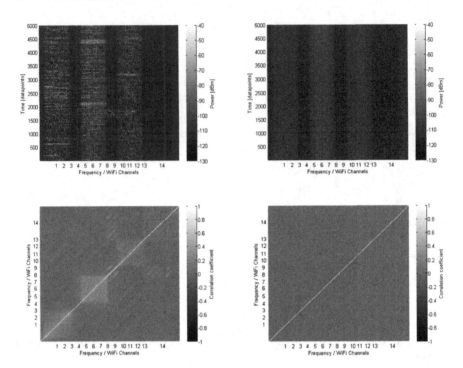

Fig. 5. Real (left) vs. synthetic (right) data: (top) waterfall fall plots, (bottom) visualization of frequency correlation coefficient matrix.

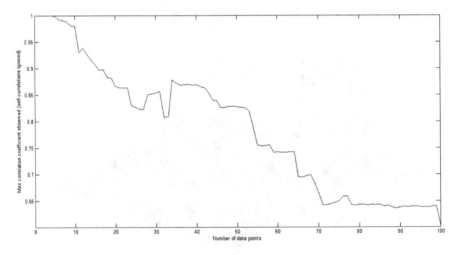

Fig. 6. Maximum correlation coefficient (between frequencies in time).

4.3   Real vs. Synthetic Data. Correlations (Dataset B)

Waterfall plots (see top section of Fig. 5) depict how details and dynamics of real-life data are lost when using a corresponding AWGN model. Bottom section of the same figure presents visualization of correlation coefficient matrices (correlation measured between traces of two frequencies). In case of real-life data correlations correspond to WiFi channels spanning over 22 MHz of bandwidth. Synthetic data does not preserve that effect.

Interestingly, maximum values of correlation coefficient remain quite high over time for real-life data (see Fig. 6) suggesting relationships between activities on certain frequencies. Corresponding effect can be observed on Fig. 7 below, where correlation coefficients are computed based on 1415486 data points per frequency (more than six days). Long-term patterns corresponding to WiFi channel 1, 6 and 11 activity emerge, which could be used by cognitive radio device to learn what kind of users are present technology-wise. As before, synthetic data does not preserve this information.

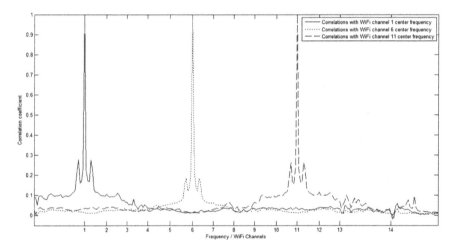

Fig. 7. Real-life data: correlations with WiFi 1, 6 and 11 channels across entire measured frequency range.

Figures 8 and 9 are plots representing duty cycle as a function of frequency and detection threshold for both real-life and synthetic data. Results are fairly comparable, which suggests that AWGN models should not be immediately dismissed in case of duty cycle-related experiments. What is interesting is the fact (see Fig. 9) that mean duty cycle (averaged over all measured frequencies) remains lower than 20% (real-life data) for detection thresholds greater than −110 dBm (and approximately −85 dBm for maximum duty cycle). 20% average spectrum utilization is consistent with results obtained through other measurement campaigns, e.g., underutilization.

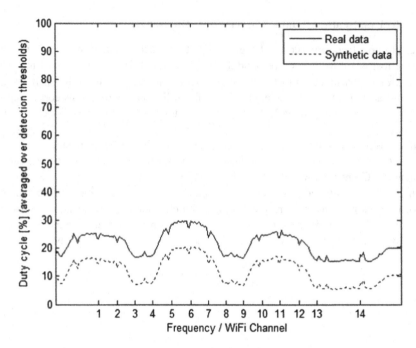

Fig. 8. Mean duty cycle (averaged over all detection thresholds).

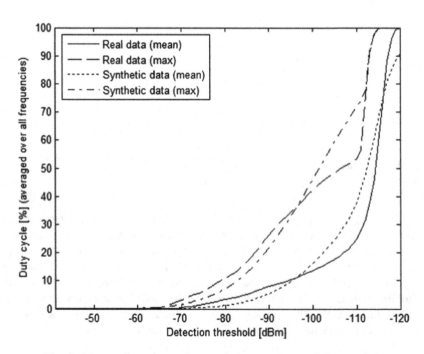

Fig. 9. Mean and maximum duty cycle (averaged over all frequencies).

5 Conclusions

Despite using a simple and relatively imprecise spectrum analyzer, collected long-term data was rich enough to notice wireless environment characteristics observed during elaborate long-term measurement campaigns, e.g. weekly and daily trends, underutilization, etc. Also, it has shown correlations between activities on different frequencies (WiFi channels in this case, but we observed the same effect in different datasets as well) that remains present over a long period of time. It could possibly be used to help identify networks with the most prominent presence within the environment. On the other hand, corresponding measurement-based AWGN models that we created failed to capture both temporal trends and correlations between individual frequencies. Information that could be used, as it was shown, to create internal models of expected daily unlicensed band activity, was not preserved in AWGN models which makes them inadequate for experimenting with certain aspects of cognitive radio development (i.e. learning, decision-making, etc.).

Robust wireless spectrum environment/occupancy models are not easy to develop and no universal model has been presented yet. Unlicensed bands, because of their complexity and dynamics, are especially challenging in this regard. Oversimplification, as we have shown, is likely to remove interesting subtleties that could be important to the overall cognitive radio behavior. While simple models remain valuable in some circumstances (e.g. when all relevant information is preserved and the model matches the experiment well), real data is richer and preserves nuances better. Given how easy it is to collect, manipulate and share WiSpy data, a publicly available repository of datasets would be an alternative to a collection of models which are likely to not be generic enough because of their spatio-temporal idiosyncrasies.

Finally, using WiSpy (or similar device) offers an additional benefit of working with data of similar quality to future consumer-end devices built with low-cost components; imprecise data adds realism in such context.

References

1. Sithamparanathan, K., Giorgetti, A.: Cognitive Radio Techniques. Spectrum Sensing, Interference Mitigation, and Localization. Artech House, Norwood (2012)
2. Chen, Y., Oh, H.S.: A Survey of measurement-based spectrum occupancy modeling for cognitive radios. IEEE Commun. Surv. Tutor. **18**(1), 848–859 (2016)
3. Bacchus, R.B., Fertner, A.J., Hood, C.S., Roberson, D.A.: Long-term, wide-band spectral monitoring in support of dynamic spectrum access networks at the IIT spectrum observatory. In: 3rd IEEE Symposium on New Frontiers in Dynamic Spectrum Access Networks, DySPAN 2008, Chicago, IL, pp. 1–10 (2008)
4. http://www.metageek.com/products/wi-spy/. Accessed 05 July 2017
5. Biggs, M., Henley, A., Clarkson, T.: Occupancy analysis of the 24 GHz ISM band. IEE Proc. - Commun. **151**(5), 481–488 (2004)
6. Lopez-Benitez, M.: Sensing-based spectrum awareness in Cognitive Radio: challenges and open research problems. In: 9th International Symposium on Communication Systems, Networks & Digital Signal Processing (CSNDSP 2014), pp. 459–464, 23–25 July 2014

7. Yilmaz, H.B., Tugcu, T., Alagöz, F., Bayhan, S.: Radio environment map as enabler for practical cognitive radio networks. IEEE Commun. Mag. **51**(12), 162–169 (2013)
8. Dzikowski, J., Hood, C.: An agent-based simulation framework for cognitive radio studies. In: Proceedings of the 2nd International Conference on Simulation Tools and Techniques (Simutools 2009). ICST (Institute for Computer Sciences, Social-Informatics and Telecommunications Engineering) (2009). Article 18
9. https://www.wi-spy.com.au/downloads/software.html. Accessed 05 July 2017

A Planning Tool for TV White Space Deployments

Mahesh Iyer[(⊠)] and Mythili Vutukuru

Department of Computer Science and Engineering,
Indian Institute of Technology Bombay, Mumbai, India
{maheshm,mythili}@cse.iitb.ac.in

Abstract. There have been numerous studies conducted on the availability of TV white spaces in India, which show that white spaces are plentiful. If one needs to harness this spectrum, there is a need for techniques to compute suitable locations where secondary base stations can be placed for providing broadband access. To address this issue, we have come up with a planning tool which determines the best locations for placement of secondary antennas based on secondary base station's coverage area, population of the region, throughput required and other such parameters. Our real-time model uses different propagation models to compute the path loss, and subsequently the throughput using Shannon's theorem, to determine the optimal placement of secondary TV white space antennas. Experiments with our tool show that it can provide good placement of secondary base stations and provide high throughput to the covered users. We believe that a tool like ours can accelerate the pace of deployment of secondary networks in the TV white space spectrum.

Keywords: White space · Real-time model
Secondary antenna placement · Planning tool · Propagation models

1 Introduction

TV white space refers to the unutilized television spectrum licensed by a regulatory authority. Within the frequency spectrum, UHF (Ultra High Frequency) band is of particular interest since it has very good wireless radio propagation characteristics. In a comprehensive study involving the estimation of available TV white space in India [4], it has been found that almost 75% of the areas in India have all the 15 channels in the 470–590 MHz spectrum available as white space. This large amount of white space spectrum can be put to use for providing internet access especially in rural areas where the broadband penetration is quite low. The goal of our work is to develop a tool for determining the optimal locations where the secondary TV antennas can be placed, in regions where primary TV transmitters are sparse. We envision that Wi-Fi access points will be available at the secondary base stations to extend the coverage of the base station to non-UHF clients.

© ICST Institute for Computer Sciences, Social Informatics and Telecommunications Engineering 2018
P. Marques et al. (Eds.): CROWNCOM 2017, LNICST 228, pp. 151–161, 2018.
https://doi.org/10.1007/978-3-319-76207-4_13

Using the tool that we have developed, TV white space researchers can get an idea of how to plan the deployment of secondary white space antennas for providing Wi-Fi coverage. Our tool makes real-time on-the-fly calculations using theoretical models, and does not require actual deployment tests. Our tool takes as input estimates of TV white spaces available at a location (e.g., using databases like [15]), and information about population density and altitude. Using this information, and the minimum required throughput to users, our tool decides on the optimal placement of secondary TV white space transmitters that can provide broadband connectivity to a region. Our tool is particularly useful to cover large swathes of rural areas in countries like India to provide broadband connectivity using TV white spaces. This work does not take into account the economic aspects involved in the deployment of TVWS antennas.

Our main contributions are as follows:

- Estimation of optimal locations of secondary base stations in the TV white space spectrum (in terms of secondary coverage area and throughput achieved) using different propagation models and demographic features like population and altitude values.
- Development of a Graphical User Interface (GUI) for easily using the above theoretical model.

The rest of the paper is organized as follows. Section 2 describes the design of the tool and the theoretical model, and presents an overview of the GUI of the tool. Section 3 describes the performance comparison of our work with other algorithms using two different datasets. Section 4 talks about work done in this field and tells how our work is different from others. Finally, Sect. 5 presents the concluding remarks and directions for future work.

2   Design

In this section, we first discuss the various metrics that can be used to pick locations for placing secondary antennas in a TV white space (TVWS) network, and propose a new metric for antenna deployment. Our work is open-source and the tool can be accessed via [16].

2.1   Criteria for Selection of Base Stations

It is a well known fact that the altitude of a place of the base station is an important factor in determining the coverage area and the end user throughput. But using just the geographic radio coverage area as a metric for TVWS antenna placement can lead to placing an antenna at a place with a high altitude and high coverage radius, but a low population being served around it. Therefore, coverage area by itself is not a good metric since it does not take into account the population of the places within its coverage. On the other hand, selecting a place for TVWS antenna based on population alone is also not a good idea since it may be the case that the place has a high population but a very low

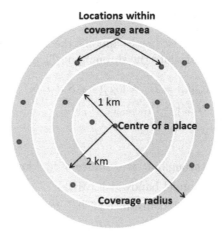

Fig. 1. Illustration of the coverage area of a place.

altitude, requiring many base stations. As a consequence, we define a metric called the *weighted utility* which takes into account both the coverage area and population while determining the places to be selected as TVWS transmitters. This metric ensures that the place selected for TVWS deployment has a proper balance between the coverage area and the population it serves. The formula for weighted utility is as follows:

$$\text{Weighted Utility} \leftarrow \frac{\text{Users}^2[\text{d}_1] \times \text{U}[\text{d}_1] + \ldots + \text{Users}^2[\text{d}_n] \times \text{U}[\text{d}_n]}{\text{Users}[\text{d}_1] + \ldots + \text{Users}[\text{d}_n]} \quad (1)$$

where

$$\text{U}[\text{d}_n] = \text{value of utility function at 'n' kms distance}$$
$$\text{Users}[\text{d}_n] = \text{number of people within 'n' kms from a place}$$

The utility function is defined by the following equation:

$$\text{U}[\text{d}_n] \leftarrow \frac{\text{Throughput at distance 'd}_n\text{'}}{\text{Bandwidth required per user} \times \text{No. of users within 'd}_n\text{'}} \quad (2)$$

In the calculation of utility function, we consider the throughput obtained at each of the locations which are within the coverage radius of a potential TVWS antenna, illustrated in Fig. 1. We then divide the throughput by the total bandwidth requirement of the population within that region. In this way, we ensure that both the coverage area and population are taken into account while calculating the utility function. In order to give more weightage to those places having a higher population, we take a weighted value of the utility function and include it while calculating our weighted utility metric.

2.2 Throughput Calculations

We use a theoretical model based on Shannon's theory to calculate the through-put at any distance. We calculate the throughput T_p at distance d_n as follows:

$$T_p[d_n] = B_w \times \log_2(1 + S[d_n]/N)$$
$$S[d_n] = P_{\text{transmit}} - L_p[d_n] \qquad (3)$$

where

$$
\begin{aligned}
T_p[d_n] &= \text{throughput at distance of 'd_n' kms (Mbps)} \\
B_w &= \text{channel bandwidth (MHz)} \\
S[d_n] &= \text{signal at distance of 'd_n' kms (Watts)} \\
P_{\text{transmit}} &= \text{Transmit Power (dBm)} \\
L_p &= \text{Path loss at distance of 'd_n' kms (dBm)} \\
N &= \text{thermal noise (Watts)}
\end{aligned}
$$

The path loss affects the utility inversely. This is because as the path loss increases, the throughput decreases, and since the utility is directly proportional to the throughput according to Eq. 2, therefore the utility decreases with the increase in path loss.

According to various field strength measurements conducted in India, it has been found that Hata model is the best suited for capturing propagation model-ing [10]. We make use of this model for calculating path loss. It is applicable to three types of environment: *urban, suburban, and rural*. The median path-loss for these environments can be calculated as described in [9] Since this model works for base station antenna heights in the range of 30 to 200 m, we therefore limit the places in our input whose altitude falls in this range. Also, we consider our secondary mobile station to be at a height of 1.5 m from the ground level.

For comparing the performance of our tool across various types of terrain considerations, we use other propagation models. Egli is a model for propagation which does not consider the elevation profile of the terrain between the sender and the receiver. It is usually applied in cases where there is a constant line-of-sight transmission between a fixed antenna and a mobile antenna and where transmission happens over an irregular terrain [8].

Free-space model is the most simple among all the propagation models and it is often used in white space availability experiments [7]. Free space model's loss is proportional to the square of the distance between the sender and receiver. It does not depend on the height of the base antenna and the mobile antenna. Also, it is proportional to the square of the channel frequency. Therefore, free space path loss increases a lot over distance and frequency [14].

Plane earth model is another propagation model we use for comparison. It considers the direct path between the sender and receiver and the reflection from ground. Its path loss does not depend on the channel frequency.

2.3   Algorithm

Our work takes the following parameters as inputs and produces secondary TVWS locations and their weighted average throughputs as output.

Input: Place, population, latitude, longitude, altitude, bandwidth requirement per user.

Output: Secondary transmitter locations, weighted average throughputs.

Following steps describe the algorithm used for computing the locations for secondary TVWS base stations. For each place given in the input

1. Calculate the coverage radius based on the altitude.
2. Find all the locations and the distances of those locations which fall within its coverage radius. See Fig. 1.
3. Within the coverage radius of each place, run the propagation model for calculating the path loss at all those distances where other locations are situated. Also, find the corresponding throughput, utility and weighted utility of each place using Eqs. 3, 2, 1 respectively.
4. We follow a greedy algorithm for white space antenna placement. From the list of places, select the place which has the highest weighted utility and cover all the locations present within its radius.
5. Remove the place which is selected as the secondary transmitter and the locations it covers from the list of places in the input.
6. Repeat the above two steps till all the places given in the input are not covered.
7. Based on the places which are selected for white space antenna placement and the locations they cover, run the propagation model again for calculating the path loss at all those distances where those locations are present.
8. Also, find the corresponding weighted average throughput for each place where the secondary antenna will be deployed.

$$\text{Weighted average throughput} \leftarrow \frac{\text{Users}[d_1] * T_p[d_1] + \ldots + \text{Users}[d_n] * T_p[d_n]}{\text{Users}[d_1] + \ldots + \text{Users}[d_n]}$$

2.4   Datasets

The TVWS tool is tested on two datasets - Thane Rural and London Urban. The Thane Rural dataset contains 400 locations along with population, latitude, longitude, and altitude information. Thane is one of the most densely populated districts in India having a large rural population. Similarly, the London Urban dataset contains 2775 locations with corresponding information. The reason for choosing London Urban dataset is to contrast the performance difference of the same propagation model in two vastly different environments, viz., rural and urban. We now describe the method of data collection for both the datasets.

The Government of India's census website [2] provides a district-wise demographic information about the list of cities/towns/villages and their corresponding population. We have the demographic information as per the 2011 census.

Table 1. Input parameters.

Parameter	Thane	London
Environment type	Rural	Urban
Receiver sensitivity	−96 dBm	−96 dBm
Secondary transmit power	36 dBm	Variable
TVWS frequency	470 MHz	770 MHz
Channel width	8 MHz	8 MHz
Bandwidth required per user	0.5 Mbps	0.5 Mbps
TVWS antenna height	30 m	7.4 m
Number of datasets	20	20
Locations within each dataset	20	140

Using this data, we run Python scripts to calculate the latitude, longitude and altitude of the places using Google's Geocoding and Elevation APIs [5,6]. For all places, we assume as input the average bandwidth (in Mbps) required per user. The information (channel availability, population etc.) regarding London Urban datasets was obtained through [3,11].

For Thane Rural datasets, we consider the input places as rural and use the path loss calculations of Hata model for rural areas. The received power or the signal power is the difference between the transmit power and the path loss. We assume a fixed secondary transmit power of 36 dBm for all the places since close to 100% places have all the white space available. As per a study conducted by the World Bank [17] about internet penetration in India, it is found that only 10% of the population had access to the internet in 2011, the year for which we have the census statistics. So we consider only 10% population as input in all the locations across Thane Rural dataset. The secondary antenna height is assumed to be 30 m.

For London Urban datasets, we use the Hata model for urban areas. The transmit power is provided as part of the input and it varies across locations. The antenna height is a fixed 7.4 m. The population having internet access is given as input for all the locations in London. Table 1 summarizes the various parameters supplied as input to both the Thane and London datasets. Section 2.3 provides a description of the placement of secondary antennas.

2.5 Graphical User Interface of the Planning Tool

The tool [16] for TVWS network deployment is integrated with Google Maps for displaying the location of secondary base stations. Figure 2 shows a sample output of the execution on our tool. The list of places to be covered for planning TVWS deployment can be either selected by using import or auto-pick option. Also, the user can easily switch between various propagation models using a drop-down list. When the front end interface is executed, PHP and MySQL scripts running at the back end determine the optimal locations for placing secondary white space antennas and display them on a Google Map.

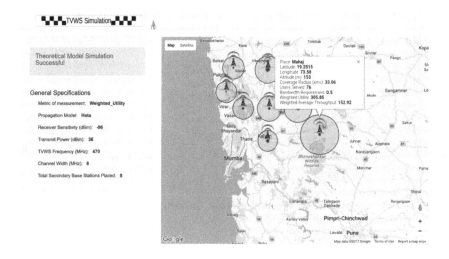

Fig. 2. Sample output of the TVWS planning tool.

3   Evaluation

We compare our weighted utility algorithm with two other algorithms - one which picks base stations based on the coverage, and the other which picks base stations using population. In coverage algorithm, we select the secondary antennas in decreasing order of coverage area while in population algorithm, we pick places according to decreasing population. Except for step 5, remaining steps are the same as described in Sect. 2.3.

For evaluation, we find that comparing the minimum of weighted average throughputs is the best indicator of the goodness of our algorithm. It is observed that the minimum weighted average throughput is maximized in the weighted utility case, as opposed to the other two algorithms.

Figure 3 depicts the CDF of minimum weighted average throughputs for coverage, weighted utility and population algorithms on 20 different datasets across Thane Rural and London Urban. Weighted utility performs the best as compared to coverage and population since it considers those locations which have a high population as well as a high altitude for TVWS placement. As a consequence, the minimum throughput obtained is the highest among all the three algorithms. The coverage algorithm performs the worst since the datasets contain many high altitude places with low population. So the weighted average throughput falls as a result of less people being present within the coverage radius of a high altitude location. For Thane Rural, population algorithm produces intermediate results as it considers the number of people around a location but does not consider altitude at all. In the case of London Urban datasets, the difference is not so pronounced owing to the fact that the London Urban datasets contain places with very little variation in population. Also, the population algorithm has the lowest minimum weighted average throughput because of almost uniform population throughout all places.

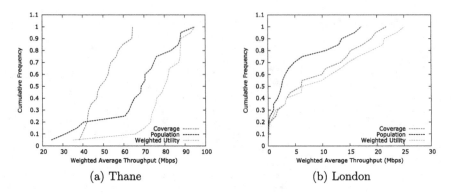

Fig. 3. CDF of minimum of weighted average throughputs across datasets for Hata model in Thane and London.

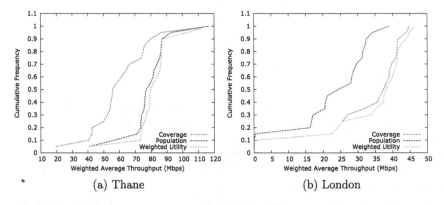

Fig. 4. CDF of minimum of weighted average throughputs across datasets for Egli model in Thane and London.

Figures 4, 5 and 6 show the CDF of minimum weighted average throughputs for Egli, Free Space and Plane Earth models respectively. We can observe that our weighted utility algorithm performs the best across all the propagation models.

Figure 7 depicts the CDF of number of secondary transmitters required for coverage, weighted utility and population algorithms on Thane Rural and London Urban datasets respectively. As expected, coverage algorithm requires the least number of TVWS antennas for both Thane and London datasets since antenna locations are selected in decreasing order of coverage area. For London datasets, population algorithm requires the most antennas. It is because there is less variation in population across various places for London. So the number of antennas required to cover the whole population is more.

Overall, we can conclude that the minimum weighted average throughput is maximum in the case of weighted utility algorithm for both Thane Rural and London Urban datasets.

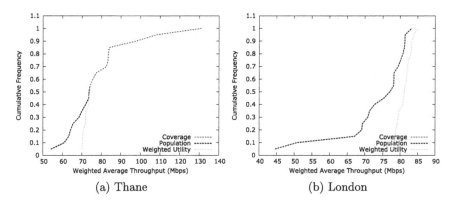

Fig. 5. CDF of minimum of weighted average throughputs across datasets for Free Space model in Thane and London.

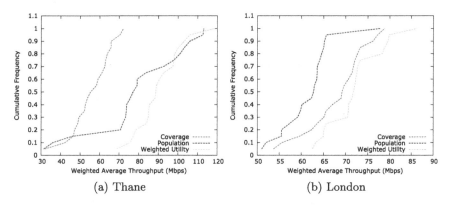

Fig. 6. CDF of minimum of weighted average throughputs across datasets for Plane Earth model in Thane and London.

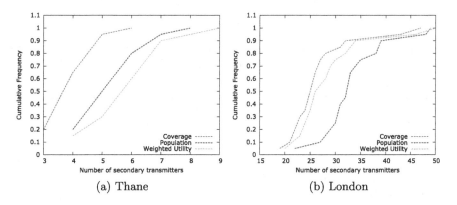

Fig. 7. CDF of number of secondary transmitters required for Hata model in Thane and London.

4   Related Work

There have been numerous studies done in the field of radio network planning tools, which optimize a number of metrics and are applicable to a wide variety of networks like GSM, UMTS, LTE, Wi-Fi etc. ASSET [1] is one such tool which has functionalities like propagation modeling, coverage map generation, traffic modeling, neighbor planning etc. Our work addresses the secondary network planning for TVWS, an area which has seen an increase in research in recent years. However, most of this research is related to spectrum sensing techniques or design enhancements in TVWS databases. KNOWS [12] deals with the design of a platform which is spectrum aware so as to utilize white spaces of varying bandwidths. In SenseLess [13], white space devices are dependent on a central database to estimate the white space availability as opposed to spectrum sensing. White space is estimated using a database of primary spectrum occupants and sophisticated propagation modeling. WISER [18] explores white spaces in indoor locations motivated by the fact that 70% of the spectrum demand comes from indoor locations. It is designed for identification and tracking of indoor white spaces, without requiring spectrum sensing.

Our work is orthogonal to these contributions in the sense that we propose a planning heuristic given that TVWS databases show the white space spectrum as available. Major research in TVWS is centered around the estimation of white space availability while our work is meant to enhance the planning efforts in using the available white space.

5   Conclusion

We have implemented a secondary white space planning tool based on a theoretical model using various propagation models (Egli, Free Space, Hata and Plane Earth) and Shannon's theorem. An algorithm to compute the optimal locations for deploying secondary antennas is also described. We put together all of this in a graphical environment which is easy to understand and use. The end user has the freedom of planning TVWS deployment for any location in India and the world provided he/she has the required input in standard format. This work can be further extended by comparing our computing tool with real deployments to see if the base station locations given by our tool make sense.

Acknowledgments. We acknowledge the contributions of Prof. Nishanth Sastry and Aravindh Raman from King's College London in various phases of this work.

References

1. ASSET Radio Network Planning Tool. http://www.teoco.com/products/planning-optimization/asset-radio-planning/
2. Census of India website. http://censusindia.gov.in
3. Connected nations 2016 downloads, Ofcom. https://www.ofcom.org.uk/research-and-data/infrastructure-research/connected-nations-2016/downloads

4. Naik, G., Singhal, G., Kumar, A., Karandikar, A.: Quantitative assessment of TV white space in India. In: 2014 Twentieth National Conference on Communications (NCC) (2014)

5. Google Maps Elevation API. https://developers.google.com/maps/documentati on/elevation/start

6. Google Maps Geocoding API. https://developers.google.com/maps/documentati on/geocoding/start

7. Mauwa, H., Bagula, A.B., Zennaro, M., Lusilao-Zodi, G.-A.: On the impact of propagation models on tv white spaces measurements in Africa. In: 2015 International Conference on Emerging Trends in Networks and Computer Communications (ETNCC) (2015)

8. Egli, J.J.: Radio propagation above 40 MC over irregular terrain. Proc. IRE **45**(10), 1383–1391 (1957)

9. Hata, M.: Empirical formula for propagation loss in land mobile radio services. IEEE Trans. Veh. Technol. **29**(3), 317–325 (1980)

10. Prasad, M., Ahmad, I.: Comparison of some path loss prediction methods with VHF/UHF measurements. IEEE Trans. Broadcast. **43**(4), 459–486 (1997)

11. Holland, O., Kokkinen, H., Wong, S., Friderikos, V., Raman, A., Dohler, M., Lema, M.: Changing availability of TV white space in the UK. Electron. Lett. **52**(15), 1349–1351 (2016)

12. Bahl, P., Chandra, R., Chou, P., Ferrell, J., Moscibroda, T., Narlanka, S., Wu, Y.: KNOWS: kognitiv networking over white spaces. In: IEEE DySPAN (2007)

13. Murty, R., Chandra, R., Moscibroda, T., Bahl, P.: Senseless: a database-driven white spaces network. IEEE Trans. Mob. Comput. **11**(2), 189–203 (2012)

14. Radio Propagation Models. http://people.seas.harvard.edu/~jones/es151/prop_ models/propagation.html

15. Ghosh, S., Naik, G., Kumar, A., Karandikar, A.: OpenPAWS: an open source PAWS and UHF TV white space database implementation for India. In: 2015 Twenty First National Conference on Communications (NCC) (2015)

16. TVWS Planning Tool. https://www.cse.iitb.ac.in/~tvws/tvws_tool/Thane/client. html

17. World Bank: Internet Users Data. http://data.worldbank.org/indicator/IT.NET. USER.P2?locations=IN

18. Ying, X., Zhang, J., Yan, L., Zhang, G., Chen, M., Chandra, R.: Exploring indoor white spaces in metropolises. In: Proceedings of the 19th Annual International Conference on Mobile Computing & Networking (2013)

Impact of Mobility in Spectrum Sensing Capacity

Luis Irio[1,2(✉)] and Rodolfo Oliveira[1,2]

[1] IT, Instituto de Telecomunicações, Lisbon, Portugal
[2] Departamento de Engenharia Electrotécnica,
Faculdade de Ciências Tecnologia, FCT,
Universidade Nova de Lisboa, 2829-516 Caparica, Portugal
l.irio@campus.fct.unl.pt

Abstract. This work evaluates the secondary users' (SUs) transmission capability considering that the primary users (PUs) can move to different positions. The transmission capability identifies the available opportunities for SU's transmission. No opportunities are available when mobile PUs are active within the SU's sensing region. We also consider the scenario when the PUs are undesirable detected active when they are not located within the SUs' sensing region. Our analysis indicate that the transmission capability increases as the average mobility of the PUs decreases, which is confirmed by simulation.

Keywords: Cognitive Radio Networks · Spectrum Sensing · Mobility

1 Introduction

In Cognitive Radio Networks (CRNs), the non-licensed users usually denominated Secondary Users (SUs) must detect the activity of the licensed users, denominated Primary Users (PUs), in order to utilize the unused spectrum bands without causing them harmful interference. Spectrum Sensing (SS) plays a central role in CRNs, since it allows to detect portions of spectrum available for transmission in the spatial sensing area of a SU. Several SS techniques were already studied and reported in the literature [1], including Waveform-based sensing [3], Energy-based sensing (EBS) [2], Cyclostationarity-based sensing (CBS) [5], and Matched Filter-based sensing (MFBS) [4]. Different surveys focused on spectrum sensing techniques are already available (e.g. [6, 7]).

Due to the path loss effect it is more difficult to detect the activity of the PUs when they move across a given region. Consequently, is more difficult to characterize the transmission capability of the SUs, denoted as Sensing Capacity (SC), when mobile PUs are considered. For static CRNs, where the nodes stay at the same position, the SC metric was defined in [8] as

$$C^{static} = \eta \cdot \zeta \cdot W \cdot P_{off}, \tag{1}$$

where η denotes the sensing efficiency, W represents the bandwidth, ζ represents the spectral efficiency of the band (bit/sec/Hz), and P_{off} is the probability of the band being

© ICST Institute for Computer Sciences, Social Informatics and Telecommunications Engineering 2018
P. Marques et al. (Eds.): CROWNCOM 2017, LNICST 228, pp. 162–172, 2018.
https://doi.org/10.1007/978-3-319-76207-4_14

accessible to SUs due to the inactivity of PUs. More recently, the SC was defined considering that several PUs act as mobile nodes [9, 10],

$$C^{mob} = \eta \cdot \zeta \cdot W \cdot P_{\mathcal{I}_{off}}, \tag{2}$$

where $P_{\mathcal{I}_{off}}$ is the probability of inactivity (i.e. not transmitting) of the PUs positioned over the SU's sensing region. While admitting multiple PUs and mobile scenarios, the SC defined in [9, 10] is not including the case when the PUs are located outside the SU's sensing region and may be anomaly detected. This effect, denominated Spatial False Alarm (SFA) effect [11], is related with the behavior of a SU misunderstanding a non-interfering PU, and was recently studied in [12] considering multiple static PUs. The SC expressed in (2) is an upper bound, because no SFA is considered. Differently from [9, 10], this work considers that the SFA effect may occur in a CRN with multiple mobile PUs, being the SC now defined as

$$C_{SFA}^{mob} = \eta \cdot \zeta \cdot W \cdot \left(P_{\mathcal{O}_{SFA}} \cdot P_{\mathcal{I}_{off}} \right), \tag{3}$$

where $P_{\mathcal{O}_{SFA}}$ is the probability of not occurring the SFA effect due to the activity of the nodes located outside the SU's sensing region.

The characterization of the sensing capacity when both mobility [9, 10] and SFA effects [11, 12] are considered has not been addressed before. The contributions of this work are summarized as follows:

- The spatial false alarm probability is derived by characterizing the aggregate interference originated by the mobile PUs not located within the SU's sensing region (i.e. when the PUs are located outside);
- The SC of CRNs, defined in [9, 10], is extended to consider the SFA effect. Both simulation and theoretical results show that SFA should not be neglected.
- We confirm that the SFA effect decreases the SC, and the results in [8–10] represent a SC's upper bound;
- Regarding the mobility of the nodes, it is shown that the SC varies inversely with the average speed of the PUs.

The paper is organized as follows. Section 2 characterizes the PUs' mobility model. The interference caused by the PUs to a SU is tackled in Sect. 3. The sensing capacity is analyzed in Sect. 4. Finally, conclusions are presented in Sect. 5.

2 System Model

2.1 System Description

This work considers that PUs are mobile nodes that move according to the Random WayPoint (RWP) mobility model [13]. By considering the RWP mobility model, we assume that n PUs move in a rectangular region with area $X_{max} \times Y_{max}$. The mobility is treated individually, and each PU is placed in a random location (x, y) in the beginning of simulation. The location of PUs is sampled from the uniform distribution characterized by $x \in [0, X_{max}]$ and $y \in [0, Y_{max}]$. (x, y) denotes the departing point.

The destination point (x', y') is also uniformly chosen as the departing point (*i.e.* $x' \in [0, X_{max}]$ and $y' \in [0, Y_{max}]$). After defining the departure and destination points a PU uniformly chooses the velocity $v \in [V_{min}, V_{max}]$ to move to the ending point. After reaching the ending point (x', y'), a PU randomly chooses a pause duration $(T_p \in [0, T_{P_{max}}])$, and during this period of time it stays at the ending point. After elapsing T_p, a PU uniformly chooses a new velocity value to move to another ending point uniformly chosen. After reaching the ending point a PU repeats the same cycle as many times as required. Nodes move with expected velocity E[V].

Figure 1 represents the system considered in this work. The static SU N_c is placed in the center of the considered scenario (in the position $(X_{max}/2, Y_{max}/2)$), and N_c senses the activity of the mobile PUs located in the circular sensing region with radius R_i^1 (characterized by the dark disk involving N_c). This work considers the SU's sensing region concept instead of the PU's protection region. However, both concepts are equivalent if the PU's protection range is equal or smaller than the SU's sensing range.

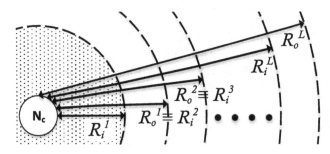

Fig. 1. Spatial scenario considered. The sensing region of the SU (node N_c) is represented by the area $A_{SR} = \pi (R_i^1)^2$. The PUs located outside the sensing region are found in the area given by $A = \pi \left((R_o^L)^2 - (R_i^1)^2 \right)$.

2.2 Distribution of the PUs Over the Simulated Region

The annulus area $A = \pi \left((R_o^L)^2 - (R_i^1)^2 \right)$ in Fig. 1 can be obtained via calculus by dividing the annulus up into an infinite number of annuli of infinitesimal width $d\chi$ and area $2\pi\chi d\chi$ and then integrating from $\chi = R_i^1$ to $\chi = R_o^L$, i.e. $A = \int_{R_i^1}^{R_o^L} 2\pi\chi \, d\chi$. Using the Riemann sum, A can be approximated by the sum of the area of a finite number (L) of annuli of width ρ,

$$A \approx \sum_{l=1}^{L} A_l, \tag{4}$$

where $A_l = \pi \left((R_o^l)^2 - (R_i^l)^2 \right)$ represents the area of the annulus l, $l \in \{1, ..., L\}$. $R_o^l = (R_i^1 + l\rho)$ and $R_i^l = (R_i^1 + (l-1)\rho)$ denotes the radius of the larger circle and smaller circle of the annulus l, respectively.

In a specific annulus l, the number of PUs is represented by the random variable (RV) X_l and is approximately described by a Poisson distribution with Probability Mass Function (PMF)

$$P(X_l = k) \approx \frac{(\beta_l A_l \tau)^k}{k!} e^{-\beta_l A_l \tau}, k = 0, 1, \ldots, n, \tag{5}$$

where β_l represents the spatial density of the PUs located in the annulus l, the number of PUs is represented by n and the probability of the PUs being active is denoted by τ. By dividing the area A in the multiple areas A_l, a different β_l is considered for each annulus A_l, which better approximates the spatial distribution of PUs in the area A.

The spatial distribution of the PUs in two dimensions (x and y) follows the result in [14, Theorem 3, $\alpha = 2$] and is given by

$$f_{XY}(x, y) = \frac{p_p}{a^2} + (1 - p_p) \frac{36}{a^4} \left(\frac{x^2}{a} - \frac{a}{4} \right) \left(\frac{y^2}{a} - \frac{a}{4} \right),$$

for $-a/2 \leq x \leq a/2, -a/2 \leq y \leq a/2, a = X_{\max} = Y_{\max}$ and where

$$p_p = \frac{(V_{max} - V_{min}) E[T_p]}{0.521405 \times a \times \ln\left(\frac{V_{max}}{V_{min}}\right) + (V_{max} - V_{min}) E[T_p]}.$$

The location of a PU within the annulus l is represented by the Bernoulli RV X_b^l and the probability of a PU being positioned within the l–th annulus is given by

$$P(X_b^l = 1) = \int\limits_{-R_o^l}^{R_o^l} \int\limits_{-\sqrt{(R_o^l)^2 - x^2}}^{\sqrt{(R_o^l)^2 - x^2}} v - \int\limits_{-R_o^l}^{R_i^l} \int\limits_{-\sqrt{(R_i^l)^2 - x^2}}^{\sqrt{(R_i^l)^2 - x^2}} v, \tag{6}$$

with $v = f_{XY}(x, y) \, dy \, dx$. The PU's spatial density of the annulus l, defined as β_l in (5), is given by $\beta_l \approx nP(X_b^l = 1)/A_l$, where $nP(X_b^l = 1)$ represents the average number of nodes located in the area A_l. In what follows (5) is adopted to characterize the number of PUs placed over the multiple annuli (L).

3 Aggregate Interference

3.1 Interference Caused by the PUs Located Within the l–th Annulus

The aggregate interference power received by the secondary user N_c placed in the center of the l–th annulus is given by

$$I = \sum_{i=1}^{n_l} I_i, \tag{7}$$

where n_l is the total number of PUs located in the annulus and I_i is the interference caused by the i-th PU. The individual interference power I_i is expressed by

$$I_i = P_{Tx}\psi_i r_l^{-\alpha}, \tag{8}$$

where P_{Tx} is the transmission power of the i-th PU[1], ψ_i is the fading observed in the channel between the PU i and SU, and r_l represents the distance between the i–th interferer and the receiver. The path-loss coefficient is represented by α.

The moment generating function (MGF) of the aggregate interference due to path loss ($\psi_i = 1$) is derived in the next steps. Let $M_I^i(s)$ denote the MGF of the i-th PU ($i = 1, \ldots, n_l$) positioned over the annulus l, given by

$$M_I^i(s) = E_{I_i}\left[e^{sI_i}\right], \tag{9}$$

where E_{I_i} denotes the expectation of I_i. The PDF of r_l can be written as the ratio between the perimeter of the circle with radius r_l and the total area A_l, being represented as follows

$$f_R(r_l) = \begin{cases} \frac{2\pi r_l}{A_l}, & R_i^l < r_l < R_o^l \\ 0, & otherwise \end{cases}. \tag{10}$$

Using (8) and (10) the MGF of the interference power received by the node N_c caused by the i-th PU is represented by

$$M_I^i(s) = \frac{2P_{Tx}^{2/\alpha}\left(\Gamma\left(-2/\alpha, P_{Tx}(R_o^l)^{-\alpha}\right)s\right) - \Gamma\left(-2/\alpha, P_{Tx}(R_i^l)^{-\alpha}s\right)\right)}{\left((R_o^l)^2 - (R_i^l)^2\right)s},$$

where $\Gamma(s,x) = \int_x^\infty t^{s-1}e^{-t}dt$ is the upper incomplete gamma function and $\Gamma(s) = \int_0^\infty t^{s-1}e^{-t}dt$ represents the gamma function.

The PDF of the aggregate interference I due to k active PUs may be defined though the convolution of the PDFs of each I_i, when the individual interference I_i is independent and identically distributed. Consequently, the MGF of I is written as follows

$$M_{I/k}(s) = M_I^1(s) \times \cdots \times M_I^k(s) = \left(M_I^i(s)\right)^k. \tag{11}$$

The PDF of the aggregate interference (I) may be stated through the Law of Total Probability as follows

---

[1] For every PU we have assumed $P_{Tx} = 10^3$ mW.

$$f_I(j) = \sum_{k=0}^{n_l} f_I(j|X_l = k)P(X_l = k), \tag{12}$$

leading to the MGF of the aggregate interference, I, which can be written as

$$E\left[e^{sI}\right] = \sum_{k=0}^{n_l} P(X_l = k)M_{I/k}(s). \tag{13}$$

Using (11), the MGF of I is given as follows

$$E\left[e^{sI}\right] = \sum_{k=0}^{n_l} P(X_l = k)e^{k\ln\left(M_I^i(s)\right)} = e^{\beta_l A_l \tau\left(M_I^i(s)-1\right)}. \tag{14}$$

The expectation of the aggregate interference, E[I], can be obtained using the Law of Total Expectation, i.e.,

$$E[I] = E[E[I|X_l]] = 2\pi\beta_l\tau P_{Tx}\left(\frac{(R_o^l)^{2-\alpha} - (R_i^l)^{2-\alpha}}{2-\alpha}\right). \tag{15}$$

Similarly, the variance of the aggregate interference can be obtained using the Law of Total Variance as follows

$$Var[I] = Var[I_i]E[X_l] + E[I_i]^2 Var[X_l]. \tag{15}$$

Since X_l is distributed according to a Poisson distribution (with mean $\beta_l A_l \tau$), the variance of the aggregate interference is expressed by

$$Var[I] = \pi\beta_l\tau P_{Tx}^2\left(\frac{(R_o^l)^{2-2\alpha} - (R_i^l)^{2-2\alpha}}{1-\alpha}\right)$$

As shown in [15], the aggregate interference due to path loss can be approximated by a Gamma distribution. Consequently the shape and the scale parameters of the Gamma distribution, denoted by k_l and θ_l, are respectively given by $k_l = E[I]^2/Var[I]$ and $\theta_l = Var[I]/E[I]$.

3.2   Aggregate Interference Due to PUs Located Within L Annuli

As shown in the previous subsection, the interference I caused to the N_c by the PUs located within the l-th annulus is approximated by a gamma distribution, with MGF

$$M_I^l(s) = (1 - \theta_l s)^{-k_l}. \tag{16}$$

The annulus of width $R_o^L - R_i^1$ s can be expressed as a summation of L annuli of width ρ. Consequently, the MGF of the aggregate interference originated by the PUs positioned over the L annuli is represented by

$$M_{I_{agg}}(s) = \prod_{l=1}^{L} (1 - \theta_l s)^{-k_l}. \tag{17}$$

3.3 Distribution of the Aggregate Interference

The interference due to the PUs located outside the SU's sensing region can be seen as the summation of the L individual aggregated interferences caused by the PUs located within L annuli. Therefore, the expressions for the cumulative distribution function (CDF) and the PDF of the summation of L independent gamma random variables are given in [16].

Defining $\{X_l\}_{l=1}^{L}$ as independent gamma variables, but not necessarily identically distributed with parameters θ_l (scale) and k_l (shape), then the PDF of $I_{agg} = \sum_{l=1}^{L} X_l$ can be expressed as [16]

$$f_{I_{agg}}(s) = \prod_{l=1}^{L} \left(\frac{\theta_1}{\theta_l}\right)^{k_l} \sum_{w=0}^{\infty} \frac{\delta_w s^{\left(\sum_{l=1}^{L} k_l + w - 1\right)} \exp\left(-\frac{s}{\theta_1}\right)}{\theta_1^{\left(\sum_{l=1}^{L} k_l + w\right)} \Gamma\left(\sum_{l=1}^{L} k_l + w\right)}, \tag{18}$$

where $\theta_1 = \min_l\{\theta_l\}$, and the coefficients δ_w are obtained recursively,

$$\delta_{w+1} = \frac{1}{w+1} \sum_{i=1}^{w+1} \left[\sum_{l=1}^{L} k_l \left(1 - \frac{\theta_1}{\theta_l}\right)^i\right] \delta_{w+1-i},$$

and $\delta_0 = 1$. $\Gamma(.)$ represents the gamma function.

4 Sensing Capacity

4.1 Formal Definition

The band licensed of the PUs is sensed by a SU to evaluate if the spectrum is vacant or occupied. The sensing decision considered in this work is computed periodically (a period of 1 s was adopted) having the amount of aggregate interference sensed outside the sensing region into account.

Departing from the definition of SC in (3), we first define $P_{\mathcal{I}_{off}}$, the probability of not occurring any activity caused by the PUs that may be located within the SU's sensing region. A PU is located within the SU's sensing region with probability $P_{\mathcal{I}}$ given by

$$P_{\mathcal{I}} = \int\limits_{-R_i^1}^{R_i^1} \int\limits_{-\sqrt{\left(R_i^1\right)^2 - x^2}}^{\sqrt{\left(R_i^1\right)^2 - x^2}} f_{XY}(x,y) dy dx. \tag{19}$$

Because all PUs move independently, the probability of $k \leq n$ PUs being positioned over the sensing region of the SU is expressed by the probability mass function

$$B(n, k, P_{\mathcal{I}}) = \binom{n}{k} (P_{\mathcal{I}})^k (1 - P_{\mathcal{I}})^{(n-k)}. \tag{20}$$

Finally, $P_{\mathcal{I}_{off}}$ is defined as

$$P_{\mathcal{I}_{off}} = \sum_{k=0}^{n} B(n, k, P_{\mathcal{I}}) \cdot (1 - \tau)^k, \tag{21}$$

since the k PUs within the sensing region of the SU are inactive with probability $(1 - \tau)^k$.

Regarding $P_{\mathcal{O}_{SFA}}$ in (3), which denotes the probability of not occurring SFA due to the PUs located outside the SU's sensing region, and following the notation in (21) we start to consider that $n - k$ PUs are located outside the sensing region. A spatial false alarm does not occur if the aggregate interference power caused by the PUs located outside the sensing region is lower than a given threshold (γ). Its probability is represented by $P(I_{agg}\{n_l = n - k\} \leq \gamma)$, where $\{n_l = n - k\}$ indicates that the parameters k_l and θ_l must be computed assuming n_l defined in Sect. 3.1 equal to $n - k$. After computing the parameters k_l and θ_l, $f_{I_{agg}}(s)$ may be also computed through (18) and

$$P(I_{agg}\{n_l = n - k\} \leq \gamma) = \int_0^{\gamma} f_{I_{agg}}(s) ds. \tag{22}$$

By considering the different number of $n - k$ PUs that may be localized outside the session region, $P_{\mathcal{O}_{SFA}}$ is given by

$$P_{\mathcal{O}_{SFA}} = \sum_{k=0}^{n} (I_{agg}\{n_l = n - k\} \leq \gamma), \tag{23}$$

and finally using (3), (21) and (23), the sensing capacity is written as follows

$$C_{SFA}^{mob} = \eta \cdot \zeta \cdot W \sum_{k=0}^{n} B(n, k, P_{\mathcal{I}}) \cdot (1 - \tau)^k \cdot P(I_{agg}\{n_l = n - k\} \leq \gamma). \tag{24}$$

Table 1. Parameters used to compute the different results.

X_{max}	1000 m	R_i^1	100 m	α	2
Y_{max}	1000 m	$T_{P_{max}}$	0 s, E[V] = 10.82 m/s	ρ	10 m
V_{min}	5 m/s	$T_{P_{max}}$	300 s, E[V] = 1.50 m/s	L	61
V_{max}	20 m/s	$\eta \cdot \zeta \cdot W$	1	γ	0.1 mW

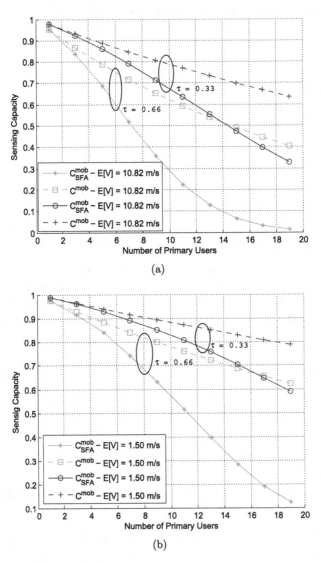

(a)

(b)

Fig. 2. Sensing capacity for different levels of PU's activity (τ): (a) high mobility scenario (E[V] = 10.82 m/s); (b) low mobility scenario (E[V] = 1.50 m/s).

4.2 Comparison Results

This subsection compares the impact of the SFA in the SU's SC. The SC is computed with (24) and compared with the results obtained with (27) in [9] (similar to (2)), which neglects the SFA effect. Different network scenarios were considered, where the number of mobile PUs were varied from a single PU to 19. The PUs moving according to the RWP mobility model achieve different average velocities, $E[V] = \{1.50, 10.82\}$ m/s, by adopting $T_{P_{max}} = \{0, 300\}$ s, respectively. Two different probabilities of PU's activity were also considered, i.e. $\tau = \{0.33, 0.66\}$. The simulations were run for each number of PUs and adopting constant $T_{P_{max}}$ and τ values. The missing parameters related with the propagation model and the computation of theoretical model are described in Table 1.

The sensing capacity results (computed with (24) and (27) in [9]) are illustrated in Fig. 2. Figure 2(a) plots the results for $E[V] = 10.82$ m/s, while 2(b) plots the result for $E[V] = 1.50$ m/s. Regarding the impact of the PUs' mobility on the SC, it is well known that the spatial density of the nodes moving according the RWP model increases within the sensing region of the node N_C as the average velocity of the nodes increase [14]. Consequently, more PUs are likely to be located within the sensing region as the average velocity of the PUs increases. In this case, the node N_c detects higher PUs' activity within its sensing region, leading to a lower SC (Fig. 2(a)), when compared to a scenario of lower average velocity (Fig. 2(b)).

Finally, the results presented in Fig. 2 show that for the two assumptions (considering/neglecting the SFA) the SC varies inversely with the number of PUs, the level of PU's activity (τ), and the average velocity of the PUs ($E[V]$). However, the SC decreases more sharply when the SFA effect is considered, and the deviation from neglecting the SFA increases when the number of PUs and PU's level of activity increase, or when the average velocity of the nodes decrease. Moreover, the deviation observed in the SC confirms that when the SFA effect is neglected the results obtained with [9] represent an upper bound of the SC.

5 Conclusions

This work characterizes the SUs sensing capacity in a CRN when are considered multiple mobile PUs. Contrarily to other works, we consider that PUs may be detected active when they are located outside the sensing region. This effect, known as SFA, degrades the sensing capacity of CRs, as demonstrated in the paper. Moreover, it is shown that the decrease of the sensing capacity due to the SFA effect may be significant, namely when the PU's activity and the number of PUs increase. Finally, due to the mobility model, the results presented in the paper indicate that the sensing capacity increases as the average velocity of the nodes decrease. This result indicates that the capacity of the SUs varies inversely with the velocity of the PUs, which confirms the importance of this work.

Acknowledgments. This work was partially supported by the Portuguese Science and Technology Foundation (FCT/MEC) under the project UID/EEA/50008/2013 and grant SFRH/BD/108525/2015. The work was also supported by the "Faculdade de Cincias e Tecnologia" - Nova University of Lisbon, through the PhD Program in Electrical and Computer Engineering.

References

1. Yucek, T., Arslan, H.: A survey of spectrum sensing algorithms for cognitive radio applications. IEEE Commun. Surv. Tutorials **11**, 116–130 (2009)
2. Urkowitz, H.: Energy detection of unknown deterministic signals. Proc. IEEE **55**, 523–531 (1967)
3. Zahedi-Ghasabeh, A., Tarighat, A., Daneshrad, B.: Spectrum sensing of OFDM waveforms using embedded pilots in the presence of impairments. IEEE Trans. Veh. Technol. **61**, 1208–1221 (2012)
4. Bouzegzi, A., Ciblat, P., Jallon, P.: Matched filter based algorithm for blind recognition of OFDM systems. In: Proceedings of IEEE VTC 2008-Fall, pp. 1–5, September 2008
5. Al-Habashna, A., Dobre, O.A., Venkatesan, R., Popescu, D.C.: Cyclostationarity- based detection of LTE OFDM signals for cognitive radio systems. In: Proceedings of IEEE GLOBECOM 2010, pp. 1–6, December 2010
6. Masonta, M.T., Mzyece, M., Ntlatlapa, N.: Spectrum decision in cognitive radio networks: a survey. IEEE Commun. Surv. Tutorials **15**, 1088–1107 (2013)
7. Sun, H., Nallanathan, A., Wang, C.-X., Chen, Y.: Wideband spectrum sensing for cognitive radio networks: a survey. IEEE Wirel. Commun. **20**, 74–81 (2013)
8. Lee, W.-Y., Akyildiz, I.F.: Optimal spectrum sensing framework for cognitive radio networks. IEEE Trans. Wireless Commun. **7**, 3845–3857 (2008)
9. Cacciapuoti, A.S., Akyildiz, I.F., Paura, L.: Primary-user mobility impact on spectrum sensing in cognitive radio networks. In: 22nd IEEE International Symposium on Personal, Indoor and Mobile Radio Communications, pp. 451–456, Toronto (2011)
10. Cacciapuoti, A.S., Akyildiz, I.F., Paura, L.: Optimal primary-user mobility aware spectrum sensing design for cognitive radio networks. IEEE J. Sel. Areas Commun. **31**, 2161–2172 (2013)
11. Han, W., Li, J., Liu, Q., Zhao, L.: Spatial false alarms in cognitive radio. IEEE Commun. Lett. **15**, 518–520 (2011)
12. Han, W., Li, J., Li, Z., Si, J., Zhang, Y.: Spatial false alarm in cognitive radio network. IEEE Trans. Sig. Process. **61**, 1375–1388 (2013)
13. Johnson, D.B., Maltz, D.A.: Dynamic source routing in ad hoc wireless networks. Mob. Comput. **353**, 153–181 (1996)
14. Bettstetter, C., Resta, G., Santi, P.: The node distribution of the random way- point mobility model for wireless ad hoc networks. IEEE Trans. Mob. Comput. **2**, 257–269 (2003)
15. Haenggi, M., Ganti, R.K.: Interference in large wireless networks. Found. Trends Netw. **3**, 127–248 (2009)
16. Moschopoulos, P.G.: The distribution of the sum of independent gamma random variables. Ann. Inst. Stat. Math. **37**, 541–544 (1985)

Multi-Armed Bandit Learning in IoT Networks: Learning Helps Even in Non-stationary Settings

Rémi Bonnefoi[1]([✉]) [iD], Lilian Besson[1,2] [iD], Christophe Moy[1], Emilie Kaufmann[2], and Jacques Palicot[1]

[1] CentraleSupélec (campus of Rennes), IETR, SCEE Team,
Avenue de la Boulaie - CS 47601, 35576 Cesson-Sévigné, France
{Remi.Bonnefoi,Lilian.Besson,Christophe.Moy,
Jacques.Palicot}@CentraleSupelec.fr
[2] Univ. Lille 1, CNRS, Inria, SequeL Team,
UMR 9189 - CRIStAL, 59000 Lille, France
Emilie.Kaufmann@Univ-Lille1.fr

Abstract. Setting up the future Internet of Things (IoT) networks will require to support more and more communicating devices. We prove that intelligent devices in unlicensed bands can use Multi-Armed Bandit (MAB) learning algorithms to improve resource exploitation. We evaluate the performance of two classical MAB learning algorithms, UCB_1 and Thomson Sampling, to handle the decentralized decision-making of Spectrum Access, applied to IoT networks; as well as learning performance with a growing number of intelligent end-devices. We show that using learning algorithms does help to fit more devices in such networks, even when all end-devices are intelligent and are dynamically changing channel. In the studied scenario, stochastic MAB learning provides a up to 16% gain in term of successful transmission probabilities, and has near optimal performance even in non-stationary and non-$i.i.d.$ settings with a majority of intelligent devices.

Keywords: Internet of Things · Multi-Armed Bandits
Reinforcement learning · Cognitive Radio · Non-stationary bandits

1 Introduction

Unlicensed bands are more and more used and considered for mobile and LAN communication standards (WiFi, LTE-U), and for Internet of Things (IoT) standards for short-range (ZigBee, Z-Wave, Bluetooth) and long-range (LoRaWAN, SIGFOX, Ingenu, Weightless) communications [1]. This heavy use of unlicensed bands will cause performance drop, and could even compromise IoT promises.

Efficient Medium Access (MAC) policies allow devices to avoid interfering traffic and can significantly reduce the spectrum contention problem in unlicensed bands. As end-devices battery life is a key constraint of IoT networks,

© ICST Institute for Computer Sciences, Social Informatics and Telecommunications Engineering 2018
P. Marques et al. (Eds.): CROWNCOM 2017, LNICST 228, pp. 173–185, 2018.
https://doi.org/10.1007/978-3-319-76207-4_15

this leads to IoT protocols using as low signaling overhead as possible and simple ALOHA-based mechanisms. In this article, we analyze the performance of Multi-Armed Bandits (MAB) algorithms [2,3], used in combination with a time-frequency slotted ALOHA-based protocol. We consider the Upper-Confidence Bound (UCB$_1$) [4], and the Thompson-Sampling (TS) algorithms [5–7].

MAB learning has already been proposed in Cognitive Radio (CR) [8], and in particular, for sensing-based Dynamic Spectrum Access (DSA) in licensed bands [9]. Recently, TS and UCB$_1$ algorithms have been used for improving the spectrum access in (unlicensed) WiFi networks [10], and the UCB$_1$ algorithm was used in a unlicensed and frequency- and time-slotted IoT network [11]. Many recent works show that MAB algorithms work well for real-world radio signal. However, even with only one dynamic user using the learning algorithm, the background traffic or the traffic of the other devices is never really stationary or $i.i.d$ (independent and identically distributed). In recent works like [11], several devices are using bandit algorithms, and the assumptions made by the stochastic bandit algorithms are not satisfied: as several agents learn simultaneously, their behavior is neither stationary nor $i.i.d.$ As far as we know, we provide the first study to confirm robustness of the use of stochastic bandit algorithms for decision making in IoT networks with a large number of intelligent devices in the network, which makes the environment not stationary at all, violating the hypothesis required for mathematical proofs of bandit algorithms convergence and efficiency.

The aim of this article is to assess the potential gain of learning algorithms in IoT scenarios, even when the number of intelligent devices in the network increases, and the stochastic hypothesis is more and more questionable. To do that, we suppose an IoT network made of two types of devices: static devices that use only one channel (fixed in time), and dynamic devices that can choose the channel for each of their transmissions. Static devices form an interfering traffic, which could have been generated by devices using other standards as well. We first evaluate the probability of collision if dynamic devices randomly select channels (naive approach), and if a centralized controller optimally distribute them in channels (ideal approach). Then, these reference scenarios allow to evaluate the performance of UCB$_1$ and TS algorithms in a decentralized network, in terms of successful communication rate, as it reflects the network efficiency.

The rest of this article is organized as follows. The system model is introduced in Sect. 2. Reference policies are described in Sect. 3, and MAB algorithms are introduced in Sect. 4. Numerical results are presented in Sect. 5.

2   System Model and Notations

As illustrated in Fig. 1, we suppose a slotted protocol. All devices share a synchronized time, and know in advance the finite number of available RF channels. In each time slot, devices try to send packets to the unique Base Station, which listens continuously to all channels, following an ALOHA-based communication (no sensing). Each time slot is divided in two parts: first for uplink communications in which data packets are sent by end-devices to the base station. If

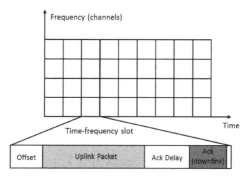

Fig. 1. The considered time-frequency slotted protocol. Each frame is composed by a fix-duration uplink slot in which the end-devices transmit their packets. If a packet is well received, the base station replies by transmitting an *Ack*, after the ack delay.

only one packet is sent in this part of the slot, the base station can decode it and sends an acknowledgement to the device in the second part. If two or more devices send an uplink packet in the same slot, the uplink packets collide (*i.e.*, there is a *collision*), and the acknowledgement *Ack* is not transmitted. This way, no collision can occur on the downlink messages, easing the analysis of collisions.

There are two types of end-devices in the network:

- *Static* end-devices have poor RF abilities, and each of them uses only one channel to communicate with the base station. Their choice is assumed to be fixed in time (stationary) and independent (*i.i.d.*). The traffic generated by these devices is considered as an interfering traffic for other devices.
- *Dynamic* (or *smart*) end-devices have richer RF abilities, they can use all the available channels, by quickly reconfiguring their RF transceiver on the fly. They can also store communication successes or failures they experienced in each channel, in order to change channel, possibly at every time slot.

There are $N_c \geq 1$ channels, $D \geq 0$ dynamic end-devices, and $S \geq 0$ static devices. Furthermore, in channel $i \in [\![1; N_c]\!]$ there are $0 \leq S_i \leq S$ static devices (so $S = \sum_{i=1}^{N_c} S_i$). We focus on *dense networks*, in which the number of devices $S + D$ is very large compared to N_c (about 1000 to 10000, while N_c is about 10 to 50). As this problem is only interesting if devices are able to communicate reasonably efficiently with the base station, we assume devices only communicate occasionally, *i.e.*, with a low *duty cycle*, as it is always considered for IoT.

We suppose that all devices follow the same emission pattern, being fixed in time, and we choose to model it as a simple Bernoulli process: all devices have the same probability to send a packet in any (discrete) temporal slot, and we denote $p \in (0, 1)$ this probability[1]. The parameter p essentially controls the frequency of communication for each device, once the time scale is fixed (*i.e.*, real time during two messages), and $1/p$ is proportional to the *duty cycle*.

---

[1] In the experiments below, p is about 10^{-3}, because in a crowded network p should be smaller than $N_c/(S + D)$ for all devices to communicate successfully (in average).

The goal is to design a simple sequential algorithm, to be applied identically by each dynamic device, in a fully distributed setting (each device runs its own algorithm, from its observations), in order to minimize collisions and maximize the fraction of successful transmissions of all the dynamic devices.

Before explaining how this goal presents similarity with a *multi-armed bandit problem*, we present some natural baseline policies (*i.e.*, algorithms).

3   Three Reference Policies

This section presents three different policies that will be used to assess the efficiency of the learning algorithms presented in the next section. The first one is naive but can be used in practice, while the two others are very efficient but require full knowledge on the system (i.e., an oracle) and are thus unpractical.

3.1   Naive Policy: Random Channel Selection

We derive here the probability of having a successful transmission, for a dynamic device, in the case where all the dynamic devices make a purely random channel selection (i.e., uniform on $i \in [\![1; N_c]\!] = \{1, \ldots, N_c\}$).

In this case, for one dynamic device, a successful transmission happens if it is the only device to choose channel i, at that time slot. The probability of successful transmission is computed as follows, because the S_i static devices in each channel i are assumed to be independent, and static and dynamic devices are assumed to *not* transmit at each time t with a fixed probability $1 - p$:

$$\mathbb{P}(\text{success}|\text{sent}) = \sum_{i=1}^{N_c} \underbrace{\mathbb{P}(\text{success}|\text{sent in channel } i)}_{\text{No one else sent in channel } i} \; \underbrace{\mathbb{P}(\text{sent in channel } i)}_{=1/N_c, \text{by uniform choice}} \quad (1)$$

All dynamic devices follow the same policy in this case, so the probability of transmitting at that time in channel i for any dynamic device is p/N_c, and there are $D - 1$ other dynamic devices. As they are independent, the probability that no other dynamic device sent in i is $q = \mathbb{P}(\bigcap_{k=1}^{D-1} \text{device } k \text{ did not sent in } i) = \prod_{k=1}^{D-1} \mathbb{P}(\text{device } k \text{ did not sent in } i)$. And $\mathbb{P}(\text{device } k \text{ sent in } i) = p \times 1/N_c$, by uniform choice on channels and the Bernoulli emission hypothesis. So $q = \prod_{k=1}^{D-1}(1 - p/N_c) = (1 - p/N_c)^{D-1}$. Thus we can conclude,

$$\mathbb{P}(\text{success}|\text{sent}) = \sum_{i=1}^{N_c} \underbrace{(1 - p/N_c)^{D-1}}_{\text{No other dynamic device}} \times \underbrace{(1 - p)^{S_i}}_{\text{No static device}} \times \frac{1}{N_c}$$

$$= \frac{1}{N_c}\left(1 - \frac{p}{N_c}\right)^{D-1} \sum_{i=1}^{N_c}(1 - p)^{S_i}. \quad (2)$$

This expression (2) is constant (in time), and easy to compute numerically, but comparing the successful transmission rate of any policy against this naive policy is important, as any efficient learning algorithm should outperform it.

3.2 (Unachievable) Optimal Oracle Policy

We investigate in this section the optimal policy that can be achieved if the dynamic devices have a perfect knowledge of everything, and a fully centralized decision making[2] is possible. We want to find the stationary repartition of devices into channels that maximizes the probability of having a successful transmission.

If the oracle draws once uniformly at random a configuration of dynamic devices, with D_i devices affected to channel i is fixed (in time, i.e., stationary), then this probability is computed as before:

$$\mathbb{P}(\text{success}|\text{sent}) = \sum_{i=1}^{N_c} \mathbb{P}(\text{success}|\text{sent in channel } i) \, \mathbb{P}(\text{sent in channel } i)$$

$$= \sum_{i=1}^{N_c} \underbrace{(1-p)^{D_i-1}}_{D_i-1 \text{ others}} \times \underbrace{(1-p)^{S_i}}_{\text{No static device}} \times \underbrace{D_i/D}_{\text{Sent in channel } i} \qquad . \qquad (3)$$

Consequently, the optimal allocation vector $(D_1, \ldots, D_{N_c})$ is the solution of the following real-valued constraint optimization problem:

$$\underset{D_1,\ldots,D_{N_c}}{\arg\max} \sum_{i=1}^{N_c} D_i(1-p)^{S_i+D_i-1}, \qquad (4a)$$

$$\text{such that } \sum_{i=1}^{N_c} D_i = D, \qquad (4b)$$

$$D_i \geq 0 \qquad \forall i \in [\![1; N_c]\!]. \qquad (4c)$$

Proposition 1. *The Lagrange multipliers method [12] can be used to solve the constraint real-valued maximization problem introduced in Eq. (4).*

It gives a closed form expression for the optimal solution $D_i^*(\lambda)$, depending on the system parameters, and the unknown Lagrange multiplier $\lambda \in \mathbb{R}$.

$$D_i^*(\lambda) = \left(\frac{1}{\log(1-p)} \left[W \left(\frac{\lambda e}{(1-p)^{S_i-1}} \right) - 1 \right] \right)^{\dagger}. \qquad (5)$$

Proof. – The objective function $f : (D_1, \ldots, D_{N_c}) \mapsto \sum_{i=1}^{N_c} D_i(1-p)^{S_i+D_i-1}$ is quasi-convex [13] in each of its coordinates, on $[0, \infty)^{N_c}$.
- The Lagrange multipliers method can be applied to the optimization problem (4a), with a quasi-convex objective function f, linear equality constraints (4b) and linear inequality constraints (4c). Thanks to Theorem 1 from [14] for quasi-convex functions, the strong duality condition is satisfied in this case, so finding the saddle points will be enough to find the maximizers.   □

---

[2] This optimal policy needs an *oracle* seeing the entire system, and affecting all the dynamic devices, once and for all, in order to avoid any signaling overhead.

Where $(a)^\dagger = \max(a, 0)$, and W denotes the W-Lambert function which is the reciprocal bijection of $x \mapsto xe^x$ on $\mathbb{R}^+ = [0, +\infty)$ [15]. Moreover, condition (4b) implies that the Lagrange multiplier λ is the solution of

$$\sum_{i=1}^{N_c} D_i^*(\lambda) = D. \tag{6}$$

Equation (6) can be solved numerically, with simple one-dimensional root finding algorithms. Solving the optimization problem provides the optimal real number value for D_i^*, which has to be rounded to find the optimal number of devices for channel i: $\widehat{D_i} = \lfloor D_i^* \rfloor$ for $1 \leq i < N_c$, and $\widehat{D_{N_c}} = D - \sum_{i=1}^{N_c-1} \widehat{D_i}$.

3.3   A Greedy Approach of the Oracle Strategy

We propose a *sequential* approximation of the optimal policy: the third solution is a sub-optimal naive policy, simple to set up, but also unpractical as it also needs an oracle. End-devices are iteratively inserted in the channels with the lowest load (*i.e.*, the index i minimizing $S_i + D_i(\tau)$ at global time step τ). Once the number of devices in each channel is computed, the probability of sending successfully a message is also given by Eq. (3). This is the policy that would be used by dynamic devices if they were inserted one after the other, and if they had a perfect knowledge of the channel loads.

4   Sequential Policies Based on Bandit Algorithms

We now present the stochastic Multi-Armed Bandit (MAB) model, and the two stochastic MAB algorithms used in our experiments [3]. While the stochastic MAB model has been used to describe some aspects of Cognitive Radio systems, it is in principle not suitable for our IoT model, due to the non-stationarity of the channels occupancy caused by the learning policy used by dynamic objects.

4.1   Stochastic Multi-Armed Bandits

A Multi-Armed Bandit problem is defined as follows [2,5,16]. There is a fixed number $N_c \geq 1$ of levers, or "arms", and a player has to choose one lever at each discrete time $t \geq 1, t \in \mathbb{N}$, denoted as $A(t) = k \in \{1, \dots, N_c\}$. Selecting arm k at time t yields a (random) *reward*, $r_k(t) \in \mathbb{R}$, and the goal of the player is to maximize the sum of his rewards, $r_{1\dots T} = \sum_{t=1}^{T} r_{A(t)}(t)$.

A well-studied version of this problem is the so-called "stochastic" MAB, where the sequence of rewards drawn from a given arm k is assumed to be independent and identically distributed (*i.i.d*) under some distribution ν_k, that has a mean μ_k. Several types of reward distributions have been considered, for example distributions that belong to a one-dimensional exponential family (*e.g.*, Gaussian, Exponential, Poisson or Bernoulli distributions). We consider

Bernoulli bandit models, in which $r_k(t) \sim \text{Bern}(\mu_k)$, that is, $r_k(t) \in \{0,1\}$ and $\mathbb{P}(r_k(t) = 1) = \mu_k$.

The problem parameters $\mu_1, \ldots, \mu_K$ are unknown to the player, so to maximize his cumulated rewards, he must learn the distributions of the channels, to be able to progressively focus on the best arm (*i.e.*, the arm with largest mean). This requires to tackle the so-called *exploration-exploitation dilemma*: a player has to try all arms a sufficient number of times to get a robust estimate of their qualities, while not selecting the worst arms too many times.

In a Cognitive Radio application, arms model the *channels*, and players are the *dynamic end-devices*. For example in the classical OSA setting with sensing [9], a single dynamic device (a player) sequentially tries to access channels (the arms), and collects a reward of 1 if the channel is available and 0 otherwise. So rewards represent the *availability* of channels, and the parameter μ_k represents the mean availability of channel k.

Before discussing the relevance of a multi-armed bandit model for our IoT application, we present two bandit algorithms, UCB1 and Thompson Sampling, which both strongly rely on the assumption that rewards are *i.i.d.*.

4.2 The UCB$_1$ Algorithm

A naive approach could be to use an empirical mean estimator of the rewards for each channel, and select the channel with highest estimated mean at each time. This greedy approach is known to fail dramatically [2]. Indeed, with this policy, the selection of arms is highly dependent on the first draws, if the first transmission in a channel fails, the device will never use it again. Rather than relying on the empirical mean reward, Upper Confidence Bounds algorithms instead use a *confidence interval* on the unknown mean μ_k of each arm, which can be viewed as adding a "bonus" exploration to the empirical mean. They follow the "*optimism-in-face-of-uncertainty*" principle: at each step, they play according to the best model, as the statistically best possible arm (*i.e.*, the highest upper confidence bound) is selected.

More formally, for one device, let $N_k(t) = \sum_{\tau=1}^{t} \mathbb{1}(A(\tau) = k)$ be the number of times channel k was selected up-to time $t \geq 1$. The empirical mean estimator of channel k is defined as the mean reward obtained by selecting it up to time t, $\widehat{\mu_k}(t) = 1/N_k(t) \sum_{\tau=1}^{t} r_k(\tau) \mathbb{1}(A(\tau) = k)$. For UCB$_1$, the *confidence* term is $B_k(t) = \sqrt{\alpha \log(t)/N_k(t)}$, giving the upper confidence bound $U_k(t) = \widehat{\mu_k}(t) + B_k(t)$, which is used by the device to decide the channel for communicating at time step $t+1$: $A(t+1) = \arg\max_{1 \leq k \leq N_c} U_k(t)$. UCB$_1$ is an *index policy*.

The UCB$_1$ algorithm uses a parameter $\alpha > 0$, originally, α set to 2 [4], but empirically $\alpha = 1/2$ is known to work better (uniformly across problems), and $\alpha > 1/2$ is advised by the theory [3]. In our model, every dynamic device implements its own UCB$_1$ algorithm, *independently*. For one device, the time t is the number of time it accessed the network (following its Bernoulli transmission process, *i.e.*, its duty cycle), *not* the total number of time slots from the beginning, as rewards are only obtained after a transmission, and IoT objects only transmit sporadicly, due to low transmission duty cycles.

4.3 Thompson Sampling

Thompson Sampling [5] was introduced in 1933 as the very first bandit algorithm, in the context of clinical trials (in which each arm models the efficacy of one treatment across patients). Given a prior distribution on the mean of each arm, the algorithm selects the next arm to draw based on samples from the *conjugated* posterior distribution, which for Bernoulli rewards is a Beta distribution.

A Beta prior $\text{Beta}(a_k(0) = 1, b_k(0) = 1)$ (initially uniform) is assumed on $\mu_k \in [0,1]$, and at time t the posterior is $\text{Beta}(a_k(t), b_k(t))$. After every channel selection, the posterior is updated to have $a_k(t)$ and $b_k(t)$ counting the number of successful and failed transmissions made on channel k. So if the *Ack* message is received, $a_k(t+1) = a_k(t)+1$, and $b_k(t+1) = b_k(t)$, otherwise $a_k(t+1) = a_k(t)$, and $b_k(t+1) = b_k(t)+1$. Then, the decision is done by *sampling* an *index* for each arm, at each time step t, from the arm posteriors: $X_k(t) \sim \text{Beta}(a_k(t), b_k(t))$, and the chosen channel is simply the channel $A(t+1)$ with highest index $X_k(t)$. For this reason, Thompson Sampling is a *randomized index policy*.

Thompson Sampling, although being very simple, is known to perform well for stochastic problems, for which it was proven to be asymptotically optimal [6,7]. It is known to be empirically efficient, and for these reasons it has been used successfully in various applications, including on problems from Cognitive Radio [10,17], and also in previous work on decentralized IoT-like networks [18].

4.4 A Bandit Model for IoT

Our IoT application is challenging in that there are *multiple* players (the dynamic devices) interacting with the *same* arms (the channels), without any centralized communication (they do not even know the total number of dynamic devices).

Considered alone, each dynamic device implements a learning algorithm to play a bandit game, the device is consequently a smart device. In each time slot, if it has to communicate (which happens with probability p), then it chooses a channel and it receives a reward 1 if the transmission is successful, 0 otherwise. Each device aims at maximizing the sum of the rewards collected during its communication instants, which shall indeed maximize the fraction of successful transmissions. Besides the modified time scale (rewards are no longer collected at every time step), this looks like a bandit problem. However, it cannot be modeled as a stochastic MAB, as the rewards are clearly *not i.i.d*: they not only depend on the (stationary, *i.i.d*) behavior of the static devices, but also on the behavior of other smart devices, that is not stationary (because of learning).

Despite this, we show in the next section that running a stochastic bandit algorithm for each device based on its own rewards is surprisingly successful.

Multi-player MAB with *collision avoidance*? Another idea could be to try to use a *multi-player MAB* model, as proposed by [19], to describe our problem.

In that case, the static and dynamic devices effect is decoupled, and arms only model the availability of the channels in the absence of dynamic devices: they are *i.i.d.* with mean $\mu_i = 1 - pS_i$. Moreover, dynamic devices are assumed to be able to *sense* a channel before sending [19], and so communicate only if no static device is detected on the channel. The smart devices try to learn the arms with highest means, while coordinating to choose different arms, *i.e.*, avoid collisions in their choice, in a decentralized manner. However, in this model it is assumed that the multiple agents can know that they experienced a collision with another agent, which is non-realistic for our problem at stake, as our model of smart device cannot do sensing nor differentiate collisions between smart and non-smart devices.

Adversarial **bandit algorithms?** Instead of using MAB algorithms assuming a stochastic hypothesis on the system, we could try to use MAB algorithms designed to tackle a more general problem, that makes no hypothesis on the interfering traffic. The *adversarial MAB* algorithms is a broader family, and a well-known and efficient example is the Exp3 algorithm [3]. Empirically, the Exp3 algorithm turned out to perform worse than both UCB$_1$ and TS in the same experiments. Contrarily to the two stochastic algorithms, the use of Exp3 is correctly justified, even in the non-stationary and non-*i.i.d*, as its performance guarantee are true in *any* setting. But it is not so surprising that it performs worse, as the theoretical performance guarantees of adversarial MAB algorithms are an order of magnitude worse than the one for stochastic ones. More is left on this aspect for our future work.

5   Experiments and Numerical Results

We suppose a network with $S + D = 2000$ end-devices, and one IoT base station. Each device sends packets following a Bernoulli process, of probability $p = 10^{-3}$ (*e.g.*, this is realistic: one packet sent about every 20 minutes, for time slots of 1s). The RF band is divided in $N_c = 10$ channels[3]. Each static device only uses one channel, and their uneven repartition (see footnote 3) in the 10 channels is: $(S_1, \cdots , S_{N_c}) = S \times (0.3, 0.2, 0.1, 0.1, 0.05, 0.05, 0.02, 0.08, 0.01, 0.09)$, to keep the same proportions when S decreases. The dynamic devices have access to all the channels, and use learning algorithms. We simulate the network during 10^6 discrete time slots, during which each device transmits on average 1000 packets (i.e., the learning time is about 1000 steps, for each algorithm).

Figure 2 presents the evolution of the successful transmission rate, as a function of time. The two MAB algorithms, UCB$_1$ and Thompson Sampling (TS), are compared against the naive random policy from below, and the two oracle policies (optimal and greedy) from above. The results are displayed when 10, 30, 50 and 100% of the traffic is generated by dynamic devices.

We can see in Fig. 2 that the TS algorithm (in red) outperforms the UCB$_1$ algorithm (in blue), when the number of end-devices is below 50%. When the

---

[3] We tried similar experiments with other values for N_c and this repartition vector, and results were similar for non-homogeneous repartitions. Clearly, the problem is less interesting for homogeneous repartition, as all channels appear the same for dynamic devices, and so even with D small in comparison to S, the system behaves like in Fig. 2d, where the performance of the five approaches are very close.

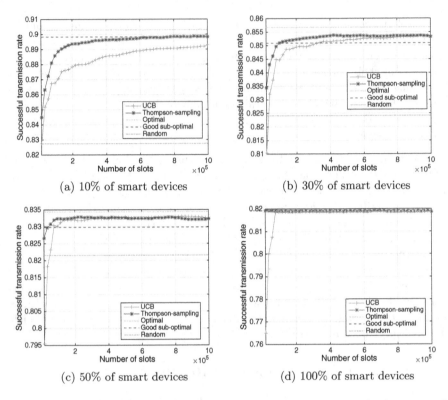

(a) 10% of smart devices

(b) 30% of smart devices

(c) 50% of smart devices

(d) 100% of smart devices

Fig. 2. Performance of 2 MAB algorithms (UCB$_1$ and Thompson Sampling), compared to extreme references without learning or oracle knowledge, when the proportion of smart end-devices in the network increases, from 10% to 100% (limit scenario). (Color figure online)

number of end-devices is higher, both algorithms have almost the same performance, and perform well after very few transmissions (quick convergence). Moreover, we can see in Figs. 2a, b, and c that both have better success rate than the random policy and the probability of successful transmission is between the oracle optimal and oracle suboptimal policies. For instance, for 10% of dynamic devices, after about 1000 transmissions, using UCB$_1$ over the naive uniform policy improved the successful transmission rate from 83% to 88%, and using Thompson Sampling improved it to 89%. Increasing the number of end-devices decreases the gap between the optimal and random policies: the more dynamic devices, the less useful are learning algorithms, and basically for networks with only dynamic devices, the random policy is as efficient as the optimal one, as seen in Figs. 2d and 3.

To better assess the evolution of the optimal policy compared to the random one, we have displayed on Fig. 3 the evolution of the gain, in term of successful transmissions rate, provided by the optimal oracle and the two learning policies, after 10^6 time slots, $i.e.$, about 1000 transmissions for each object. We can see

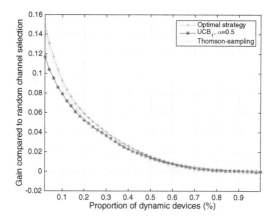

Fig. 3. Learning with UCB$_1$ and Thomson Sampling, with many smart devices.

that when the proportion of end-devices is low (*e.g.*, 1% of devices are dynamic), the optimal policy provides an improvement of 16% compared to random channel selection. The TS algorithm always provides near-optimal performance, but the UCB$_1$ algorithm has a lowest rate of convergence and performs consequently worse after 1000 transmissions, for instance it only provides a gain of 12% for the same proportion of dynamic devices (1%).

Figure 3 also shows that learning keeps near-optimal performance even when the proportion of devices becomes large. Note that when this proportion increases, the assumptions of a stochastic MAB model are clearly violated, and there is no justification for the efficiency of TS and UCB$_1$ algorithms. Hence, it is surprising to have near optimal performance with stochastic MAB algorithms applied to partly dynamic and fully dynamic scenarios.

6   Conclusion

In this article, we proposed an evaluation of the performance of MAB learning algorithms in IoT networks, with a focus on the convergence of algorithms, in terms of successful transmission rates, when the proportion of intelligent dynamic devices changes. Concretely, increasing this probability allows to insert more objects in the same network, while maintaining a good Quality of Service. We show that UCB$_1$ and TS have near-optimal performance, even when their underlying *i.i.d.* assumption is violated by the many "intelligent" end-devices.

This is both a surprising and a very encouraging result, showing that application of bandit algorithms tailored for a stochastic model is still useful in broader settings. The fully *decentralized* application of classic stochastic MAB algorithms are almost as efficient as the best possible centralized policy in this setting, after a short learning period, even though the dynamic devices *can not* communicate with each others, and *do not* know the system parameters. We will investigate this behavior in order to understand it better theoretically. We will also experiment more with adversarial algorithms, to confirm that they work less efficiently than stochastic bandit algorithms in our non-stochastic setting.

Moreover, for sake of simplicity we supposed that all devices use the same standard. Our future work will consider more realistic interference scenarios and IoT networks, with, *e.g.*, non-slotted time, more than one base station etc.

Acknowledgements. This work is supported by the French National Research Agency (ANR), under the projects SOGREEN (grant coded: N ANR-14-CE28-0025-02) and BADASS (N ANR-16-CE40-0002), by Région Bretagne, France, by the French Ministry of Higher Education and Research (MENESR) and ENS Paris-Saclay.

References

1. Centenaro, M., Vangelista, L., Zanella, A., Zorzi, M.: Long-range communications in unlicensed bands: the rising stars in the IoT and smart city scenarios. IEEE Wirel. Commun. **23**(5), 60–67 (2016)
2. Lai, T.L., Robbins, H.: Asymptotically efficient adaptive allocation rules. Adv. Appl. Math. **6**(1), 4–22 (1985)
3. Bubeck, S., Cesa-Bianchi, N., et al.: Regret analysis of stochastic and non-stochastic multi-armed bandit problems. Found. Trends® Mach. Learn. **5**(1), 1–122 (2012)
4. Auer, P., Cesa-Bianchi, N., Fischer, P.: Finite-time analysis of the multi-armed bandit problem. Mach. Learn. **47**(2), 235–256 (2002)
5. Thompson, W.R.: On the likelihood that one unknown probability exceeds another in view of the evidence of two samples. Biometrika **25**, 285–294 (1933)
6. Agrawal, S., Goyal, N.: Analysis of Thompson sampling for the multi-armed bandit problem. In: Conference on Learning Theory, JMLR, p. 39-1 (2012)
7. Kaufmann, E., Korda, N., Munos, R.: Thompson sampling: an asymptotically optimal finite-time analysis. In: Bshouty, N.H., Stoltz, G., Vayatis, N., Zeugmann, T. (eds.) ALT 2012. LNCS (LNAI), vol. 7568, pp. 199–213. Springer, Heidelberg (2012). https://doi.org/10.1007/978-3-642-34106-9_18
8. Haykin, S.: Cognitive radio: brain-empowered wireless communications. IEEE J. Sel. Areas Commun. **23**(2), 201–220 (2005)
9. Jouini, W., Ernst, D., Moy, C., Palicot, J.: Upper confidence bound based decision making strategies and dynamic spectrum access. In: 2010 IEEE International Conference on Communications, pp. 1–5 (2010)
10. Toldov, V., Clavier, L., Loscrí, V., Mitton N.: A Thompson sampling approach to channel exploration-exploitation problem in multihop cognitive radio networks. In: PIMRC, pp. 1–6 (2016)
11. Bonnefoi, R., Moy, C., Palicot, J.: Advanced metering infrastructure backhaul reliability improvement with cognitive radio. In: SmartGridComm, pp. 230–236 (2016)
12. Boyd, S., Vandenberghe, L.: Convex Optimization. Cambridge University, Cambridge (2004)
13. Luenberger, D.G.: Quasi-convex programming. SIAM J. Appl. Math. **16**(5), 1090–1095 (1968)
14. Arrow, K.J., Enthoven, A.C.: Quasi-concave programming. Econometrica **29**(4), 779–800 (1961)

15. Corless, R., Gonnet, G., Hare, D., Jeffrey, D., Knuth, D.: On the lambert $\mathcal{W}$ function. Adv. Comput. Math. **5**(1), 329–359 (1996)
16. Robbins, H.: Some aspects of the sequential design of experiments. Bull. Am. Math. Soc. **58**(5), 527–535 (1952)
17. Maskooki, A., Toldov, V., Clavier, L., Loscrí, V., Mitton, N.: Competition: channel exploration/exploitation based on a Thompson sampling approach in a radio cognitive environment. In: EWSN (2016)
18. Moy, C., Palicot, J., Darak, S.J.: Proof-of-concept system for opportunistic spectrum access in multi-user decentralized networks. EAI Endorsed Trans. Cogn. Commun. **2**, 1–10 (2016)
19. Liu, K., Zhao, Q.: Distributed learning in multi-armed bandit with multiple players. IEEE Trans. Sig. Process. **58**(11), 5667–5681 (2010)

Inter-operator Interference Coordination in the Spectrum-Sharing Overlapping Area

Yiteng Wang[1], Youping Zhao[1($\boxtimes$)] (iD), Xin Guo[2], and Chen Sun[2]

[1] School of Electronic and Information Engineering,
Beijing Jiaotong University, Beijing, China
yozhao@bjtu.edu.cn
[2] Sony China Research Laboratory, Sony (China) Ltd., Beijing, China
{Xin.Guo,Chen.Sun}@sony.com

Abstract. With the widespread application of dynamic spectrum access technology, sharing spectrum with the same primary systems by multiple operators will become a common scenario. Serious co-channel interference (CCI) needs to be mitigated if there is no coordination among the operators. In this paper, a cluster-based interference management algorithm is proposed to reduce the inter-operator CCI in the spectrum-sharing overlapping area. The proposed algorithm consists of two major steps: (1) undirected weighted graph-based clustering and spectrum allocation; (2) signal to interference and noise ratio (SINR) margin-based power adjustment. A novel weight is defined and employed in the clustering procedure to take the SINR requirement of each secondary user (SU) into account. Simulation results show that the ratio of satisfied SUs (whose SINR exceeds their SINR thresholds) can be increased while the sum of co-channel interference is significantly reduced. Furthermore, by introducing a third-party agent, direct exchange of sensitive SU information between different operators can be avoided for better privacy protection.

Keywords: Dynamic Spectrum Access (DSA) · Inter-operator interference
Spectrum Access System (SAS) · Undirected weighted graph

1 Introduction

Cognitive radio (CR) technology, or more specifically, dynamic spectrum access (DSA) is one of the key technologies to address the spectrum shortage problem. In the DSA systems, a spectrum management mechanism named as spectrum access system (SAS) is proposed to authorize and manage the spectrum access with the goal of better spectrum utilization [1]. SAS can serve as "an information and control clearinghouse for the band-by-band registrations and conditions of use that will apply to all users with access to each shared Federal band under its jurisdiction" [1]. How to use the limited

This work is supported in part by Sony China Research Laboratory, Sony (China) Ltd. Prof. Zhao's work is also supported in part by Beijing Natural Science Foundation (4172046).

© ICST Institute for Computer Sciences, Social Informatics and Telecommunications Engineering 2018
P. Marques et al. (Eds.): CROWNCOM 2017, LNICST 228, pp. 186–199, 2018.
https://doi.org/10.1007/978-3-319-76207-4_16

spectrum more efficiently is also the key to successfully apply CR to the fifth-generation (5G) mobile communication systems. With the widespread application of DSA technology, spectrum sharing with the same primary systems by multiple operators will be inevitable.

In the inter-operator spectrum sharing system, also known as the co-primary spectrum sharing system [2], multiple secondary users (SUs) controlled by different SASs coexist with the same primary system (PS) or these SUs share the same spectrum pool. In this case, SASs may be developed by different operators or spectrum policies, resulting in various coexistence scenarios. The common issue to be addressed is the serious inter-operator co-channel interference (CCI) if the SUs belonging to different SASs share the same spectrum without any coordination. Given the quality of service (QoS) requirement of PU, how to mitigate the CCI and increase the number of allowable SUs through the cooperation among SASs is the major issue investigated in this paper.

In this paper, a cluster-based interference management algorithm is proposed, which consists of two major steps: (1) undirected weighted graph-based clustering and spectrum allocation; (2) signal to interference and noise ratio (SINR) margin-based power adjustment. The major contributions of this work are summarized as follows.

(1) A clustering-based spectrum allocation and power adjustment algorithm is proposed to ensure the coexistence of SUs in the spectrum sharing overlapping area of different operators;
(2) A novel weight is defined and employed in the clustering procedure, which takes the SINR requirement of each SU into account;
(3) A new parameter termed as "*SINR margin*" is introduced into the power adjustment procedure to avoid the unnecessary power waste and further reduce the CCI in the spectrum-sharing overlapping area;
(4) A public SAS, which could be an authorized "third-party" agent, is proposed to avoid the direct exchange of sensitive information between SASs for better privacy and security.

Note that the proposed scheme is different from the well-known medium access control (MAC) protocol-carrier sense multiple access with collision avoidance (CSMA/CA). CSMA/CA is a contention-based MAC protocol, while the proposed scheme enables simultaneous transmissions in the same channel and takes the QoS requirements of the spectrum-sharing SUs into account.

The remainder of this paper is organized as follows. In Sect. 2, we briefly summarize the existing work on user clustering and inter-operator interference management. Section 3 provides an overview of the multiple SASs-based spectrum sharing systems and the CCI model. Section 4 discusses the clustering procedure and the clustering-based spectrum allocation. Section 5 discusses the power adjustment procedure based on the newly proposed SINR margin. Simulation results are presented in Sect. 6. Finally, Sect. 7 concludes the paper.

2 Related Works

In this section, literature survey consists of the following three parts: (1) general interference management approaches; (2) clustering-based spectrum allocation and interference management; and (3) inter-operator interference management.

Generally speaking, interference management algorithms can be designed from different domains such as time, space, frequency, and power. Classical interference mitigation approaches in spectrum sharing systems mainly include the precoding algorithm, interference avoidance algorithm and transmit power control algorithm. Precoding algorithm is an interference suppression algorithm by designing the proper precoding matrix according to the specific criteria [3]. Because of the dependence on the spatial freedom, precoding algorithm is applied to the multiple input multiple output (MIMO) systems. Block diagonalization, minimum mean square error (MMSE), signal to the interference leakage and interference (SLNR) maximization and interference alignment are the most commonly used precoding algorithms [4–7]. Interference avoidance algorithms result in the minimum distance between co-channel users to avoid the interference. In [14], the authors design the primary exclusion zone to avoid the PU's interference caused by the SUs and the secondary exclusion zone to avoid the CCI between the co-channel SUs. However, setting the minimum distance between users will lead to lower spatial utilization of the spectrum. Transmit power control method is also a simple but effective interference suppression method by limiting the transmit power [8]. However, sometimes the transmit power might be too low to satisfy the QoS requirement of users.

Various methods for clustering-based spectrum allocation or interference management are also investigated. In [9], a graph-based clustering resource allocation scheme is proposed. However, the interference graph in [9] only contains the interference relationship. In other words, the information conveyed from the graph in [9] is whether there exists interference between two users. The diverse QoS requirements of the users cannot be inferred from the interference graph. As a result, the graph-based clustering resource allocation scheme may not be able to meet the different QoS requirements of the users. A graph-based two-step resource allocation scheme is proposed in [10]. The first step is clustering the users based on the interference graph, and the second step is to allocate the resources within the cluster. Clustering-based interference alignment shows excellent performance in interference management except for the channel information dependence and antenna limitation [11]. The undirected weighted graph in [11] also takes the path loss experienced by the desired signal and co-channel interference into consideration to better reflect the impact of interference.

Inter-operator interference management is different from the intra-operator interference management. Coordination between different operators is necessary, especially in the spectrum-sharing overlapping areas. Resource allocation with concurrent learning for heterogonous long term evolution (LTE) small cells is proposed in [12], which is a dynamic resource allocation scheme with a distributed two-level learning procedure. However, the convergence speed of learning is quite a drawback. In [13], a hierarchical game approach for multi-operator spectrum sharing is proposed to avoid the inter-operator interference. A Kalai-Smorodinsky bargaining game among leaders and a Stackelberg game between operators and mobile users are employed in this approach. The co-primary spectrum sharing scenario is a new spectrum access mode to enable two or more operators to share spectrum resource with the same primary system [2]. In [2], each operator accesses the shared spectrum pool in a non-orthogonal manner with asymmetric power levels to solve the inter-operator interference. But such approach is suitable for the operators with the same priority in spectrum sharing. In summary, the above-mentioned three papers treat the SUs equally, and the various QoS requirements from different users are not considered yet in the proposed algorithms. How to design an interference coordination algorithm with consideration of the various QoS requirements in the spectrum-sharing overlapping area is the major problem to be addressed in this paper. More specifically, the U.S. Federal Communications Commission has proposed a dynamic spectrum management framework for a Citizen Broadband Radio Service (CBRS) governed by SAS [15]. Coexistence of CBRS networks offered by different operators is such an application scenario.

3 System Scenario and Interference Model

In this section, the system scenario of SAS-based spectrum sharing systems with multiple operators is presented and the co-channel interference model is discussed.

3.1 System Scenario

As shown in the Fig. 1, two SAS operators (namely, SAS_1 and SAS_2) coexist with the same PS, and each SAS is in charge of multiple SUs. Each SU consists of a pair of transmitter and receiver. In this paper, "Public SAS" is introduced as an authorized "third-party" agent to coordinate the SASs and exchange necessary information in between. With the "Public-SAS", exchange of sensitive SU information between SASs can be avoided, thus protecting the SUs' privacy.

3.2 Interference Model

As Fig. 1 shows, the management areas of SAS_1 and SAS_2 are overlapped. Serious CCI may exist if there is no coordination between the SASs. The CCI at the i-th SU receiver is defined as follows:

$$I_i = \sum_{j \in A} P_j d_{ij}^{-\alpha_{ij}} \tag{1}$$

where I_i is the CCI of the i-th SU receiver; A is the index set of all co-channel SU transmitters in the overlapping area; P_j is the transmit power of the j-th SU; d_{ij} is the distance between the i-th SU receiver and the j-th SU transmitter; α_{ij} is the path loss exponent corresponding to the radio link between the i-th SU receiver and j-th SU transmitter.

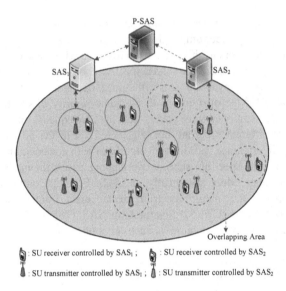

Fig. 1. Inter-operator interference coordination in the spectrum-sharing overlapping area. Note: "P-SAS" is the proposed third-party agent to coordinate the different SASs.

The SINR of a satisfied SU should be no less than its SINR threshold, i.e., $SINR \geq SINR_{th}$. The main problem to be solved is how to increase the ratio of satisfied SUs and reduce the CCI in the overlapping area of different SASs.

The SINR of the i-th SU is calculated by

$$SINR_i = 10 \lg \left(\frac{P_{\max i} d_{ii}^{-\alpha_{ii}}}{\sum_{j \in A} P_{\max j} d_{ij}^{-\alpha_{ij}} + N_0} \right) \tag{2}$$

where $SINR_i$ is the SINR of the i-th SU receiver; P_{maxi} is the maximum transmit power of the i-th SU transmitter; d_{ii} is the distance between the i-th SU receiver and the i-th SU transmitter; α_{ii} is the path loss exponent corresponding to the radio link between the i-th SU receiver and i-th SU transmitter; A is the index set of all co-channel SU transmitters in the overlapping area; P_{maxj} is the maximum transmit power of the j-th SU; d_{ij} is the distance between the i-th SU receiver and the j-th SU transmitter; α_{ij} is the path loss exponent corresponding to the radio link between the i-th SU receiver and j-th SU transmitter; N_0 is the noise power of the i-th SU receiver.

4 Clustering-Based Spectrum Allocation

In this section, the undirected weighted graph is firstly introduced, and then an undirected weighted graph-based clustering procedure is proposed. Finally, the clustering-based spectrum allocation method is introduced.

4.1   Undirected Weighted Graph

As shown in Fig. 2, the undirected weighted graph G = (V, E, W) consists of all secondary systems (SS) in the spectrum-sharing overlapping area, and each SS consists of a pair of SU transmitter and SU receiver. V is the set of vertices and each vertex is corresponding to a SS. E is the set of edges between two SSs. W is the weight set, i.e., W = $\{w_{ij}\}$.

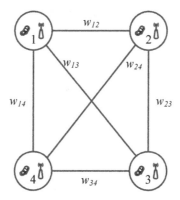

Fig. 2. Undirected weighted graph considering four spectrum-sharing secondary systems

The weight (w_{ij}) can be defined in different ways. The weight defined by (3) reflects the relative interference level to the desired signal. Bigger weight represents the relatively weaker interference. Considering the SUs usually have different QoS requirement, e.g., SINR threshold, the weight in (3) treats the SUs equally. This observation motivated us to define a novel weight which takes the SUs' different QoS requirements into consideration. The newly proposed weight is defined by (4). The weight in (4) is normalized by each SU's SINR threshold, therefore, the weight can reflect the relative interference to the desired signal as well as the SINR requirement. Generally, bigger weight indicates relatively smaller interference.

$$w_{ij} = \frac{P_{\max i} d_{ii}^{-\alpha_{ii}}}{P_{\max j} d_{ij}^{-\alpha_{ij}}} + \frac{P_{\max j} d_{jj}^{-\alpha_{jj}}}{P_{\max i} d_{ji}^{-\alpha_{ji}}}, \tag{3}$$

$$w_{ij} = \frac{P_{\max i} d_{ii}^{-\alpha_{ii}}}{P_{\max j} d_{ij}^{-\alpha_{ij}} SINR_{thi}} + \frac{P_{\max j} d_{jj}^{-\alpha_{jj}}}{P_{\max i} d_{ji}^{-\alpha_{ji}} SINR_{thj}}, \tag{4}$$

where w_{ij} is the weight between the i-th SU pair and the j-th SU pair; $SINR_{thi}$ is the SINR threshold of the i-th SU receiver; $SINR_{thj}$ is the SINR threshold of the j-th SU receiver; the definitions of the other parameters are the same as (2).

4.2   Undirected Weighted Graph-Based Clustering Approach

As shown in Figs. 3 and 4, in order to take the SUs' different QoS requirements (more specifically, SUs' SINR requirements) into account, a clustering procedure is proposed. In some sense, the undirected weighted graph-based clustering procedure can be viewed as a greedy algorithm. The most demanding SU, which has the highest SINR threshold in the un-clustered set, is selected as the first cluster member. Then, select the other members in an order such that the sum of weights remains the largest.

To explain the proposed clustering procedure, a step-by-step illustration is shown in Fig. 3 and discussed as follows. In Fig. 3, as a simple example, there are 4 SSs in the un-clustered set. To establish the first cluster, i.e., Cluster-1, the SINR thresholds of these four SSs are compared and then pick out the most demanding SS, i.e., the SS with the maximal SINR threshold as the first member of Cluster-1. For this example, SS_1 has the highest SINR threshold. Therefore, SS_1 is selected as the first cluster member of Cluster-1. Next, the weights between SS_1 and the other three SSs, i.e., $\{w_{12}, w_{13}, w_{14}\}$, are calculated. Assuming w_{13} is the largest weight among w_{12}, w_{13} and w_{14}, the SS_3 is picked out and put into Cluster-1. Then, the SINR of all SSs in Cluster-1 (i.e., SS_1 and SS_3) are estimated and compared against their corresponding SINR thresholds. If every SS in the Cluster-1 meets its SINR threshold, it confirms that SS_3 can be successfully put into Cluster-1; otherwise, when there is additional channel available, a new cluster (Cluster-2) can to be created to accommodate SS_3. For this example, SS_3 can be successfully put into Cluster-1.

Repeat the same procedure for the remaining SSs in the un-clustered set. The sum of weights between SS_2 and the SSs in Cluster-1 are calculated (i.e., $w_{12} + w_{23}$), which is then compared with the sum of weights between SS_4 and the SSs in Cluster-1 (i.e., $w_{14} + w_{34}$). Assuming $w_{12} + w_{23} > w_{14} + w_{34}$, SS_2 is picked out and put into Cluster-1. The SINR of all SS in Cluster-1 (i.e., SS_1, SS_3, and SS_2) are estimated again and compared against their corresponding SINR thresholds. If all SSs in the Cluster-1 still meet their SINR thresholds, SS_2 can be successfully put into Cluster-1. Otherwise, as long as there is additional available channel, a new cluster needs to be created. Finally, check whether the last SS left in the un-clustered set can be successfully put into Cluster-1. For this example, a new cluster (i.e., Cluster-2) needs to be created to accommodate SS_4. Note: when there is no additional channel available for creating a new cluster, the SSs left in the un-clustered set might be put into the last cluster.

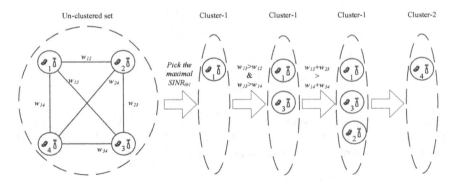

Fig. 3. Illustration of the proposed clustering procedure

In the proposed clustering procedure, each SS's SINR requirement and the interference between different SSs are considered altogether. In this way, the number of satisfied SSs can be increased while reducing the sum of co-channel interference.

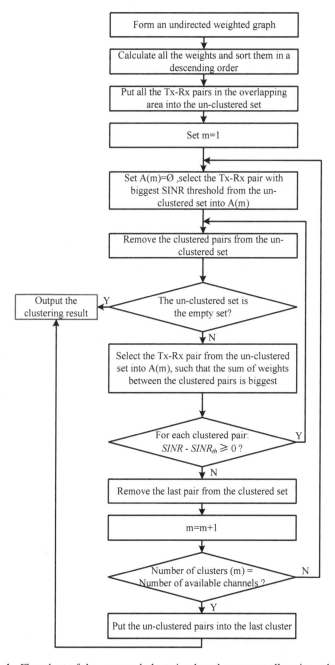

Fig. 4. Flowchart of the proposed clustering-based spectrum allocation scheme

4.3 Clustering-Based Spectrum Allocation Method

Spectrum allocation is based on the clustering result. As the SUs in the same cluster have relatively low interference, SUs in the same cluster can share the same spectrum whereas SUs in different clusters should use different spectrum. SUs are marked by the corresponding cluster index, therefore, SASs can allocate available spectrum to each SU based on its associated cluster index.

The flowchart of the proposed clustering-based spectrum allocation scheme is shown in Fig. 5. Predefined events, such as the change of SINR threshold, may trigger the start of interference coordination by sending the event indicator. An SAS, say, SAS_1, in the overlapping area sends the related information to the public-SAS for clustering. The public-SAS process the received information and then collects the needed information from other SAS, say, SAS_2. Each SAS allocates spectrum to each SU according to the received cluster information from the public-SAS. It's worth noting that the received cluster information of each SAS doesn't contain any user information of the other SASs, thus protecting the privacy of user information.

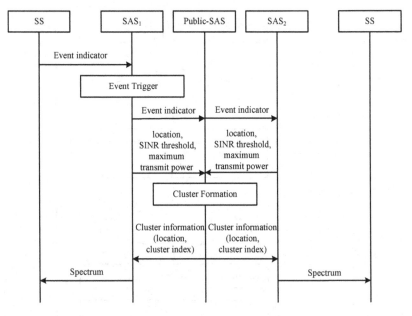

Fig. 5. Flowchart of the proposed clustering-based spectrum allocation scheme. Note that "Public-SAS" is the proposed third-party agent to coordinate the different SASs in the overlapping areas.

5 Power Adjustment Procedure

Once the clustering-based spectrum allocation is completed, power adjustment can be applied to further reduce the sum of CCI.

SINR margin is a newly proposed parameter, which is defined as the difference between the actual SINR and the SINR threshold. In a cluster, it is possible that the actual SINR of some SUs are much bigger than their SINR thresholds. Based on such observation, SINR margin-based power adjustment approach is proposed to reduce the unnecessary SINR margin. By decreasing the transmit power of SU, SINR margin can be reduced to the SINR margin threshold.

SINR margin can be determined for each cluster. For example, when we set the SINR margin threshold to be 0 dB, it means that each SU needs to reduce the transmit power until the SINR of an SU is equal to its SINR threshold.

The flowchart of the clustering-based spectrum allocation and power adjustment scheme is shown in the Fig. 6. After clustering and spectrum allocation, SINR margin threshold of each cluster is determined according to the information of cluster members. And then SUs should reduce their transmit power until its SINR margin is equal to the SINR margin threshold.

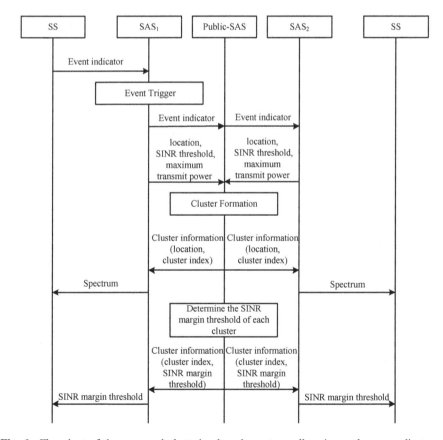

Fig. 6. Flowchart of the proposed clustering-based spectrum allocation and power adjustment scheme. Note that "Public-SAS" is the proposed third-party agent to coordinate the different SASs in the overlapping areas.

6 Performance Simulations

Simulations are conducted to evaluate the performance of the proposed algorithms.

6.1 Simulation Scenario

In the simulation, 12 SSs belonging to different SASs coexist in an area of 100 m × 100 m. For a given time instance, it is assumed that there is only one pair of SU transmitter and receiver in each SS. SSs in the spectrum sharing overlapping area are small cells with various SINR requirements, and the radius of each SS is assumed to be 20 m. The transmitter is at the cell center and the receiver is at the cell edge.

6.2 Simulation Parameters

Major simulation parameters are listed in Table 1. The SINR thresholds of 12 SUs are different from each other, ranging from 9 dB to 20 dB with a step size of 1 dB.

Table 1. List of simulation parameters

Symbol	Definition	Value
N_p	Number of secondary systems (SU Tx-Rx pairs)	12
N_c	Number of available channels	3
NF	Noise figure of SU receiver	5 dB
$SINR_{th}$	SINR threshold	9 dB–20 dB
P_{max1}	Maximum transmit power of the former 6 SUs	3 dBm
P_{max2}	Maximum transmit power of the latter 6 SUs	0 dBm
$\alpha_{ii} = \alpha_{jj}$	Path loss exponent	2.5
$\alpha_{ij} = \alpha_{ji}$	Path loss exponent	3.5
$SINR_{th\_margin}$	SINR margin threshold	0 dB

6.3 Ratio of Satisfied SUs

In this simulation, we only change the random locations of the 12 SUs in 10000 simulation runs, and get the ratio of satisfied SUs (i.e., $SINR \geq SINR_{th}$). As shown in Table 2, the ratio of satisfied SUs can be increased with the proposed weight setting and it can be further increased with the power adjustment.

Table 2. Ratio of satisfied SUs

Algorithm in use	Sequential Coloring [9]	Using the proposed clustering procedure with the existing weight as defined by (3) (without power adjustment)	Using the proposed clustering procedure with the proposed weight as defined by (4) (without power adjustment)	Using the proposed clustering procedure with the proposed weight as defined by (4) (with power adjustment)
Ratio of satisfied SUs	82%	84%	95%	96%

6.4   Comparison of the CDF of SINR

In this simulation, SU_1 has the highest SINR requirement, i.e., 20 dB. In Fig. 7, the SINR cumulative distribution function (CDF) curve corresponding to SU_1 is plotted. As shown in Fig. 7, in sense of probability of satisfying the SINR threshold, the proposed weight scheme results in better performance than the existing weight. The probability of failing to meet the SINR requirement is about 6% with the sequential coloring algorithm when using the existing weight, while it is reduced to 0% when adopting the proposed weight setting. In addition, the SINR values are more concentrated after applying the power adjustment.

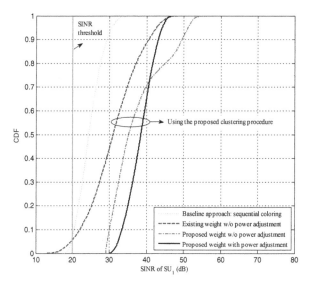

Fig. 7. CDF of SINR of SU_1

6.5   Sum of Co-channel Interference

In this simulation, the sum of co-channel interference is defined by (5).

$$I_{sum} = \sum_{m=1}^{Nc} \sum_{i,j \in C_m} P_j d_{ij}^{-\alpha_{ij}} \tag{5}$$

where C_m represents the m-th cluster; N_c is total number of the clusters in the overlapping area; P_j is the transmitting power of the j-th SS; d_{ij} is the distance between the transmitter in the j-th SS to the receiver in the i-th SS; α_{ij} is the path loss exponent between the transmitter in the j-th SS to the receiver in the i-th SS.

Figure 8 shows the sum of co-channel interference when using different algorithms. Simulation results demonstrate that the proposed weight leads to better performance in terms of sum interference as compared to the traditional weight. Furthermore, the sum of interference can be further reduced with the power adjustment according to the SINR margin.

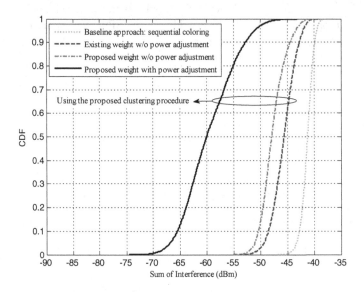

Fig. 8. CDF of the sum of interference

7   Conclusion

In this paper, the inter-operator interference in the overlapping area of different SASs is addressed without directly exchanging SUs' sensitive information between SASs. A clustering-based spectrum allocation and power adjustment scheme is proposed to improve the ratio of satisfied SUs while reducing the sum of co-channel interference. In the clustering procedure, a novel weight is defined and employed in the undirected weighted graph, which takes each SU's SINR requirement into account. Furthermore, the SINR margin-based power adjustment is employed to further reduce the sum interference. Simulation results, such as the ratio of satisfied SUs, the CDF of SINR and the sum interference, demonstrate the effectiveness and advantages of the proposed algorithm. The proposed scheme is also applicable to scenarios with mobile SUs. The only difference is that the clustering algorithm needs to be conducted periodically in response to the topology changes due to UE mobility. Given the limited number of available channels, when the number of SUs keeps increasing, not all SUs' QoS requirements could be satisfied through clustering and power adjustment. Further interference management (such as interference alignment) can be applied within each cluster to accommodate even more SUs, which is worthy investigation in the future.

References

1. PCAST Report to the President. Realizing the Full Potential of Government-Held Spectrum to Spur Economic Growth. Executive Office of the President and President's Council of Advisors on Science and Technology, July 2012

2. Yu, Q., Wang, J., Yang, X., Zhu, Y., Teng, Y., Kari, H.: Inter-operator interference coordination for co-primary spectrum sharing in UDN. China Commun. **12**, 104–112 (2015)

3. Jung, M., Hwang, K., Choi, S.: Interference minimization approach to precoding scheme in MIMO-based cognitive radio networks. IEEE Commun. Surv. Tutor. **15**(8), 789–791 (2011)

4. Lee, K.-J., Lee, I.: MMSE based block diagonalization for cognitive radio MIMO broadcast channels. IEEE Trans. Multimedia **10**(10), 3139–3144 (2011)

5. Park, J., Lee, B., Shim, B.: A MMSE vector precoding with block diagonalization for multiuser MIMO downlink. IEEE Trans. Commun. **60**(2), 569–577 (2012)

6. Sun, C., Ge, J., Bao, X., Shi, X.: A leakage-based precoding scheme for cognitive multiuser MIMO systems. In: IEEE 4th International Conference on Intelligent Networking and Collaborative Systems, Salerno, pp. 562–565 (2012)

7. Xu, Y., Mao, S.: Distributed interference alignment in cognitive radio networks. In: IEEE 22nd International Conference on Computer Communications and Networks (ICCCN), Nassau, pp. 1–7 (2013)

8. Yeh, S., Shilpa, T., Nageen, H., Kerstin, J.: Power control based interference mitigation in multi-tier networks. In: IEEE GLOBECOM Workshops, Miami, USA, pp. 701–705 (2010)

9. Zhang, Q., Zhu, X., Wu, L., Sandrasegaran, K.: A coloring-based resource allocation for OFDMA femtocell networks. In: IEEE Wireless Communications and Networking Conference (WCNC), pp. 673–678 (2013)

10. Pateromichelakis, E., Shariat, M., Quddus, A., Tafazolli, R.: Dynamic clustering framework for multi-cell scheduling in dense small cell networks. IEEE Commun. Lett. **17**(9), 1802–1805 (2013)

11. Chen, S., Cheng, R.S.: Clustering for interference alignment in a multiuser interference channel. In: Proceedings of the IEEE VTC, Yokohama, Japan, pp. 1–5, May 2012

12. Bikov, E., Ghamri-Doudane, Y., Botvich, D.: Smart resource allocation with concurrent learning scheme for heterogeneous LTE small cell networks. In: IEEE Global Communications Conference (GLOBECOM), San Diego, California, USA (2015)

13. Zhang, H., Xiao, Y., Cai, L.X., Niyato, D., Song, L., Han, Z.: A hierarchical game approach for multi-operator spectrum sharing in LTE unlicensed. In: IEEE GLOBECOM, San Diego, California, USA (2015)

14. Tefek, U., Lim, T.J.: Interference management through exclusion zones in two-tier cognitive networks. IEEE Trans. Wireless Commun. **15**(3), 2292–2302 (2016)

15. Sohul, M.M., Yao, M., Yang, T., Reed, J.H.: Spectrum Access System for the Citizen Broadband Radio Service. IEEE Commun. Mag. **53**(7), 18–25 (2015)

Blind Symbol Rate Estimation of Faster-than-Nyquist Signals Based on Higher-Order Statistics

Albert Abelló[1,2](✉) [ID], Damien Roque[2] [ID], and Jean-Marie Freixe[1]

[1] Eutelsat S.A., Paris, France
aabellob@eutelsat.com
[2] Institut Supérieur de l'Aéronautique et de l'Espace (ISAE-SUPAERO),
Université de Toulouse, Toulouse, France

Abstract. Both faster-than-Nyquist (FTN) and cognitive radio go towards an efficient use of spectrum in radio communications systems at the cost of an added computational complexity at the receiver side. To gain the maximum potential from these techniques, non-data-aided receivers are of interest. In this paper, we use fourth-order statistics to perform blind symbol rate estimation of FTN signals. The estimator shows good performance results for moderate system's densities beyond the Nyquist rate and for a reasonable number of received samples.

Keywords: Blind symbol rate estimation · Spectrum sensing
Faster-than-Nyquist signaling · Cyclostationary signals
Higher-order statistics

1 Introduction

Cognitive radio (CR) is primarily intended to improve the utilization of the radio electromagnetic spectrum [8]. To this end, a CR system can be basically described by a two-step process: (i) radio scene analysis (*i.e.*, detection of spectrum holes, estimation of the signal-to-interference-plus-noise ratio...) and (ii) selection and operation of an appropriate waveform (*i.e.*, channel estimation, transmit power control...). Among the constraints to be fulfilled by the chosen waveform, flexibility and spectral efficiency are found at the top of the list [2].

In the past decades, radio transmission systems were tied to the Nyquist criterion to ensure perfect reconstruction of the symbols with the help of linear systems. The symbol rate was thus bounded by the bilateral bandwidth of the transmitted signal and the only way to increase the spectral efficiency was to increase the constellation size. Even if significant improvements in the receivers sensitivity justify this approach, one may still wonder if the Nyquist criterion is a necessary condition for reliable transmission of information.

The idea of "faster-than-Nyquist" (FTN) signaling was first developed by Mazo [11] in 1975: the symbol rate is increased such that interpulse interference

© ICST Institute for Computer Sciences, Social Informatics and Telecommunications Engineering 2018
P. Marques et al. (Eds.): CROWNCOM 2017, LNICST 228, pp. 200–210, 2018.
https://doi.org/10.1007/978-3-319-76207-4_17

cannot be cancelled by linear filtering at the receiver side. However, FTN systems operating below the Mazo limit may preserve similar performance to that of Nyquist systems, at the cost of non-linear processing [6]. Unfortunately, the additional algorithmic complexity induced has delayed the implementation of FTN systems for several decades. Iterative equalization and decoding techniques [5,19] combined with increasing computational capabilities have renewed the interest in FTN signaling, enabling spectral efficiency gains up to 8–20 % [1,10, 12,14,15].

In most applications, pilots and preambles are usually inserted to assist synchronization in receivers. However, it is preferable not to send these helper elements to preserve the spectral efficiency brought by FTN. It is thus desirable to perform non-data-aided (*i.e.*, blind) spectrum sensing, synchronization, channel estimation... However, FTN signaling rises several challenges due to the absence of second-order cyclic-correlation features, as it will be shown in the following. In particular, state of the art signal detection and blind symbol rate estimation techniques using second-order cyclostationarity do not apply in the FTN case [9,13,18].

In this paper, we show that a fourth-order extension of the symbol rate estimator presented in [4] is required to operate on FTN signals. We discuss the performance of our estimator in terms of dynamic range with respect to several parameters such as the transmission density or the number of received symbols.

The paper is organized as follows. Section 2 first defines a single-carrier FTN signal model and analyzes the conditions under which higher-order cyclostationary features are present. Secondly, a blind symbol rate estimator for FTN signals is proposed using the reduced-dimension cyclic temporal moment function. Section 3 discusses the performance of the proposed estimator by means of simulations over an additive white Gaussian noise (AWGN) channel. Concluding remarks and insights are presented in Sect. 4.

2 System Model: Single-Carrier Linear Transmitter

2.1 Faster-than-Nyquist Signaling

Let $\{c_k\}_{k\in\mathbb{Z}}$ be a square summable sequence of independent and identically distributed (IID) symbols to be transmitted. Each complex symbol c_k is taken in a constellation $\mathbb{A}$. The complex baseband signal at the output of the transmitter is obtained by associating each c_k with a pulse shape $h(t) \in \mathbb{C}$ of finite energy

$$s(t) = \sum_{k=-\infty}^{\infty} c_k\, h(t - kT_s), \quad t \in \mathbb{R} \tag{1}$$

with T_s the elementary symbol spacing.

For this system, we can define the transmission density as $\rho = 1/(T_s B)$ where B is the transmitted signal bandwidth (assumed finite). Based on the frame theory [3, Chap. 7], one can note that:

– if $\rho \leq 1$, perfect symbol recovery can be obtained using a linear receiver;
– if $\rho > 1$, inter-symbol interference unconditionally appears at the output of a linear receiver, but symbols may still be recovered by using a nonlinear post-processing, knowing the initial constellation [6].

The former category includes traditional Nyquist systems while the latter defines FTN systems throughout this paper.

2.2 Higher-Order Statistics of FTN Signals

The nth-order statistical moment of the transmitted signal is given by [7]

$$
R_s(t, \boldsymbol{\tau})_n = \mathrm{E}\left\{\prod_{i=1}^{n} s^{(*)i}(t + \tau_i)\right\} = \mathrm{E}\left\{\prod_{i=1}^{n} \sum_{k=-\infty}^{\infty} c_k^{(*)i} h^{(*)i}(t - kT_s + \tau_i)\right\}
$$

$$
= \sum_{k_1 \in \mathbb{Z}} \cdots \sum_{k_n \in \mathbb{Z}} \mathrm{E}\left\{c_{k_1}^{(*)1} \ldots c_{k_n}^{(*)n}\right\} h^{(*)1}(t - k_1 T_s + \tau_1) \ldots h^{(*)n}(t - k_n T_s + \tau_n) \quad (2)
$$

where $(\cdot)^{(*)i}$ indicates an optional conjugation on the ith factor and $\boldsymbol{\tau} = [\tau_1, \ldots, \tau_n]^T$, with $(\cdot)^T$ the transpose operator. In the following, we consider any conjugation set that allows the expectation in (2) being non-zero for some combination $k_1, \ldots, k_n$. A discussion on this choice can be found in [16]. The second and higher-order moment functions of a linearly modulated signal have been widely described in [17]. One remarks from (2) that $R_s(t + T_s, \boldsymbol{\tau})_n = R_s(t, \boldsymbol{\tau})_n$. We consider that $R_s(t, \boldsymbol{\tau})_n$ is absolutely integrable over a period T_s so that we can develop the Fourier series with coefficients

$$
R_s^{\alpha}(\boldsymbol{\tau})_n = \frac{1}{T_s} \int_{-T_s/2}^{T_s/2} R_s(t, \boldsymbol{\tau})_n e^{-j2\pi\alpha t} \mathrm{d}t \quad (3)
$$

where α denotes the cyclic frequency which may be non-zero for particular values $p/T_s, p \in \mathbb{Z}$. The expression in (3) is commonly referred to as the cyclic temporal moment function (CTMF). The transmitted signal is said nth order cyclostationary if there exists some non-zero α such that (3) is non-zero. To prove that higher-order cyclostationary features are present in FTN signals, let us consider the case $k_1 = k_2 = \cdots = k_n = k$ yielding

$$
R_s(t, \boldsymbol{\tau})_n = R_{c,n} \sum_{k=-\infty}^{\infty} \prod_{i=1}^{n} h^{(*)i}(t - kT_s + \tau_i) \quad (4)
$$

where we define $R_{c,n} = \mathrm{E}\left\{|c_k|^n\right\}$ assumed non-zero in the following. Without loss of generality and for the sake of simplicity, we consider here the reduced-dimension cyclic temporal moment function (RD-CTMF) by setting $\tau_n = 0$

$$
R_s^{\alpha}(\boldsymbol{\tau}')_n = \frac{1}{T_s} \int_{-T_s/2}^{T_s/2} R_s(t, \boldsymbol{\tau}')_n e^{-j2\pi\alpha t} \mathrm{d}t
$$

$$
= \frac{R_{c,n}}{T_s} \int_{-\infty}^{\infty} h^{(*)n}(t) \prod_{i=1}^{n-1} h^{(*)i}(t + \tau_i) e^{-j2\pi\alpha t} \mathrm{d}t \quad (5)
$$

where $\boldsymbol{\tau}' = [\tau_1, \ldots, \tau_{n-1}]^T$, are the reduced-dimension time lags. Since linearly modulated signals considered here are assumed bandlimited, a frequency representation of the RD-CTMF is of interest. To this extent, we introduce the reduced-dimension cyclic spectral moment function (RD-CSMF):

$$S_s^\alpha(\boldsymbol{f}')_n = \int_{\boldsymbol{\tau}'} R_s^\alpha(\boldsymbol{\tau}')_n \, e^{-j2\pi \boldsymbol{f}'^T \boldsymbol{\tau}'} \mathrm{d}\boldsymbol{\tau}' \tag{6}$$

where $\boldsymbol{f}' = [f_1, \ldots, f_{n-1}]^T$ are the reduced-dimension frequency lags. Let us define $\boldsymbol{1} = [1, \ldots, 1]^T$ the indicator column vector function of size $n-1$. For the sake of notation simplicity, we consider in the following that the pulse shape takes values in the real field (*i.e.*, $h(t) \in \mathbb{R}$). It can be then shown [17] that

$$S_s^\alpha(\boldsymbol{f}')_n = \frac{R_{c,n}}{T_s} H(\alpha - \boldsymbol{1}^T \boldsymbol{f}') \prod_{i=1}^{n-1} H(f_i) \tag{7}$$

where $H(f)$ is the Fourier transform of the impulse response $h(t)$, assumed bandlimited such that $H(f) = 0$ if $f \notin [-B/2; B/2]$. After having derived the nth order RD-CSMF, we focus on two particular cases, $n = 2$ and $n = 4$.

Example 1 (Second-order cyclostationarity). We obtain from (7):

$$S_s^\alpha(\boldsymbol{f}')_2 = \frac{R_{c,2}}{T_s} H(\alpha - f_1) H(f_1), \quad \alpha = \frac{p}{T_s}, \ p \in \mathbb{Z}. \tag{8}$$

One remarks that

- if $\rho \leq 1$ (non-FTN case), then $1/T_s \leq B$ and there exists $f_1 \in \mathbb{R}, p \in \mathbb{Z}^*$ such that $S_s^\alpha(\boldsymbol{f}')_2 \neq 0$;
- if $\rho > 1$ (non-FTN case), then $1/T_s > B$ and $S_s^\alpha(\boldsymbol{f}')_2 = 0$ for any $f_1 \in \mathbb{R}$ and $p \in \mathbb{Z}^*$.

In other words, the transmitted signal is not cyclostationary at the second order for FTN signals. This fact is crucial and makes it theoretically impossible to blindly estimate the symbol rate of FTN systems by means of a second order cyclostationary analysis of the received signals.

Example 2 (Fourth-order cyclostationarity). We obtain from (7):

$$S_s^\alpha(\boldsymbol{f}')_4 = \frac{R_{c,4}}{T_s} H(\alpha - (f_1 + f_2 + f_3)) H(f_1) H(f_2) H(f_3) \tag{9}$$

One remarks that independently of the value of ρ, there exists $\boldsymbol{f}', p \in \mathbb{Z}^*$ such that

$$S_s^\alpha(\boldsymbol{f}')_4 \neq 0. \tag{10}$$

Therefore, a fourth-order analysis of the received signals allows blind symbol rate estimation for both non-FTN and FTN signals by means of an appropriate processing to be specified in the next Section.

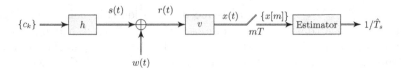

Fig. 1. Linear transmission system over a bandlimited AWGN channel.

2.3   Proposed Estimator over the AWGN Channel

System model is depicted in Fig. 1. White noise with spectral density $2N_0$ is added to the linearly modulated signal:

$$r(t) = s(t) + w(t). \tag{11}$$

An ideal bandlimiting filter with frequency response $V(f) = 1/\sqrt{B}$ if $|f| \leq B/2$ and $V(f) = 0$ otherwise is then applied to the received signal so that

$$x(t) = (r * v)(t) = \sum_{k=0}^{K-1} c_k (h * v)(t - kT_s) + (w * v)(t)$$

$$= \sum_{k=0}^{K-1} c_k g(t - kT_s) + n(t) \tag{12}$$

where $g(t) = (h*v)(t)$, $n(t) = (w*v)(t)$ and where K is the number of transmitted symbols. The signal is sampled at instants mT. We consider without loss of generality that T_s is a multiple of T:

$$x(mT) = \sum_{k=0}^{K-1} c_k g(mT - kT_s) + n(mT) \tag{13}$$

with $n(mT) \sim \mathcal{CN}(0, \sigma_n^2)$. Due to the finite impulse response of the transmission filter, we consider that $x(mT)$ can be truncated to M non-zero samples. At the receiver, an estimation of the RD-CTMF (5) is obtained by [17]

$$\hat{R}_x^\alpha(\tau') = \frac{1}{T} \sum_{m=0}^{M-1} x^{(*)n}(mT) \prod_{i=1}^{n-1} x^{(*)i}(mT + \tau_i) e^{-j2\pi \frac{\alpha}{M} mT}. \tag{14}$$

where the transmitted signal is assumed to be nth order cycloergodic so that the expectation in (2) can be replaced by a time average [16]. The chosen blind symbol rate estimator based on [4] first computes (14) for all discrete delay vectors τ' taken in $\mathcal{T} = \{-\Delta\tau/2, -\Delta\tau/2 + 1, \ldots, \Delta\tau/2\}^n$ with $\Delta\tau$ a positive integer. Secondly, the sum of squared absolute values from the previous step is maximized with respect to the (non-zero) cyclic frequency:

$$1/\hat{T}_s = \operatorname*{argmax}_{\alpha \neq 0} \Psi(\alpha) \tag{15}$$

with

$$\Psi(\alpha) = \sum_{\tau' \in \mathcal{T}} |\hat{R}_x^\alpha(\tau')|^2. \tag{16}$$

In the following, the transmitted signal is built using a binary phase-shift keying (BPSK) constellation and a pulse shaping filter $h(t)$ chosen as a square-root-raised cosine (SRRC) with roll-off factor 0.2. Considering this excess bandwidth, the inter-symbol interference (ISI)-free reference is at $\rho = 0.83$. The oversampling factor is given by $T_s/T = 10$ and we set $T = 1$. Furthermore, (14) is implemented with a discrete Fourier transform so that $\alpha \in \mathcal{F}$ with $\mathcal{F} = \{-1/2, -1/2 + 1/M, \dots, 1/2 - 1/M\}$. Subsequent notation assumes that $0, -1/T_s, 1/T_s \in \mathcal{F}$. However, approximate values do not change significantly the results as M gets large enough.

To illustrate the previous analysis, the empirical fourth-order RD-CTMF is depicted in Fig. 2 in an FTN case ($\rho = 1.2$). A peak at $\alpha = 1/T_s$ confirms the ability to blindly estimate the symbol rate in the absence of noise. In Fig. 3, the signal-to-noise ratio is given by $E_b/N_0 = 5$ dB with E_b the energy per transmitted bit. Clearly, an observation of length $K = 600$ symbols is not sufficient to reveal cyclic features while $K = 60000$ seems sufficient.

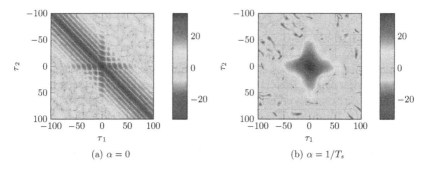

(a) $\alpha = 0$ (b) $\alpha = 1/T_s$

Fig. 2. Estimated fourth-order RD-CTMF, $10 \log \left(\hat{R}_s^\alpha(\tau') \right)$, after $K = 60000$ transmitted symbols, $\rho = 1.2$, section $\tau_3 = 0$.

We note that for $\alpha = 1/T_s$, the energy is distributed over a given delay span bounded by $\Delta\tau$. This observation will allow us in the following Section to configure the proposed ad-hoc symbol rate estimator.

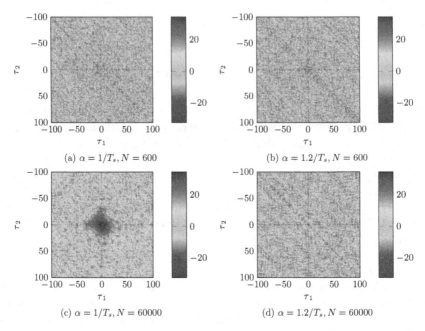

(a) $\alpha = 1/T_s, N = 600$

(b) $\alpha = 1.2/T_s, N = 600$

(c) $\alpha = 1/T_s, N = 60000$

(d) $\alpha = 1.2/T_s, N = 60000$

Fig. 3. Estimated fourth-order RD-CTMF, $10\log\left(\hat{R}_x^\alpha(\tau')\right)$ for $E_b/N_0 = 5$ dB, $\rho = 1.2$, section $\tau_3 = 0$.

3   Simulations

As stated before, the proposed estimator sums the available estimated RD-CTMFs over the delay span $\Delta\tau$ to produce a peak at the transmitted symbol rate. The estimated symbol rate corresponds to the cyclic frequency that maximizes $\Psi(\alpha)$. Figure 4 shows the aforementioned function to be maximized (excluding the continuous component $\alpha = 0$). Consequently, the estimator performance may be roughly measured through the dynamic range of $\Psi(\alpha)$, defined as the ratio between its value at the actual symbol rate and its mean:

$$R = \frac{\Psi(1/T_s)}{\bar{\Psi}(\alpha)} \tag{17}$$

where

$$\bar{\Psi}(\alpha) = \frac{1}{M-1} \sum_{\alpha \in \mathcal{F}\backslash\{0\}} \Psi(\alpha). \tag{18}$$

Figure 5 shows the dynamic range of the blind symbol rate estimator for different values of the maximum delay span $\Delta\tau$. As the span increases, the performance increases as well since the received white noise samples are averaged in time. In the following simulations, the time lag span is fixed to 10 samples.

Figure 6 shows the dynamic range of the blind symbol rate estimator for different system's densities. The dynamic range decreases with system's density

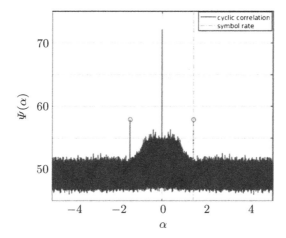

Fig. 4. Sum over $\tau_1, \ldots, \tau_3$ of the estimated fourth-order RD-CTMF, $E_s/N_0 = 5\,\mathrm{dB}$, $\rho = 1.2$, $K = 60000$ received symbols.

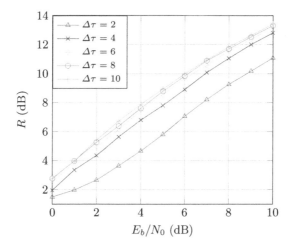

Fig. 5. Dynamic range of the symbol rate estimator for $\rho = 1.2$ and $K = 60000$.

and increases with E_b/N_0. After evaluating the dynamic range for various system densities, we observe that it is not linear in ρ and that density values above $\rho = 1.4$ yield a dynamic range close to $0\,\mathrm{dB}$ making impossible the symbol rate estimation with the values of E_b/N_0 and K considered so far.

The impact of the observed frame length on the dynamic range is shown in Fig. 7 for $\rho = 1.2$. We show that for a given frame length, there is an E_b/N_0 threshold from which correct estimation is possible.

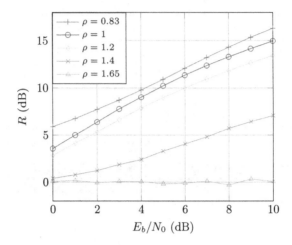

Fig. 6. Dynamic range of the symbol rate estimator for $K = 60000$.

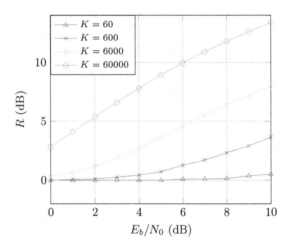

Fig. 7. Dynamic range of the symbol rate estimator for $\rho = 1.2$.

4   Conclusion

In this paper, we have addressed the problem of blind symbol rate estimation of FTN signals using fourth-order statistics. After showing that at least fourth-order statistics are required in the FTN case, we have evaluated by simulation the performance of an ad-hoc blind symbol rate estimator. Simulations show that performance is highly dependent on system's density, available frame length, and signal-to-noise ratio. In particular, the fourth-order symbol rate estimator shows good performance results for moderate system's densities (up to $\rho = 1.4$) and for high frames length (around $K = 60000$ received symbols). Future work should address the high density and short-length case by introducing other than fourth-order statistical signatures of the received signals. In addition to the dynamic range measurement, it would also be appropriate to extend the estimator performance evaluation to the calculation of its statistics. This work could also be extended to the case of general channel models.

Acknowledgements. The authors would like to thank Nghia Pham from Eutelsat S.A. and Thomas Gilles from ISAE-SUPAERO for their valuable comments and remarks. This work has been supported by the *Direction Générale de l'Armement* (DGA) under the CIFRE grant 10/2015/DGA.

Appendix: Statistical Moments for Different Conjugations

Below are listed all possible conjugation combinations and the resulting expectation term in the autocorrelation function in (2). We restrict our analysis up to fourth-order statistics of BPSK and quadrature phase-shift keying (QPSK) constellations. The expectation term has been defined as

$$R_{c,n} = \mathrm{E}\left\{ c_{k_1}^{(*)1} \ldots c_{k_n}^{(*)n} \right\}.$$

For a given constellation, we list below all possible combinations for the particular case $k_1 = k_2, \ldots, k_n = k$:

$R_{c,1} \in \{\mathrm{E}\{c_k\}, \mathrm{E}\{c_k^*\}\},$

$R_{c,2} \in \{\mathrm{E}\{c_k c_k\}, \mathrm{E}\{c_k^* c_k\}, \mathrm{E}\{c_k^* c_k^*\}\},$

$R_{c,3} \in \{\mathrm{E}\{c_k c_k c_k\}, \mathrm{E}\{c_k^* c_k c_k\}, \mathrm{E}\{c_k^* c_k^* c_k\} \mathrm{E}\{c_k^* c_k^* c_k^*\}\},$

$R_{c,4} \in \{\mathrm{E}\{c_k c_k c_k c_k\}, \mathrm{E}\{c_k^* c_k c_k c_k\}, \mathrm{E}\{c_k^* c_k^* c_k c_k\}, \mathrm{E}\{c_k^* c_k^* c_k^* c_k\}, \mathrm{E}\{c_k^* c_k^* c_k^* c_k^*\}\}.$

For a BPSK constellation with $c_k \in \{1, -1\}$, we have $R_{c,1} = \{0, 0\}$, $R_{c,2} = \{1, 1, 1\}$, $R_{c,3} = \{0, 0, 0, 0\}$, $R_{c,4} = \{1, 1, 1, 1, 1\}$.

For a QPSK constellation with $c_k \in \{1 + j, 1 - j, -1 + j, -1 - j\}/\sqrt{2}$, we obtain $R_{c,1} = \{0, 0\}$, $R_{c,2} = \{0, 1, 0\}$, $R_{c,3} = \{0, 0, 0, 0\}$, $R_{c,4} = \{-1, 0, 1, 0, -1\}$.

Odd orders lead to all statistical moments being zero for zero-mean constellations. For the fourth-order statistical moments, additionally, the particular cases $k_1 = k_2, k_3 = k_4$ and $k_1 = k_3, k_2 = k_4$ are not zero and yield the same statistical moments presented before.

References

1. Abello, A., Roque, D., Freixe, J.M., Mallier, S.: Faster-than-Nyquist signaling: on linear and non-linear reduced-complexity turbo equalization. Analog Integr. Circ. Sig. Process. **91**, 1–10 (2017)
2. Arslan, H.: Cognitive Radio, Software Defined Radio, and Adaptive Wireless Systems, vol. 10. Springer, Heidelberg (2007). https://doi.org/10.1007/978-1-4020-5542-3

3. Christensen, O.: Frames and Bases: An Introductory Course. Applied and Numerical Harmonic Analysis. Springer/Birkhäuser, Boston/London (2008). https://doi. org/10.1007/978-0-8176-4678-3. OHX

4. Ciblat, P., Loubaton, P., Serpedin, E., Giannakis, G.B.: Asymptotic analysis of blind cyclic correlation-based symbol-rate estimators. IEEE Trans. Inf. Theory **48**(7), 1922–1934 (2002)

5. Douillard, C., Jézéquel, M., Berrou, C., Picart, A., Didier, P., Glavieux, A.: Iterative correction of intersymbol interference: turbo-equalization. Euro. Trans. Telecommun. **6**(5), 507–511 (1995)

6. Forney, G.: Maximum-likelihood sequence estimation of digital sequences in the presence of intersymbol interference. IEEE Trans. Inf. Theory **18**(3), 363–378 (1972)

7. Gardner, W.A., Spooner, C.M.: The cumulant theory of cyclostationary timeseries. I. Foundation. IEEE Trans. Signal Process. **42**(12), 3387–3408 (1994)

8. Haykin, S.: Cognitive radio: brain-empowered wireless communications. IEEE J. Sel. Areas Commun. **23**(2), 201–220 (2005)

9. Jallon, P., Chevreuil, A.: Estimation of the symbol rate of linearly modulated sequences of symbols. Sig. Process. **88**(8), 1971–1979 (2008)

10. Maalouli, G., Bannister, B.A.: Performance analysis of a MMSE turbo equalizer with LDPC in a FTN channel with application to digital video broadcast. In: 2014 48th Asilomar Conference on, Signals, Systems and Computers, pp. 1871–1875, November 2014

11. Mazo, J.E.: Faster-than-Nyquist signaling. Bell Syst. Tech. J. **54**(8), 1451–1462 (1975)

12. McGuire, M., Sima, M.: Discrete time faster-than-Nyquist signalling. In: 2010 IEEE Global Telecommunications Conference (GLOBECOM 2010), pp. 1–5, December 2010

13. Napolitano, A.: Cyclostationarity: new trends and applications. Sig. Process. **120**, 385–408 (2016)

14. Pham, N., Anderson, J.B., Rusek, F., Freixe, J.M., Bonnaud, A.: Exploring fasterthan-Nyquist for satellite direct broadcasting. In: AIAA International Communications Satellite Systems Conference, pp. 16–26 (2013)

15. Prlja, A., Anderson, J.: Reduced-complexity receivers for strongly narrowband intersymbol interference introduced by faster-than-Nyquist signaling. IEEE Trans. Commun. **60**(9), 2591–2601 (2012)

16. Renard, J., Verlant-Chenet, J., Dricot, J.M., De Doncker, P., Horlin, F.: Higherorder cyclostationarity detection for spectrum sensing. EURASIP J. Wirel. Commun. Netw. **2010**(1), 721695 (2010)

17. Spooner, C.M., Gardner, W.A.: The cumulant theory of cyclostationary timeseries. II. development and applications. IEEE Trans. Signal Process. **42**(12), 3409–3429 (1994)

18. Turunen, V., Kosunen, M., Huttunen, A., Kallioinen, S., Ikonen, P., Parssinen, A., Ryynanen, J.: Implementation of cyclostationary feature detector for cognitive radios. In: 2009 4th International Conference on Cognitive Radio Oriented Wireless Networks and Communications, pp. 1–4, June 2009

19. Tüchler, M., Singer, A.C.: Turbo equalization: an overview. IEEE Trans. Inf. Theory **57**(2), 920–952 (2011)

Impact of Uncertainty About a User to be Active on OFDM Transmission Strategies

Andrey Garnaev$^{(\boxtimes)}$, Wade Trappe, Ratnesh Kumbhkar,
and Narayan B. Mandayam

WINLAB, Rutgers University, North Brunswick, USA
garnaev@yahoo.com, {trappe,ratnesh,narayan}@winlab.rutgers.edu

Abstract. In this paper we investigate the impact that incomplete knowledge regarding user activity can have on the equilibrium transmission strategy for an OFDM-based communication system. The problem is formulated as a two user non-zero sum game for independent fading channel gains, where the equilibrium strategies are derived in closed form. This allows one to show that a decrease in uncertainty about the user activity could reduce the number of subcarriers jointly used by the users. For the boundary case (with complete information, which reflects a classical water-filling game) the equilibrium strategies are given explicitly. The necessary and sufficient conditions, when channels sharing strategies are optimal, is established as well as the set of shared subcarriers is identified. The stability of the upper bound of the size of this set with respect to power budgets is derived.

Keywords: OFDM · Nash equilibrium · NC-OFDM
Multicarrier modulation

1 Introduction

Multiuser power control problems in wireless networks employing orthogonal frequency division multiplexing (OFDM) technology [15] and its variants like noncontiguous orthogonal frequency division multiplexing (NC-OFDM), where only a subset of all subcarriers are used due to either to avoid incumbent transmissions or tactical considerations [19] have received significant research interest in current and future wireless communication systems due to their reliability, adaptability and spectral efficiency. Selfish behaviour of users in OFDM style systems has been extensively studied in the literature (see, for example [11], and references therein). An important tool for designing optimal power allocation as well as estimating their effectiveness is game theory. This is due to the fact that, in general, such systems are multi-agent systems where each agent has its own (selfish) goal to achieve. Game theory supplies solutions for such multi-agent problems as well as methods to find them (see, for example [11] as a survey for such concepts and applications to wireless problems). In [21], a multiuser power control problem in a frequency-selective interference channel was modeled by a

© ICST Institute for Computer Sciences, Social Informatics and Telecommunications Engineering 2018
P. Marques et al. (Eds.): CROWNCOM 2017, LNICST 228, pp. 211–222, 2018.
https://doi.org/10.1007/978-3-319-76207-4_18

two-player game. A condition on fading channel gains was derived to guarantee existence of a Nash equilibrium as well as that this equilibrium is unique and stable, i.e., an iterative water-filling algorithm can efficiently reach the Nash equilibrium. In [12], a power allocation problem in the downlink of wireless networks, where multiple access points send independent coded network information to multiple mobile terminals through orthogonal channels was formulated as non-zero sum game. It was proven that this is a potential game having a unique equilibrium with probability one. In [16], a problem to maximize information rates for the Gaussian frequency-selective interference channel was formulated as a noncooperative game of complete information and an asynchronous iterative water-filling algorithm was proposed to achieve the Nash equilibria. In [1], closed form solutions for the symmetric water-filling game with equal crosstalk coefficients was obtained. This allows one to derive the conditions for which there is a unique solution or multiple solutions. In [17], the saddle point was found explicitly in a jamming game where a user and a jammer has enough energy to employ all the channels in their optimal behaviour. In [3,4], a game theoretic analysis of secret and reliable communication under combined jamming and eavesdropping attack was given. In [18], a problem of multiband transmission under hostile jamming modeled by zero-sum game was solved. In [9], a bargaining solution over the fair trade-off between secrecy and throughput was derived.

In this paper, we investigate the impact that incomplete knowledge about user activity can have on the equilibrium OFDM transmission strategy. The problem is formulated as a two user non-zero sum game for independent fading channel gains. This impact is investigated by means of two algorithms developed to find equilibrium strategies. The first is the best response strategies algorithm illustrating learning mechanism to reach an equilibria. The second one is a superposition of two bisection methods based describing the equilibrium in closed form. For the case of complete knowledge about whether a user is active (which corresponds to classical water-filling problem) the equilibrium strategies are given explicitly. To the best of our knowledge, this classical water-filling game has not been yet solved explicitly in the literature. The necessary and sufficient conditions for when subcarrier sharing strategies are optimal is established, as well as the set of shared subcarriers is identified.

The organization of this paper is as follows: in Sect. 2, a model of transmission with incomplete information is formulated, and the convergence of the best response algorithm is proven. In Sect. 3, the equilibrium strategies are derived in closed form as well as an algorithm to find them based on superposition of bisection methods is given. In Sect. 4, for the boundary case of complete information the strategies are found explicitly. Finally, in Sect. 5, conclusions are offered, and in Appendix sketch of the proof of the obtain results are given.

2   Formulation of the Problem

We assume that the total spectrum band that can be used jointly by *two users* for communication with *one receiver* is split into n subcarriers. *One of the users (called, user 1) is active, i.e., he communicates with certainty.* User 1 has only a priori knowledge about the other user (called, user 2) being active. Namely, *user 1 knows that with a priori probability q^1 that user 2 will be active, while with probability q^0 user 2 will not be active.*

The strategy of user j ($j = 1, 2$) is a power allocation vector $\boldsymbol{P}^j = (P_1^j, \ldots, P_n^j)$ with $P_i^j \geq 0$ is the power assigned to transmit in subcarrier i, $\sum_{i=1}^n P_i^j = \overline{P}^j$ where $\overline{P}^j$ is the total power to transmit. Let Π^j be the set of all feasible strategies for user j. The payoff v^1 to user 1 is the expected throughput, while the payoff v^2 to user 2 is the throughput given as follows:

$$
\begin{aligned}
v^1(\boldsymbol{P}^1, \boldsymbol{P}^2) &= q^1 \sum_{i=1}^n \ln\left(1 + \frac{h_i^1 P_i^1}{\sigma^2 + h_i^2 P_i^2}\right) + q^0 \sum_{i=1}^n \ln\left(1 + \frac{h_i^1 P_i^1}{\sigma^2}\right), \\
v^2(\boldsymbol{P}^1, \boldsymbol{P}^2) &= \sum_{i=1}^n \ln\left(1 + \frac{h_i^2 P_i^2}{\sigma^2 + h_i^1 P_i^1}\right),
\end{aligned}
\tag{1}
$$

where h_i^j is the fading channel gains and σ^2 is the background noise power. Thus, in (1), we deal with the scenario involving independent fading channels.

Since user 1 has only a priori knowledge about whether user 2 is active, while user 2 knows about his activity, this is a *Bayesian game* [11]. Bayesian approaches have been widely used for modeling network problems, such as to incorporate an incentive mechanism in a cooperative medium access scheme in a wireless relaying network [13], to design anti-eavesdropping strategies when eavesdropper might be an active adversary [6], and for intrusion detection in wireless ad hoc networks [20].

We look for (Nash) equilibrium strategies. Recall that $(\boldsymbol{P}_*^1, \boldsymbol{P}_*^2)$ is an equilibrium if and only if for any $(\boldsymbol{P}^1, \boldsymbol{P}^2)$ the following inequalities holds: $v^1(\boldsymbol{P}^1, \boldsymbol{P}_*^2) \leq v^1(\boldsymbol{P}_*^1, \boldsymbol{P}_*^2)$ and $v^2(\boldsymbol{P}_*^1, \boldsymbol{P}^2) \leq v^2(\boldsymbol{P}_*^1, \boldsymbol{P}_*^2)$. Thus, $(\boldsymbol{P}_*^1, \boldsymbol{P}_*^2)$ is an equilibrium if and only if they are the best response strategy to each other. i.e., $\boldsymbol{P}_*^1 = \mathrm{BR}^1(\boldsymbol{P}_*^2) := \arg_{\boldsymbol{P}^1 \in \Pi^1} \max v^1(\boldsymbol{P}^1, \boldsymbol{P}_*^2)$ and $\boldsymbol{P}_*^2 = \mathrm{BR}^2(\boldsymbol{P}_*^1) := \arg_{\boldsymbol{P}^2 \in \Pi^2} \max v^2(\boldsymbol{P}_*^1, \boldsymbol{P}^2)$.

Theorem 1

(a) *The considered game has an equilibrium.*

(b) *The best response strategies* $(\boldsymbol{P}^1, \boldsymbol{P}^2) = (\mathrm{BR}^1(\boldsymbol{P}^2), \mathrm{BR}^2(\boldsymbol{P}^1))$ *can be found in water-filling form as follows:*

$$
P_i^1 = P_i^1(\omega) := \left\lfloor \frac{1}{2\omega} - \frac{h_i^2 P_i^2 + 2\sigma^2}{2h_i^1} + \frac{1}{2}\sqrt{\left(\frac{1}{\omega} - \frac{h_i^2 P_i^2}{h_i^1}\right)^2 + 4q^0 \frac{h_i^2 P_i^2}{(h_i^1)^2}} \right\rfloor_+, i = 1, \ldots, n
$$

with ω being the unique root of the equation $\sum_{i=1}^n P_i^1(\omega) = \overline{P}^1$ and

$$
P_i^2 = P_i^2(\omega) := \lfloor 1/\omega - (\sigma^2 + h_i^1 P_i^1)/h_i^2 \rfloor_+, i = 1, \ldots, n
$$

with ω being the unique root of the equation $\sum_{i=1}^n P_i^2(\omega) = \overline{P}^2$.

(c) *The best-response algorithm converges to an equilibrium. Namely, let $\boldsymbol{P}_0^2$ be any strategy of user 2, $\boldsymbol{P}_1^1 = \mathrm{BR}^1(\boldsymbol{P}_0^2)$, $\boldsymbol{P}_1^2 = \mathrm{BR}^2(\boldsymbol{P}_1^1)$ and so on. Then, $(\boldsymbol{P}_k^1, \boldsymbol{P}_k^2)$ converges to an equilibrium.*

3   Equilibrium Strategies in Closed Form

In this section, we obtain the solution in closed form as a function of two auxiliary parameters. This allows us to examine the structure of the strategies as well as to design an alternative algorithm based on the bisection method, which can find these parameters and thereby determine the equilibrium strategies.

Theorem 2. *The equilibrium strategies $(\boldsymbol{P}^1, \boldsymbol{P}^2)$ of the considered game with $q^0 > 0$ must have the following form with ω^1 and ω^2 as positive parameters:*

$$
P_i^1 = P_i^1(\omega^1, \omega^2) := \begin{cases} \dfrac{q^0}{\omega^1 - q^1 h_i^1 \omega^2/h_i^2} - \dfrac{\sigma^2}{h_i^1}, & i \in I_{11}(\omega^1, \omega^2), \\[2mm] \dfrac{1}{\omega^1} - \dfrac{\sigma^2}{h_i^1}, & i \in I_{10}(\omega^1, \omega^2), \\[2mm] 0, & i \in I_{00}(\omega^1, \omega^2) \cup I_{01}(\omega^1, \omega^2), \end{cases}
$$

$$\tag{2}$$

$$
P_i^2 = P_i^2(\omega^1, \omega^2) := \begin{cases} \dfrac{1}{\omega^2} - \dfrac{h_i^1}{h_i^2}\dfrac{q^0}{\omega^1 - q^1 h_i^1 \omega^2/h_i^2}, & i \in I_{11}(\omega^1, \omega^2), \\[2mm] \dfrac{1}{\omega^2} - \dfrac{\sigma^2}{h_i^2}, & i \in I_{01}(\omega^1, \omega^2), \\[2mm] 0, & i \in I_{00}(\omega^1, \omega^2) \cup I_{10}(\omega^1, \omega^2), \end{cases}
$$

$$\tag{3}$$

with

$$
\begin{aligned}
I_{00}(\omega^1, \omega^2) &= \{i : 1/\sigma^2 \le \omega^1/h_i^1, 1/\sigma^2 \le \omega^2/h_i^2\}, \\
I_{10}(\omega^1, \omega^2) &= \{i : 1/\sigma^2 > \omega^1/h_i^1, \omega^1/h_i^1 \le \omega^2/h_i^2\}, \\
I_{01}(\omega^1, \omega^2) &= \{i : 1/\sigma^2 > \omega^2/h_i^2, q^1\omega^2/h_i^2 + q^0/\sigma^2 \le \omega^1/h_i^1\}, \\
I_{11}(\omega^1, \omega^2) &= \{i : \omega^2/h_i^2 < \omega^1/h_i^1 < q^1\omega^2/h_i^2 + q^0/\sigma^2\}.
\end{aligned}
$$

In particular, Theorem 2 (and subsequently Theorem 4) specify the subcarriers that are either not used (I_{00}), or used by just one of the users (I_{10}) and (I_{10}), or by both users (I_{11}). The strategies can be considered *subcarrier-sharing* if the set of the shared subcarriers I_{11} is empty.

Theorem 3. *The set of subcarriers $I_{11}(\omega^1, \omega^2)$ employed by the users for joint use is non-decreasing in probability q^0.*

The value of the parameters ω^1 and ω^2 are defined based on the condition that the power resources $H^1(\omega^1, \omega^2)$ and $H^2(\omega^1, \omega^2)$ employed by $\boldsymbol{P}^1(\omega^1, \omega^2)$ and $\boldsymbol{P}^2(\omega^1, \omega^2)$ have to be equal to $\overline{P}^1$ and $\overline{P}^2$, i.e.,

$$
H^k(\omega^1, \omega^2) := \sum_{i=1}^{n} P_i^k(\omega^1, \omega^2) = \overline{P}^k, k = 1, 2. \tag{4}
$$

In the following Proposition, which follows directly from Theorem 2, auxiliary properties of the functions H^1 and H^2 are given.

Proposition 1

  (a) For a fixed ω^2, $H^1(\omega^1, \omega^2)$ is continuous on ω^1 and decreasing from infinity for $\omega^1 \downarrow 0$ to zero for $\omega^1 \geq \max_i(q^0/\sigma^2 + q^1\omega^2/h_i^2)$.

  (b) For a fixed ω^1, $H^1(\omega^1, \omega^2)$ is continuous and increasing on ω^2 such that

$$H^1(\omega^1, 0) = \sum_{i=1}^{n} \lfloor q^0/\omega^1 - \sigma^2/h_i^1 \rfloor_+,$$

$$H^1(\omega^1, \omega^2) = \sum_{i=1}^{n} \lfloor 1/\omega^1 - \sigma^2/h_i^1 \rfloor_+ \text{ for } \omega^2 \geq \omega^1 \max_i(h_i^2/h_i^1).$$

  (c) For a fixed ω^2 there is an $\Omega^1(\omega^2)$ such that

$$H^1(\Omega^1(\omega^2), \omega^2) = \overline{P}^1. \tag{5}$$

  (d) $\Omega^1(\omega^2)$ is continuous and increasing on ω^2 such that $\Omega^1(0) = \underline{\omega}^1$ and $\Omega^1(\infty) = \overline{\omega}^1$ with $\underline{\omega}^1$ and $\overline{\omega}^1$ uniquely given as roots of the equations:

$$\sum_{i=1}^{n} \lfloor q^0/\underline{\omega}^1 - \sigma^2/h_i^1 \rfloor_+ = \overline{P}^1 \text{ and } \sum_{i=1}^{n} \lfloor 1/\overline{\omega}^1 - \sigma^2/h_i^1 \rfloor_+ = \overline{P}^1. \tag{6}$$

  (e) For a fixed ω^1, $H^2(\omega^1, \omega^2)$ is continuous on ω^2 and decreasing from infinity for $\omega^2 \downarrow 0$ to zero for $\omega^2 \geq \underline{\omega}^2 := \max_i h_i^2 \max\{1/\sigma^2, \omega^1/h_i^1\}$.

  (f) $H^2(\Omega^1(\omega^2), \omega^2)$ is continuous on ω^2 such that $H(\Omega^1(\omega^2), \omega^2)$ tends to infinity for ω^2 tending to zero, and $H^2(\Omega^1(\omega^2), \omega^2) = 0$ for $\omega^2 \geq \underline{\omega}^2$. Thus, the root of the following equation exists and it can be found by bisection method:

$$H^2(\Omega^1(\omega^2), \omega^2) = \overline{P}^2. \tag{7}$$

Proposition 2 and Theorem 2 directly imply the following main result:

Theorem 4. *For $q^0 > 0$ the equilibrium strategies are given by (2) and (3), where $\omega^1 = \Omega^1(\omega^2)$ with Ω^1 given by (5), while ω^2 is given by (7). Due to the monotonic properties of H^1 and H^2 the $\Omega^1(\omega^2)$ can be found by the bisection method for each fixed ω^2, while the optimal ω^2 can be found by the superposition of two bisection methods.*

As an illustrative example throughout the paper we consider the total spectrum band consisting of five subcarriers, i.e., $n = 5$, the background noise power is $\sigma^2 = 1$ and the fading channel gains are $h^1 = (0.2, 0.5, 0.4, 0.1, 0.6)$, $h^2 = (0.23, 0.1, 0.5, 0.15, 1)$. Figure 1 illustrates an increase in the payoff to user 1 and a decrease in the payoff to user 2 with an increase in a priori probability q^0 for user 2 to be non-active. Of course, an increase in the power resource of user 2 leads to an increase in his payoff and in a reduction of the payoff to user 1. Figure 2 illustrates that for small power budget of user 2 ($\overline{P}^2 = 0.5$) the users employ subcarrier sharing strategies (i.e. I_{11} is empty). An increase in his power budget makes the user to employ the subcarriers user 1 also uses. Namely, for

$\overline{P}^2 = 1$ the set I_{11} is empty for $q^0 < 0.57$ and $I_{11} = \{5\}$ for $q^0 > 0.57$. While for $\overline{P}^2 = 1.5$ the set $I_{11} = \{3\}$ for $q^0 < 0.75$ and $I_{11} = \{3,5\}$ for $q^0 > 0.75$. Thus, an increase in the probability q^0 leads to an increase in interference reflected by an increase in number of the subcarriers involved in being jointly employed by both users.

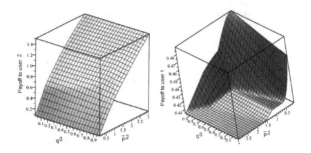

Fig. 1. The payoff to user 2 (left) and the payoff to user 1 (right) as functions on a priori probability q^0 and power budget $\overline{P}^2$ with $\overline{P}^1 = 1$.

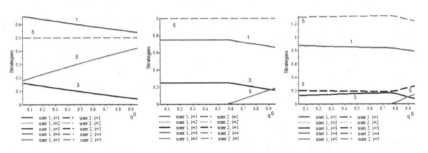

Fig. 2. Strategies of users for $\overline{P}^2 = 0.5$ (left), $\overline{P}^2 = 1$ (center) and $\overline{P}^2 = 1.5$ (right) with $\overline{P}^1 = 1$.

4   Both Users Always are Active: Explicit Solution

In this section we obtain the equilibrium strategies explicitly in an important boundary case for the a priori probability $q^0 = 0$, i.e., when both users always are active. This case coincides with two-person water-filling game in classical framework with independent fading channel gains. To get the equilibrium explicitly let us introduce an auxiliary notations. First, to avoid bulkiness in formulas we assume that all the subcarriers are different in ratio of fading channel gains for the users, i.e., $h_i \neq h_j$ with $i \neq j$, where $h_i := h_i^2/h_i^1$. Then, without loss of generality we can assume that the subcarriers are arranged in increasing order on ratio

$$h_1 < h_2 < \ldots < h_n < h_{n+1} := \infty. \tag{8}$$

$$\sum_{i=1}^{k} \left\lfloor \frac{1}{\omega_k^1} - \frac{\sigma^2}{h_i^1} \right\rfloor_+ = \overline{P}^1 \text{ and } \sum_{i=k+1}^{n} \left\lfloor \frac{1}{\omega_k^2} - \frac{\sigma^2}{h_i^2} \right\rfloor_+ = \overline{P}^2. \tag{9}$$

Due to the left side of the first equation (9) is decreasing on ω and increasing on k we have that $\omega_{k+1}^1 > \omega_k^1$. While due to the left side of the second equation (9) is decreasing on ω and k we have that $\omega_{k+1}^2 < \omega_k^2$. Thus, ξ_k is decreasing on k where

$$\xi_k := \omega_k^2/\omega_k^1 \text{ for } k = 1, \dots, n-1 \text{ and } \xi_0 = \infty \text{ and } \xi_n = 0. \tag{10}$$

Theorem 5. *The considered game with $q^0 = 0$ has the unique equilibrium $(\boldsymbol{P}^1, \boldsymbol{P}^2)$.*
    (a) If

$$h_k \le \xi_k < h_{k+1} \tag{11}$$

then

$$P_i^1 = \begin{cases} \left\lfloor \dfrac{1}{\omega_k^1} - \dfrac{\sigma^2}{h_i^1} \right\rfloor_+, & i \le k, \\ 0, & i \ge k+1, \end{cases} \text{ and } P_i^2 = \begin{cases} 0, & i \le k, \\ \left\lfloor \dfrac{1}{\omega_k^2} - \dfrac{\sigma^2}{h_i^2} \right\rfloor_+, & i \ge k+1. \end{cases} \tag{12}$$

    (b) If

$$\xi_k < h_k < \xi_{k-1} \tag{13}$$

then

$$P_i^1 = \begin{cases} \left\lfloor \dfrac{1}{\omega^1} - \dfrac{\sigma^2}{h_i^1} \right\rfloor_+, & i \le k-1, \\ \overline{P}^1 - \displaystyle\sum_{j=1}^{k-1} \left\lfloor \dfrac{1}{\omega^1} - \dfrac{\sigma^2}{h_i^1} \right\rfloor_+ & i = k, \\ 0, & i \ge k+1, \end{cases} \quad P_i^2 = \begin{cases} 0, & i \le k-1, \\ \overline{P}^2 - \displaystyle\sum_{j=1}^{k-1} \left\lfloor \dfrac{1}{\omega^2} - \dfrac{\sigma^2}{h_i^2} \right\rfloor_+, & i = k, \\ \left\lfloor \dfrac{1}{\omega^2} - \dfrac{\sigma^2}{h_i^2} \right\rfloor_+, & i \ge k+1, \end{cases} \tag{14}$$

with

$$\omega^2 = h_k \omega^1 \tag{15}$$

and ω^1 is the unique positive root of the equation

$$F(\omega^1) := \sum_{j=1}^{k} \left\lfloor \frac{1}{\omega^1} - \frac{\sigma^2}{h_i^1} \right\rfloor_+ + \sum_{j=k+1}^{n} \left\lfloor \frac{1}{\omega^1} - \frac{\sigma^2 h_k}{h_i^2} \right\rfloor_+ = \overline{P}^1 + h_k \overline{P}^2. \tag{16}$$

Since ξ_i is decreasing while h_i is increasing, the condition (11) and (13) uniquely define the switching subcarrier k. The equilibrium strategies cannot jointly employ more than one subcarrier. It is interesting to note that a similar band sharing phenomena we can observe in bandwidth scanning strategy under incomplete information about adversary's activity [5,7,8]. If (11) holds than the strategies are subcarrier sharing while if (13) holds the equilibrium strategies subcarrier sharing except the only subcarrier k which they use jointly. Thus, (11) is the necessary and sufficient condition for the equilibrium strategy to be subcarrier sharing. Figure 3(left) illustrates that an increase in power budget of user 2 leads to a decrease in switching subcarrier while an increase in power budget of user 1 impacts on switching subcarrier in opposite way. Also, it illustrates sequential switching between the criteria with an increase of users' power budgets. Figure 3(center) illustrates that an increase in power budget to user 2 leads to an increase in switching subcarrier k, while an decrease in power budget to user 1 yields into an increase in k. An increase of power budget to a user leads to an increase in his payoff and in a decrease in the payoff to the other (Fig. 3(right)). A surprising property of the equilibrium strategies is that an increase in power budgets cannot lead to employing more than one subcarrier for joint using. This is quite different from the scenario with one of the users being malicious where an increase in power budgets make the users employ more and more subcarriers [10, 17].

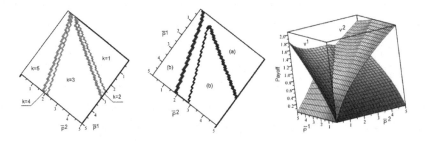

Fig. 3. The switching subcarrier k (left) and the cases of Theorem 5 (center) and payoffs to the users (right) as functions on $\overline{P}^1$ and $\overline{P}^2$.

5   Conclusions

In this paper, by means of a two users non-zero sum OFDM transmission game with independent fading channel gains, we investigate an impact of incomplete knowledge about whether a user is active on the equilibrium transmission strategy. Two algorithms to find equilibrium strategies are given. The first is the best response strategies algorithm illustrating learning mechanism to reach an equilibria. The second one is a superposition of two bisection methods based describing the equilibrium in on closed form. It allows to show that an decrease in uncertainty about the user to be active reduces size of the set of shared subcarriers. For the boundary case (i.e. complete knowledge about a user to be present, which reflects a classical water-filling game) the equilibrium strategies are given explicitly. The necessary and sufficient conditions, when subcarrier sharing strategies are optimal, is established, as well as the set of shared subcarriers is identified. Stability of the upper bound of size of this subcarriers' set to an increase of users' power budgets is proven, what can be applicable for NC-OFDM networks.

Acknowledgments. This work is supported in part by a grant from the U.S. Office of Naval Research (ONR) under grant number N00014-15-1-2168.

A Appendix

Proof of Theorem 1: Since $v^j(\boldsymbol{P}^1, \boldsymbol{P}^2)$ is concave on $\boldsymbol{P}^j$, (a) follows [2]. The KKT Theorem straightforward implies (b).

(c) It is clear that the sets of equilibrium coincide for the games with payoffs scaled by positive multiplies. That is why, to find equilibrium instead of the original game with payoffs (v^1, v^2) we can consider equivalent game with payoffs $(V^1, V^2) = (v^1, q^1 v^2)$. The last game is an exact potential game [14], and so, the best response algorithm converges. Recall that the game with payoffs (V^1, V^2) is an exact potential game if and only if there is a function $V(\boldsymbol{P}^1, \boldsymbol{P}^2)$ such that for any strategies $(\boldsymbol{P}^1, \boldsymbol{P}^2)$ and $(\boldsymbol{P}^1_*, \boldsymbol{P}^2_*)$ the following conditions hold:

$$V(\boldsymbol{P}^1_*, \boldsymbol{P}^2) - V(\boldsymbol{P}^1, \boldsymbol{P}^2) = V^1(\boldsymbol{P}^1_*, \boldsymbol{P}^2) - V^1(\boldsymbol{P}^1, \boldsymbol{P}^2),$$
$$V(\boldsymbol{P}^1, \boldsymbol{P}^2_*) - V(\boldsymbol{P}^1, \boldsymbol{P}^2) = V^2(\boldsymbol{P}^1, \boldsymbol{P}^2_*) - V^2(\boldsymbol{P}^1, \boldsymbol{P}^2). \tag{17}$$

It is clear for the function

$$V(\boldsymbol{P}^1, \boldsymbol{P}^2) = q^1 \sum_{i=1}^{n} \ln(\sigma^2 + h_i^1 P_i^1 + h_i^2 P_i^2) + q^0 \sum_{i=1}^{n} \ln(\sigma^2 + h_i^1 P_i^1)$$

the condition (17) holds, and the result follows. ∎

Proof of Theorem 2: Since $v^j(\boldsymbol{P}^1, \boldsymbol{P}^2)$ is concave on $\boldsymbol{P}^j$, by KKT Theorem, $(\boldsymbol{P}^1, \boldsymbol{P}^2)$ is an equilibrium if and only if there are ω^1 and ω^2 (Lagrangian multipliers) such that the following conditions hold:

$$\frac{q^1 h_i^1}{\sigma^2 + h_i^1 P_i^1 + h_i^2 P_i^2} + \frac{q^0 h_i^1}{\sigma^2 + h_i^1 P_i^1} \begin{cases} = \omega^1, & P_i^1 > 0, \\ \leq \omega^1, & P_i^1 = 0, \end{cases} \tag{18}$$

$$\frac{h_i^2}{\sigma^2 + h_i^1 P_i^1 + h_i^2 P_i^2} \begin{cases} = \omega^2, & P_i^2 > 0, \\ \leq \omega^2, & P_i^2 > 0. \end{cases} \tag{19}$$

Thus, by (18) and (19), we have that

(a) if $P^1 = 0$ and $P^2 = 0$ then $h_i^1/\sigma^2 \leq \omega^1$ and $h_i^2/\sigma^2 \leq \omega^2$,

(b) if $P^1 > 0$ and $P^2 = 0$ then $P_i^1 = 1/\omega^1 - \sigma^2/h_i^1$ with $h_i^1/\sigma^2 > \omega^1$ and $h_i^2/h_i^1 \leq \omega^2/\omega^1$.

(c) if $P^1 = 0$ and $P^2 > 0$ then $P_i^2 = 1/\omega^2 - \sigma^2/h_i^2$ with $h_i^2/\sigma^2 > \omega^2$ and $q^1 h_i^1/h_i^2 \omega^2 + q^0 h_i^1/\sigma^2 \leq \omega^1$.

(d) if $P^1 > 0$ and $P^2 > 0$ then

$$P_i^1 = \frac{q^0}{\omega^1 - q^1 h_i^1 \omega^2/h_i^2} - \frac{\sigma^2}{h_i^1} \quad \text{and} \quad P_i^2 = \frac{1}{\omega^2} - \frac{h_i^1}{h_i^2} \frac{q^0}{\omega^1 - q^1 h_i^1 \omega^2/h_i^2},$$

and the result follows. ∎

Proof of Theorem 3: The set of the channels jointly used by both users is $I_{11}(\omega^1, \omega^2) = \{i : \omega^2/h_i^2 < \omega^1/h_i^1 < q^1 \omega^2/h_i^2 + q^0/\sigma^2\}$. First, note that due to $q^1 \omega^2/h_i^2 + q^0/\sigma^2 > \omega^2/h_i^2$ and $q^0 + q^1 = 1$ yield that $\sigma^2 > \omega^2/h_i^2$. Then, $q^1 \omega^2/h_i^2 + q^0/\sigma^2 = q^0(1/\sigma^2 - \omega^2/h_i^2) + \omega^2/h_i^2$ is increasing on q^0, and the result follows. ∎

Proof of Theorem 5: Since $v^j(\boldsymbol{P}^1, \boldsymbol{P}^2)$ is concave on $\boldsymbol{P}^j$, by KKT Theorem, $(\boldsymbol{P}^1, \boldsymbol{P}^2)$ is an equilibrium if and only if there are ω^1 and ω^2 (Lagrangian multipliers) such that the following conditions hold for $m = 1, 2$:

$$\frac{h_i^m}{\sigma^2 + h_i^1 P_i^1 + h_i^2 P_i^2} \begin{cases} = \omega^m, & P_i^m > 0, \\ \leq \omega^m, & P_i^m = 0. \end{cases} \tag{20}$$

Then, by (20),

$$(P_i^1, P_i^2) = \begin{cases} (0, 0), & h_i^1/\omega^1 \leq \sigma^2 \text{ and } h_i^2/\omega^2 \leq \sigma^2, \\ \left(\dfrac{1}{\omega^1} - \dfrac{\sigma^2}{h_i^1}, 0\right), & h_i^1/\omega^1 > \sigma^2 \text{ and } h_i^2/\omega^2 \leq h_i^1/\omega^1, \\ \left(0, \dfrac{1}{\omega^2} - \dfrac{\sigma^2}{h_i^2}\right), & h_i^2/\omega^2 > \sigma^2 \text{ and } h_i^1/\omega^1 \leq h_i^2/\omega^2, \\ \sigma^2 + h_i^1 P_i^1 + h_i^2 P_i^2 = \dfrac{h_i^1}{\omega^1} = \dfrac{h_i^2}{\omega^2}, & h_i^1/\omega^1 = h_i^2/\omega^2 > \sigma^2. \end{cases} \tag{21}$$

By (21), if $P_i^1 > 0$ and $P_i^2 > 0$ then $h_i^2/h_i^1 = \omega^2/\omega^1$. Thus, by (8), both strategies can employ only at most one channel for joint use. Moreover, there is a k such that

$$P_i^1 \begin{cases} > 0, & i < k - 1, \\ \geq 0, & i = k, \\ = 0, & i > k, \end{cases} \quad \text{and } P_i^2 \begin{cases} = 0, & i < k - 1, \\ \geq 0, & i = k, \\ > 0, & i > k, \end{cases} \tag{22}$$

where (a) $P_k^1 > 0$ and $P_k^2 > 0$ if $h_k^2/h_k^1 = \omega^2/\omega^1$, (b) $P_k^1 > 0$ and $P_k^2 = 0$ if $h_k^2/h_k^1 < \omega^2/\omega^1$, and (c) $P_k^1 = 0$ and $P_k^2 > 0$ if $h_k^2/h_k^1 > \omega^2/\omega^1$.

Thus, by assumption (8), we have to consider separately two cases: (A) there is a k such that $h_k < \omega^2/\omega^1 < h_{k+1}$, (B) there is a k such that $h_k = \omega^2/\omega^1$.

(A) Let there exist a k such that $h_k < \omega^2/\omega^1 < h_{k+1}$. Then, by (21), (22) and the fact that $\boldsymbol{P}^1 \in \Pi^1$ and $\boldsymbol{P}^2 \in \Pi^2$, we have that $\boldsymbol{P}^1$ and $\boldsymbol{P}^2$ have to be given by (12), and $\omega^1 = \omega_k^1$ and $\omega^2 = \omega_k^2$. Thus, (11) also has to hold.

(B) Let there exist a k such that $h_k = \omega^2/\omega^1$. Thus, (15) holds. Also, by (21), (22) and the fact that $\boldsymbol{P}^1 \in \Pi^1$ and $\boldsymbol{P}^2 \in \Pi^2$, we have that $\boldsymbol{P}^1$ and $\boldsymbol{P}^2$ have to be given by (14) and also the following condition has to hold:

$$\sigma^2 + h_k^1 P_k^1 + h_k^2 P_k^2 = \frac{h_k^1}{\omega^1} = \frac{h_k^2}{\omega^2} \tag{23}$$

By (23) with right side h_k^1/ω^1, $P_k^1 = 1/\omega^1 - (\sigma^2 + P_k^2)/h_k^1 < 1/\omega^1 - \sigma^2/h_k^1$. Substituting this P_k^1 into (14) and taking into account that $\boldsymbol{P}^1 \in \Pi^1$ yield that

$$\omega^1 \leq \omega_k^1. \tag{24}$$

Similarly, dealing with strategy $\boldsymbol{P}^2$ in condition (23) with right side h_k^2/ω^2 implies that

$$\omega^2 \leq \omega_{k-1}^2. \tag{25}$$

By (14), the condition (23) with right side h_k^1/ω^1 is equivalent to

$$\sigma^2 + h_k^1\left(\overline{P}^1 - \sum_{j=1}^{k-1}\left\lfloor\frac{1}{\omega^1} - \frac{\sigma^2}{h_i^1}\right\rfloor_+\right) + h_k^2\left(\overline{P}^2 - \sum_{j=k+1}^{n}\left\lfloor\frac{1}{\omega^2} - \frac{\sigma^2}{h_i^2}\right\rfloor_+\right) = \frac{h_k^1}{\omega^1}.$$

(26)

Substituting (15) into (26) implies (16).

Since the left side of Eq. (16) is decreasing on ω^1, by (24), it has a root if and only of $F(\omega_k^1) < \overline{P}^1 + h_k\overline{P}^2$. This condition is equivalent to

$$\overline{P}^2 > \sum_{j=k+1}^{n}\left\lfloor\frac{1}{\omega^1 h_k} - \frac{\sigma^2}{h_i^2}\right\rfloor_+ = (\text{by } (15)) = \sum_{j=k+1}^{n}\left\lfloor\frac{1}{\omega^2} - \frac{\sigma^2}{h_i^2}\right\rfloor_+.$$

Thus, $\omega^2 > \omega_k^2$. Substituting (15) in the last inequality and taking into account (24) implies that

$$\xi_k < h_k.$$

(27)

By (14) and (15), the condition (23) with right side h_k^2/ω^2 is equivalent to

$$G(\omega^2) := \sum_{j=1}^{k-1}\left\lfloor\frac{1}{\omega^2} - \frac{\sigma^2}{h_i^1 h_k}\right\rfloor_+ + \sum_{j=k}^{n}\left\lfloor\frac{1}{\omega^2} - \frac{\sigma^2}{h_i^2}\right\rfloor_+ = \overline{P}^1/h_k + \overline{P}^2.$$

(28)

Thus, by (25), this equation has a positive root if and only if $G(\omega_{k-1}^2) < \overline{P}^1/h_k + \overline{P}^2$. By (15) and (28), this is equivalent to $\omega_{k-1}^1 < \omega^1$. This, jointly with (15) and (25), implies that $\xi_{k-1} > h_k$. Then, taking into account (27) yields (13), and the result follows. ∎

References

1. Altman, E., Avrachenkov, K., Garnaev, A.: Closed form solutions for water-filling problems in optimization and game frameworks. Telecommun. Syst. **47**, 153–164 (2011)
2. Fudenberg, D., Tirole, J.: Game Theory. MIT Press, Boston (1991)
3. Garnaev, A., Baykal-Gursoy, M., Poor, H.V.: A game theoretic analysis of secret and reliable communication with active and passive adversarial modes. IEEE Trans. Wirel. Commun. **15**, 2155–2163 (2016)
4. Garnaev, A., Trappe, W.: The eavesdropping and jamming dilemma in multichannel communications. In: IEEE International Conference on Communications (ICC), pp. 2160–2164. Budapest, Hungary (2013)
5. Garnaev, A., Trappe, W.: Stationary equilibrium strategies for bandwidth scanning. In: Jonsson, M., Vinel, A., Bellalta, B., Marina, N., Dimitrova, D., Fiems, D. (eds.) MACOM 2013. LNCS, vol. 8310, pp. 168–183. Springer, Cham (2013). https://doi.org/10.1007/978-3-319-03871-1_15
6. Garnaev, A., Trappe, W.: Secret communication when the eavesdropper might be an active adversary. In: Jonsson, M., Vinel, A., Bellalta, B., Belyaev, E. (eds.) MACOM 2014. LNCS, vol. 8715, pp. 121–136. Springer, Cham (2014). https://doi.org/10.1007/978-3-319-10262-7_12

7. Garnaev, A., Trappe, W.: One-time spectrum coexistence in dynamic spectrum access when the secondary user may be malicious. IEEE Trans. Inf. Forensics Secur. **10**, 1064–1075 (2015)
8. Garnaev, A., Trappe, W.: A bandwidth monitoring strategy under uncertainty of the adversary's activity. IEEE Trans. Inf. Forensics Secur. **11**, 837–849 (2016)
9. Garnaev, A., Trappe, W.: Bargaining over the fair trade-off between secrecy and throughput in OFDM communications. IEEE Trans. Inf. Forensics Secur. **12**, 242–251 (2017)
10. Garnaev, A., Trappe, W., Petropulu, A.: Equilibrium strategies for an OFDM network that might be under a jamming attack. In: 51st Annual Conference on Information Systems and Sciences (CISS) (2017)
11. Han, Z., Niyato, D., Saad, W., Basar, T., Hjrungnes, A.: Game Theory in Wireless and Communication Networks: Theory, Models, and Applications. Cambridge University Press, New York (2012)
12. He, G., Cottatellucci, L., Debbah, M.: The waterfilling game-theoretical framework for distributed wireless network information flow. EURASIP J. Wirel. Commun. Netw. **1**, 124–143 (2010)
13. Ju, P., Song, W., Jin, A.L.: A Bayesian game analysis of cooperative MAC with incentive for wireless networks. In: IEEE Global Communications Conference (GLOBECOM) (2014)
14. Monderer, D., Shapley, L.S.: Potential games. Games Econ. Behav. **14**, 124–143 (1996)
15. Prasad, R.: OFDM for Wireless Communications Systems. Artech House, Boston (2004)
16. Scutari, G., Palomar, D.P., Barbarossa, S.: Asynchronous iterative water-filling for Gaussian frequency-selective interference channels. IEEE Trans. Inf. Theory **54**, 2868–2878 (2008)
17. Slimeni, F., Scheers, B., Le Nir, V., Chtourou, Z., Attia, R.: Closed form expression of the saddle point in cognitive radio and Jammer power allocation game. In: Noguet, D., Moessner, K., Palicot, J. (eds.) CrownCom 2016. LNICSSITE, vol. 172, pp. 29–40. Springer, Cham (2016). https://doi.org/10.1007/978-3-319-40352-6_3
18. Song, T., Stark, W.E., Li, T., Tugnait, J.K.: Optimal multiband transmission under hostile jamming. IEEE Trans. Commun. **64**, 4013–4027 (2016)
19. Sridharan, G., Kumbhkar, R., Mandayam, N.B., Seskar, I., Kompella, S.: Physical-layer security of NC-OFDM-based systems. In: IEEE Military Communications Conference (MILCOM), pp. 1101–1106 (2016)
20. Wei, H., Sun, H.: Using Bayesian game model for intrusion detection in wireless Ad Hoc networks. Int. J. Commun. Netw. Syst. Sci. **3**(7), 602–607 (2010)
21. Yu, W., Ginis, G., Cioffi, J.M.: Distributed multiuser power control for digital subscriber lines. IEEE J. Sel. Areas Commun. **20**, 1105–1115 (2002)

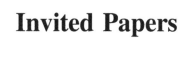

Invited Papers

Reliable and Reproducible Radio Experiments in FIT/CorteXlab SDR Testbed: Initial Findings

Leonardo S. Cardoso$^{(\boxtimes)}$ ⓘ, Othmane Oubejja, Guillaume Villemaud,
Tanguy Risset, and Jean Marie Gorce

Univ Lyon, INSA Lyon, Inria, CITI, 69621 Villeurbanne, France
leonardo.cardoso@insa-lyon.fr

Abstract. The FIT/CorteXlab platform is a wireless testbed situated in Lyon, France, where all radio nodes are confined to an electro-magnetically (EM) shielded environment and have flexible radio-frequency (RF) front-end for experimenting on software defined radio (SDR) and cognitive radio (CR). A unique feature of this testbed is that it offers roughly 40 SDR nodes that can be accessed from anywhere in the world in a reproducible manner: the electro-magnetic shield prevents from external interference and channel variability. In this paper we show why it is important to have such a reproducible radio experiment testbed and we highlight the reproducibility by the channel characteristics between the nodes of the platform. We back our claims with a large set of measurements done in the testbed, that also refines our knowledge on the propagation characteristics of the testbed.

Keywords: Reproducibility · Software defined radio
Cognitive radio · Wireless testbed · FIT/CorteXlab

1 Introduction

Low cost and accessible SDR platforms have fostered more than a decade of radio communication proof of concepts and experiments, as of the writing of this work. This development is comparable to the early days of personal computers, back in the mid 1970s. These platforms span a wide audience, be it radio amateurs, enthusiasts, hackers, and of course, wireless communications researchers. In particular, wireless communications researchers have greatly gained from using these devices, allowing a complete development cycle, that now spans from theoretical development of techniques and algorithms all the way to a proof of concept. This ability was once restricted to industries, military and government institutes, due to their hard and expensive nature.

The FIT/CorteXlab testbed is a part of the Future Internet of Things (FIT) project and federation of testbeds. This work has been supported by the FIT project.

© ICST Institute for Computer Sciences, Social Informatics and Telecommunications Engineering 2018
P. Marques et al. (Eds.): CROWNCOM 2017, LNICST 228, pp. 225–236, 2018.
https://doi.org/10.1007/978-3-319-76207-4_19

As communications systems and techniques evolve, so do radio platforms required to test them. The new era of radio communication systems relies on their multi-user capabilities, including interference avoidance, cooperation, relaying, or simple co-existence. Many interesting research topics are under investigation in a multi-user context, from its most fundamental aspect in network information theory, or on the use of machine learning for radio system design [1], to more practical designs, including new waveforms, cooperative multi-user communications, caching for wireless systems [2], massive simultaneous transmission of very small-packets for the Internet of things (IoT), massive multiple input - multiple output (MIMO) systems [3] and distributed MIMO, physical layer (PHY) network coding, millimeter wave, and agile spectrum sensing systems. All these topics can profit from the evaluation on real systems. To reflect these advances, the market for radio platforms is quickly adapting to accommodate the needs of wireless researchers. In the specific case of multi-user techniques, a researcher must own and control experiments over a multitude of radio platforms, which can become prohibitively expensive and complex to manage. This is where wireless testbeds come in. Wireless testbeds allow anyone aiming to experiment with multi-user wireless techniques to access a large number of high performance radio nodes in a controlled environment and with an accessible interface, that takes care of all non-essential aspects of running these kinds of experiments.

In recent years, a number of large-scale wireless radio testbeds have been developed. Most of these testbeds focus on computation and networking aspects, with only a few targeting the wireless PHY layer. Consequently, only a few of them count with full SDR capabilities. It was with the development of high end flexible transceivers, such as the USRP, the PicoSDR, and more recently the BladeRF, that the opportunity to build larger SDR testbeds became a reality. The software part of SDR also played an essential role in its growing popularity. The development of signal processing and communication toolkits and frameworks such as GNU Radio [4], IRIS [5] or OpenAir Interface [6] enabled the easy development of communication systems for these testbeds, that can now be prototyped by wireless communications researchers all over the world.

There are several PHY-centric testbeds in operation today. A pioneer wireless testbed was ORBIT [7]. Initially a network level testbed, ORBIT quickly updated its nodes with SDRs as soon as they became available. It counts with hundreds of nodes, not all being SDR capable. The Cornet testbed was among the first testbeds fully dedicated to SDR. It counts with 48 SDR nodes deployed in one of Virginia Tech's buildings, spread over 4 floors. Stemming from the Cornet testbed, the CREW project [8] offers a facility that concentrates on the IRIS toolkit to offer waveform development capabilities over its approximately 16 SDR nodes. On these testbeds, registered users can remotely access and run experiments on flexible radio platforms. These testbeds are certainly among the most advanced in the world, however none of them propose an electro-magnetically shielded environment.

Focus of this work, the FIT/CorteXlab[1] testbed is a facility situated at the INSA Lyon campus in France, in the basement of the Telecommunications Department, and operated by Inria. It is composed of 38 SDR nodes that can be accessed remotely and freely from anywhere in the world. Currently, its SDR nodes can be divided into two types: 22 USRP model 2932 and 16 PicoSDR (four of them 4×4 MIMO, 12 of them 2×2 MIMO). Keeping the spirit of an open testbed, GNU Radio is used as its main SDR toolkit. One very important aspect of the FIT/CorteXlab testbed is its experiment room, of roughly $180\,m^2$, where all the radio nodes were deployed in a confined EM shielded environment, as seen in Fig. 1. FIT/R2Lab is a sister testbed to FIT/CorteXlab, also belonging to the FIT banner, and counting with some models of USRPs in a shielded room. It was partly inspired by FIT/CorteXlab, with the main difference being that focuses on 5G, and to that end, OpenAirInterface was made available as the standard radio framework. To the best of our knowledge this is the only other large-scale testbed that offers a shielded environment.

Choosing a shielded environment for radio experimentation allows for relaxed experimentation frequencies and scenarios, while contributing to reproducible experiments as well. This decision comes from fact that non-shielded radio experiments are subject to interference as well as to non-stationary radio propagation characteristics, hence being inherently random in nature. This becomes a critical issue when these experiments are necessary to validate wireless communications algorithms, since the scientific method relies on *reproducibility of experiments*. Furthermore, how can we compare the results of different algorithms when we can not distinguish its effects, from uncontrollable effects of the surroundings? As we see, reproducibility is a key aspect of experimenting in wireless communications.

In a previous work [9], we have provided initial findings of a channel sounding campaign in FIT/CorteXlab's experimentation room. We focused on the channel impulse response in time and frequency, trying to understand how the shielding influences the diversity of the channels in the room. That work has not studied the coverage profiles of nodes in the room as well as the path-loss between any pair of nodes. In this work, by means of a measurement campaign, we provide further information on the propagation environment of FIT/CorteXlab's experimentation room as well as the coverage-to-transmitted-power relation of the communications done in FIT/CorteXlab for the USRP nodes. Finally, we take a step back and provide results that corroborate our claim that FIT/CorteXlab's experimentation room can indeed be used for reproducible experiments.

The remainder of this work is divided as follows. In Sect. 2 we discuss on when and how FIT/CorteXlab can provide reproducibility. Section 3 describes the characterization of the path-loss for FIT/CorteXlab and details the experimentation setup used. On Sect. 4 we present some initial results to support our claims. Finally, we draw some conclusions and delineate further steps in Sect. 5.

---

[1] For more information on FIT/CorteXlab, please refer to the website: http://www.cortexlab.fr/.

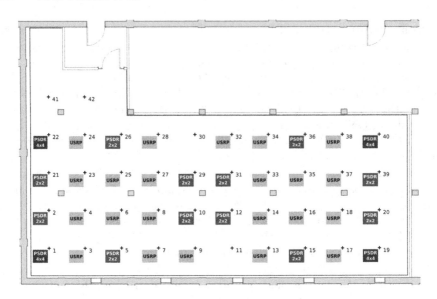

Fig. 1. Node positions in the FIT/CorteXlab testbed.

2   Experimental Reproducibility

The bridge between theory and experimentation is always hard to build properly. Reproducibility is a key point to ensure an effective analysis of experimentations. Field testing is, of course, always necessary to perform a final validation of a wireless system or a complete network. But in a real radio environment, it is impossible to ensure reproducibility, and the overwhelming amount of uncontrolled parameters increase the complexity of analysis. The main intent of a controlled environment like FIT/CorteXlab experimentation room is to offer both EM isolation and reproducibility and this is the main focus of this section.

The first point is EM isolation. It guarantees no external signals are received during an experimentation, which in turn means that all signals measured in the testbed *could only be generated in the testbed*. This avoids interference from outside wireless systems, and ensures that all received interference is created by radio nodes (or other equipment) inside the experimentation room of the testbed. To that intent three measures were taken to ensure EM shielding: (1) the FIT/CorteXlab experimentation room was installed in the underground of the building that hosts it; (2) it is entirely shielded with a metallic tissue that covers all sides and; (3) partially covered with EM absorbers. Furthermore, all networking connections enter the room through fiber optics and there is a 13.2 kW power filter installed in the incoming electrical circuit. The outside-to-inside (and vise-versa) attenuation is greater than 80 dB on the whole frequency range of operation (roughly 300 MHz to 4 GHz). This value is large enough to consider that any signal coming from outside will be attenuated to under the noise floor of the receivers installed in the room. This environment allows experiments on any frequency within the capabilities of the SDR platforms, while protecting from outside interference, as well as from generating interference on sensitive frequencies, i.e., military, radar, mobile, etc.

The second point is on reproducibility. Of course, isolation is already a necessary condition to offer reproducibility, but not sufficient. We also need that the global link budget is both stable and reversible. Many PHY and MAC layer mechanisms rely on an evaluation of the link budget quality, i.e., radio signal strength indicator (RSSI), signal-to-noise ratio (SNR) or signal-to-interference plus noise ratio (SINR). Therefore, to analyze the behavior of such wireless systems, it's essential to build experimentation with a fine control on this link budget, and with the capability of reproducing the same link budget several times with different scenarios.

In Sect. 4 we will see that FIT/CorteXlab offers a very good reproducibility in terms of global path-loss between each nodes. This reproducibility comes from several characteristics that will be detailed here. The first one is the isolation of the room, already explained before. EM absorbers also contribute and are considered not only for isolation, but also to reduce multi-paths reflexions in the testbed. Without absorbers, the FIT/CorteXlab room would face excessive reflexions, creating an unrealistic radio channel. Thus, the semi-anechoic characteristic enables the wireless path-losses to be stable, while preserving a few reflexions in order to avoid a complete free-space propagation. Two other important aspects are the fixed node positions and omni-directional wide-band antennas. They allow a fixed link budget, irrespective of the relative position of nodes and selected transmission frequency. Finally, the nodes' transceivers are of high quality and possess relatively stable RF characteristics. Section 3.1 will deal with the RF transceivers in more detail.

Last but not least, a reproducible testbed is crucial for the analysis of interference issues. Interference control is a key optimization issue for large-scale wireless networks, be it inter-standard interference or intra-standard interference. If all individual link budgets between all nodes are sufficiently stable, then we can also assess that interference level can be managed, tuned and reproduced. This is clearly impossible in a real world experimentation, striving to build a bridge between theory, simulation and experimentation.

3   Path-Loss Characterization in FIT/CorteXlab

To provide reliable path-loss measurements for the FIT/CorteXlab experimentation room, we must first properly characterize the overall transmitter (TX) and receiver (RX) chains used for the measurements. We must be able to clearly estimate the absolute transmission and reception powers, in decibel-milliwatt (dBm), taking into account the antenna gains and RF characteristics of the radio nodes. As we will see in the following, all characterization and path-loss measurements were done for the USRPs only. The PicoSDRs, with its 3-stage RF amplifier and filtering, require a more complex approach and will be the focus of a future work.

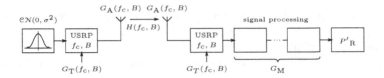

Fig. 2. TX and RX chains used for the hardware characterization.

A simple TX and RX chain was devised to aid in characterizing the radio nodes under transmission and reception and can be seen in Fig. 2. The power at the TX side P_T in dBm, whose signal is at central frequency f_c and bandwidth B, can be modeled as:

$$P_\text{T} = G_\text{A}(f_c, B) + G_\text{T}(f_c, B) + P_\text{s}, \tag{1}$$

where G_A is the antenna gain in dB, G_T is the USRP TX gain in dB, P_s is the power of the Gaussian circularly symmetric transmitted signal $s \sim \mathcal{CN}(0, \sigma)$. Then, $P_s = 10\log(\sigma^2)$, with log the logarithm function on base 10. A Gaussian source signal was selected for its flat power spectrum density and will give a flat response whatever band used in the measurements. For the receiver part, the following model was adopted

$$P'_\text{R} = G_\text{A}(f_c, B) + G_\text{R}(f_c, B) + G_\text{M}(f_c, B) + H(f_c, B) + P_\text{T}, \tag{2}$$

where P'_R is the measured received power in dBm, G_R is the USRP RX gain in dB, G_M is the gain of the signal processing part of the measurement chain (filtering, FFT, etc.) in dB, and H is channel gain in dB. Since the same antennas are used at both sides of the link, G_A is the same for the TX and the RX.

3.1   TX-RX Gain-Power Characterization

Measurements were performed initially for the TX followed by the RX side. A summary of the relevant parameters for both set of measurements are shown in Table 1. All USRPs were pre-calibrated using the universal hardware driver (UHD) calibration tool. The TX and RX chains were developed in GNU Radio following the description in Fig. 2. The same attenuator and RF cable were used throughout the study, to guarantee a constant connector and cable loss reference.

For the TX measurements, a spectrum analyzer was connected through the attenuator to the RF output port of the USRP. This can be seen as taking $G_\text{A} = 0$ dBi in (1). The TX gain was configured in the "UHD sink" GNU Radio block. Finally, three individual USRPs were tested to check for significant differences in the measurements. In Fig. 3a, we see the measured TX powers with respect to the gain $G_\text{T}(f_c, B)$, set at the TX. The measured powers already take into account the attenuation in the measurements (-30 dB for the attenuator). The expected behavior can be seen, with the power linearly increasing with the gain, until it reaches the non-linear region where the amplifier saturates.

Table 1. Configured parameters for the TX and RX characterization.

Parameter	Range of values
Source type	0-mean Gaussian noise
Amplitude (of I and Q)	1
B (sample rate)	1 MHz
f_c central frequency	2.45 GHz
Channel bandwidth (filter)	10 MHz
Attenuator	30 dB
RF cable	RADIALL R286300752 (1 m)
TX and RX gain values G_R and G_T	0 to 44 dB
Signal processing gain G_M at the RX	−12 dB

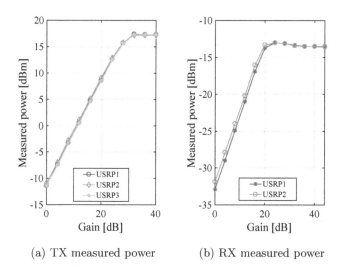

(a) TX measured power   (b) RX measured power

Fig. 3. TX and RX characterization for the USRP NI 2932 at $f_c = 2.45$ GHz and $B = 1$ MHz.

Interestingly, all measured USRPs never reach the maximum power given in the specifications, of 20 dBm, for this specific model. Nevertheless, all three USRPs deliver the same behavior with very little variation. We can also notice that for the different USRPs used in this study, a measured power difference of at most 1 dB can be observed. This suggests that for precise power measurements, a more refined study is necessary to better characterize these measured power levels. This study is however, out of the scope of this work.

For the RX, a Gaussian signal with the fixed characteristics and a known power of 9.1 dBm was provided at the input port of the USRP through the attenuator. As for the TX case, this can be seen as taking $G_A = 0$ dBi in (2). The RX gains were configured in the "UHD source" GNU Radio block. Unlike in the TX study, only two USRPs were evaluated. We can see in Fig. 3b, that the USRPs also behave as expected in RX mode. Here, the measured powers also take into account the attenuation in the measurements (-30 dB for the attenuator). The same pattern of amplification, with a linear increase and a non-linear part can be observed. As for the TX case, we can also notice a difference in the received powers, of approx. 1 dBm, between both tested USRPs for a given gain value.

3.2   Path-Loss Measurement Campaign

Having characterized the TX and RX powers with respect to the TX and RX gains, we can now proceed to measuring the path-loss $H(f_c, B)$. As stated before, the path-loss measurements were made only for the USRPs. They were performed pairwise, considering every TX - RX combination possible in the FIT/CorteXlab experimentation room. To that aim, 22 experimentation tasks were created in which each one of the 22 USRP nodes behave as a TX while the remaining USRP nodes behaving as RXs. The TXs send the signal described in Sect. 3.1 with a constant power, given for a transmit gain of $G_T = 20$ dB. Each RX measures P'_R and calculates $H(f_c, B)$ from (2), by replacing all known gain values. For these experiments air was used as the transmission medium, and therefore the cable and the attenuator were not used. The antenna gain considered is $G_A(f_c, B) =$ 4.3 dBi, given by the antenna manufacturer. Finally, the physical positions of each node is given in Fig. 1. The actual antenna positions are marked by a "+" in Fig. 1, along with the node number. The horizontal and vertical steps between adjacent nodes are regular and equal to 1.8 m.

4   Experimental Results

With the exception of the attenuator, cable and TX and RX gain values, all experimentation parameters are the same as in Table 1. In Figs. 4 and 5 we see three examples of selected TX - RX settings, namely with node 3, 16 and 38 as TXs, respectively. Each bar corresponds to the measured path-loss for each one of the receiving USRPs. The PicoSDR's path-losses are set to zero in these figures, to highlight the fact that they were not measured. The behavior of the observed path-losses are as expected and increase with the distance of the transmitter nodes, going from around 67 to 73 dB, when next to the transmitter, to 85 to 104 dB, when farthest away from the transmitter, depending on the position of the node. It should be noted that the presence of structural columns (seen in Fig. 1 as grey squares surrounded by a red line) affect the path-loss, as expected. Take for example, the path-loss between TX 3 and RX 34 in Fig. 4 with respect to several other neighboring nodes, as seen in Table 2. We clearly see that the path-loss between TX 3 and RX 34 is of the same order as the path-loss between TX 3 and RX 38, which is in stark contrast with the path-loss between TX 3 and RXs 32 and 33, the immediate neighbors of 34. A similar behavior can be observed over all experiments and can also be seen in Fig. 5a and b.

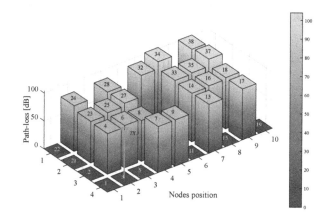

Fig. 4. Example of path-loss measured between node 3 and all other USRP nodes.

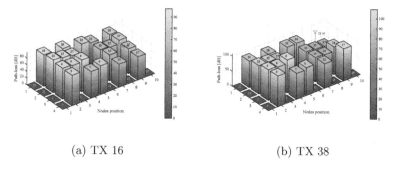

(a) TX 16   (b) TX 38

Fig. 5. Example of path-loss measured between node 16 and all other USRP nodes (left) and between node 38 and all other USRP nodes (right).

To sum up all path-loss findings, Fig. 6 shows the path-loss distribution over same-distance pairs of nodes. This figure was compiled over all experimentation runs and all TX configurations, for a total of 176 measurement runs (3696 individual measurements). The horizontal axis compiles the distance from the TX in each run to a RX. The discrete distances in this figure account for the grid structure of the FIT/CorteXlab experimentation room. On the vertical axis all path-loss measurements for nodes of a certain distance are given, as well their the average value, marked with a triangle. As we can see, the relatively high spread in path-losses for same-distance pairs of nodes, take into consideration different propagation characteristics, such as multipath fading (reflexions) and shadowing due to the structural columns. Even though these characteristics highly affect the average, we can still observe a rather linear tendency over distance as expected. Moreover, the slope of this tendency shows that the path-loss exponent experienced in that room is greater than 2, thus showing that the propagation conditions are harder than free-space. The high variability of these measured path-losses indicate that a FIT/CorteXlab user might want to take this information into consideration before planning his or her experiment scenario.

Table 2. Path-losses of several nodes with respect to TX node 3

RX node number	Distance	Path-loss
34	**10.5 m**	**102 dB**
32	9.0 m	89 dB
33	9.7 m	89 dB
38	13.7 m	104 dB

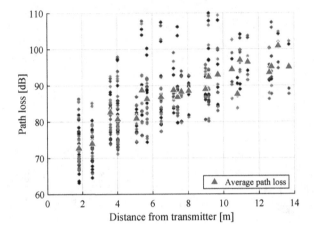

Fig. 6. Compilation of all path-losses measured between same-distance pairs of nodes

Finally, we fixed the TX configuration and looked over the 8 runs of the same configuration. Each measurement run took place at least 1 h apart from the previous run. This time, instead of looking at the actual values of the path-losses in dB, we looked at their variability between same node pairs over each run. The idea is to see the impact of consecutive runs over the actual value of the path-loss. Figure 7 presents the standard deviation of the measured path-loss around the average value, for any pair of TX-RX nodes. The diagonal values are missing from the figure since we have restricted a node from simultaneously being a TX and an RX. A color code was added to enhance the readability of the figure, with colors toward the red meaning a higher standard deviation, while colors leaning toward the green mean a lower one. Due to size restrictions only the first 9 USRP nodes are present in the figure, however, the observations and conclusions are extensible to all nodes. We can see that all standard deviations are confined to within several tenths or hundredths of a dB (aways less than 1 dB), which indicate the tightness of the path-loss measurements. This means that the path-losses remain rather stable throughout experiments spanning several hours apart. Interestingly, when looking at a specific pair of nodes, we observe a symmetric pattern in the standard deviation of the path-loss. This happens in spite of different TX and RX chain characteristics for a given radio node, which also

RX TX	3	4	6	7	8	9	13	14	16
3		0.104	0.122	0.124	0.036	0.077	0.080	0.086	0.074
4	0.105		0.058	0.111	0.277	0.113	0.136	0.194	0.072
6	0.064	0.033		0.088	0.151	0.106	0.245	0.125	0.118
7	0.126	0.122	0.065		0.229	0.056	0.863	0.569	0.070
8	0.030	0.312	0.162	0.204		0.177	0.137	0.207	0.295
9	0.148	0.129	0.117	0.063	0.209		0.197	0.027	0.106
13	0.074	0.092	0.206	0.634	0.137	0.108		0.134	0.029
14	0.108	0.145	0.109	0.528	0.197	0.030	0.144		0.044
16	0.090	0.067	0.134	0.072	0.255	0.091	0.039	0.040	

Fig. 7. Standard deviation of the measured path-loss for over all experiment runs, for a selected pair of TX-RX.

explains why the values are not exactly the same. If we account only for the channel and the TX and RX antennas (each node share the same antenna for TX and RX), we see that the channel is rather reversible. These two results clearly corroborate our claim that the FIT/CorteXlab experimentation room is indeed a reproducible experimentation environment and are in accordance to what previously stated in Sect. 2.

5 Conclusions and Perspectives

In this work we have provided experimental measurements that clarify the path-loss distribution in the FIT/CorteXlab experimentation room. These results will serve as a reference for users wanting to better understand their experimental results with respect to the radio environment, as well as for users willing to properly decide on a scenario configuration for their experiments. Furthermore, we have provided additional findings that complement the ones published before [9], that points toward a reproducible environment inside of the FIT/CorteXlab experimentation room. The ensemble of these findings will help FIT/CorteXlab users to move onto experimentation on advanced radio techniques for future wireless communications. Finally, we have provided all raw measurements and related code as an open-source downloadable package, that can be explored by users aiming to better understand the propagation environment in the FIT/CorteXlab experimentation room, producing insights more relevant to them.

The forthcoming goal will be twofold. Firstly, we need to implement this path-loss evaluation as a routine of the FIT/CorteXlab testbed, in order to regularly update the coverage map of each node, taking into consideration the maintenance related replacement of equipment. This routine will also serve as benchmarking purposes, allowing FIT/CorteXlab administrators and users to quickly identify radio nodes with faulty or underperforming RF stages. Secondly, the findings herein are a part of an ongoing study, that will eventually include a time-frequency characterization to complete our knowledge about the various radio channels that can be encountered in this testbed as well as the PicoSDR nodes. As stated before, in [9] we have already performed some channel sounding based on OFDM waveforms. This preliminary work has demonstrated that, even if in most cases are LOS (line of sight) conditions with a flat channel on the whole usable bandwidth, in some particular combinations we have NLOS (non line of sight) with more diversity (and lower coherence bandwidth). Reversely, finding ways of increasing the diversity of links in our testbed while preserving the reproducibility of experimentation is also an interesting perspective.

References

1. O'Shea, T.J., Hoydis, J.: An introduction to machine learning communications systems. arXiv preprint arXiv:1702.00832 (2017)
2. Fadlallah, Y., Tulino, A.M., Barone, D., Vettigli, G., Llorca, J., Gorce, J.-M.: Coding for caching in 5G networks. IEEE Commun. Mag. **55**(2), 106–113 (2017)
3. Alexandropoulos, G.C., Ferrand, P., Gorce, J.-M., Papadias, C.B.: Advanced coordinated beamforming for the downlink of future LTE cellular networks. IEEE Commun. Mag. **54**(7), 54–60 (2016)
4. Blossom, E.: GNU radio: tools for exploring the radio frequency spectrum. Linux J. **2004**(122), 4 (2004)
5. Finn, D., Tallon, J., DaSilva, L.A., Van Wesemael, P., Pollin, S., Liu, W., Bouckaert, S., Vanhie-Van Gerwen, J., Michailow, N., Hauer, J.-H., Willkomm, D., Heller, C.: Experimental assessment of tradeoffs among spectrum sensing platforms. In: Wintech 2011, Las Vegas, Nevada, September 2011
6. Nikaein, N., Marina, M.K., Manickam, S., Dawson, A., Knopp, R., Bonnet, C.: Openairinterface: a flexible platform for 5G research. SIGCOMM Comput. Commun. Rev. **44**(5), 33–38 (2014)
7. Raychaudhuri, D., Seskar, I., Ott, M.: ORBIT: wireless experimentation. In: McGeer, R., Berman, M., Elliott, C., Ricci, R. (eds.) The GENI Book, pp. 63–95. Springer, Cham (2016). https://doi.org/10.1007/978-3-319-33769-2_4
8. DaSilva, L.A., Doyle, L., Finn, D., Tallon, J., Moerman, I., Bouckaert, S.: Crew: building a cognitive radio federation. In: IC0902, Bologna, Italy, November 2010
9. Mouaffo, A., Cardoso, L., Boeglen, H., Villemaud, G., Vauzelle, R.: Radio link characterization of the CorteXlab testbed with a large number of software defined radio nodes. In: 2015 9th European Conference on Antennas and Propagation (EuCAP), Lisbon, Portugal, April 2015

Spectrum Broker Service for Micro-operator and CBRS Priority Access Licenses

Topias Kokkinen[1]([✉]), Heikki Kokkinen[1], and Seppo Yrjölä[2]

[1] Fairspectrum, Otakaari 5, 02150 Espoo, Finland
{info,heikki.kokkinen}@fairspectrum.com
[2] Nokia, Kaapelitie 4, 90620 Oulu, Finland
seppo.yrjola@nokia.com

Abstract. This paper discusses a spectrum broker service for micro-operator and Citizens Broadband Radio Service (CBRS) Priority Access Licenses (PAL). The spectrum broker service provides a marketplace for selling and leasing of spectrum resources. The micro-operator licenses are regional, and possibly temporal, mobile network spectrum licenses for a confined service area like for a factory, a campus, or a hospital. CBRS opens the 3.5 GHz band for Dynamic Spectrum Access (DSA) in the US. PAL is the middle priority level license in CBRS. The paper introduces a new service model for spectrum brokering. The required functionalities of the service are described, and a new automated spectrum pricing model is proposed for the broker service.

Keywords: Spectrum broker · Dynamic Spectrum Access · Micro-operator
CBRS

1 Introduction

Traditional spectrum allocation for Mobile BroadBand networks (MBB) is mainly done in the primary market where the government authorities sell long term licenses by auctions. While these auctions have many benefits and are accepted as the standard method, they still lead to inefficient situations in particular circumstances. The demand for the spectrum can change rapidly and drastically due to factors such as changes in traffic demand, spectrum applications, and technologies. However, the static long term licenses do not adapt to these changes [1]. This leads to situations where the licenses are not held by the parties that value them the most. Another problem that Berry et al. [1] recognize is that the packaging of licenses to large blocks leads to oligopolies where there are only few large license holders. The winning bidder might not need all bundled licenses so parts of the spectrum remain unused. Additionally, restricted competition and static licenses hinder new innovation.

A solution to this problem is to establish a secondary market for the licenses. Cramton and Doyle [2] state that an open access market for spectrum would increase competition and make the process more efficient, transparent, fair, and simple. Chapin and Lehr [3] found that there are three enablers for market liquidity in the secondary spectrum access market: available spectrum by increasing achievable Quality of Services (QoS) and hence, demand, and low transaction costs and risks. On the other hand,

© ICST Institute for Computer Sciences, Social Informatics and Telecommunications Engineering 2018
P. Marques et al. (Eds.): CROWNCOM 2017, LNICST 228, pp. 237–246, 2018.
https://doi.org/10.1007/978-3-319-76207-4_20

Xavier and Ypsilanti [4] discuss issues related to introduction of secondary markets. The following relevant concerns were highlighted: uncertainty regarding the future primary allocations leading to incorrect estimations of spectrum scarcity and value; lack of information on available spectrum; risks of increased interference; coordination, harmonization, and controlling mechanisms; anti-competitive conduct, in particular concentration of spectrum and hoarding; disruptive effects on end users; and ability to achieve public interest objectives. Based on this, Ballon and Delaere [5] suggest the use of coordinating or enabling mechanisms and entities contributing to efficient spectrum management through providing information to stakeholders, interference mitigation, frequency harmonization, combating anti-competitive behavior, and pursuing public interest and consumer protection. Governmental or privately operated automated systems can contribute to regulation through monitoring compliance with policies and regulations, act in case of violations, and support public policy objectives. This potentially results lower cost, more efficiently utilized spectrum, and embedded management, and further helps to define the 'rules of the spectrum game' for co-operative interactions contributing to business aspects.

There are many proposals of real-time secondary marketplaces where capacity is auctioned according to current demand, for example [6]. Yoon et al. [7] examined the effects of three different frameworks, direct trading, auction. and brokerage for the secondary spectrum use and considered changes in market conditions and institutional limitation. They suggested that direct trading optimizes social welfare, considering current technical, economical and policy factors, while more complex trading mechanism may not yet achieve the optimal benefits due to implementation costs. In these studies, marketplaces were mainly designed for liquid licenses. However, this paper answers the research question: *How to facilitate the exchange of spectrum resources that are used for applications such as micro-operator licenses or Priority Access Licenses (PAL) in Citizens Broadband Radio System (CBRS)* [8]. These licenses are often *illiquid micro licenses*. Thus, we introduce a non-real-time marketplace for buying and leasing both exclusive and shared access to spectrum. The main function of the marketplace is to allow fast, convenient, and low-cost exchange of local licenses. If there is a high demand for a particular micro-license, sellers can use auction instead of a buy now price. Auctions can be used to find the equilibrium price but they do not work as efficiently if there are only few buyers [9]. It is reasonable to assume that the number of buyers is relatively small in micro licensing cases, because the licenses are local and they benefit only few buyers.

Additionally, this paper examines the pricing of illiquid micro-licenses. The price of liquid licenses can be determined for example by auctions or by comparing the sales prices of similar licenses. However, when there are not enough buyers or sellers, market based methods are not reliable. The valuation can also be done by evaluating factors such as the potential economic benefit of the license and the opportunity costs of alternative options. However, this is a labor-intensive method and might not be economically worthwhile when considering the size of the micro licenses. This paper introduces an automatic valuation method for these small, illiquid licenses.

First, this paper will consider the uses for a secondary market. Then, it will describe the key functions of the marketplace such as listing, buying, and valuation. It then proposes a few revenue models for the marketplace and describes some of the existing open source platforms that could be used for developing the marketplace. Finally, the paper concludes that the proposed marketplace could be a viable method for allocating the illiquid micro licenses.

2 Brokering Business and CBRS

The proposed marketplace facilitates the secondary exchange of small, illiquid licenses. It could be used to allocate spectrum resources for the local networks used by clients such as event organizers, education facilities, and manufacturing companies. Matinmikko et al. [10] introduce a new local operator model for the deployment of ultra-dense small cell radio networks in specific locations. In this concept, a micro operator buys or leases spectrum access from the current license holder such as a large network operator. They then provide the required service and infrastructure for a client that needs a local network solution. The proposed marketplace allows micro operators to gain access to spectrum conveniently.

Another example, which could benefit from this kind of secondary marketplace is CBRS Priority Access Licenses [8]. The Federal Communications Commission (FCC) [11] licenses for the PAL layer users will be assigned via competitive bidding. They are allowed to operate up to a total of 70 MHz of the 3550–3650 MHz spectrum segment, and they are protected from General Authorized Access (GAA) interference. A PAL non-renewable authorization is for a 10 MHz channel in a single census track for three years, with the ability to aggregate up to six years up-front. To ensure availability of PAL spectrum to at least two licensed users in the highest demand areas, licenses will be permitted to hold no more than four PALs in one census track at once, and no licenses are granted if there is only one applicant, except in rural areas. The PAL layer may cover critical access users like utilities, Internet of Things (IoT) verticals, governmental users, and non-critical users e.g., Mobile Network Operators (MNOs) and Wireless Broadband Service (WBS) providers on the 3650–3700 MHz band after the final five-year term. PALs are auctioned to the licensee within their service area on a census track basis but the specific channels are assigned, re-assigned, and terminated by the Spectrum Access System (SAS) at the end of the term. The PAL will be opened for the third opportunistic licensed-by-rule GAA tier users when unused and further automatically terminated and may not be renewed at the end of its term. PAL licensees report their *PAL Protection Areas* (PPAs) on the basis of actual network deployments., SAS does not authorize other Citizens Broadband radio Service Devices (CBSD) on the same channel in geographic areas and at maximum power levels that would cause aggregate interference within a PPA.

The FCC revisited rules for CBRS in 2016, and introduced the *light-touch leasing process* to enable secondary markets for the spectrum use rights held by PAL licensees [11]. Under the framework, no FCC oversight is required for partitioning and disaggregation of PAL licenses. PAL licensees are free to lease any portion of their spectrum or license outside of their PPA. The PPA can be self-reported by the PAL owner or calculated by the SAS. The PAL radio frequency channel can be re-allocated beyond the PPA, but within the census tract. Introduced low additional administrative burden with a minimum availability of 80 MHz GAA spectrum in each license area will provide the increased flexibility to serve targeted quantities of spectrum or services to geographic areas. Furthermore, the FCC will permit stand-alone or an SAS-managed spectrum exchange and let market forces determine the role of the SAS value added services.

Berry et al. [1] state that the current secondary spectrum exchange is inefficient because of regulation and transaction costs. There is a need for a more systematic method of allocation, where the process is highly automated to reduce delays, search costs, and transaction costs. This can be achieved with a marketplace that helps to automate many labor intensive and time-consuming parts of the exchange. Tonmukayakul and Weiss [9] use Agent-based Computational Economics (ACE) to study when a secondary market is a viable option i.e., when the license holders are willing to supply licenses and when the secondary users are willing to buy them. The paper concludes that there is a demand for secondary use licenses when buyers find exclusive licenses too expensive or when the unlicensed spectrum is crowded. These conditions are likely to happen in the case of local networks. According to Peha and Panichpapiboon [12], it is profitable for the seller to share spectrum access even if the price is quite low. If the spectrum is unused, the license holders have incentives to sell or lease the license to gain extra revenue and to cover the costs of holding the license. If the transaction is done through an efficient marketplace, the sellers are able to lease or sell even very small licenses with profit.

3   Spectrum Broker Service Concept

To increase the efficiency and to make the process more dynamic, the service automates many labour-intensive processes. For example, it generates the contract between the buyer and the seller automatically. It stores the required documentation like CE (Conformité Européenne) certificates and regulator licenses. It also checks that the sale complies with all regulatory rules and possible standards requirements, e.g. regarding to power density and installation parameters. By predicting the aggregated field strengths, the service checks and avoids the harmful interference impact of the buyer network on other licensed radio users in geographic, frequency, and time domains. The service may also visualize the protection and exclusion zones and the respective coverage area of the new license. The estimation of interference protection may include both computed and measured data. Spectrum sales require that documentation concerning the sale is filed to the regulatory authorities. To make the process dynamic, the service creates these documents automatically. The marketplace can also be connected to Enterprise Resource Planning (ERP) software to increase efficiency of accounting. The spectrum broker service is an essential tool in offering Spectrum as a Service (SaaS). The marketplace could offer various additional services to improve the exchange process. It could provide consulting about the pricing, legal processes, or technology. It could also provide advanced information such as sales and sourcing analytics to sellers and buyers, respectively. The marketplace could also include financing services and it could host advertisements and premium listings.

The user interface and the service backend have to be customizable so that they can facilitate the needs of the market for radio spectrum resources. They should allow both selling and leasing as well as allow pricing that is determined flexibly by the pricing formula. Additionally, there has to be a possibility to integrate a map function to the platform. An open source software platform for a marketplace like Cocorico [13], Sharetribe [14], or Spree [15] could form the basis for an early implementation of the service.

Listing

License holders have two options to list their licenses on the marketplace. If they choose to list them automatically, the system determines the base price of the license according to an automated process explained in the valuation section. This allows the license holders to list large amounts of micro licenses conveniently. Alternatively, license holders can list micro licenses manually, one area at a time, allowing them to make a more detailed listing and use a more elaborate pricing method.

Sellers can determine whether they want to lease or sell the license. Both leasing and selling are subject to the legal regulative status of the radio licenses in the particular jurisdiction, and specific radio license terms. It is possible to offer an exclusive license, where only the buyer has access to the spectrum, or a shared license, where many users use the license simultaneously. In the case of a lease, the seller can assume a spectrum manager role where it is responsible of ensuring compliance with terms, regulations, and reporting duties. The exchange can also be a de facto transfer, where all the rights and responsibilities are transferred to the buyer. It should be noted, that the parties must agree who pays the frequency fee.

The marketplace offers analytics tools to sellers to help them monitor the sales. Additionally, it offers an availability management system that helps sellers to manage their available and reserved licenses. An illustration of user interface for listing can be found in Fig. 1.

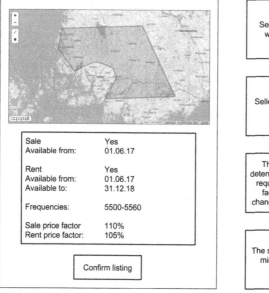
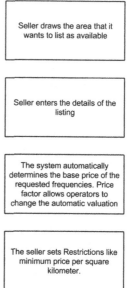

Fig. 1. User interface for listing spectrum resources

Buying and leasing

The marketplace enables the buyers or leasers to search for license holders and select custom coverage areas. The buyer enters information about planned use, which can be used by the seller to estimate the value of the spectrum use, cost for the frequency fee, and potential for harmful interference. A detailed search engine helps the buyers to find all potential listings. It can automatically combine or divide licenses even from different sellers so that the license matches the needs of the buyer. If the seller uses the auto-mated pricing method or has individually priced the license in question, the service shows the prices immediately and thus allows competitive tendering between different license holders. If there is no available price for the searched license, buyer can ask for a quote from the seller. The buyer has the option to either lease or buy the license. An example of a user interface for searching spectrum resources and the search results can be found in Figs. 2 and 3, respectively.

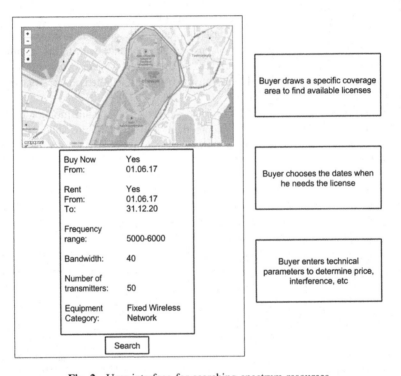

Fig. 2. User interface for searching spectrum resources

Real-time markets are mainly proposed to maximize the spectrum utilization during short term changes in the spectrum demand. For example, an operator might lease more capacity during peak hours through the market. However, our proposed market is mainly meant to allocate spectrum to projects and events which are planned in advance or which require a long term license. Because of this, a non-real-time market is sufficient.

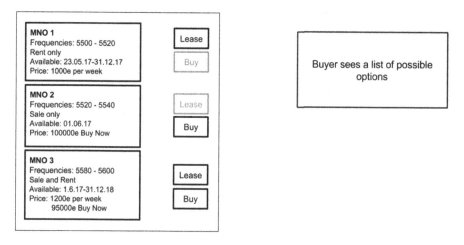

Fig. 3. Results from spectrum search

The marketplace acts as an independent third-party broker in the process. There are different possibilities how the marketplace generates revenue. It could take commission from successful transactions. It could charge monthly fees or fees from making listings. The fees from using the basic services of the marketplace should not be too high to drive away the potential buyers or sellers. Fees from the above-mentioned additional services would generate revenue without raising the costs of basic transactions.

4 Automatic Spectrum Valuation

In the current proposals of secondary markets, the valuation of the licenses is mainly done by auctions. However, Tonmukayakul and Weiss [9] state that auctions work only when the licenses are liquid, i.e. when there are enough buyers and sellers. In many cases, there are only one or a small number of buyers in the context of licenses for local networks and micro operators. For example, in a case where a factory wants to deploy a local network to its own property, there are no other buyers because the property is only used by the factory.

This paper introduces a new automatic valuation method for these relatively illiquid licenses. The method is based on factors such as availability, usability, and the number of frequency bands in the license. This kind of automated pricing allows license holders to list large areas to the marketplace conveniently. The automatic valuation of a base price can for example be done by using the formula that Finnish Communications Regulatory Authority (FICORA) uses to determine frequency fees [16], see Fig. 4. This formula takes into account the frequency band, population density, number of transmitters, relative bandwidth and used radio equipment. This base price is used to determine the leasing and selling prices in the proposed spectrum broker service.

Fee = C1 · Cinh · C6b · B0 · S · P, where

C1 = <u>frequency band coefficient</u>
Cinh = <u>population coefficient</u>
C6b = <u>system coefficient</u>
B0 = <u>relative band width</u>
S = <u>basic fee coefficient</u>
P = <u>basic fee</u>

Fig. 4. FICORA's formula for computing spectrum resource fee [16]

The buyer's input parameters, like the type of equipment, are used to calculate coefficients such as the basic fee coefficient. The system automatically calculates a part of the factors like the number of inhabitants in the area. This is done by using the selected area and population density data. The license holders can choose to charge a premium on top of the base price. The license holders can further set a minimum price based on area to make sure that the price is high enough for the transaction to be profitable.

Alden [17] analyses many factors that affect the valuation of the spectrum. The paper concludes that the process is complex and often very unique. Because of this, the automated valuation method cannot be applied in every situation. It does not work well in situations where the true valuation is not driven by technical factors such as number of transmitters in use. It is hard if not impossible to automatically evaluate the fair price of the spectrum if the true value is driven by factors such as speculation about future benefits and motives to limit competition. This kind of scenarios are likely to happen for example in campuses and cities. Because of this, the pricing method requires further consideration and can only be used only in limited situations. Alden [17] classifies two different methods for valuing spectrum: direct and indirect method. He states that indirect method, such as benchmarking, is often not viable because comparable cases might not exist. This is especially true in these illiquid micro licenses. Direct method considers opportunity costs and potential revenues. Opportunity costs can be evaluated by determining the costs or profits of the alternative options that the buyer and seller have. These include for example the cost of alternative license that the buyer could use. Potential revenues include for example calculating the net present value of the revenues that the buyer will generate with the license. These kinds of methods might lead to accurate estimates but they are very labour intensive and time consuming. Because of this, these methods most likely cannot be used when determining the price of micro licenses. Using the above-mentioned formula offers an automated and efficient approach to valuation that could be accurate enough for the purposes of illiquid micro license exchange.

Here we consider how the formula recognises the main factors that affect the value of the license according to Alden. Intrinsic factors, such as the unequal capabilities of different frequencies can automatically be taken into account and they are recognised in the pricing method of the FICORA. Namely, frequency band and relative band width coefficients measure these properties.

Some extrinsic factors are also recognised in the pricing method. These include physical characteristics like geography and some socio-economic characteristics such as the number of users in the area. This is mainly recognised in the population coefficient. If the marketplace operates in a specific regulatory environment, extrinsic factors such as market specific regulations are most likely constant and thus they can be recognised as well.

However, some extrinsic factors are hard to calculate automatically. These include, for example, the economic benefit that companies get from using the spectrum. Furthermore, it is not straightforward to evaluate the competitive environment of the specific location. Locations where there are many competitors or just a few dominating ones are not attractive locations for new investments. Furthermore, selling licenses to competitors increases competition in the market and this might generate negative effects for the seller. It is better for the seller to price the licenses manually in situations where this kind of problems arise.

5 Conclusions

To enable the efficient employment of local networks and allocation of priority access licenses, a marketplace for illiquid micro licenses is needed. The proposed, non-real-time secondary market is a solution for this challenge. It lowers the transaction costs and inconvenience in the spectrum exchange. Thus, it allows small scale sales that would not be profitable with current transaction costs.

The paper introduces a new automatic method for the valuation of micro licenses. It is based on the frequency fee formula used by the Finnish Communications Regulatory Authority. The method allows license holders to list illiquid micro licenses efficiently. Additionally, it allows buyers to search specific licenses and get the price quotes immediately.

We list a number of features that the proposed system has. To increase efficiency, the marketplace automates labour-intensive processes by filing regulatory documents and checking compliance with the law. Additional services, such as analytics tools and consulting could provide additional value for both the buyer and the seller. The paper shows how the marketplace could be developed by providing examples of the interfaces for both the buyer and the seller. We conclude that an existing open-source platform could be used in the development of the platform. The revenue section shows that there are different business models that could be used to generate revenue without raising the prices too high for the buyers or the sellers.

Future work could consider applying the CBRS brokering concept in to European Licensed Shared Access spectrum sharing concepts evolving from static uses case to more dynamic concept [18]. Finally, the successful deployment of the spectrum trading and leasing framework calls for a collaborative effort from the government, industry, and academia to build dynamic capabilities and technology enablers needed to incubate and accelerate the development. One potential joint topic to study is the utilization of blockchain technology to reduce transaction costs through automatization of business-to-business complex multi-step workflows in contracting and data exchange, while transforming spectrum regulation from administrative to more dynamic market based approach.

References

1. Berry, R., Honig, M., Vohra, R.: Spectrum markets motivation challenges and implications. IEEE Commun. Mag. **48**(11), 146–155 (2010)
2. Cramton, P., Doyle, L.: An Open Access Wireless Market, white paper (2015)
3. Chapin, J.M., Lehr, W.H.: Cognitive radios for dynamic spectrum access – The path to market success for dynamic spectrum access technology. IEEE Commun. Mag. **45**(5), 96–103 (2007)
4. Xavier, P., Ypsilanti, D.: Policy issues in spectrum trading. INFO **8**(2), 34–61 (2006)
5. Ballon, P., Delaere, S.: Flexible spectrum and future business models for the mobile industry. Telematics Inform. **26**(3), 249–258 (2009)
6. Toth, P., Vološin, M., Zoričak, M., Zausinová, J., Gazda, V.: Frequency spectrum allocation in an agent-based model of real-time spectrum secondary market. In: 2017 IEEE 15th International Symposium Applied Machine Intelligence and Informatics, pp. 000129–000136 (2017)
7. Yoon, H., Hwang, J., Weiss, M.B.: An analytic research on secondary-spectrum trading mechanisms based on technical and market changes. Comput. Netw. **56**(1), 3–19 (2012)
8. CFR 47 §§96.23-32. The Code of Federal Regulations of the USA. Title 47 Part 96 Citizens Broadband Radio Service. Subpart C - Priority Access §§96.23-32 (2015)
9. Tonmukayakul, A., Weiss, M.B.: A study of secondary spectrum use using agent-based computational economics. Netnomics **9**(2), 125–151 (2008)
10. Matinmikko, M., Latva-aho, M., Ahokangas, P., Yrjölä, S., Koivumäki, T.: Micro operators to boost local service delivery in 5G. Wirel. Pers. Commun. J. **95**, 69–82 (2017)
11. FCC 16-55: The Second Report and Order and Order on Reconsideration finalizes rules for innovative Citizens Broadband Radio Service in the 3.5 GHz Band (3550–3700 MHz) (2016)
12. Peha, J.M., Panichpapiboon, S.: Real-time secondary markets for spectrum. Telecommun. Policy **28**(7), 603–618 (2004)
13. Cocorico. http://www.cocolabs.io/en/. Accessed 07 July 2017
14. Sharetribe. https://www.sharetribe.com/ Accessed 07 July 2017
15. Spree. https://spreecommerce.com/. Accessed 07 July 2017
16. Finnish Communications Regulatory Authority. Frequency fees guide spectrum use. https://www.viestintavirasto.fi/en/spectrum/radiolicences/frequencyfees.html. Accessed 26 May 2017
17. Alden, J.: Exploring the value and economic valuation of spectrum. Report prepared for the ITU (2012). http://www.itu.int/ITU-D/treg/broadband/ITU-BB-Reports_SpectrumValue.pdf. Accessed 25 May 2017
18. ETSI RRS DTR/RRS-0148: Feasibility study on temporary spectrum access for local high-quality wireless networks. Early draft 0.0.6 (2017)

Designing a Testbed Infrastructure for Experimental Validation and Trialing of 5G Vertical Applications

Juha Kalliovaara[1(✉)][iD], Reijo Ekman[1][iD], Jarkko Paavola[1][iD], Tero Jokela[1][iD], Juhani Hallio[1], Jani Auranen[1], Pekka Talmola[2][iD], and Heikki Kokkinen[3]

[1] Turku University of Applied Sciences, Turku, Finland
juha.kalliovaara@turkuamk.fi
[2] Nokia, Espoo, Finland
[3] Fairspectrum, Helsinki, Finland

Abstract. This paper describes the design of a testbed for experimental validation and trialing of 5G vertical applications. The paper introduces the challenges that 5G aims to solve with regard to the spectrum demand and the convergence of different wireless communication services. The European-level 5G research program 5G Public Private Partnership (5G-PPP) is a coordinated European approach to secure European leadership in 5G. The 5G-PPP has developed a 5G Pan-European Trials Roadmap, which includes a comprehensive strategy for coordinated international preliminary and pre-commercial trials. The objective in designing Turku University of Applied Sciences (TUAS) testbed infrastructure in Turku, Finland, has been in building a testbed that can be used to contribute to the development, standardization and trialing of wireless communications in a diverse selection of scenarios and vertical applications. In addition, the paper describes the spectrum monitoring capabilities at TUAS facilities.

Keywords: 5G · Testbed · Field trials · Experimental validation
Field measurements · TVWS · LTE · DTT broadcasting · LSA · LoRa

1 Introduction

Designing a 5th generation mobile networks (5G) testbed infrastructure for experimentations and trials is far from a trivial task. It requires theoretical knowledge on wireless networks, engineering knowledge to build and operate the testbed and professional level measurement equipment and skilled personnel to operate them. 5G will not only be a New Radio [1], but also an umbrella under which the newly developed and existing technologies are converged to meet the requirements of 5G applications [2]. Thus, it is essential to know the limitations of the current technologies and to accurately define the requirements of the 5G applications.

© ICST Institute for Computer Sciences, Social Informatics and Telecommunications Engineering 2018
P. Marques et al. (Eds.): CROWNCOM 2017, LNICST 228, pp. 247–263, 2018.
https://doi.org/10.1007/978-3-319-76207-4_21

The 5G Public Private Partnership (5G-PPP) [3] funded by European Union is a major initiative aiming to secure European leadership in 5G. The public and private sectors in Europe work together to develop 5G in several different projects on different topics, such as overall architecture, physical layer, Network Function Virtualization (NFV), software-defined networking (SDN), and network slicing. European Commission has created a coordinated 5G action plan (5GAP) [4], which promotes preliminary trials under the 5G-PPP arrangement to take place from 2017 onward and pre-commercial trials from 2018 onward.

To address the key elements in 5GAP, a high-level 5G Pan-European Trials Roadmap [5] was released in May 2017. The main objectives of the Trials Roadmap are the following:

1. Support global European leadership in 5G technology, 5G networks deployment and profitable 5G business.
2. Validate benefits of 5G to vertical sectors, public sector, businesses and consumers.
3. Initiate a clear path to successful and timely 5G deployment.
4. Expand commercial trials and demonstrations as well as national initiatives.

The Finnish Funding Agency for Innovation (Tekes) [6] funds a 5thGear programme [7], which gathers Finnish companies and research institutes together with the aim to solve the challenges of next generation wireless communications, create new business and international collaboration. 5G Test Network Finland (5GTNF) [8] coordinates the integration of the 5G testbeds in 5thGear programme to create a joint open 5G technology and service development innovation platform to support the vision of 5G-PPP in Finland.

This paper introduces the approach chosen by Turku University of Applied Sciences (TUAS) for the evolution and design of testbed infrastructure, which will be used in the European 5G development through experimental validation and trialing of 5G vertical applications and is also a part of the 5GTNF.

The rest of the paper is organized as follows: Sect. 2 describes the previous TUAS research and available test networks, which form a basis of the TUAS testbed. Section 3 discusses the spectrum issues in 5G, while Sect. 4 describes the proposed testbed infrastructure on a high level. Section 5 describes the required spectrum monitoring capabilities and Sect. 6 concludes the paper.

2   TUAS Test Networks and Field Measurement Activities

As the 5G is expected to be able to provide optimized support for a variety of different services and applications [9], understanding the limitations in the current technologies is essential in building a converged 5G ecosystem. Depending on the use case and application, 5G should be able to simultaneously support multiple combinations of reliability, latency, throughput, positioning, and availability [10].

Testbed development requires knowledge on different use cases and vertical applications. TUAS has wide experience in the following vertical applications:

- TV content distribution and reception (broadcasting).
- IoT devices communicating data to the cloud service.
- Video surveillance streams in high definition.

The previous TUAS research and testbeds in digital terrestrial television (DTT) broadcasting, TV White Space (TVWS) and licensed spectrum sharing are described in Sects. 2.1 and 2.2, while Sect. 2.3 describes the recently planned industrial Internet of Things (IoT) testbeds.

2.1 Digital Terrestrial Television and TV White Spaces

TUAS radio laboratory has strong traditions in DTT broadcasting research during the past 10 years. Interoperability tests, mobility tests, verification and validation of rotated constellations and measurements of interference and coverage for DVB-T/H/T2 (Digital Video Broadcasting - Terrestrial/Handheld/Second Generation Terrestrial) have been conducted in several different projects, including EUREKA-Celtic projects WING-TV [11], B21C [12] and ENGINES [13].

Since 2010, the focus of TUAS research has been in spectrum sharing, especially in TVWS and LSA. In spectrum sharing, it is essential to study the technical protection conditions to enable the coexistence between secondary and primary (incumbent) users through field measurements in real test network environments. Field measurements are very time-consuming and expensive to conduct as they require substantial human resources, test network infrastructure, professional level measurement devices and radio licenses [14,15]. Field measurements are rare in the literature. Especially in spectrum sharing, the studies are typically based on simulations and laboratory measurements in controlled environments.

Turku TVWS test environment [16] was set up during in White Space Test Environment for Broadcast Frequencies (WISE), WISE2 and ReWISE (Reliability Extension to White Space Test Environment) projects (2011–2014) [17] to develop and validate technical solutions, accelerate commercial utilization of white spaces, and to contribute to the regulation and standardization work [18–29]. The test network and associated radio laboratory are located in Turku, Finland. TVWS equipment has also been installed and trialed in the use-case pilots of WISE2 project in different locations in Helsinki [16]. The test network was the first in Europe to have a full geolocation-based radio license for the TVWS frequency range 470 MHz–790 MHz [30] in the 40 × 40 km area shown in Fig. 1.

TUAS participated in Horizon 2020 Collaborative Spectrum Sharing competition with a proposal called DISTRIBUTE, which won the competition [31]. The highly innovative view on distributed spectrum sharing in DISTRIBUTE uses solutions involving licensed spectrum and is based on forms of geolocation databases. DISTRIBUTE adapted the geolocation database concept to be entirely decentralized, operating in a distributed way solely on the nodes or terminals that are sharing the spectrum. The approach is consistent with regulation

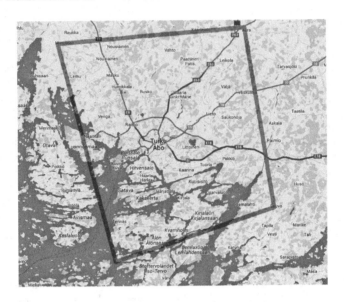

Fig. 1. 40 × 40 km Turku TVWS network radio license area.

and policy. Regulatory constraints might be even conveyed by the regulator at a higher level, and the distributed database solution will always operate within those local constraints. The approach is applicable to sharing of licensed spectrum, such as licensed devices operating in TVWS and Licensed Shared Access (LSA), and license-exempt spectrum sharing such as conventional TVWS and Spectrum Access System (SAS)-supported license-exempt access.

2.2 Licensed Spectrum Sharing

The Future of UHF Frequency Band (FUHF) project [32] continued to study spectrum sharing in ultra high frequency (UHF) TV band. The main focus was on field measurements [15] to study the feasibility of exclusive shared spectrum access through Long Term Evolution (LTE) Supplemental Downlink (SDL) concept [33–37]. The project also observed the regulatory and technical developments to determine the most feasible spectrum utilization methods for the UHF TV broadcasting band. The potential developments in the use of the band and candidate technologies such as WiB [38] and Tower Overlay over LTE-Advanced+ (TOoL+) [39–41] were considered in [15].

TUAS also co-operated with CORE+ project through WISE2 project and was a full project consortium partner in the follow-up project CORE++ [42]. These projects studied the LSA [43–51] and SAS [52–54] concepts by developing the framework, participating in the regulatory work and field trialing the developed systems. TUAS participated in the development of repositories for both LSA and SAS and in developing the spectrum sensing system fulfilling the requirements of Environmental Sensing Capability (ESC) in SAS. The European

Telecommunications Standards Institute (ETSI) work on defining LSA for 2300–2400 MHz band was recently finished [55–58] and is expected to evolve into a spectrum sharing method which could assist in meeting the spectrum demand for 5G [59].

2.3 Industrial IoT

There are two separate private networks for industrial IoT validation and trialing purposes in the TUAS test environment. The first network is a LoRa [60] low power wide area network (LPWAN) to study deep indoor propagation characteristics of a LoRa network. The network consists of two base stations at TUAS premises in ICT-City and Sepänkatu (locations are shown in Fig. 5), one base station at Kuusisto TV-mast and additional base stations operated by a private corporation. The network is operated on three 200 kHz channels at 868.1, 868.3 and 868.5 MHz. The transmissions have a 125 kHz bandwidth and a maximum duty-cycle constraint of 1%.

The second network consists of industrial radio modems, which provide a mission-critical communications solution and are based on private radio networking technology [61]. They provide reliable long-range data connectivity and very high availability for mission-critical applications under severe circumstances. The radio modems allow to build a private network that is not dependent on mobile network operators. The master base station is installed at ICT-city. The network consists of 5 base stations and is operated at 428 MHz.

3 Spectrum Issues in 5G

The main drivers for 5G are the constantly increasing requirements for higher bit rates, shorter latency, reliability, and support for a larger number of devices, as wireless services, especially video streaming and emerging massive IoT, are being adopted at an accelerating pace. The mobile network interface becomes more and more common not just in mobile phones, but also in laptops, tablets, and other end user equipment.

The quality of available content and services also improves and results in a rapid increase in the amount of traffic in mobile networks. The trend is predicted to continue [62–64] in the foreseeable future. Due to the existing base of end user equipment supporting only earlier mobile network generations, 5G systems cannot be allocated on the existing mobile network frequency bands, but they require new spectrum allocations. The increased demand of mobile network capacity can partially be solved by more efficient coding, though the main growth in capacity will take place by decreasing the average cell size and using higher frequency bands.

The European Commission Radio Spectrum Policy Group issued an opinion paper stating that the 5G pioneer bands in Europe are 700 MHz, 3.4–3.8 GHz (the 3.5 GHz band), and 24.25–27.5 GHz [65]. In the countries where the 700 MHz band can be cleared in the coming years, the band will mainly be taken into

LTE use. Otherwise and on longer term, the 700 MHz band, already allocated for mobile broadband (MBB), will be critical in providing nationwide and indoor coverage for 5G [4, 65].

The bands above 24 GHz require a completely new radio access network (RAN) structure due to a large difference in propagation characteristics compared to the currently used mobile bands. Thus, the 3.5 GHz band will be the first strategic band for the 5G launch in Europe [4]. World Radiocommunication Conference 2019 (WRC-19) will decide about European 5G spectrum allocation above 24 GHz, including the pioneer 5G band above 24 GHz [66]. 5G operating in the frequencies between 24 and 86 GHz [4, 67] can provide the large bandwidths and high data rates required by the increasing amount of MBB traffic. In addition to the 24.25–27.5 GHz band, also 31.8–33.4 GHz and 40.5–43.5 GHz are considered to be promising candidates for 5G in Europe.

The frequencies below 6 GHz are essential for 5G [68], as they can provide the needed coverage and reduce the cost of building mobile networks due to their better propagation characteristics. The current 3.5 GHz band allocation differs significantly in European countries. Some countries will be able to clear the band within a few years, but most of the countries have spectrum allocations which cannot be cleared in several years. Some of the countries which cannot clear the band completely consider making spectrum resources within the band available through static or dynamic spectrum sharing. Several European countries also consider regional radio licenses in addition or instead of nationwide radio licenses in the 3.5 GHz band. In general, spectrum sharing [69, 70] methods may play a role in meeting the spectrum demand for 5G [59, 71, 72] especially in the frequencies below 6 GHz.

In the United States (US), a broadcast television spectrum incentive auction [73] was made to reorganize the DTT transmissions to the lower parts of the UHF TV frequency band and create contiguous blocks of cleared spectrum to the upper parts of the frequency band to be auctioned for the mobile network operator (MNOs). The process comprised of two separate auctions: a reverse auction for broadcasters to determine the price at which they would be willing to relinquish their spectrum usage rights and a forward auction to determine the prices MNOs are willing to pay for the spectrum. The auctions were interdependent and consisted of several rounds until the set goals regarding the economics and the amount of spectrum to be cleared were achieved. The auction was formally closed in April 2017 and resulted in a reallocation of 84 MHz of DTT spectrum and began a 39-month transition period, during which some television (TV) stations need to take their new channel assignments into use [74]. It is possible that Europe and the rest of the world could follow the US in reallocating the 600 MHz band for MBB to obtain more spectrum for 5G in frequencies below 1 GHz.

4   TUAS Testbed for 5G Vertical Applications

The current research activities at TUAS are largely focused on the development of a converged 5G ecosystem: Tekes-funded [6] WIVE (Wireless for Verticals)

[75], CORNET (Critical Operations over Regular Networks) [76], RAMP (Industrial Internet Reference Architecture for Medical Platforms) [77] and EU-funded 5G-PPP phase 2 project 5G-XCAST (Broadcast and Multicast Communication Enablers for the Fifth Generation of Wireless Systems) [78].

The TUAS testbed will support the following 5G verticals [79,80]:

- Smart cities [80].
- Media and entertainment [81].
- Factories of the future [82].

The TUAS 5G testbed focus will be on spectrum below 6 GHz. The frequencies of the current test network components are illustrated in Fig. 2. Radio licenses need to be acquired for each of the frequency bands, and permission from the MNOs is needed in the bands which have been allocated to LTE. As can be seen from Fig. 6, the 700 MHz band does not have any transmissions and is available for testbed use for the time being even though it has already been auctioned to the MNOs. The 5G candidate band 3.4–3.8 GHz is the main candidate for a future testbed extension, while the 2.5–2.69 GHz band is a backup frequency band if radio licenses cannot be obtained to the desired frequency bands.

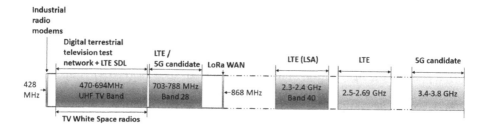

Fig. 2. TUAS testbed service frequencies.

The overall TUAS 5G testbed service architecture is illustrated in Fig. 3. The testbed infrastructure, backbone and the Operations, Administration, and Maintenance (OAM) are located in the TUAS radio laboratory at ICT-city building in Turku, Finland. The internal LTE virtual Evolved Packet Core (vEPC) and the LSA are operated on servers of the TUAS radio laboratory network. The ETSI LSA architecture reference model described in [57] is used. The blocks in grey color describe the equipment under the management of TUAS radio laboratory and the blocks in white the equipment outside TUAS control. Thus, the LSA controller is currently an external service. The Microsoft Azure portal and the external LTE Evolved Packet Cores (EPCs) are connected to the TUAS radio laboratory infrastructure through a firewall and a Virtual Private Network gateway (VPN-GW). The green blocks illustrate the air interfaces of different testbed services and the orange box the spectrum monitoring and sensing systems described in Sect. 5.

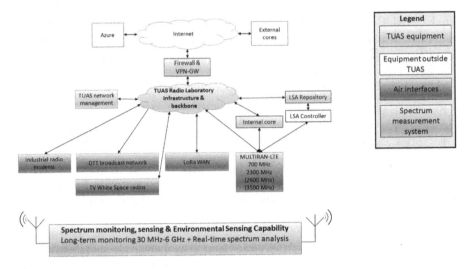

Fig. 3. Block diagram of overall TUAS testbed service architecture. (Color figure online)

One of the major challenges in the 5G experimentations and trials will be the user terminals. Especially the supported frequency ranges, the level of flexibility the terminals allow and the available software applications will largely determine for which purposes the terminals can be used for.

Figure 4 gives a more detailed description of the LTE part of the testbed along with a plan for the installation of first LTE Evolved Node Bs (eNBs). Two small-cell eNBs will be installed at ICT-city premises for indoor trialing purposes, one rooftop eNB will be installed at ICT-city and a second rooftop eNB at TUAS premises at Sepänkatu. The test network infrastructure includes an optical transport network (OTN) between the premises at ICT-city and Sepänkatu.

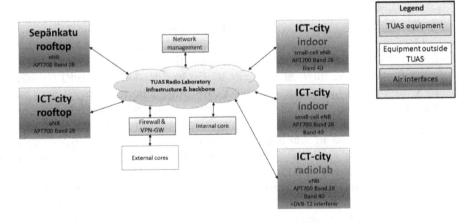

Fig. 4. LTE network architecture block diagram.

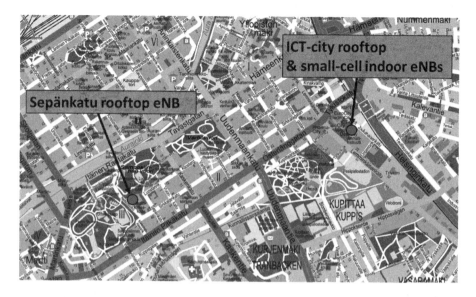

Fig. 5. LTE eNB geographical locations in Turku, Finland.

The geographical locations of the eNBs in Turku, Finland, are shown in Fig. 5. In addition to LTE eNBs, the locations have the following services:

- Sepänkatu: long-term radio spectrum observatory system, LoRa base station and industrial radio modem base station.
- ICT-city radio laboratory: on-demand real-time spectrum analysis, LoRa base station, industrial radio modem base station and DTT transmitter.

Instead of being only a new radio access technology for LTE, 5G will be an integration of several different services and networks. Thus, the overall system will be a completely redesigned programmable multi-service architecture [83–85] which uses network slicing. Network slicing means that the system can run multiple service instances (slices) on the same physical infrastructure. Network slices can be configured for each application, use case or service of 5G to meet its specific requirements and to serve different groups of users. The flexibility and programmability needed to create the network slices are provided by NFV and SDN.

5G-XCAST project [78] aims to design a dynamically adaptable 5G network architecture, which has layer independent network interfaces that are capable of dynamically and seamlessly switching between unicast, multicast and broadcast modes or using them in parallel. For example, the TUAS 5G testbed will be used for demonstrating point-to-multipoint Public Warning Systems (PWS) capabilities developed in the project.

The TUAS testbed can be flexibly extended as new network functionalities are developed and new equipment becomes available. The testbed infrastructure allows to test various Proof of Concepts (PoCs) from different 5G vertical applications.

5   Radio Spectrum Monitoring and Sensing

A spectrum observatory network was built in a GlobalRF Spectrum Opportunity Assessment project [86–92] in Wireless Innovation between Finland and the US (WiFiUS) program [93], which was jointly funded by the National Science Foundation (NSF) [94] and Tekes [6]. The project built an international network of radio frequency (RF) spectrum observatories continuously collecting long-term spectrum data to study the trends in spectrum utilization and to identify frequency bands where spectrum sharing could be feasible.

Three spectrum observatories are operational in Chicago, US, Virginia, US, and Turku, Finland. The measurement data from the spectrum observatories in Finland and the US is collected and stored into a single location at Illinois Institute of Technology [95] in Chicago. The RFeye nodes manufactured by CRFS [96] measure the whole frequency band from 30 MHz to 6 GHz in each of the locations.

Figure 6 shows the Turku spectrum observatory power spectral density (PSD) from June 26th 2017 for 470–900 MHz. The 700 MHz band was allocated to MBB [97,98] and in Finland the band has been cleared and auctioned for MNOs [99]. As can be seen from the figure, the 5 DTT multiplexes have been regrouped to the 470–694 MHz UHF TV broadcasting frequency range, but the 700 MHz MBB is not operational yet. Three 10 MHz blocks of frequency division duplex (FDD)-LTE downlink transmissions are active in the 800 MHz band [100].

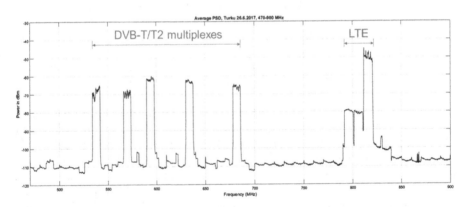

Fig. 6. 470–900 MHz UHF spectrum average PSD on June 26th 2017.

ICT-City site is equipped with several on-demand spectrum monitoring systems, which can distinguish different signals operating in the same frequency band [101], as shown in Fig. 7. The wideband signal in Fig. 7 is a 10 MHz LTE downlink signal and the two low-power transmissions are Programme Making and Special Events (PMSE) wireless microphones with 200 kHz bandwidth. The y-axis represents the signal strength in dBm and the x-axis the frequency. The center frequency is 783 MHz and the span 20 MHz. TUAS has also participated in the development of distributed spectrum sensing system with low cost hardware [102] and Environmental Sensing Capability (ESC) in SAS [54].

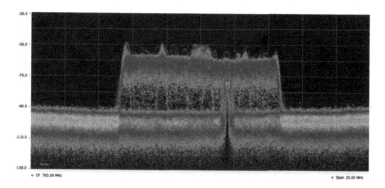

Fig. 7. On-demand spectrum monitoring is capable of distinguishing different signals operating in the same frequency band.

6   Conclusions

5G can be seen as an umbrella, which converges all the current wireless network systems, services and frequency ranges into one ecosystem. The ecosystem includes the evolution of the old technologies and completely new technologies and architectures, all of which need to meet the key performance indicators (KPIs) set in 5G-PPP for different vertical applications and services. The presented TUAS 5G testbed is a case study, which demonstrates how a testbed can be built for the purposes of the 5G research projects TUAS is involved in. The testbed allows to use different LTE ePCs and frequency ranges, which allows to support a range of different vertical applications.

Acknowledgements. Turku University of Applied Sciences is grateful for companies, especially Nokia, Teleste, Digita, Fairspectrum, and Satel, that have supported testbed infrastructure development in EUREKA-Celtic [103], 5thGear [7], Trial [104] and Industrial Internet [105] programs funded in Finland by the Finnish Funding Agency for Innovation (Tekes) [6]. The testbed will be further developed. This work is supported in part by Tekes under the project Wireless for Verticals (WIVE). WIVE is a part of 5G Test Network Finland (5GTNF), and in part by the European Commission under the 5G-PPP project 5G-Xcast (H2020-ICT-2016-2 call, grant number 761498). The views expressed in this contribution are those of the authors and do not necessarily represent the projects.

References

1. Lien, S.Y., Shieh, S.L., Huang, Y., Su, B., Hsu, Y.L., Wei, H.Y.: 5G new radio: waveform, frame structure, multiple access, and initial access. IEEE Commun. Mag. **55**(6), 64–71 (2017)
2. 5G-PPP Architecture Working Group: View on 5G Architecture, Version 1.0, July 2016
3. The 5G Infrastructure Public Private Partnership. https://5g-ppp.eu/
4. European Commission: COM (2016) 588 final: 5G for Europe: An Action Plan, September 2016

5. 5G Infrastructure Association (5G-IA): 5G Pan-European trials roadmap version 1.0, May 2017
6. Tekes. https://www.tekes.fi/en/
7. Tekes: 5thGear programme, 2014–2019. https://www.tekes.fi/en/programmes-and-services/tekes-programmes/5thgear/projects/
8. 5G Test Network Finland. http://5gtnf.fi/
9. 3GPP: 3GPP TS 22.261 V16.0.0: Technical Specification Group Services and System Aspects; Service requirements for the 5G system; Stage 1 (Release 16), June 2017
10. NGMN Alliance: NGMN 5G White Paper v1.0, February 2015
11. Celtic-Plus: The B21C project (Broadcast for the 21st Century). https://www.celticplus.eu/project-wing-tv/
12. Celtic-Plus: The B21C project (Broadcast for the 21st Century). https://www.celticplus.eu/project-b21c/
13. Celtic-Plus: The ENGINES project. https://www.celticplus.eu/project-engines/
14. Kalliovaara, J.: Field measurements in determining incumbent spectrum utilization and protection criteria in wireless co-existence studies. Ph.D. dissertation, University of Turku (2017). ISBN 978-951-29-6825-1
15. Kalliovaara, J., Ekman, R., Talmola, P., Höyhtyä, M., Jokela, T., Poikonen, J., Paavola, J., Jakobsson, M.: Coexistence of DTT and mobile broadband: a survey and guidelines for field measurements. Wirel. Commun. Mob. Comput. **2017**, 19 p. (2017). https://doi.org/10.1155/2017/1563132. Article no. 1563132
16. Kalliovaara, J., Paavola, J., Ekman, R., Kivinen, A., Talmola, P.: TV White Space Network Interference Measurements and Application Pilot Trials. Final report from field measurement campaigns and application pilot trials in WISE projects during 2011–2014, November 2016
17. White Space test environment for broadcast frequencies (WISE) projects. http://wise.turkuamk.fi
18. Holland, O., Sastry, N., Ping, S., Knopp, R., Kaltenberger, F., Nussbaum, D., Hallio, J., Jakobsson, M., Auranen, J., Ekman, R., Paavola, J., Kivinen, A., Tran, H.N., Ishizu, K., Harada, H., Chawdhry, P., Chareau, J.M., Bishop, J., Bavaro, M., Anguili, E., Gao, Y., Dionisio, R., Marques, P., Kokkinen, H., Luukkonen, O.: A series of trials in the UK as part of the Ofcom TV white spaces pilot. In: 1st International Workshop on Cognitive Cellular Systems (CCS), pp. 1–5, September 2014
19. Holland, O., Ping, S., Sastry, N., Chawdhry, P., Chareau, J.M., Bishop, J., Xing, H., Taskafa, S., Aijaz, A., Bavaro, M., Viaud, P., Pinato, T., Anguili, E., Akhavan, M.R., McCann, J., Gao, Y., Qin, Z., Zhang, Q., Knopp, R., Kaltenberger, F., Nussbaum, D., Dionisio, R., Ribeiro, J., Marques, P., Hallio, J., Jakobsson, M., Auranen, J., Ekman, R., Kokkinen, H., Paavola, J., Kivinen, A., Solc, T., Mohorcic, M., Tran, H.N., Ishizu, K., Matsumura, T., Ibuka, K., Harada, H., Mizutani, K.: Some initial results and observations from a series of trials within the Ofcom TV white spaces pilot. In: 2015 IEEE 81st Vehicular Technology Conference (VTC Spring), pp. 1–7, May 2015
20. Ojaniemi, J., Kalliovaara, J., Alam, A., Poikonen, J., Wichman, R.: Optimal field measurement design for radio environment mapping. In: 2013 47th Annual Conference on Information Sciences and Systems (CISS) (2013)
21. Ojaniemi, J., Kalliovaara, J., Poikonen, J., Wichman, R.: A practical method for combining multivariate data in radio environment mapping. In: IEEE International Symposium on Personal, Indoor and Mobile Radio Communications (PIMRC), pp. 729–733 (2013)

22. Talmola, P., Kalliovaara, J., Paavola, J., Ekman, R., Vainisto, A., Aurala, N., Kokkinen, H., Heiska, K., Wichman, R., Poikonen, J.: Field measurements of WSD-DTT protection ratios over outdoor and indoor reference geometries. In: 2012 7th International ICST Conference on Cognitive Radio Oriented Wireless Networks and Communications (CROWNCOM), June 2012
23. Paavola, J., Kalliovaara, J., Poikonen, J.: Section 6.1.2 'TVWS Coexistence with Incumbents'. In: Medeisis, A., Holland, O. (eds.) Cognitive Radio Policy and Regulation: Techno-Economic Studies to Facilitate Dynamic Spectrum Access. Signals and Communication Technology. Springer, Cham (2014)
24. CEPT: CEPT/SE43(11)36 WSD Maximum Power Considerations, 10th SE43 meeting, Bologna, Italy, July 2011
25. CEPT: CEPT/ECC SE43(11)Info 08 WSD Maximum Power Measurement Report, 10th SE43 meeting, Bologna, Italy, July 2011
26. CEPT: CEPT/ECC SE43(11)81 Wise-Project Measurement Report: WSD maximum Power Indoor Measurements in Turku Test Network, 12th SE43 meeting, Cambridge, UK, December 2011
27. CEPT: CEPT/ECC SE43(11)81 WSD maximum power measurements in indoor 2 m reference geometry, 12th SE43 meeting, Cambridge, UK, December 2011
28. CEPT: CEPT/ECC SE43(11)82 PMSE protection measurements in Helsinki City Theatre, 12th SE43 meeting, Cambridge, UK, December 2011
29. CEPT: CEPT/ECC SE43(11)82AP1 Wise-Project Measurement Report: PMSE Measurements in Helsinki City Theatre, 12th SE43 meeting, Cambridge, UK, December 2011
30. Kokkinen, H.: Fairspectrum provides TV white space database for Europe's first geolocation radio license. Press Release, Helsinki, Finland (2012)
31. European Commission: Collaborative spectrum sharing. https://ec.europa.eu/research/horizonprize/index.cfm?prize=spectrum-sharing
32. The Future of UHF Frequency Band project. http://fuhf.turkuamk.fi
33. Kalliovaara, J., Ekman, R., Jokela, T., Jakobsson, M., Talmola, P., Paavola, J., Huuhka, E., Jokisalo, M., Meriläinen, M.: Suitability of ITU-R P.1546 propagation predictions for allocating LTE SDL with GE06. In: 2017 IEEE International Symposium on Broadband Multimedia Systems and Broadcasting (BMSB), June 2017
34. Yrjölä, S., Mustonen, M., Matinmikko, M., Talmola, P.: LTE broadcast and supplemental downlink enablers for exploiting novel service and business opportunities in the flexible use of the UHF broadcasting spectrum. IEEE Commun. Mag. 54(7), 76–83 (2016)
35. Yrjölä, S., Huuhka, E., Talmola, P., Knuutila, T.: Coexistence of digital terrestrial television and 4G LTE mobile network utilizing supplemental downlink concept: a real case study. IEEE Trans. Veh. Technol. PP(99), 1 (2016)
36. Yrjölä, S., Ahokangas, P., Matinmikko, M., Talmola, P.: Incentives for the key stakeholders in the hybrid use of the UHF broadcasting spectrum utilizing Supplemental Downlink: a dynamic capabilities view. In: 2014 1st International Conference on 5G for Ubiquitous Connectivity (5GU), pp. 215–221, November 2014
37. Yle: Yle, Qualcomm and Nokia Announce Worlds First Demonstration of LTE Supplemental Downlink in a TV Broadcast Band, September 2016. http://yle.fi/aihe/artikkeli/2016/09/02/yle-qualcomm-and-nokia-announce-worlds-first-demonstration-lte-supplemental
38. Stare, E., Gimenez, J., Klenner, P.: WIB: a new system concept for digital terrestrial television (DTT). In: IBC 2016 Conference, September 2016

39. Juretzek, F.: Integration of high tower, high power LTE-advanced broadcast into mobile networks. In: 2016 IEEE International Symposium on Broadband Multimedia Systems and Broadcasting (BMSB), pp. 1–6, June 2016

40. Ilsen, S., Rother, D., Juretzek, F., Brtillon, P., Seccia, J., Ripamonti, S.: Tower overlay over LTE-Advanced+ (TOoL+) - field trial results. In: 2015 IEEE 5th International Conference on Consumer Electronics - Berlin (ICCE-Berlin), pp. 369–373, September 2015

41. Ilsen, S., Juretzek, F., Richter, L., Rother, D., Brtillon, P.: Tower overlay over LTE-Advanced+ (TOoL+): results of a field trial in Paris. In: 2016 IEEE International Symposium on Broadband Multimedia Systems and Broadcasting (BMSB), pp. 1–6, June 2016

42. Cognitive Radio Trial Environment CORE+. http://core.willab.fi/

43. Palola, M., Rautio, T., Matinmikko, M., Prokkola, J., Mustonen, M., Heikkilä, M., Kippola, T., Yrjölä, S., Hartikainen, V., Tudose, L., Kivinen, A., Paavola, J., Okkonen, J., Mäkeläinen, M., Hänninen, T., Kokkinen, H.: Licensed shared access (LSA) trial demonstration using real LTE network. In: 2014 9th International Conference on Cognitive Radio Oriented Wireless Networks and Communications (CROWNCOM), pp. 498–502, June 2014

44. Paavola, J., Kivinen, A.: Device authentication architecture for TV white space systems. In: 2014 9th International Conference on Cognitive Radio Oriented Wireless Networks and Communications (CROWNCOM), pp. 460–465, June 2014

45. Palola, M., Matinmikko, M., Prokkola, J., Mustonen, M., Heikkilä, M., Kippola, T., Yrjölä, S., Hartikainen, V., Tudose, L., Kivinen, A., Paavola, J., Heiska, K.: Live field trial of licensed shared access (LSA) concept using LTE network in 2.3 GHz band. In: 2014 IEEE International Symposium on Dynamic Spectrum Access Networks (DySPAN), pp. 38–47, April 2014

46. Mustonen, M., Matinmikko, M., Palola, M., Yrjölä, S., Paavola, J., Kivinen, A., Engelberg, J.: Considerations on the licensed shared access (LSA) architecture from the incumbent perspective. In: 2014 9th International Conference on Cognitive Radio Oriented Wireless Networks and Communications (CROWNCOM), pp. 150–155, June 2014

47. Palola, M., Matinmikko, M., Prokkola, J., Mustonen, M., Heikkilä, M., Kippola, T., Yrjölä, S., Hartikainen, V., Tudose, L., Kivinen, A., Paavola, J., Heiska, K., Hänninen, T., Okkonen, J.: Description of finnish licensed shared access (LSA) field trial using TD-LTE in 2.3 GHz band. In: 2014 IEEE International Symposium on Dynamic Spectrum Access Networks (DySPAN), pp. 374–375, April 2014

48. Kalliovaara, J., Jokela, T., Ekman, R., Hallio, J., Jakobsson, M., Kippola, T.: Interference measurements for licensed shared access (LSA) between LTE and wireless cameras in 2.3 GHz band. In: 2015 IEEE International Symposium on Dynamic Spectrum Access Networks (DySPAN), pp. 128–134 (2015)

49. Matinmikko, M., Palola, M., Mustonen, M., Rautio, T., Heikkilä, M., Kippola, T., Yrjölä, S., Hartikainen, V., Tudose, L., Kivinen, A., Kokkinen, H., Mäkeläinen, M.: Field trial of licensed shared access (LSA) with enhanced LTE resource optimization and incumbent protection. In: 2015 IEEE International Symposium on Dynamic Spectrum Access Networks (DySPAN), pp. 263–264, September 2015

50. Yrjölä, S., Hartikainen, V., Tudose, L., Ojaniemi, J., Kivinen, A., Kippola, T.: Field trial of Licensed Shared Access with enhanced spectrum controller power control algorithms and LTE enablers. J. Sig. Process. Syst. 89(1), 119–132 (2017). https://doi.org/10.1007/s11265-016-1170-1

51. Luttinen, E., Matinmikko, M., Ahokangas, P., Katz, M., Yrjölä, S.: Feasibility assessment of Licensed Shared Access (LSA) concept - case of a finish mobile network operator (MNO). In: 2014 1st International Conference on 5G for Ubiquitous Connectivity (5GU), pp. 252–257, November 2014
52. Aho, P., Palola, M., Kippola, T., Heikkilä, M., Mäkeläinen, M., Hänninen, T., Tudose, L., Hartikainen, V., Yrjölä, S., Kivinen, A., Paavola, J.: Field trial of Citizens Broadband Radio Service (CBRS)/Spectrum Access System (SAS). In: Wireless Innovation Forum European Conference on Communications Technology and Software Defined Radio (WInnComm-Europe 2016), Paris, France, October 2016
53. Palola, M., Hartikainen, V., Mäkeläinen, M., Kippola, T., Aho, P., Lähetkangas, K., Tudose, L., Kivinen, A., Joshi, S., Hallio, J.: The first end-to-end live trial of CBRS with carrier aggregation using 3.5 GHz LTE equipment. In: 2017 IEEE International Symposium on Dynamic Spectrum Access Networks (DySPAN), pp. 1–2, March 2017
54. Palola, M., Höyhtyä, M., Aho, P., Mustonen, M., Kippola, T., Heikkilä, M., Yrjölä, S., Hartikainen, V., Tudose, L., Kivinen, A., Ekman, R., Hallio, J., Paavola, J., Mäkeläinen, M., Hänninen, T.: Field trial of the 3.5 GHz citizens broadband radio service governed by a spectrum access system (SAS). In: 2017 IEEE International Symposium on Dynamic Spectrum Access Networks (DySPAN), pp. 1–9, March 2017
55. ETSI: ETSI TR 103 113 V1.1.1., Mobile Broadband services in the 2300–2400 MHz frequency band under Licensed Shared Access regime, July 2013
56. ETSI: ETSI TS 103 154 V1.1.1, Reconfigurable Radio Systems (RRS); System requirements for operation of Mobile Broadband Systems in the 2300 MHz–2400 MHz band under Licensed Shared Access (LSA), October 2014
57. ETSI: ETSI TS 103 235 V1.1.1, Reconfigurable Radio Systems (RRS); System architecture and high level procedures for operation of Licensed Shared Access (LSA) in the 2300 MHz–2400 MHz band, October 2015
58. ETSI: ETSI TS 103 379 V1.1.1, Reconfigurable Radio Systems (RRS); Information elements and protocols for the interface between LSA Controller (LC) and LSA Repository (LR) for operation of Licensed Shared Access (LSA) in the 2300 MHz–2400 MHz band, January 2017
59. ETSI releases specifications for Licensed Shared Access, April 2017. http://www.etsi.org/news-events/news/1181-2017-04-news-etsi-releases-specifications-for-licensed-shared-access
60. Gregora, L., Vojtech, L., Neruda, M.: Indoor signal propagation of LoRa technology. In: 2016 17th International Conference on Mechatronics - Mechatronika (ME), pp. 1–4, December 2016
61. SATEL: SATEL XPRS radio networking technology. https://xprs.satel.com/
62. Cisco: White Paper: Cisco Visual Networking Index: Forecast and Methodology, 2016–2021, June 2017
63. Ericsson: Ericsson Mobility Report 2017, June 2017
64. ITU-R: Report ITU-R M.2290, Future spectrum requirements estimate for terrestrial IMT, December 2013
65. Radio Spectrum Policy Group: RSPG16-032 final: Strategic roadmap towards 5G for Europe, Opinion on spectrum related aspects for next generation wireless systems (5G), November 2016
66. Marcus, M.J.: WRC-19 issues: a survey. IEEE Wirel. Commun. **24**(1), 2–3 (2017)
67. EU project METIS-II: White paper: Preliminary Views and initial considerations on 5G RAN Architecture and Functional Design, March 2016

68. Badic, B., Drewes, C., Karls, I., Mueck, M.: Rolling Out 5G: Use Cases, Applications, and Technology Solutions. Apress, New York (2016)

69. European Commission: COM/2012/478 Promoting the Shared Use of Radio Spectrum Resources in the Internal Market, September 2012

70. Presidents Council of Advisors on Science and Technology: Realizing the full potential of government-held spectrum to spur economic growth, July 2012

71. Mueck, M., Jiang, W., Sun, G., Cao, H., Dutkiewicz, E., Choi, S.: White Paper: Novel Spectrum Usage Paradigms for 5G, November 2014

72. Morgado, A., Gomes, A., Frascolla, V., Ntougias, K., Papadias, C., Slock, D., Avdic, E., Marchetti, N., Haziza, N., Anouar, H., Yang, Y., Pesavento, M., Khan, F., Ratnarajah, T.: Dynamic LSA for 5G networks the ADEL perspective. In: 2015 European Conference on Networks and Communications (EuCNC), pp. 190–194, June 2015

73. Gómez-Barquero, D., Caldwell, M.W.: Broadcast television spectrum incentive auctions in the U.S.: trends, challenges, and opportunities. IEEE Commun. Mag. **53**(7), 50–56 (2015)

74. Federal Communications Commission: Broadcast Incentive Auction. https://www.fcc.gov/about-fcc/fcc-initiatives/incentive-auctions. Accessed 20 June 2017

75. WIVE project. http://5gtnf.fi/projects/wive/

76. Critical Operations over Regular Networks (CORNET) project. http://www.oulu.fi/cornet/

77. Industrial Internet Reference Architecture for Medical Platforms (RAMP) project. http://ramp.turkuamk.fi/

78. 5G-Xcast project. http://5g-xcast.eu

79. 5G-PPP: White paper: 5G empowering vertical industries, February 2016

80. NGMN Alliance: Perspectives on Vertical Industries and Implications for 5G v2.0, September 2016

81. 5G-PPP: White paper: 5G and Media & Entertainment, January 2016

82. 5G-PPP: White paper: 5G and the Factories of the Future, October 2015

83. Nokia: Nokia white paper: 5G - a System of Systems for a programmable multi-service architecture (2016)

84. 5G Americas: 5G Americas White Paper Network Slicing for 5G and Beyond, November 2016

85. 3GPP: 3GPP TS 23.501 V1.0.0: 3rd Generation Partnership Project; Technical Specification Group Services and System Aspects; System Architecture for the 5G System; Stage 2 (Release 15), June 2017

86. Taher, T., Attard, R., Riaz, A., Roberson, D., Taylor, J., Zdunek, K., Hallio, J., Ekman, R., Paavola, J., Suutala, J., Roning, J., Matinmikko, M., Höyhtyä, M., MacKenzie, A.: Global spectrum observatory network setup and initial findings. In: 2014 9th International Conference on Cognitive Radio Oriented Wireless Networks and Communications (CROWNCOM), June 2014

87. Attard, R., Kalliovaara, J., Taher, T., Taylor, J., Paavola, J., Ekman, R., Roberson, D.: A high-performance tiered storage system for a global spectrum observatory network. In: Proceedings of the 9th International Conference on Cognitive Radio Oriented Wireless Networks (CROWNCOM) (2014)

88. Noorts, G., Engel, J., Taylor, J., Roberson, D., Bacchus, R., Taher, T., Zdunek, K.: An RF spectrum observatory database based on a hybrid storage system. In: 2012 IEEE International Symposium on Dynamic Spectrum Access Networks (DySPAN), October 2012

89. Abdallah, A., MacKenzie, A.B., Marojevic, V., Kalliovaara, J., Bacchus, R., Riaz, A., Roberson, D., Juhani, H., Ekman, R.: Detecting the impact of human mega-events on spectrum usage. In: 2016 13th IEEE Annual Consumer Communications Networking Conference (CCNC), pp. 523–529, January 2016

90. Höyhtyä, M., Matinmikko, M., Chen, X., Hallio, J., Auranen, J., Ekman, R., Röning, J., Engelberg, J., Kalliovaara, J., Taher, T., Riaz, A., Roberson, D.: Spectrum occupancy measurements in the 2.3-2.4 GHz band: guidelines for licensed shared access in Finland. EAI Endorsed Trans. Cogn. Commun. 1(2), e2, 11 p. (2015). http://eudl.eu/issue/cogcom/1/2

91. Höyhtyä, M., Matinmikko, M., Chen, X., Hallio, J., Auranen, J., Ekman, R., Roning, J., Engelberg, J., Kalliovaara, J., Taher, T., Riaz, A., Roberson, D.: Measurements and analysis of spectrum occupancy in the 2.3–2.4 GHz band in Finland and Chicago. In: 2014 9th International Conference on Cognitive Radio Oriented Wireless Networks and Communications (CROWNCOM), pp. 95–101, June 2014

92. Höyhtyä, M., Mämmelä, A., Eskola, M., Matinmikko, M., Kalliovaara, J., Ojaniemi, J., Suutala, J., Ekman, R., Bacchus, R., Roberson, D.: Spectrum occupancy measurements: a survey and use of interference maps. IEEE Commun. Surv. Tutor. 18(4), 2386–2414 (2016)

93. Wireless Innovation between Finland and US (WiFiUS). http://209.140.21.224/~jwifiusa/

94. National Science Foundation. http://www.nsf.gov/

95. Illinois Institute of Technology. http://web.iit.edu/

96. CRFS: CRFS RFeye Node 20-6. https://us.crfs.com/en/products/nodes/node-20-6/

97. ITU: Resolution 232 [COM5/10] (WRC-12) - Use of the frequency band 694–790 MHz by the mobile, except aeronautical mobile, service in Region 1 and related studies (2012)

98. CEPT: CEPT Report 53: Report A from CEPT to the European Commission in response to the Mandate To develop harmonised technical conditions for the 694–790 MHz (700 MHz) frequency band in the EU for the provision of wireless broadband and other uses in support of EU spectrum policy objectives, November 2014

99. Finnish Communications Regulatory Authority: 703–733 MHz/758–788 MHz spectrum auction. https://www.viestintavirasto.fi/en/spectrum/radiospectrumuse/spectrumauction.html. Accessed 30 June 2017

100. Finnish Communications Regulatory Authority: End of 4G spectrum auction. https://www.viestintavirasto.fi/en/ficora/news/2013/endof4gspectrumauction.html. Accessed 30 June 2017

101. Tektronix: RSA306B USB Spectrum Analyzer. http://www.tek.com/spectrum-analyzer/rsa306. Accessed 20 June 2017

102. Grönroos, S., Nybom, K., Björkqvist, J., Hallio, J., Auranen, J., Ekman, R.: Distributed spectrum sensing using low cost hardware. J. Sig. Process. Syst. 83(1), 5–17 (2016)

103. Celtic-Plus: Celtic-Plus web page. https://www.celticplus.eu

104. Tekes: Trial Environment for Cognitive Radio and Networks 2011–2014. https://www.tekes.fi/en/programmes-and-services/recently-ended-programmes/trial/

105. Tekes: Team Finland Industrial Internet Program 2014–2019. https://www.tekes.fi/en/programmes-and-services/tekes-programmes/industrial-internet-business-revolution/

Interference Study of Micro Licensing for 5G Micro Operator Small Cell Deployments

Marja Matinmikko[1]([⊠]), Antti Roivainen[2], Matti Latva-aho[1], and Kimmo Hiltunen[1]

[1] Centre for Wireless Communications (CWC),
University of Oulu, Oulu, Finland
{marja.matinmikko,matti.latva-aho,
kimmo.hiltunen}@oulu.fi
[2] Keysight Technologies Finland Oy, Oulu, Finland
antti.roivainen@keysight.com

Abstract. 5G brings along very dense small cell deployments in specific locations such as hospitals, campuses, shopping malls, and factories. This will result in a novel 5G deployment scenario where different stakeholders, i.e., micro operators, are issued local spectrum access rights in the form of micro licenses, to deploy networks in the specific premises. This new form of sharing-based micro licensing guarantees that the local 5G networks remain free from harmful interference from each other and also protects potential incumbent spectrum users' rights. It admits a larger number of stakeholders to gain access to the 5G spectrum to serve different vertical sectors' needs beyond traditional mobile network operators (MNO) improving the competition landscape. We characterize the resulting interference scenarios between the different micro operators' deployments and focus on the building-to-building scenario where two micro operators hold micro licenses in separate buildings in co-channel and adjacent channel cases. We analyze the resulting allowable transmit power levels of a base station from inside one building towards an end user mobile terminal inside another building as a function of the minimum separation distance between the two micro operator networks. Numerical results are provided for the example case of the 3.5 GHz band with different building entry losses characterizing the impact of propagation characteristics on the resulting interference levels. The results indicate that the building entry losses strongly influence the interference levels and resulting required minimum separation distances, which calls for flexibility in determining the micro license conditions for the building specific situation.

Keywords: 5G · Interference management · Micro operator
Spectrum sharing

1 Introduction

Next generation mobile communication networks known as 5G are expected to drive industrial and societal transformations and economic growth with high quality mobile broadband offerings and supporting of new types of high demand applications.

© ICST Institute for Computer Sciences, Social Informatics and Telecommunications Engineering 2018
P. Marques et al. (Eds.): CROWNCOM 2017, LNICST 228, pp. 264–275, 2018.
https://doi.org/10.1007/978-3-319-76207-4_22

Provisioning of high quality wireless connectivity in specific locations such as schools, transport hubs, public service providers' units, and enterprises has become a key societal objective in Europe as the enabler for new services [1]. The location specific needs for wireless connectivity have become a major design criteria in the development of 5G networks and their applications in different vertical sectors [2]. There is a growing need for locally operated wireless network deployments by different stake-holders to meet ever increasing requirements for higher capacity, higher data rate, lower latency, massive device density, and reduced capital and operational costs as discussed in [3].

Timely availability of 5G spectrum will be critical for the roll out of the new networks. These networks are expected to be deployed in a wide range of frequency bands with different propagation characteristics including existing spectrum bands for mobile below 1 GHz and between 1–6 GHz, as well as new spectrum above 6 GHz especially in the millimeter wave range (24–86 GHz) as expected from the World Radiocomunication Conference in 2019 (WRC-19). While regulators are globally committed to making new 5G spectrum available, the authorization models to use the 5G spectrum is an open topic and will include a mix of licensed and unlicensed models [1, 4]. New sharing based spectrum authorization models for granting access rights to use the 5G bands among the applicants in an objective, transparent, non-discriminatory and proportionate way are urgently needed to support innovation and market entry as outlined in [4].

Several spectrum sharing models have been introduced in regulation to consider different spectrum authorization regimes to admit additional users while protecting the incumbents in the band. European Licensed Shared Access (LSA) discussed in the 2.3–2.4 GHz and 3.6–3.8 GHz bands introduces additional licensed users while protecting the existing incumbent users and giving quality of service guarantees also for the new LSA license holders [5]. However, the authorization model for granting the LSA licenses is determined to be a national matter left for the national regulators and has not been discussed yet. A three-tier sharing model for Citizens Broadband Radio Service (CBRS) by the Federal Communications Commission (FCC) in US introduces two layers of additional users under licensed or general authorization regimes in the 3.55–3.7 GHz band while protecting the incumbents [6]. The priority access layers (PAL) introduces new local spectrum licenses of 10 MHz bandwidth to be granted via auctions for three-year license period over a geographic area of census tract. Both the LSA and CBRS models introduce additional local users since country-wide spectrum availability cannot be guaranteed due to incumbent activity that needs to be protected.

In the research domain, there have been studies on sharing between mobile network operators (MNO) in a so called co-primary shared model [7] where several MNOs access a common band with equal access rights. This model has also been considered for the millimeter wave bands in [8, 9] requiring either complex coordination mechanisms between MNOs or resulting in interference between them. In particular, new sharing-based local spectrum authorization models are needed for ultra-dense small cell deployments in specific buildings where venue owners role becomes increasingly important as discussed in [10]. To this end, the development of suitable spectrum authorization models for 5G is an open topic in terms of the level of exclusivity in spectrum use and resulting mechanisms for protection from harmful interference. The use of higher carrier frequencies for 5G inherently assumes local network deployments due the propagation characteristics, which needs to be properly taken into account in designing the authorization mechanisms.

There is a growing pressure to preserve a competitive environment open the mobile connectivity market to new entrants [1]. Future 5G networks will be able to share various resources establishing end-to-end network slices particularly in the higher frequency bands where the new networks will consist of very dense deployments of small cells connected with high capacity backhauls [2]. The concept of micro operators as new entrants to the mobile market were discussed in [3, 11] to establish local network deployments to complement traditional MNO offerings. Their appearance is highly dependent on the local availability of 5G spectrum and the ability to lease the required parts of the infrastructure on-demand as a service without high upfront investments.

In the development of new spectrum sharing and authorization models for 5G, interference characterization between the systems involved in sharing is critical and requires proper modeling of the wireless propagation characteristics in the specific frequency bands and deployment scenarios. This paper introduces a novel deployment scenario for 5G where local indoor small cell networks are deployed in separate buildings by different micro operators with locally issued spectrum *micro licenses*. Interference scenarios between the two different operators having local indoor small cell deployments in co-channel and adjacent channel cases are modeled and numerical examples of allowed interfering power levels are calculated in the 3.5 GHz band.

The rest of this paper is organized as follows. In Sect. 2 we introduce the system model of micro operator indoor small cell networks with micro licensing and the resulting interference scenarios. Section 3 presents the interference calculation methodology, followed by numerical results in Sect. 4. Finally, conclusions are drawn in Sect. 5 together with future research directions.

2 Local Micro Operator Deployments

5G will introduce small cell deployments that will serve the versatile needs of different vertical sectors as described in [2]. These local cellular network deployments could in the future be operated by different stakeholders in addition to the currently dominant MNOs. In this section we present the new micro operator concept described in [3] for the establishment of local small cell deployments and characterize the resulting interference scenarios between the different micro operator networks as outlined in Fig. 1.

2.1 Micro Operator Concept

The authorization mechanisms to assign spectrum access rights to those requesting it are in the key position to shape the future 5G mobile communication market. Traditional spectrum authorization models for providing mobile services include granting of individual access rights typically through auctions leading to a small number of MNOs to deploy nation-wide networks with high infrastructure investments. Currently, the

only option for non-MNOs to deploy local networks is through the general authorization (unlicensed) model for the establishment of wireless local area networks
(WLAN) without quality guarantees. These models will need to be rethought in 5G as
these networks are envisaged to operate also in considerably higher carrier frequencies
with smaller coverage areas, which calls for new sharing based spectrum authorization
models.

The concept of micro operators was recently proposed in [3, 11] to allow different
stakeholders to establish locally operated small cell networks in various places such as
shopping malls, hospitals, sports arenas, and industry plants based on local spectrum
availability. Since these different deployment areas require high-quality guaranteed
wireless connectivity, which is only possible when operations are free from harmful
interference from other wireless systems, it is justified that the micro operators obtain
spectrum *micro licenses* with local exclusive access rights to deploy and operate small
cell 5G networks in a specific location for a given license duration. This model presents
a major paradigm shift in spectrum authorization by combining the benefits of both
exclusive licensing and unlicensed models by allowing a larger number of stakeholders
to get quality guaranteed local spectrum access rights. The proposed micro licenses can
become a key enabler to allow various stakeholders taking up the micro operator role to
deploy 5G small cell networks in specific high-demand areas to serve different vertical
sectors' needs. These new micro operators can provide a wide variety of tailored
services in specific locations to complement traditional mobile broadband offerings to
realize the 5G deployment plans set, e.g., in [4].

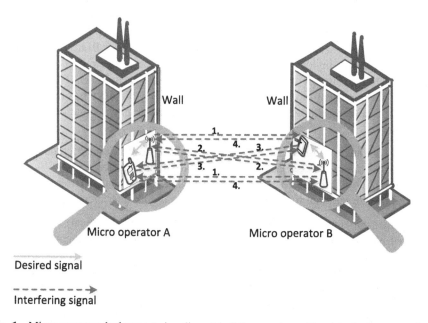

Fig. 1. Micro operator deployments in adjacent buildings and resulting interference scenarios.

2.2 Interference Characterization

Industry, regulators and MNOs are seeking for spectrum for 5G networks from various frequency ranges including existing bands below 1 GHz and between 1–6 GHz as well as new bands above 6 GHz [4]. For the regulators to allow 5G networks to access the bands, they will need to carefully conduct sharing and coexistence studies to ensure the feasibility of sharing between entrant 5G networks and incumbent systems as well as between the entrant system deployments in co-channel and adjacent channel cases. In these studies, interference characterization between the different systems is critical, which in turn requires proper propagation modeling and characterization of the systems involved in spectrum sharing.

In cellular deployments, the macro and micro base stations have typically larger transmission power and antenna gain than indoor base stations resulting in higher coverage areas to serve the mobile terminals. In the worst case where the different MNOs are exploiting the same or adjacent frequency bands, this leads to extremely harmful interference and long separation distances between networks in outdoor environment. In order for two operators to deploy their networks close to each other, the interference caused by one network on the other must be at pre-define tolerable level.

The proposed locally issued spectrum micro licenses require interference coordination between the different license holders and potential incumbent spectrum users in the band to guarantee that their operations remain free from harmful interference. Spectrum sharing (i.e., co-channel case) and coexistence (i.e., adjacent channel case) between different micro license holders requires identification of the different interference scenarios to develop rules and conditions for the micro licensing that guarantee that the networks remain free from harmful interference. Figure 1 illustrates a simplified interference scenario where two micro operators A and B are granted micro licenses in different buildings in the same channel to operate their own time division duplex (TDD) small cell indoor networks that are unsynchronous. This results in potential interference from one indoor network in one building to another indoor network in another building and vice versa. These interference scenarios include the following:

1. From base station to mobile terminal (downlink to downlink interference)
2. From base station to base station (downlink to uplink interference)
3. From mobile terminal to mobile terminal (uplink to downlink interference)
4. From mobile terminal to base station (uplink to uplink interference).

In characterizing the resulting interferences between the local 5G networks deployed by the different micro operators, the modeling of the propagation environment is of great importance. Several radio channel measurement campaigns have been carried out to characterize propagation environment in different frequency bands. For the interference characterization, the most important propagation characteristics are path loss (PL) and shadow fading. Several PL models, e.g., ITU-R models [12], have been reported for various scenarios for the frequency bands below 6 GHz. Recently, the extensions of PL models have been proposed for millimeter bands, e.g., in [13]. However, the PL model for building-to-building scenario has not received much attention in the existing research literature.

3 Calculation of Maximum Allowable Transmit Power

For two radio systems to operate in the same frequency band geographically close to each other, there is a need to define an interference threshold so that a victim receiver is protected from harmful interference from an interfering transmitter. In case there are two micro licensee deployments run by different micro operators, the protection can be achieved by defining a sufficient separation distance between the interfering transmitter and the victim receiver such that the PL between two systems is high enough.

In this paper we study the maximum allowable transmit power caused by a micro operator that results in protection from harmful interference at another micro operator. We focus on the interference scenario where the transmission from a base station of one micro operator is interfering a victim mobile terminal of another micro operator, and investigate the required minimum separation distance between the two micro operator networks. This interference scenario is selected as it presents a worst case scenario since the transmission power of an base station is higher than an mobile terminal and a victim mobile terminal is more vulnerable to interference than a victim base station. This study serves as the starting point for more complicated interference characterizations in 5G for spectrum sharing between small cell deployments of different operators. The minimum separation distance based calculation methodology has been adopted and derived from [14, 15]. The minimum required PL including the effect of shadow fading is determined based on minimum coupling loss (MCL) using

$$MCL_{95} = MCL_{50} + \sigma \cdot \sqrt{2} \cdot \text{erf}^{-1}(2 \cdot 0.95 - 1), \tag{1}$$

where erf^{-1} is the inverse error function, σ is the standard deviation of shadow fading, and MCL_{50} is the minimum required median MCL. The isotropic antennas are used for base station and mobile terminal [12]. Therefore, the transmit and receive antenna gains and directivity losses can be ignored in the analysis. Furthermore, the feeder loss of base station is set 0 dB [16]. Thus, MCL_{50} [14, 15] can be presented as

$$MCL_{50} = P_t - ACIR - IC - G_b, \tag{2}$$

where P_t is effective transmitted interfering power, $ACIR$ is adjacent channel interference ratio in the case where the operators are deployed in adjacent frequency bands (if the operators are assumed to be serving in the same frequency band, the $ACIR$ can be ignored), IC is interference criterion, i.e., maximum allowable received interference power, and G_b is bandwidth mitigation factor expressed as

$$G_b = \max(0; 10 \cdot \log_{10}(B_t/B_r)), \tag{3}$$

where B_t and B_r are the bandwidths of interfering base station and victim mobile terminal, respectively. Typically, IC is set 6 dB below receive noise power N

$$IC = N - 6\,\text{dB}, \tag{4}$$

where

$$N = -174 + 10 \cdot \log_{10}(B_r) + F, \tag{5}$$

where F is receiver noise figure. Due to lack of PL model in the building-to-building scenario, we carry out the analysis by assuming free space loss for outdoor propagation environment, and that the interfering base station and victim mobile terminal are located close to the external wall. Therefore, the path loss is presented as

$$PL = -27.55 + 20 \cdot \log_{10}(f) + 20 \cdot \log_{10}(d) + L_{W1} + L_{W2}, \tag{6}$$

where f is carrier frequency in MHz, d is the minimum separation distance between interfering base station and victim mobile terminal in meters, and L_{W1} and L_{W2} are the propagation losses caused by the first and the second wall, respectively. By substituting (6) to the left side of (1), the effective transmitted interfering power, i.e., the allowable transmitted interfering power can be expressed as

$$P_t = ACIR + PL + IC + G_B - \sigma \cdot \sqrt{2} \cdot \text{erf}^{-1}(2 \cdot 0.95 - 1). \tag{7}$$

4 Results

Next, we analyze the maximum allowable transmit power levels that result in interference protection at the victim receiver for the example case of 3.5 GHz band. The considered scenario includes interference modeling from a base station of one micro licensee network inside one building towards a mobile terminal of another small cell network inside another building. We use different building penetration losses characterizing the impact of propagation characteristics on the interference levels. The base station and mobile terminal parameters are taken from [16] and presented in Table 1. Due to the lack of propagation channel characterization in the case where the transmitter is located in a different building than the receiver, we use σ given in [12] for indoor hotspot scenario. It is worth noting that this parameter affects significantly to the presented results. However, the presented PL models for line-of-sight case have shown small σ in the existing literature. Moreover, since we use the free space loss for outdoor propagation and base station and mobile terminal are located close to the walls, the σ can be assumed to be realistic.

Four different combinations are considered for wall penetration losses ($L_{W1} + L_{W2}$): 10 dB, 25 dB, 40 dB, and 48.1 dB. These attenuation levels can be assumed to be caused by different types of wall construction materials in buildings [12, 17]:

- standard multi-pane glass windows in both buildings (2 × SG), 5 dB loss per window,

- standard multi-pane glass window in one building and 20 dB loss caused by concrete wall in another building, (SG + C),
- concrete walls in both buildings (2 × C),
- infrared reflective glass wall (2 × IG) in both buildings, 24.05 dB loss per wall.

In this study, the micro operators are assumed to be deployed either in the same frequency band (co-channel) or in the adjacent frequency bands (adjacent channel). In the adjacent channel case, the same bandwidths are assumed for interfering base station and victim mobile terminal. Therefore, G_B can be omitted from (7) in the adjacent channel case. In the co-channel case, the bandwidths of interfering base station and victim mobile terminal might be different. This leads to different bandwidth mitigation factors G_B. However, the maximum allowable received interference power changes equivalently. Therefore, the number of results in the co-channel case are reduced to the maximum bandwidth of interfering base station and victim mobile terminal.

Parameter ACIR takes into account both the adjacent channel leakage power ratio (ACLR) of the transmitter, assumed to be equal to 45 dB [18], and the adjacent channel selectivity (ACS) of the receiver, equal to 33 dB (for bandwidths equal to 5 MHz and 10 MHz) or 27 dB (20 MHz) [19]. With the assumed values, the ACIR becomes equal to 32.7 dB (5 MHz, 10 MHz) or 26.9 dB (20 MHz).

Figure 2 presents the maximum allowable transmit power as a function of minimum separation distance in the co-channel case. If the construction material of both walls is concrete (2 × C) and standard transmission power of 24 dBm [16] is assumed for base station, the minimum separation distance between victim mobile terminal and interfering base station must be already over 200 m. If the wall attenuation is lower, e.g., the wall consists of standard multi-pane glass window, the allowable transmit power is significantly smaller. In other words, the transmit power of the base station resulting in interference at the victim mobile terminal must be reduced or the minimum separation distance between the interfering base station and the victim mobile terminal must be significantly increased. This means that, in practice, two indoor operators in different buildings will not be able to operate in the vicinity with respect to each other if they share the same frequency band.

Table 1. Link parameters used in interference analysis

Parameter	Value
Carrier frequency, f	3 500 MHz
Bandwidth, BW	5 MHz, 10 MHz, or 20 MHz
Feeder loss	0 dB
Base station and mobile terminal antenna type	isotropic
Adjacent channel interference ratio (ACIR)	32.7 dB for 5 MHz 32.7 dB for 10 MHz 26.9 dB for 20 MHz
Mobile terminal noise figure, F	9 dB
Mobile terminal noise power, N	−98 dBm for 5 MHz, −95 dBm for 10 MHz, −92 dBm for 20 MHz
Standard deviation of shadow fading, σ	4 dB

For the adjacent channel case, the maximum allowable transmit power that results in interference protection at the victim receiver as a function of minimum separation distance is shown in Fig. 3. With a single interfering base station having the transmission power of 24 dBm, the minimum separation distances are less than 100 m already with low wall attenuation levels, i.e., with standard multi-pane glass windows in both buildings (2 × SG). If the wall construction materials are standard multi-pane glass window in one building and concrete wall in another building, the allowable transmit power would be larger in the order of 30 dBm when the minimum separation distance is 25 m or longer.

While the present analysis is conducted only for a single interfering base station, the results in Fig. 3 indicate that there could be several base stations of one micro operator, each having 24 dBm maximum transmission power, without causing harmful interference to the mobile terminal of another micro operator if they are located at least 25 m away from the mobile terminal. Especially, several base stations could operate simultaneously without interfering with the victim mobile terminal in the case of larger attenuations caused by, e.g., concrete walls in both buildings. This leads to the conclusions that a few base stations of one operator do not cause critical interference to the mobile terminal of another operator if the attenuation caused by walls is 25 dB or larger and operators are deployed in adjacent frequency bands.

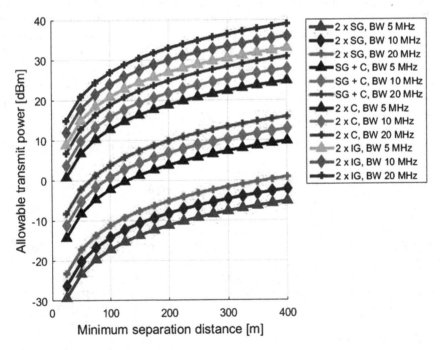

Fig. 2. Maximum allowable transmit power in co-channel case as a function of minimum separation distance with different types of building wall materials.

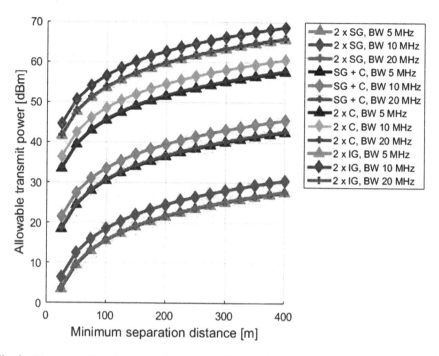

Fig. 3. Maximum allowable transmit power in adjacent channel case as a function of minimum separation distance with different types of building wall materials.

5   Conclusions and Future Work

Local small cell deployments will become an important operational mode in the future 5G networks especially when deployed in the higher carrier frequencies where coverages are inherently limited by the radio propagation characteristics. This calls for the development of new sharing-based spectrum authorization models for granting access right to deploy local 5G networks with a certain level of protection from harmful interference. Therefore, the characterization of the resulting interferences between local small cell deployments of different operators in co-channel and adjacent channel cases will be important to allow a wide variety of stakeholders become micro operators and to gain access to 5G spectrum to deploy and operate local small cell networks.

This paper has introduced a new deployment scenario for 5G small cells where two micro operators deploy local indoor small cell networks in separate buildings with locally issued spectrum micro licenses proposed in this paper. The presented study serves as the starting point for the more complicated interference characterizations in the 5G networks for spectrum sharing between small cell deployments with the new locally issued micro licenses. The example numerical results provided for the 3.5 GHz band indicate that two networks of different micro operators cannot be deployed in the neighboring buildings if they share the same frequency band. If the micro operators' networks are deployed in the adjacent frequency bands, they could operate in close vicinity with respect to each other.

Future research is needed to introduce the micro operator concept with local spectrum micro licensing into the mainstream 5G development. In particular, the development of the entire micro licensing model including its rules and conditions as well as steps is currently an open topic. Future research is also needed in characterizing the interference from multiple base stations and mobile terminals between the different micro licensee deployments in co-channel and adjacent channel cases. As the carrier frequency significantly influences the propagation loss and resulting interference levels, it is important to properly characterize the frequency band and the systems in question to derive actual protection requirements. In determining the actual license conditions that guarantee the operators free from harmful interference, there is a need for accurate propagation loss modeling based on radio channel measurements that characterizes the different interference scenarios. Moreover, since the propagation loss is significantly larger at millimeter wave bands, there is a need to study the use of highly directive antennas at base station and model them properly in the interference studies at the higher frequency bands.

Acknowledgment. This work was supported by Tekes – the Finnish Funding Agency for Innovation in MOSSAF (Multi-Operator Spectrum Sharing for Future 5G Networks) and uO5G (Micro-Operator Concept for Boosting Local Service Delivery in 5G) projects.

References

1. EC: Communication from the Commission to the Parliament, the Council, the European Economic and Social Committee and the Committee of the Regions. Connectivity for a competitive digital single market - Towards a European gigabit society. European Commission, COM (2016) 587 Final (2016)
2. 5GPPP: 5G empowering vertical industries: Roadmap paper. The 5G Infrastructure Public Private Partnership (5GPPP), Brussels (2016)
3. Matinmikko, M., Latva-aho, M., Ahokangas, P., Yrjölä, S., Koivumäki, T.: Micro operators to boost local service delivery in 5G. Wirel. Pers. Commun. **95**(1), 69–82 (2017)
4. EC: 5G for Europe: An action plan, Communication from the Commission to the European Parliament, the Council, the European Economic and Social Committee and the Committee of the Regions. COM (2016) 588 Final, Brussels, 14th September 2016
5. ECC: Licensed shared access (LSA), ECC Report 205. Electronic Communications Committee (ECC) of European Conference of Postal and Telecommunications Administrations (CEPT) (2014)
6. FCC: Amendment of the Commission's Rules with regard to commercial operations in the 3550–3650 MHz band, Order of reconsiderations and second report and order. Federal Communications Commission, FCC-16-55 (2016)
7. Tehrani, R.H., Vahid, S., Triantafyllopoulou, D., Lee, H., Moessner, K.: Licensed spectrum sharing schemes for mobile operators: a survey and outlook. IEEE Commun. Surv. Tutor. **18**(4), 2591–2623 (2016)
8. Gupta, A.K., Andrews, J.G., Heath, R.W.: On the feasibility of sharing spectrum licenses in mmWave cellular systems. IEEE Trans. Commun. **64**(9), 3981–3995 (2016)
9. Gupta, A.K., Alkhateeb, A., Andrews, J.G., Heath, R.W.: Restricted secondary licensing for mmWave cellular: How much gain can be obtained? In: IEEE Global Communications Conference (GLOBECOM), 4–8 December 2016, Washington, DC, USA, pp. 1–6 (2016)

10. Zander, J.: Beyond the ultra-dense barrier: Paradigm shifts on the road beyond 1000x wireless capacity. IEEE Wirel. Commun. **24**(3), 96–102 (2017)
11. Ahokangas, P., Moqaddamerad, S., Matinmikko, M., Abouzeid, A., Atkova, I., Gomes, J., Iivari, M.: Future micro operators business models in 5G. In: 6th International Conference on the Restructuring of the Global Economy (ROGE), University of Oxford, UK, 20–21st June 2016
12. ITU-R M.2135: Guidelines for evaluation of radio interface technologies for IMT-Advanced. Technical Report (2009)
13. Aalto University: BUPT, CMCC, Nokia, NTT DOCOMO, New York University, Ericsson, Qualcomm, Huawei, Samsung, INTEL, University of Bristol, KT Corporation, and University of Southern California, "5G channel model for bands up to 100 GHz, version 2.3." In: 2nd Workshop on Mobile Communications in Higher Frequency Bands (MCHFB) in GLOBECOM, 6–10 December 2015, San Diego, CA, USA, pp. 1–102 (2015)
14. ECC Report 172: Broadband wireless systems usage in 2300–2400 MHz, March 2012
15. Jokinen, M., Mäkeläinen, M., Hänninen, T., Matinmikko, M., Mustonen, M.: Minimum separation distance calculations for incumbent protection in LSA. In: Noguet, D., Moessner, K., Palicot, J. (eds.) CrownCom 2016. LNICST, vol. 172, pp. 116–128. Springer, Cham (2016). https://doi.org/10.1007/978-3-319-40352-6_10
16. ECC Report 203: Least restrictive technical conditions suitable for mobile/fixed communication networks (MFCN), including IMT, in the frequency bands 3400–3600 MHz and 3600–3800 MHz, March 2014
17. 3GPP TR 38.901: Study on channel model for frequencies from 0.5 to 100 GHz 3GPP. Technical Report, March 2017
18. 3GPP TS 36.104: Base Station (BS) radio transmission and reception, 3GPP. Technical Specification, March 2017
19. 3GPP TS 36.101: User Equipment (UE) radio transmission and reception, 3GPP. Technical Specification, March 2017

Check for updates

Using Deep Neural Networks for Forecasting Cell Congestion on LTE Networks: A Simple Approach

Pedro Torres[1]([✉]), Hugo Marques[1,2], Paulo Marques[1,2],
and Jonathan Rodriguez[2]

[1] Instituto Politécnico de Castelo Branco, Castelo Branco, Portugal
{pedrotorres,hugo,paulomarques}@ipcb.pt
[2] Instituto de Telecomunicações, Campus de Santiago, Aveiro, Portugal
jonathan@av.it.pt

Abstract. Predicting short-term cellular load in LTE networks is of great importance for mobile operators as it assists in the efficient managing of network resources. Based on predicted behaviours, the network can be intended as a proactive system that enables reconfiguration when needed. Basically, it is the concept of self-organizing networks that ensures the requirements and the quality of service. This paper uses a dataset, provided by a mobile network operator, of collected downlink throughput samples from one cell in an area where cell congestion usually occurs and a Deep Neural Network (DNN) approach to perform short-term cell load forecasting. The results obtained indicate that DNN performs better results when compared to traditional approaches.

Keywords: LTE · SON · Machine learning · Deep learning · Forecasting

1 Introduction

With the constant demanding for high-speed data applications (e.g., high-quality wireless video streaming, social networking, machine-to-machine communication, IoT, etc.), LTE micro and femto cells, as well as relay nodes, are being relied upon to ensure that the required overall network capacity can be met. This, however, increases the challenges in terms of network planning and specially on management. As the network complexity increases, mobile network operators (MNOs) are required to invest more in network optimization processes and automation. Hence, reducing operational costs can be done automatically through Self-Organizing Networks (SON) strategies, which allow the network to heal and improve itself, based, for example, on forecasted behaviours. SON, therefore, minimizes rollout delays and operational expenditures associated with ongoing LTE deployments.

The fast-technological development rate, we have been assisting on the last years, had led to a strong interdependence of the new emerging technologies, examples are: 5G mobile broadband (5G), IoT, Big Data Analytics (Big Data), Cloud Computing (Cloud) and SDN. For the MNO, new interests are related to knowing more information on their costumers (e.g., known locations, used services and other customer related patterns such as data consumption trends).

© ICST Institute for Computer Sciences, Social Informatics and Telecommunications Engineering 2018
P. Marques et al. (Eds.): CROWNCOM 2017, LNICST 228, pp. 276–286, 2018.
https://doi.org/10.1007/978-3-319-76207-4_23

One key task for MNOs is the correct dimensioning of their network capacity. Network load forecasting can assist in guaranteeing network resources are available to consumers, ensuring quality of service is met, therefore, avoiding consumer complaints. Improving the accuracy of load forecasting in a short period of time is a challenging open problem due to the variety of factors that influence data traffic and throughput.

Forecasting has been widely studied in deafferents areas, since the 1970s. Traditional methods introduced linear models for time series forecasting, such as autoregressive (AR), autoregressive with moving average (ARMA) and the derivations of these [1]. Currently, nonlinear forecasting models have generally obtained better accuracy than linear models. These nonlinear models are based on machine learning methods such as neural networks [2] or support vector machines [3]. Neural networks have been used widely in data forecasting due to their ability to approximate complex nonlinear relationships. However, neural network methods have some potential drawbacks such as overfitting of the model, sensitivity to random weight initialization and tendency to convergence to local optima. To address these limitations, recently new approaches, called Deep Neural Networks (DNN) [4], have been proposed. DNN, with additional nonlinear levels, can better represent complex features from their inputs and obtain a more general model with the ability to learn, from the data, these complex features.

One potential use for DNN based forecast methods, that we foresee in this paper, is to predict data access patterns on mobile networks, as MNOs heavily invest in network dimensioning to avoid congestion. Typical actions include: making use of additional spectrum carriers (whenever possible), installing more cell sites and performing traffic offloading onto other networks such as Wi-Fi. In the identification of cell congestion two things need to be considered: throughput and latency. For subscribers, when an access node is near capacity, the rapid increase in latency causes a substantial deterioration of QoE for latency-sensitive applications. One of the most common congestion detection mechanisms is based on real-time measurements of access round trip time (RTT).

In the literature, there are currently not many works related to forecasting cell congestion, however there are some research studies addressing similar topics. In [6] the authors are motivated by the fact that cellular radio networks are seldom uniformly loaded, hence propose a reactive load-balancing algorithm that adjusts the cell individual offset parameter between the serving cell and all its neighbours by a fixed step. The authors claim that the best step depends on the load conditions in both the serving cell and its neighbours as well as on the serving cell's user distribution. This is the basis for their proposed Q-Learning algorithm, that learns the best step values to apply for different load conditions and demonstrate that the Q-Learning based algorithm performs better than the best fixed φ algorithm in virtually all scenarios. In [5] the authors analyse different algorithms to match traffic demands with network resources. The compared techniques are implemented by a modified version of the Q-Learning algorithm, called the reinforcement Q-Learning algorithm, that forecasts load status for every node and that when combined with the SON may improve network performance. In [7] the autoregressive integrated moving average (ARIMA) model and exponential smoothing model are used to predict the throughput in a single cell and whole region in a LTE network.

This paper, on the other hand, describes a deep learning approach to predict cell congestion events based on the downlink average throughput. A cell congestion event was considered when we measured a drop of at least 50% (based on Service Level Agreement values) on the average download speed per user (considering an average of 20 Mbps per user during off-peak hours).

This work was developed in the scope of MUSCLES project (Mobile Ubiquitous Small Cells for Low-cost Energy and Spectrum efficient cloud service delivery) [8]. MUSCLES aims to research, implement and test a platform of LTE mobile networks autonomous management, with capabilities of self-organization, detection and automatic troubleshooting which are still being manually addressed by many MNOs. These capabilities have the potential to substantially reduce operational costs and are to be aligned with the new developments of SON technology proposed by 3GPP standardization organization.

The remaining of the paper is organized as follows: Sect. 2 summarizes the state of the art in what respects forecasting with focus in the classical methods and new deep learning trends; Sect. 3 explains the used methodology and methods; Experimental results are described and presented in Sect. 4 and; the conclusions are given in Sect. 5.

2 State of the Art Related to Forecast

In the context of forecasting, a time series is a sequence of periodic observations of a random variable (e.g., monthly energy consumption, the annual number of passengers in an airport, the daily temperature). Time series are important for applied-research because they are often the drivers of decision models. Time series analysis provides tools for selecting a model that best describes the time series and the model is then used to forecast future events in the time series. Modelling the time series is a statistical problem because observed data is used in computational procedures to estimate the coefficients of a supposed model. Models assume that observations vary randomly about an underlying mean value that is a function of time. In this work, the downlink average throughput of a single LTE cell was considered an observation of a time series. Next subsections introduce the time series forecasting traditional methods and the new trends based on deep neural networks.

2.1 Classical Framework

The classical forecasting framework uses traditional methods that are exhaustively described in the literature and with good practical applications demonstrated. Typically, these methods consist of defining a parametric model that is supposed to generate data. Based on a given sample, the unknown parameters of the model are estimated and the estimated model is used to make predictions. The following are the most popular classical methods.

An autoregressive (AR) model specifies that the output variable depends linearly on its own previous values and on a stochastic term (an imperfectly predictable term). $AR(p)$ model is a linear generative model based on the pth order Markov assumption:

$$\forall t, Y_t = \sum_{i=1}^{p} a_i Y_{t-i} + \varepsilon_t \tag{1}$$

where ε_t are zero mean uncorrelated random variables with variance σ. $a_1, \ldots, a_p$ are autoregressive coefficients. Y_t is observed stochastic process.

The moving-average (MA) model specifies that the output variable depends linearly on the current and various past values of a stochastic (imperfectly predictable) term. $MA(q)$ model is a linear generative model for the noise term based on the q th order Markov assumption:

$$\forall t, Y_t = \varepsilon_t + \sum_{j=1}^{q} b_j \varepsilon_{t-j} \tag{2}$$

where $b_1, \ldots, b_q$ are moving average coefficients.

Combined $AR(p)$ and $MA(q)$ models can be obtained through the autoregressive-moving-average ($ARMA(p,q)$) model:

$$\forall t, Y_t = \sum_{i=1}^{p} a_i Y_{t-i} + \varepsilon_t + \sum_{j=1}^{q} b_j \varepsilon_{t-j} \tag{3}$$

ARMA model is a weakly stationary process. When data show evidence of non-stationarity, an initial differencing step (corresponding to the "integrated" part of the model) can be applied one or more times to eliminate the non-stationarity and we are in the presence of an autoregressive integrated moving average (ARIMA) model.

Other extensions can be extensively used, such as models with seasonal components (SARIMA), models with side information (ARIMAX), models with long-memory (ARFIMA), multi-variate time series models (VAR), models with time-varying coefficients and other non-linear models.

There are different methods for estimating model parameters, such as Maximum likelihood estimation, method of moments or Conditional and unconditional least square estimation.

2.2 Deep Neural Networks

Another branch of time series forecasting consists in using machine learning techniques, such as support vector machines or artificial neural networks (ANN) [9]. The most common type of ANNs is a multilayer perceptron (MLP) that forecasts a profile using previous data. A deep neural network (DNN) [10] is an ANN with more layers than the typical three layers of MLP. The deep structure increases the feature abstraction capability of neural networks. Deep learning algorithms use multiple-layer architectures or deep architectures to extract inherent features in data from the lowest level to the highest level, and they can discover huge amounts of structure in the data. Figures 1 and 2, illustrate typical architectures of the ANN and DNN.

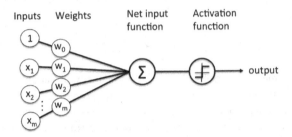

Fig. 1. Traditional neural network architecture, perceptron node

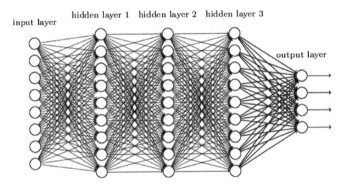

Fig. 2. Deep Neural Network architecture

3   Methodology and Methods

3.1   Methodology

The methodology used in this work consists of analysing the historical throughput data coming from one cell to train the forecasting methods to learn trends and predict future events, considering also the seasonality. Our dataset consists of hourly samples over a period of a month. The dataset was broken into 2 parts for training (75% of the dataset size) and validation and testing (25%). A Recurrent Neural Network (RNN) [11] using the Long Short-Term Memory (LSTM) [12] architecture was implemented using TensorFlow [13] to train and create our model.

A summary on the used methodology:

- Use of a dataset of historic measurements (four weeks), coming from 1 cell;
- The measurements were collected through an automated process and averages were computed on each hour;
- The measurements were used as the input for forecasting future network behaviour (time series analysis);

- The forecasting approach is to train by three weeks and computed for the 4th week;
- Forecasting is computed and validated, by comparing the obtained results with the real measurements, obtained for the 4th week;
- Results are ready to be exploited by the MNOs SON strategies.

3.2 Method

The deep learning method used consists in a RNN with a LSRM architecture. The LSTM network is a type of recurrent neural network used in deep learning because very large architectures can be successfully trained.

In a traditional RNN, during the gradient back-propagation phase, the gradient signal can end up being multiplied many times (as many as the number of timesteps) by the weight matrix associated with the connections between the neurons of the recurrent hidden layer. This means that, the magnitude of weights in the transition matrix can have a strong impact on the learning process.

If the weights in this matrix are small (or, more formally, if the leading eigenvalue of the weight matrix is smaller than 1.0), it can lead to a situation called vanishing gradients, where the gradient signal gets so small that learning either becomes very slow or stops working altogether. It can also make more difficult the task of learning long-term dependencies in the data. Conversely, if the weights in this matrix are large (or, again, more formally, if the leading eigenvalue of the weight matrix is larger than 1.0), it can lead to a situation where the gradient signal is so large that it can cause learning to diverge. This is often referred to as exploding gradients.

These issues are the main motivation behind the LSTM model which introduces a new structure called a memory cell (see Fig. 3 below).

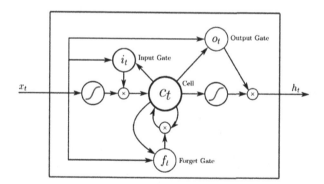

Fig. 3. LSTM memory cell, with input, output and forget gates

A memory cell is composed of four main elements: an input gate, a neuron with a self-recurrent connection (a connection to itself), a forget gate and an output gate. The self-recurrent connection has a weight of 1.0 and ensures that, barring any outside interference, the state of a memory cell can remain constant from one timestep to another. The gates serve to modulate the interactions between the memory cell itself and its environment. The input gate can allow incoming signal to alter the state of the memory cell or block it. On the other hand, the output gate can allow the state of the memory cell to influence other neurons or prevent it. Finally, the forget gate can modulate the memory cell's self-recurrent connection, allowing the cell to remember or forget its previous state, as needed.

In LSTM, the update of a layer of memory cells, at every timestep t, can be described as follows:

1. Compute the values for i_t, the input gate, and $\tilde{C}_t$ the candidate value for the states of the memory cells at time t:

$$i_t = \sigma(W_i x_t + U_i h_{t-1} + b_i) \tag{4}$$

$$\tilde{C}_t = tanh(W_c x_t + U_c h_{t-1} + b_c) \tag{5}$$

2. Compute the value for f_t, the activation of the memory cells forgets the gates at time t:

$$f_t = \sigma\left(W_f x_t + U_f h_{t-1} + b_f\right) \tag{6}$$

3. Given the value of the input gate activation i_t, the forget gate activation f_t and the candidate state value $\tilde{C}_t$, we can compute C_t the memory cells' new state at time t:

$$C_t = i_t * \tilde{C}_t + f_t * C_{t-1}) \tag{7}$$

4. With the new state of the memory cells, we can compute the value of their output gates and, subsequently, their outputs:

$$O_t = \sigma(W_O x_t + W_O h_{t-1} + V_O C_t + b_O) \tag{8}$$

$$h_t = O_t * tanh(C_t) \tag{9}$$

where x_t is the input of the memory cell layer at time t. W_i, W_f, W_C, W_O, U_i, U_f, U_C, U_O and V_O are weight matrices. b_i, b_f, b_c and b_O are bias vectors.

The model is composed of a single LSTM layer followed by an average pooling and a logistic regression layer as illustrated in Fig. 4 below. Thus, from an input sequence $x_0, x_1, \ldots, x_n$, the memory cells in the LSTM layer will produce a representation sequence $h_0, h_1, \ldots, h_n$. This representation sequence is then averaged over all timesteps resulting in representation h. Finally, this representation is fed to a logistic regression layer whose target is the class label associated with the input sequence.

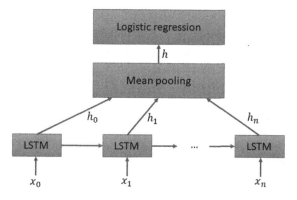

Fig. 4. Concept for the DNN based LSTM forecast model used in this paper. It is composed of a single LSTM layer followed by mean pooling over time and logistic regression

4 Experimental Results

This section presents the forecasting results obtained with a Deep Learning approach and the comparison with two classical methods, ARIMAX model and Naïve persistence model [14]. The goal is to forecast one entire week of the cell average downlink (DL) throughput, with a resolution of one hour. The input dataset for our model was provided by a MNO, originating from 1 cell in a dense urban area, where congestion problems typically occur. Three weeks of historical collected measurements have been used for training the prediction models and one week was used to compare the observed throughput with the forecast values.

Figure 5 depicts the forecasting results obtained from the deep learning method. The dataset is split, the data is separated into training datasets, where 75% of the dataset size was used to train the model, leaving the remaining 25% for validating the results.

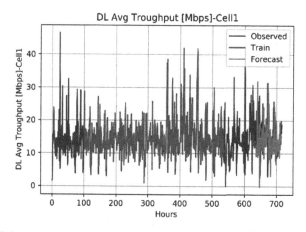

Fig. 5. Downlink average throughput observation for cell 1 (blue line) with the training (orange line) and forecast (green line) results. (Color figure online)

Table 1. Forecasting errors (MSE) expressed in Mbps

Method	MSE [Mbps]
ARIMAX model	7.16
Naïve persistence model	6.90
Deep learning	1.01

To measure the model accuracy, the Mean Squared Error (MSE) is computed and compared with 2 classical methods. The results presented in Table 1, show that the deep learning method is more accurate than the other methods, for this dataset. However, the computational cost associated to this method is higher in comparison to the classical methods.

Based on the more detailed forecasting results, in Fig. 6, it is possible predicted situations of cell congestion and proactively actuate in the network through SON functions that can change key network configuration parameters. For example, for this cell the average download speed, per user, on an LTE network on off-peak hours is around 20 Mbps. Cell congestion was considered when we observed a 50% reduction of this speed (identified in Fig. 6 by the asterisk symbol). Furthermore, measured values of 10 Mbps or lower, have been consistently observed on short periods (30 min to 1 h) during commonly identified peak-hours (e.g., 7:00 a.m. to 9:00 p.m.). In such cases, the network configuration parameters, for example a network carrier activation (if available), could be activated 1 h before the predicted event. The dots in Fig. 6 represent this decision point where something must be changed in the network to avoid the identified problems (asterisks) in the network.

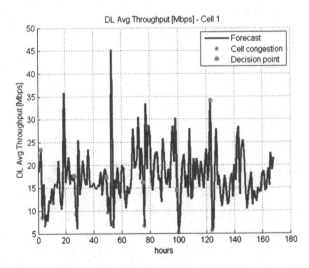

Fig. 6. Identification of cellular congestion (asterisks) and decision points (dots) to actuate on the network in order to avoid congestion. In the provided example, the actuation event occurs 1 h before the predicted congestion event.

It is important to note that the cellular congestion does not only depend on the download speed, it is however a very important key performance indicator (KPI) to be considered. The same method can be applied to forecast other network KPIs and the correlation between the different KPIs further improves the problem detection algorithm.

5 Conclusions

This work describes a deep neural network data analytics methodology and model, capable of forecasting the average downlink throughput of one LTE cell based on historic measurements. The obtained results have shown that, in comparison with other traditional forecasting methods, if an appropriate dataset of samples is provided, the proposed model is able to forecast with high accuracy the cell downlink throughput. We were able to predict a cell congestion event up to 30 h in advance which provides SON strategies enough time to react (e.g., by shifting coverage and capacity to areas in need), before subscribers have been impacted by dropped calls or reduced data speeds and therefore making MNOs happy by anticipating network problems and avoiding customer complaints. The current model is still prone to further improvements by refining the deep neural network algorithm. Furthermore, the authors are currently implementing the algorithm in an LTE system-level simulator to quantify network performance improvements based on cell congestion prediction and SON strategies.

Acknowledgments. This work is funded by the Operational Competitiveness and Internationalization Programme (COMPETE 2020) [Project Nr. 17787] (POCI-01-0247-FEDER-MUSCLES).

References

1. Deb, C., Zhang, F., Yang, J., Lee, S.E., Shah, K.W.: A review on time series forecasting techniques for building energy consumption. Renew. Sustain. Energy Rev. **74**, 902–924 (2017)
2. Zhang, G., Patuwo, B.E., Hu, M.Y.: Forecasting with artificial neural networks: the state of the art. Int. J. Forecast. **14**(1), 35–62 (1998)
3. Sapankevych, N.I., Sankar, R.: Time series prediction using support vector machines: a survey. IEEE Comput. Intell. Mag. **4**(2), 24–38 (2009)
4. Dalto, M., Matusko, J., Vasak, M.: Deep neural networks for ultra-short-term wind forecasting. In: Proceedings of the 2015 IEEE International Conference on Industrial Technology (ICIT), Seville, Spain, 17–19 March 2015, pp. 1657–1663 (2015)
5. Xu, J., Tang, L., Chen, Q., Yi, L.: Study on based reinforcement Q-Learning for mobile load balancing techniques in LTE-A HetNets. In: 2014 IEEE 17th International Conference on Computational Science and Engineering, Chengdu, pp. 1766–1771 (2014)
6. Mwanje, S.S., Mitschele-Thiel, A.: A Q-Learning strategy for LTE mobility load balancing. In: 2013 IEEE 24th Annual International Symposium on Personal, Indoor, and Mobile Radio Communications (PIMRC), London, pp. 2154–2158 (2013)

7. Dong, X., Fan, W., Gu, J.: Predicting LTE throughput using traffic time series. ZTE Commun. **4** (2015)
8. MUSCLES project. https://www.celticplus.eu/project-muscles/
9. Moreno, J.J.M., Poll, A.P., Gracia, P.M.: Artificial neural networks applied to forecasting time series. Psicothema **23**(2), 322–329 (2011)
10. Gu, J., Wang, Z., Kuen, J., Ma, L., Shahroudy, A., Shuai, B.: Recent Advances in Convolutional Neural Networks, (2015) arXiv:1512.07108
11. Dorffner, G.: Neural networks for time series processing. Neural Netw. World (1996)
12. Hochreiter, S., Schmidhuber, J.: Long short-term memory. Neural Comput. **9**, 1735–1780 (1997)
13. TensorFlow. https://www.tensorflow.org/
14. Torres, P., Marques, P., Marques, H., Dionísio, R., Alves, T., Pereira, L., Ribeiro, J.: Data analytics for forecasting cell congestion on LTE networks. In: IEEE/IFIP Workshop on Mobile Network Measurement (MNM 2017), Dublin, June 2017

Radio Hardware Virtualization for Coping with Dynamic Heterogeneous Wireless Environments

Xianjun Jiao$^{(\boxtimes)}$ (iD), Ingrid Moerman, Wei Liu,
and Felipe Augusto Pereira de Figueiredo

IDLab, Department of Information Technology, Ghent University - imec,
Technologiepark-Zwijnaarde 15, 9052 Ghent, Belgium
{xianjun.jiao,ingrid.moerman,wei.liu,
felipe.pereira}@ugent.be

Abstract. Diverse wireless standards, designed for diverse traffic types, operate in the same wireless environment without coordination, often leading to interference and inefficient spectrum usage. Although C-RAN (Cloud/centralized RAN) is a promising architecture to achieve intra-operator network coordination, the architecture encounters challenge when low latency services and diverse access technologies are expected over non-fiber fronthaul. So, multi-standard multi-channel access point with low processing latency is preferred to be at the edge of network instead of central cloud. But, developing this kind of equipment is difficult as multiple radio chips and drivers have to be integrated and coordinated. In ORCA (Orchestration and Reconfiguration Control Architecture) project, a SDR architecture is developed on a single chip radio platform including hardware accelerators wrapped by unified software APIs, which offer the following capabilities: (1) concurrent data transmission over multiple virtual radios; (2) runtime composition and parametric control of radios; and (3) radio resource slicing, supporting independent operation of multiple standards in different bands, time slots or beams. Such an architecture offers a fast development cycle, as only software programming is required for creating and manipulating multiple radios. The architecture further achieves an efficient utilization of hardware resources, as accelerators can be shared by multiple virtual radios.

Keywords: Coexistence · SDR · Resource slicing · FPGA · C-RAN
Virtualization · CPRI

1 Introduction

Our world is increasingly defined by software. Even sectors that used to rely mainly on hardware are evolving rapidly. From use cases like self-driving cars to the inspection of factory plants, digital assets make the difference.

Software Defined Radio (SDR) [1] is a typical case of "softwarized" hardware: transceiver components (such as mixers, demodulators or decoders) that are typically implemented on hardware are now possible to be implemented by means of software.

© ICST Institute for Computer Sciences, Social Informatics and Telecommunications Engineering 2018
P. Marques et al. (Eds.): CROWNCOM 2017, LNICST 228, pp. 287–297, 2018.
https://doi.org/10.1007/978-3-319-76207-4_24

C-RAN (Cloud/centralized Radio Access Network) [2] is a typical application of SDR in wireless industry. In C-RAN architecture, RRH (Remote Radio Head, including antennas) is connected to software BBU (Base Band Unit) in cloud center via digitalized IQ sample fiber link (CRPI or OBSAI) [3]. Each RRH covers a sector or a cell. Because all cells' BBUs are resident in the same cloud center, it brings benefits [4] to operator, such as allocating processing and frequency resources to different cell dynamically according to traffic variation (day VS night; street VS stadium; etc.); coordinate interference among different cells in a more efficient way; multi-cell cooperated transmitting and receiving for UE (User Equipment) and etc. A drawback of C-RAN for operator is that high quality fronthaul is needed to connect RRH at antenna side and BBU in the cloud. The link needs to be low latency and low jitter [5]. When there isn't fiber available, fronthaul will be challenging.

Advanced technologies in computer science, such as virtualization [4], can be easily applied to C-RAN, since all layers of RAN protocol, including L1 – physical layer, are implemented in software running in cloud center. By virtualization, it is no longer necessary to map each BBU software instance to one physical server. Multiple BBU instances can share the same physical server, or multiple physical servers can serve as a super computer to run an ultra-high bandwidth BBU. BBU instance can be created, destroyed or migrated according to dynamic requirement.

In parallel with operators' RAN, there are many other types of wireless networks/standard, such as Wi-Fi [6] for internet or intranet access, 802.15.4/Zigbee [7] and 802.11ah [8] for short-to-middle range IoT (Internet of Things) applications, as well as LoRa [9] and SigFox [10] for long range IoT, remain competitive. In addition, new applications are emerging, serving as driving force of network technologies, which include robot or UAV (Unmanned Aerial Vehicle) control, vehicle-to-vehicle communication for autopilot, Virtual Reality (VR) and real-time gaming. So, new standards or new features are needed over existing standards to interact with diverse physical world.

Furthermore, spectrum sharing is a common issue for many technologies mentioned above, especially for those operating in the ISM (Industrial, Scientific and Medical) bands. In practice, the coordination among these technologies is either very hard to achieve or not present at all. Unlike the case of C-RAN, an operator can run multiple standards and base stations at one location – cloud center, the application here run in different physical access-point/gateways, which are owned by different enterprises or even private home. This situation may lead to inefficient usage of spectrum, and severe QoS (Quality of Service) degradation for specific application due to interference from heterogeneous technologies.

An equipment supporting parallel operation of multiple standards and multiple channels is a promising approach to deliver services with diverse QoS, in terms of optimized wireless access and spectrum utilization efficiency. For low latency application, hardware solution, which could be ASIC (Application-Specific Integrated Circuit) or FPGA (Field-Programmable Gate Array), is more appropriate than software. A problem is that, one chip always is implemented for one or few standard, and operates on one frequency channel at a time. One option is to construct an equipment with multiple chips to support multiple standards and channels, though this will be not only costly but also inconvenient to program and coordinate from the perspective of the developer—ASICs with dedicated configurations, drivers and inter-chip communication link become necessary prerequisites. For a multi-chip design, features commonly supported in C-RAN, such as dynamic computing resource sharing and migrating among cells/channels, are very hard to realize (if not impossible). This is because multi-chip hardware design implies fixed hardware resources allocation. An integrated new ASIC could be designed to merge multiple chips to single chip, but simply chip merging won't give dynamic resource manipulation among intra ASIC blocks. In addition, long design cycle and high development cost of ASIC would be a big obstacle on the road.

In this paper, an architecture supporting low latency processing via hardware (FPGA) accelerators, which is still flexible enough to support multi-standard multi-channel virtualization, is proposed to meet the requirement of diverse wireless access at the network edge. An initial demo is also implemented based on SDR platform composed by Xilinx Zynq SoC and Analog devices RF frontend.

2 Latency Analysis

Latency is one of key factors for different types of standards and application. System architecture of wireless technology is influenced by the latency requirements and implementation feasibility of specific latency target. In this section, we first investigate the latency requirements of mainstream wireless standards (Sect. 2.1), and then present the latency measurements of two types of SDR platforms, namely the USRP (Sect. 2.2), and Xilinx Zynq SoC based SDR (Sect. 2.3).

2.1 Latency Requirement of Wi-Fi and LTE

According to Wi-Fi standard [6], the most critical latency requirement is from SIFS (Short Interframe Space). The concept of interframe space is shown in Fig. 1, which is from "Fig. 10-4—Some IFS relationships" of 802.11-2016 standard.

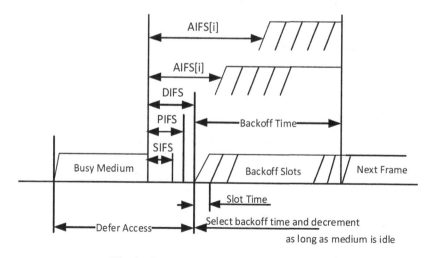

Fig. 1. 802.11 interframe space relationships

As explained in the standard: "The SIFS is the time from the end of the last symbol, or signal extension if present, of the previous frame to the beginning of the first symbol of the preamble of the subsequent frame as seen on the WM. The SIFS shall be used prior to transmission of an Ack frame...". The SIFS specified in the standard is 10 μs or 16 μs, depending on band (2.4 GHz or 5 GHz) and PHY type (DSSS, OFDM, etc.). For the 60 GHz band system, which has directional multi-gigabit ability, SIFS is only 3 μs.

Unlike Wi-Fi's CSMA/CA MAC mechanism, in LTE system everything is scheduled in advance, including acknowledgement of HARQ (Hybrid Automatic Repeat Request) process. Figure 2 shows LTE uplink HARQ procedure (Fig. 10.14 of [11]).

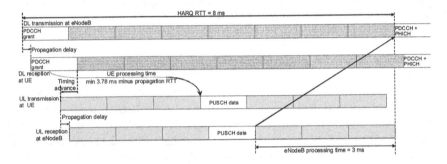

Fig. 2. Timing diagram of the uplink HARQ (SAW – Stop And Wait) protocol

In uplink HARQ, base station has 3 ms to make acknowledgement in downlink PHICH (Physical Hybrid ARQ Indicator Channel) after it receives uplink IQ samples of PUSCH (Physical Uplink Shared Channel). According to the C-RAN white paper [2], base station needs 800–900 μs after receiving IQ samples of each 1 ms. So the round trip latency budget between RRH and BBU is around 100–200 μs.

According to CPRI over fiber specification [3], maximum one-way latency of CPRI link is 5 μs. Besides CPRI latency, other latency overheads between RRH and BBU include physical distance, buffers, switches, cloud computer interface (Ethernet/PCIe/OS), etc. All together should less than round trip latency budget of C-RAN fronthaul. CPRI over Ethernet [12] is a hot topic in C-RAN fronthaul area, because not every places/areas have fiber coverage.

2.2   Latency Measurement Results of USRP + Host Computer

USRP (Universal Software Radio Peripheral) [13] SDR platform is the most widely used platform in research community. In most cases, it is used jointly with host computer, which can be (to some extent) regarded as a minimum version of C-RAN. The latency test is provided by the UHD (USRP Hardware Driver) [14] native example: latency_test [15]. Table 1 shows the measurement results of different USRPs combined with different computer communication links. Each latency result is measured and averaged over 10 round tests of 5 M, 10 M and 25 M sampling rates.

Table 1. Round trip latency between RF frontend and host computer software.

USRP type	Link type	Latency (us)	Host computer configuration
X310	PCIe	79	Intel i7-6700 3.4 GHz, NI PCIe ×4 card
X310	10 Gbps Ethernet	106	Intel E5-2650 v4 2.2GH, Qlogic 57810 Eth
X310	1 Gbps Ethernet	101	Intel i7-6700 3.4 GHz, Intel i219-v Eth
B210/200mini	USB 3.0	66	Intel i7-6700 3.4 GHz, Intel controller
N210	1 Gbps Ethernet	103	Intel i7-6700 3.4 GHz, Intel i219-v Eth

The latency measurement results show that the host computer based SDR architecture can't meet SIFS requirement of Wi-Fi system, but it is good enough to be used for current LTE system, because latency of ~ 100 μs only consumes tiny portion of LTE processing time needed by HARQ process. That is why there are already several host-computer based LTE systems, such as srsLTE [16], OAI (Open Air Interface) [17] and amarisoft [18], which work quite well. On the contrary, almost all Wi-Fi SDR implementations, such as NI 802.11 Application Framework [19] and WARP (Wireless Open-Access Research Platform) [20], use FPGA to do processing instead of host computer.

2.3   Latency Measurement Results of Xilinx Zynq-7000 SoC

Xilinx Zynq-7000 All Programmable SoC (System on Chip) [21] includes two parts: PL (Programmable Logic) and PS (Processing System). PL actually is a traditional FPGA, which can do computation intensive operation and latency critical tasks. PS is a multi-cores ARM cortex AP (Application Processor), which is suitable to run control program, higher layer protocol and oeprating system. PL and PS are connected by multiple AXI (Advanced eXtensible Interface) high speed buses, which have low latency and high throughput performance. We evaluate its latency using a dummy FPGA block interacting with an ARM testing program in bare metal mode.

The testing system was constructed as in Fig. 3. The dummy FPGA acceleration block was designed by Xilinx HLS (High Level Synthesis) tool. The block receives data from PS in streaming manner via Xilinx DMA (Direct Memory Access) module, and stream the processed result (same amount of data as input) back to PS via DMA. It takes 654 clock cycles for this FPGA block to process 128 input samples, each sample is represented as a 32-bit word on the 32-bit AXI stream bus. The configuration interface between PS, PL and DMA controller is AXI_LITE, which is connected to M_AXI_GP port of ARM. Data link is AXI stream, which is connected to S_AXI_HP port of ARM. A DMA controller was used to convert AXI Memory Mapped interface (needed by PS) to AXI Stream interface (needed by streaming mode FPGA accelerator).

ZC706 Evaluation Board [22] for the Zynq-7000 XC7Z045 SoC is used to do the evaluation. Clock speeds of our design are as follows: AXI buses and PL run at 200 MHz, and ARM cortex-A9 processor run at 800 MHz. Xilinx ILA (Integrated Logic Analyzer) is inserted to the design for event recording with 5 ns resolution. The ARM software event is recorded by writing special value to PL register and detecting this value via ILA. The latency profiling result is shown in Fig. 4.

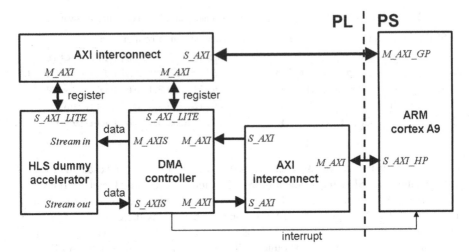

Fig. 3. Diagram of Latency test for Zynq-7000 Platform. M_* – master AXI interface; S_* – Slave AXI interface; AXIS – AXI streaming interface; *_GP – General Purpose (for register read/write); *_HP – High Performance (for data transfer)

Figure 4 shows the event log of the entire round trip delay test captured by Xilinx ILA. First, the software start DMA transmission at −0.135 μs; then DMA controller receives the instruction at 0 μs via AXI LITE register interface; After some internal preparation and buffering operation, the actual DMA transmission on the AXIS bus starts at 0.3 μs; After 3.295 μs, which is caused by the accelerator processing latency of 654 clocks at 200 MHz, the accelerator completes the data transfer of processing results back to DMA controller in streaming manner; Then DMA controller raises interrupt to PS at 4.48 μs; Finally, software becomes aware of this event at 4.595 μs. So the round trip latency between the FPGA accelerator and software in PS is 4.595 + 0.135 − (3.595 − 0.3) = 1.435 μs. Note that this is superior performance comparing to the latency of USRP variants, and it is even not a significant overhead compared to the Wi-Fi SIFS requirement (16 μs or 10 μs).

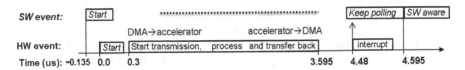

Fig. 4. Latency test result of Zynq-7000 SoC Platform

3   Architecture Design

Hardware/FPGA implementation or hardware/FPGA accelerated software is necessary to achieve realtime operation of certain wireless standards, such as Wi-Fi. Even for mobile operator, in the era of beyond LTE, 5G is also considering much lower latency

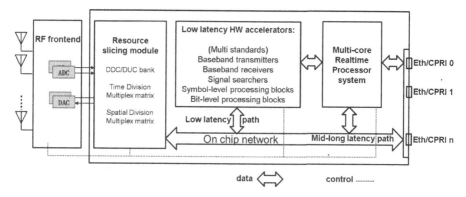

Fig. 5. ORCA Architecture supports both hardware-like low latency performance and software-like flexibility

(at sub millisecond) than LTE. All these trends imply that pure centralized/cloud based software solution won't be the silver bullet. However, simply using pure ASCI/FPGA design to meet performance/latency requirement will lose software-like flexibility, such as virtualization and effective coordination among channels and standards. Exploring an architecture, which has both hardware/FPGA performance and software flexibility, would be a more attractive option for next generation wireless network.

Figure 5 shows an architecture design to meet diverse requirements in a flexible way. First, the wideband multi-antenna RF frontend is connected to a resource slicing module. Then, resource slicing module handles IQ samples to/from specific slice, such as a channel, time slot, antenna/beam, under the software control of PS. Next, slice specific IQ samples are routed via on chip network to/from different destinations according to latency requirements. If the IQ samples belong to a low latency service (UAV/self-driving-car control) or standard (Wi-Fi), their destination/source will be likely other on-chip hardware accelerators. For IQ samples of radio slices which carry mid-long latency service (watching TV) or standard (LTE), they can be routed to pure software domain: either on-chip processor system or off-chip network interface (Ethernet, CPRI, etc.) until a processing unit in a host computer is reached.

To support pure-software-like virtualization and flexibility characteristic for the on-chip hardware accelerator, the accelerator design and on-chip real-time scheduling are the two key enablers. Besides the fact that the accelerator itself needs to meet latency/performance requirement, but also be general enough so that it can be shared by multiple standards. Thanks to that OFDM has been widely adopted by many standards, different standards do share some common processing units. Furthermore, a special issue needs to be addressed when sharing accelerators among multiple slices, this is context saving and restoring of the accelerators. Because when an accelerator is used among multiple slices in TDM (Time Division Multiplex) mode, it has to maintain context internally for each slice it serves. This is necessary to resume accelerator execution for a specific slice from its previous state before interruption. Needless to say, the software design to schedule diverse accelerators for different slices is also a challenging task on its own. This software is essential to achieve effective spectrum utilization with multiple standards/channels coordinated.

4   Demonstration

A demo is setup as shown in Fig. 6 to proof the concept of radio hardware virtualization. The SDR platform is composed by Xilinx zc706 evaluation board together with
Analog Devices fmcomms2 RF front end [23]. A host computer is connected to the
SDR platform for visualization and processing mid-long latency task. Three standards
are covered in the demo: Wi-Fi/802.11 20 MHz mode, Zigbee/802.15.4 2.4 GHz
version, and BLE.

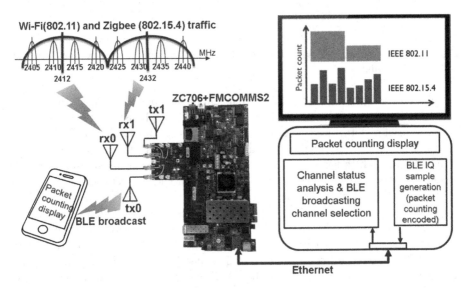

Fig. 6. Radio hardware virtualization demo setup

Ten virtualized preamble detection instances and one BLE (Bluetooth Low Energy)
[24] broadcaster instance are created from resource slicing module and a dual-mode
preamble detector (as accelerator) in FPGA under the scheduling software in ARM
processor. RF front end has two receiving antennas and two transmitting antennas(rx0,
rx1 and tx0, tx1 in Fig. 6), and works in 40 MHz bandwidth mode. For each rx
antenna, resource slicing module creates one 20 MHz Wi-Fi channel and four 5 MHz
Zigbee channels (overlapped with Wi-Fi) by five DDC (Digital Down Converter).
Central frequency of each rx antenna's DDC can be tuned independently inside the
range of 40 MHz bandwidth. In the demo, rx0 is tuned to cover upper 20 MHz of
40 MHz; rx1 is tuned to cover lower 20 MHz of 40 MHz. Ten (five per rx antenna)
slices' IQ sample are routed to ARM processor, then fed one by one to the preamble
detector by control software for preamble searching. 9.6Gbps AXI bus is used to
construct on chip network. Dedicated AXI links are setup between resource slicing,
preamble detector and ARM processor.

ARM reports Wi-Fi and Zigbee packet counting results of each slice to host
computer via Ethernet. A program in computer analyzes channel status according to

packet counting report, then it will: (1) select a good BLE broadcasting channel from three options: 2402 MHz, 2426 MHz, 2480 MHz; (2) generate IQ samples for BLE broadcasting packet [25] with Wi-Fi and Zigbee packet counting information encoded; (3) Send BLE IQ samples to ARM processor in the SDR platform via Ethernet. Resource slicing module broadcasts the BLE packet into the air via the right tx slice (frequency, timing and antenna) under ARM software control. Finally, a user can read the BLE message, which contains Wi-Fi and Zigbee packet counting information, on their equipment (phone, pad) screen by general purpose BLE scanner App, for instance, LightBlue and BLE Scanner. In the demo, BLE broadcasting is an example of mid-long latency service which is handled by host computer instead of FPGA.

A dual-mode preamble detector (16-sample auto-correlation algorithm) is designed based on similar structure of Wi-Fi and Zigbee's preamble. According to the standards, at Wi-Fi baseband rate 20 Msps and Zigbee half baseband rate 1 Msps, both preambles have the form of repeating 16-sample random signal. The only difference is that: Wi-Fi' preamble has 160 samples which is generated by repeating 16-sample signal 10 times; Zigbee repeats 8 times, which results in 128-sample preamble.

C language is used to develop both FPGA and ARM software. By Xilinx HLS C, resource slicing and preamble detector blocks achieve 200 MHz clock speed. AXI bus run at 64-bit 200 MHz mode. Each AXI 64-bit word contains two IQ samples (16-bit I and 16-bit Q sample for each antenna). To process 512 samples, which means 25.6 µs under Wi-Fi baseband rate, 512 µs under half Zigbee baseband rate, preamble detector needs only 1094 clocks, i.e. 5.47 µs, according to FPGA synthesis report. So, it is fast enough to handle two Wi-Fi slices and ten Zigbee slices. Because the speed of accelerator consuming IQ sample is higher than speed of ten rx slices generating IQ sample. The whole processing system won't lose any IQ-sample/signal, as if there are ten preamble detector running in fully parallel (logically). Different from technology in [26], multiple virtual AP (Access Point) share one Wi-Fi channel by time division, our implementation allows running multiple APs in multiple channels concurrently without implementing standalone FPGA block for each channel.

For the control software, a basic control slot length is 25.6 µs (512 samples of Wi-Fi), which is also the basic time slot length of resource slicing. 20 slots compose a control period. Different tasks, such as ten preamble detection tasks, one BLE broadcasting task, host computer communication task, tx/rx frequency tuning task, are scheduled in different time slots according to upstream producing rate and latency requirement, just like a computer running multiple programs. By carefully arranging the schedule, there are ten rx instances and one tx instances running in fully parallel from the end user point of view. In this way, a set of radio hardware resources (RF front end, accelerator, etc.) get virtualized to multiple instances.

5   Conclusion and Future Work

ORCA project tries to push the virtualization in cloud/host-computer domain to radio hardware level to solve the spectrum sharing issue under diverse wireless access scenario. By building a platform with a software-hardware co-design philosophy, developer can use the platform to create multiple concurrent virtualized instances from the low latency high performance hardware/FPGA accelerator. A hierarchical latency handling methodology is proposed to utilize different characters of hardware/FPGA and host computer. With this architecture, multiple wireless accesses run fully in parallel, just like running multiple programs on the same CPU, to maximize utilization of FPGA accelerators. A demo showcase is made to proof the concept by running concurrent two Wi-Fi, eight Zigbee and one BLE instances in 40 MHz bandwidth from the same set of FPGA resource. During the demo development, high level synthesis and processor controlled on chip network are used to shorten the development cycle significantly compared with traditional HDL (Hardware Description Language) based development method. Demonstration results show that this high level design methodology can also generate high performance FPGA blocks.

In the future, software framework and API will be refined in a more formatted way to abstract on chip resources, such as accelerator and on-chip high-speed network. By doing so, FPGA developer and software developer can design platform compatible accelerator and virtualized wireless access service in the more efficient and coordinated way.

Acknowledgment. The project leading to this application has received funding from the European Union's Horizon 2020 research and innovation programme under grant agreement No. 732174 (ORCA project).

References

1. Wyglinski, A.M., et al.: Revolutionizing software defined radio: case studies in hardware, software, and education. IEEE Commun. Mag. **54**(1), 68–75 (2016)
2. C-RAN: The Road Toward Green RAN. http://labs.chinamobile.com/cran/wp-content/uploads/2014/06/20140613-C-RAN-WP-3.0.pdf
3. Common Public Radio Interface (CPRI); Interface Specification. http://www.cpri.info/downloads/CPRI_v_6_0_2013-08-30.pdf
4. Checko, A., Christiansen, H.L., Yan, Y., Scolari, L., Kardaras, G., Berger, M.S., Dittmann, L.: Cloud RAN for mobile networks a technology overview. IEEE Commun. Surv. Tutorials **17**(1), 405–426 (2015)
5. de la Oliva, A., Hernandez, J.A., Larrabeiti, D., Azcorra, A.: An overview of the CPRI specification and its application to C-RAN-based LTE scenarios. IEEE Commun. Mag. **54**(2), 152–159 (2016)
6. Part 11: Wireless LAN Medium Access Control (MAC) and Physical Layer (PHY) Specifications. http://standards.ieee.org/getieee802/download/802.11-2016.pdf
7. IEEE Standard for Low-Rate Wireless Networks. http://standards.ieee.org/getieee802/download/802.15.4-2015.pdf
8. Taneja, M.: 802.11ah—LPWA interworking. In: Proceedings of IEEE NetSoft Conference on Workshops (NetSoft), Seoul, South Korea, pp. 441–446, June 2016
9. Lora Alliance. https://www.lora-alliance.org/
10. Sigfox. http://www.sigfox.com/
11. Sesia, S., Toufik, I., Baker, M.: LTE - The UMTS Long Term Evolution From Theory to Practice, 2nd edn. Wiley, Hoboken (2011)

12. Wan, T., Ashwood-Smith, P.: A performance study of CPRI over Ethernet with IEEE 802.1Qbu and 802.1Qbv enhancements. In: 2015 IEEE Global Communications Conference (GLOBECOM), San Diego, CA, pp. 1–6 (2015)
13. USRP. https://www.ettus.com/product
14. UHD. https://www.ettus.com/sdr-software/detail/usrp-hardware-driver
15. Latency_test.cpp in UHD. https://github.com/EttusResearch/uhd/blob/maint/host/examples/latency_test.cpp
16. srsLTE. https://github.com/srsLTE
17. Open Air Interface. http://www.openairinterface.org/
18. Amrisoft. https://www.amarisoft.com/
19. LabVIEW Communications 802.11 Application Framework. http://sine.ni.com/nips/cds/view/p/lang/en/nid/213084
20. WARP: Wireless Open Access Research Platform. http://warpproject.org/trac/
21. Xilinx Zynq-7000 All Programmable SoC. https://www.xilinx.com/products/silicon-devices/soc/zynq-7000.html
22. Xilinx Zynq-7000 All Programmable SoC ZC706 Evaluation Kit. https://www.xilinx.com/products/boards-and-kits/ek-z7-zc706-g.html
23. FMCOMMS2. https://wiki.analog.com/resources/eval/user-guides/ad-fmcomms2-ebz/quick start/zynq
24. Bluetooth Low Energy. https://www.bluetooth.com/specifications/adopted-specifications
25. BLE (Bluetooth Low Energy) transmitter and sniffer. https://github.com/JiaoXianjun/BTLE
26. Bhanage, G., Vete, D., and Seskar, I.: SplitAP: leveraging wireless network virtualization for flexible sharing of WLANs. In: Global Telecommunications Conference. IEEE (2010)

TV White Spaces and Licensed Shared Access Applied to the Brazilian Context

Raphael B. Evangelista$^{(\boxtimes)}$, Carlos F. M. e Silva,
Francisco R. P. Cavalcanti, and Yuri C. B. Silva

Federal University of Ceará, Fortaleza, CE, Brazil
raphael@gtel.ufc.br

Abstract. The spectrum "scarcity" problem can be tackled by promoting a more efficient use of this resource. Spectrum sharing techniques, e.g. TV White Spaces (TVWS) and Licensed Shared Access (LSA), are good solutions for this problem and there are already regulation and standardization efforts worldwide. The Brazilian regulatory scenario is not that advanced regarding spectrum sharing, but there are already some actions towards the adoption of this concept for the Brazilian reality. This paper gives an overview of the spectrum sharing concept and the Brazilian telecommunications regulatory scenario. Case studies regarding the employment of both TVWS and LSA in the Brazilian scenario are also presented as a way to bring more attention to the adoption of those concepts in the country.

Keywords: Spetrum sharing · TVWS · LSA

1 Introduction

There is a considerable increase in mobile data traffic. According to forecasts [8], this traffic will grow sevenfold between 2016 and 2021, and it will reach, by the end of 2021, 49 exabytes per month. This extra boom is mainly due to the popularization and proliferation of devices worldwide, like smartphones and tablets, as well as the development of data-hungry applications.

On one hand it is expected that there will be 29 billion connected devices in the whole world by 2022, thanks to the advancements in technology and development of concepts, like Machine-to-Machine (M2M), Internet of Things (IoT), and Internet of Vehicles (IoV), to name a few [9]. On the other hand, applications which demand high data rate, like video streaming and online gaming, are becoming more common. In order to be capable of dealing with this high traffic, the next generation of communication systems, Fifth Generation (5G), predicted to be launched by 2020, expects to provide a capacity increase of one to ten thousandfold compared to the previous generation, Fourth Generation (4G) technology [24]. As a consequence of this, a huge demand on Radio Frequency (RF) spectrum is also expected. However, this natural resource is limited, and

© ICST Institute for Computer Sciences, Social Informatics and Telecommunications Engineering 2018
P. Marques et al. (Eds.): CROWNCOM 2017, LNICST 228, pp. 298–309, 2018.
https://doi.org/10.1007/978-3-319-76207-4_25

currently it is suffering from scarcity. Actually, this is an apparent scarcity, since there are lots of bands (generally high GHz bands) not explored by any service.

The easiest way of trying to solve this "scarcity" problem is to explore the higher frequency bands, in particular cm and mm wave bands, which have a lot of spectrum available [2]. However, this approach does not cover all use cases, since waves in high bands present hostile propagation characteristics, e.g. strong pathloss, atmospheric and rain absorption, low diffraction around obstacles, etc.; and therefore may not always be compatible with all applications, for example, communications where devices are found in a mobile and very dynamic environment.

The massive Multiple Input Multiple Output (MIMO) technique is a very good approach to deal with the propagation characteristics in higher bands. The utilization of large antenna arrays allows a better steering of the signal transmission power towards the direction of interest, enhancing the transmission gain. Furthermore, it allows the interference to be better managed, which also improves the wireless communication in a network [2].

Another solution is to promote a more efficient spectrum use in frequencies which are overused, typically the lower ones. The traditional way the spectrum is managed in most countries, even in Brazil, is through the granting of spectrum licenses for exclusive use on a long-term basis. However, in some cases, a spectrum owner does not use the resource assigned to him during all the time and in all geographical areas. Despite the fact that this static approach is very robust in the avoidance of harmful interference among services, it leads to the underutilization of spectrum.

Spectrum sharing comes out as a very good option to solve this inefficiency problem, enabling a more dynamic access to the RF spectrum and allowing this resource to be shared in a flexible way. This concept should not be confused with the unlicensed use of spectrum, e.g. Industrial, Scientic and Medical (ISM) applications, where the spectrum in specific bands is shared without the need of license and with services being subject to interference of other services.

This work is focused on two concepts of different generations of spectrum sharing: TV White Spaces (TVWS), being part of the first generation, and Licensed Shared Access (LSA), of the following one. Each one having its particularities and well-defined use cases.

Brazil, as a geographically extensive country, has serious problems regarding the digital inclusion, mostly in rural or remote parts of it. In these regions, generally, there is no broadband Internet access or it is expensive and with poor quality.

Either TVWS or LSA could be used in different use cases, as it is presented in this work, to solve the problems previously exposed. It should be emphasized that the contributions of this work related to both techniques are focused on the Brazilian context.

The rest of the paper is organized as follows. Section 2 discusses about the spectrum sharing concept and describes TVWS and LSA approaches. Section 3 presents the spectrum regulatory scenario in Brazil. A discussion about the application of spectrum sharing concepts in the Brazilian scenario is made in Sect. 4. The paper is finally concluded in Sect. 5.

2 Spectrum Sharing

Spectrum Sharing has different meanings. For a National Regulatory Authority (NRA), it means to provide more spectrum for a service without interfering or bringing harm to the existing users of that resource.

The focus of this work is on Dynamic Spectrum Access (DSA), where the sharing is organized among users and depends on demands of systems that share the resources, with the allocations changing with time in a dynamic manner. This branch of spectrum sharing should not be confused with the co-existence concept, where the shared spectrum is provided in a fixed or static manner, in a way that there is no interference among users using the same or adjacent spectrum [22].

The main problem that comes with the DSA employment is the interference that new users (also called secondary users) of the spectrum can bring to the original users (or primary users) of this resource. For the traditional case where a service has an exclusive license to the spectrum, the unwanted emissions that can cause interference in other services in the same or adjacent bands are regulated through spectral masks, which are generally harmonized across the world regions. For DSA, there is a sharing of spectrum in different radio technologies, then some limits should be established regarding the transmit power and/or the sharing distance, so that one service does not cause interference to the others and viceversa, compromising the communication.

The two spectrum sharing techniques addressed in this section are TVWS and LSA.

2.1 TVWS

TVWS is a portion of spectrum in the range of Very High Frequency (VHF) and Ultra High Frequency (UHF) that is not in use at a particular time and location and, therefore, it represents a new opportunity for wireless communication systems in a frequency band that has good propagation characteristics. They emerge as a by-product of the Digital Switchover (DSO), also known as the digital television transition; a process in which analog Television (TV) broadcasting is replaced by the digital one. The DSO has been successfully completed in various countries and it is still in progress in some others. In Brazil, for example, the Ministry of Communications established in 2014 a DSO plan, starting in 2015 and gradually to be implemented until December 2018 [25].

The basic principle of TVWS consists of allowing unlicensed, secondary users to access spectrum at specific geographic locations and/or during specific time intervals, not interfering with terrestrial TV transmission or reception, or any other primary service. Importantly, the TVWS regulations require White

Space Devices (WSDs) to obtain authorization before they can transmit, and require those devices to cease operation when they are located within protected areas [26].

Since waves at the frequency range of TVWS have good propagation characteristics, the application of this concept is more envisioned for use cases where there is a need for wireless coverage extension. For example, TVWS can be used to improve the coverage of a 4G network of a mobile operator in rural locations.

The potential uses of TVWS are still being considered by the industry and regulatory bodies, because there are still uncertainties about what sort of TVWS availability is realistic, and the amount of TVWS spectrum available can change significantly from one country to another [17]. Many countries have studied the use of TVWS, but only two of them currently have a proper regulation model that permits the license-exempt use of TVWS: the United States of America (USA) with Federal Communications Commission (FCC), and the United Kingdom (UK) with Office of Communications (Ofcom).

The extension of spectrum occupancy of TVWS has opened up a new dimension for a variety of potential applications. The merit of TVWS exploitation is to provide innovative applications not fully supported by existing technologies, and to offer resource expansion to existing applications for enhanced performance [1]. One company that has begun developing rural broadband equipment using TVWS is Carlson Wireless Technologies[1] from USA. The company has more than a decade of experience in developing effective rural solutions. These wireless radios can provide broadband data rate over much larger distances than the existing Wireless Fidelity (Wi-Fi) routers, and in December 2013, FCC approved its commercial and unlicensed use in the USA.

2.2 LSA

While TVWS is considered a technology of the first generation of spectrum sharing, LSA is the key example of a concept of the next generation [24].

LSA, firstly known as Authorized Shared Access (ASA), is defined as a new complementary regulatory framework which was developed in Europe as a joint effort of the Electronic Communications Committee (ECC), the European Conference of Postal and Telecommunications (*Conférence Européenne des administrations des Postes et des Télécommunications*, CEPT) and the European Telecommunications Standards Institute (ETSI). This framework allows the so-called LSA licensee (secondary user) to access additional spectrum resources, which are underutilized by its incumbent user. It is based on an agreement called sharing framework which is defined by three stakeholders: incumbent user (primary user), LSA licensee, and NRA. The sharing framework includes technical and operational conditions which the users are subject to, aiming at the protection from harmful interference for both incumbent and LSA licensee.

The main feature which differentiates LSA from the other spectrum sharing techniques is its individual licensing regime, which means that the licensee in

---

[1] http://www.carlsonwireless.com/.

order to use the spectrum needs an individual authorization that contains its rights and obligations. The advantage of this regime is that these sharing rules, which the licensees must follow, guarantee that the interference might be managed, enabling protection from interference and predictable Quality of Service (QoS) for both primary and secondary users [15].

Differently from TVWS, LSA is not expected to be applied to enhance wireless coverage. The application of this concept is more related to the provision of additional spectrum access and predictable QoS for services. The first use case of LSA is the application of the concept to provide additional spectrum for mobile broadband services in the 2300 MHz to 2400 MHz band. This band is defined by the Generation Partnership Project (3GPP) as Long-Term Evolution (LTE) Band 40, allocated to mobile services and identified for International Mobile Telecommunications (IMT) globally in the International Telecommunication Union (ITU) Radio Regulations [11]. It should be mentioned that the basic principles for the LSA operation are not dependent on the frequency, allowing it to be applied to other bands [24].

The system components are standardized by ETSI and described in [11]. The system requirements and architecture are specified in [10, 12].

The basic architecture of the LSA system is composed by a database called LSA repository, which manages the LSA spectrum. Besides that entity, there is the LSA controller, which communicates directly with the LSA repository and, according to the information in the last entity, it grants access or requests the evacuation of the band by an LSA licensee through a control mechanism.

3   Brazilian Regulation Scenario

The NRA in charge of the regulation of telecommunications in Brazil is the National Telecommunications Agency (*Agncia Nacional de TelecomuniÇões*, Anatel) which was created in 1997 by the (*Lei Geral de TelecomunicaÇões*, LGT), a very important law for the regulation of this sector, providing the ground rules for the telecommunications market and contributing to the development of the country [4].

Anatel is an independent agency linked to the former Ministry of Communications (currently Ministry of Science, Technology, Innovation and Communications), which is in charge of establishing the public policy of the telecommunications sector in Brazil.

Among the attributions of the Brazilian NRA, can be highlighted, the management of the RF spectrum, being Anatel responsible for its rules and regulation. Anatel designs and updates the RF spectrum allocation, distribution and destination plan. The attributions follow the ITU recommendations defined for region 2. The distribution and destinations of RF bands for the services and telecommunications activities consider the present needs and future expansion [28].

According to the LGT and established by Anatel, as previously mentioned, RF bands are designated to specific telecommunications services, and, hence, companies exploiting a service using a given band can only be granted license for a spectrum designated for that band. Furthermore, as the RF spectrum is a limited resource and a public property, its economic exploitation is only allowed by Anatel grant through concession, permit, or authorization [4], obtained generally through bidding processes, so that there is fairness in the competition among stakeholders.

Still, according to the LGT, there are two exceptions where the exploitation of the RF spectrum is allowed without the need of authorization: the use of this resource by the army and by restricted radiation equipment.

Regulation for the use of the RF spectrum went through recent modifications in 2016 under an Anatel Resolution [5]. From that time on there are some possibilities for a kind of secondary market of spectrum, since it enables the spectrum that was licensed to a primary user to be explored in a secondary basis by another player upon a prior authorization of Anatel, if the incumbent is not yet utilizing the resource properly.

Another step towards spectrum sharing was recently taken by Anatel, when two mobile operators were allowed to perform an agreement in the sharing of a Radio Access Network (RAN) of the 450 MHz band in order to improve rural coverage. With that, Anatel considered the benefits, like price reductions, and gain in QoS, that the sharing of infrastructure and spectrum could bring to the telecommunications sector through efficient resources usage [28].

These efforts show a certain progress towards a more efficient RF spectrum management in Brazil, and it places both TVWS and LSA in the Brazilian regulation horizon, since these concepts are very good options for more efficiency in the utilization of the spectrum.

4   Spectrum Sharing Trends in Brazil

The access to information and knowledge are essential for a country to be competitive in a globalized economy. In this sense, broadband Internet becomes a very important element for the country infrastructure nowadays [14]. Hence, the economic, social and political development of Brazil can be accelerated by improving the broadband access, speed, quality and decreasing its cost. This enhancement can be translated into technological advances, cost reduction and service quality improvements in various areas, e.g. health, education, and public security. Furthermore, it can be considered an investment in the research field.

Brazil has achieved considerable advances in broadband, but in comparison with other countries, it is still expensive, slow and usually of poor quality. In [13] the rank of Brazil in 2015 with regard to other countries can be seen for different categories, like fixed broadband Internet prices, fixed and mobile broadband Internet subscriptions, mobile network coverage, etc. The status of broadband in Brazil is shown in [20], comparing some statistics from 2006 to 2014. It can be noticed a certain progress in digital inclusion but at a slow pace, and the situation in rural and remote regions and for poor people is still far from being acceptable. While there is Internet access in 54% of urban households, this percentage is just

22% in rural ones. Furthermore, in households of economically disadvantaged individuals, there is Internet access in just 14% of cases.

For rural or remote areas, a critical reason that makes the broadband access very difficult is the lack of interest from service providers in such areas. Brazil is a geographically extensive country, hence, an investment on providing such service in various regions (mostly rural or remote) would imply in an enormous expenditure on telecommunications infrastructure, what makes this practice very unattractive. As it can be seen in [25], there is poor coverage of Third Generation (3G) and 4G services of a Brazilian mobile operator in an important state of the country.

One way to increase the provision of wireless broadband in general is the employment of techniques or technologies to allow the RF spectrum to be used more dynamically and efficiently, so a broader range of stakeholders could have access to and explore wireless broadband. Either TVWS or LSA are very good tools for reaching this efficiency and dynamism of spectrum use.

At the moment, it seems that Anatel is particularly interested in fostering the development of telecommunications/broadband in rural and remote areas. This can be attested in the Anatel regulatory agenda, which indicates a movement towards the regulation of the use of TVWS for the development of broadband of Brazilian rural areas, as a regulatory impact analysis on the use of white spaces in VHF and UHF bands is expected to happen by the second semester of 2018 [30].

In Brazil, there is still no ongoing regulatory actions related to LSA, but there is already research regarding the application of this concept in the Brazilian scenario. In [27] there is a spectrum sharing proposal based on the LSA concept with its specificities, in order for it to be more appropriate to the Brazilian reality. The candidate frequency bands for LSA in Brazil are: 1.4 GHz (L-Band), 2.7 GHz (2500 MHz to 2690 MHz) and 3.5 GHz (3565 MHz to 3650 MHz). Furthermore, the effort in the direction of TVWS regulation is the first step towards the use of the spectrum sharing concept, hence there is some hope in the Brazilian regulatory scenario for LSA implementation in the near future.

4.1 TVWS Case Study

As previously mentioned, Brazil presents some problems related to Internet access in rural and remote areas. With the DSO in Brazil happening and expected to be concluded by the end of 2018, the opportunity for reallocating the TV spectrum is a reality, which opens opportunities to introduce new business models, players and technologies like TVWS into the Brazilian market [25]. One of the major obstacles to providing mobile broadband connectivity in semi-urban and rural areas of Brazil is the weak economic appeal of such areas for operators to deploy their telecommunications infrastructure.

This case study idealizes the use of TVWS to address the challenge in providing mobile broadband to rural or remote areas in the Ceará state in the regions around the Digital Belt of Ceará (*Cinturão Digital do Ceará*, CDC), since there are many white space channels available in such areas [25]. The good propagation characteristics at the TVWS band compared with the current band used in LTE in Brazil means less base stations covering larger spaces, which is a better scenario to attract the attention of mobile operators to invest in such areas.

The CDC was implemented in 2010 and the investments in such infrastructure were about R$ 70 million. The project managed to reach 48% reduction in expenditures with Ceará state Operational Expenditure (OPEX), attending, at the beginning, Governing bodies, schools, hospitals and police departments. The "excess" of fibers enabled partnerships with the private sector, which brought financial and technological development to some rural and suburban regions of the state. The CDC infrastructure is made of redundant fiber optic ring and ramifications comprising more than 3000 km, with 24 optical fiber cables and branches with 12 fibers; and the access in the last mile is made through Worldwide Interoperability for Microwave Access (WiMAX) technology [29]. The use case consists in using the CDC infrastructure to provide LTE services using the white space channels available in each location (LTE over TVWS scenario). This case serves as a basis to be implemented in any other region with similar characteristics.

Since the locations of licensed Digital TV (DTV) transmitters and their corresponding service areas are known, it is reasonable to assume that a database with maps of possible locations for TVWS networks could be implemented (Geolocation Database (GLDB)). In this scenario, the WSDs obtain the available TV channels via querying a certified GLDB, instead of sensing the local spectrum environment. Due to this fact, the GLDB needs to have updated information about the TVWS availability.

The TVWS applied along with the CDC infrastructure opens up a new dimension for a variety of potential applications. Another possibility to provide digital inclusion in such regions could be the deployment of a Super Wi-Fi scenario using the TVWS as backhaul, following the idea implemented in India [21]. This solution could use modems in indoor environments to receive TVWS signal sent by Internet service providers. The receiving equipment would process this signal and forward it to 2.4 GHz or 5.8 GHz, providing wireless Internet services to the end users.

4.2 LSA Case Study

Brazil is very rich in natural resources, holding a very large mineral repository. The Brazilian mining industry has a great importance worldwide, producing and exporting high quality ores, which makes mining a very important activity for the Brazilian economy. Brazil is very well ranked in the world for different minerals regarding its production and reserves. Forecasts show excellent perspectives for this economic activity for the next decades [23].

The importance of the mining industry makes the development of this activity crucial for Brazilian economy growth. In the current globalized world, to face competition, the industry must be in constant development so that the productivity is maximized. The Industry 4.0 is the concept used for the following industrial revolution that is about to happen and which was defined in Germany, one of the world top competitive manufacturing industries. This concept is expected to improve the "industrial processes involved in manufacturing, engineering, material usage and supply chain and life cycle management" [19].

The key feature of Industry 4.0 and the enabler of such improvements is what has been called the smart factory, which is a factory that assists people and machines in performing their tasks through the awareness of the physical and virtual world. This awareness is allowed thanks to a network compatible equipment called Cyber-Physical Systems (CPS) supplied with sensors and actuators, which monitor physical industrial processes, helping to decentralize decisions. In the smart factories, these CPSs are interconnected using the concept of IoT, so the industry is a network of automated machines and people, with the possibility of some activities being controlled remotely by the latter [16].

Regarding the automation process envisioned by Industry 4.0, the wireless factory automation is recently drawing more interest than the wired one, since the former presents attractive advantages, e.g. low installation and maintenance cost, higher flexibility.

One main challenge of wireless factory automation is its requirements regarding communications latency and reliability. Industrial applications like packaging machines need very strict requirements (latency less than 1 ms and block error probability around 10^{-8} or 10^{-9}) [3]. Such services with very rigorous requirements, mainly in respect to latency and reliability, were defined by ITU as Ultra-Reliable and Low-Latency Communications (uRLLC) [18].

In recent years, there were some advances in wireless technologies for factory applications, e.g. WirelessHART, ISA 100.11a, Industrial WLAN [7]. However, these solutions together with other proprietary ones operate mostly on unlicensed RF spectrum, and, hence, there are no QoS guarantees, since there is interference from other services using the shared band.

The employment of the Industry 4.0 concept to the mining industry in Brazil is a process that needs to occur in order to keep this sector competitive in the world market [6], and the application of the LSA framework concept is a good approach to address the challenges mentioned previously. The LSA band would be made available to the mining companies with QoS guarantees, since this is a key feature of the exclusive licensing basis of this concept. Despite that, this solution facilitates the granting of spectrum license to the companies, in comparison with the traditional bidding process, which happens not so often and has quite expensive bids.

The flexibility of LSA is another advantage for this case study. The definition of the sharing framework by the stakeholders facilitates that the conditions of the parts are met. For example, a mining company would require the spectrum just for a specific part of the country, for a certain time and with a particular bandwidth size.

The interference that one service could generate on another is an issue that needs to be considered carefully, since the interference management is made using data that is present at the LSA repository (e.g., incumbent location, maximum Effective Isotropic Radiated Power (EIRP)) together with a propagation model. Since the mining sites are very particular, with a irregular relief and big depressions, the propagation model is very different from the ones already studied and available in the literature. Therefore, it represents a critical part for which a certain importance must be given.

Using this approach, all the stakeholders are contemplated. The financial investment of the mining company would be addressed to the incumbent. The LSA licensee would have the access to the licensed spectrum with the QoS guarantees that it needs. The advantage for Anatel would be a more efficient use of the spectrum, alleviating, in this sense, the spectrum "scarcity" problem.

The same idea could also be employed to other industrial activities in which the application of the concept of Industry 4.0 is envisioned, e.g. agriculture and metallurgy.

5   Conclusions

Significantly more spectrum and much wider bandwidth than what is available today will be needed in order to reach the targets of future mobile broadband systems. It is visible that the fixed allocation scheme of frequency has resulted in an underutilization of the spectrum both spatially and temporally.

The spectrum sharing concept is an innovative option to solve the spectrum "scarcity" problem by promoting a more efficient use of this resource.

Brazil still has a lot to advance in the adoption of the spectrum sharing concept, as there were very few regulatory actions in that direction. The modifications in the regulation for the use of RF spectrum demonstrates a modest progress towards the secondary market, and TVWS regulation studies are already expected to happen by 2018. Nevertheless, there is still no visible effort related to the employment of the LSA concept in the Brazilian scenario.

This paper presents two case studies about the application of TVWS and LSA concepts for the Brazilian context. It is expected that this work brings the attention of Anatel and other Brazilian stakeholders to the application of those concepts and the benefits they could bring not only for the telecommunications sector, but also for the whole country economy.

As a future work, it can be performed a more quantitative approach, evaluating the case studies presented in this paper in terms of Capital Expenditure (CAPEX) and OPEX. Similar studies could not be found in literature, what makes such work of relevant importance for the development of spectrum sharing concept in the country.

Acknowledgment. The research leading to these results received funding from the European Commission H2020 programme under grant agreement no. 688941 (FUTE-BOL), as well from the Brazilian Ministry of Science, Technology, Innovation, and Communication (MCTIC) through RNP and CTIC.

References

1. Alemseged, Y.D., et al.: TV White Space Spectrum Technologies: Regulations, Standards, and Applications. Ed. by Saeed, R.A., Shellhammer, S.J. CRC Press, Boca Raton (2012). ISBN 978-1-4398-4880-7
2. Andrews, J.G., et al.: What will 5G be? IEEE J. Sel. Areas Commun. **32**(6), 1065–1082 (2014). https://doi.org/10.1109/JSAC.2014.2328098. ISSN 0733-8716
3. Ashraf, S.A., et al.: Ultra-reliable and low-latency communication for wireless factory automation: from LTE to 5G. In: 2016 IEEE 21st International Conference on Emerging Technologies and Factory Automation (ETFA), pp. 1–8, September 2016. https://doi.org/10.1109/ETFA.2016.7733543. ISBN 978-1-5090-1314-2
4. República Federativa do Brasil - Imprensa Nacional, ed. DOU - Seção 1 135, July 1997. Lei no 9.472, de 16 de julho de 1997
5. República Federativa do Brasil - Imprensa Nacional, ed. DOU - Seção 1 213, November 2016. Resolução no 671, de 03 de novembro de 2016. ISSN 1677-7042
6. Agência Brasil.: Brazil: innovation key to mining and metallurgical industry to compete abroad, September 2016. https://goo.gl/EZELV2. Accessed July 2017
7. Christin, D., Mogre, P.S., Hollick, M.: Survey on wireless sensor network technologies for industrial automation: the security and quality of service perspectives. In: Future Internet 2010, pp. 96–125, 2 April 2010. ISSN 1999-5903. https://doi.org/10.3390/fi2020096
8. Cisco.: Cisco Visual Networking Index: Global Mobile Data Traffic Forecast Update, 2016–2021, White paper. Cisco, February 2017
9. Ericsson.: Ericsson Mobility Report. Ericsson, June 2017
10. ETSI.: System architecture and high level procedures for operation of Licensed Shared Access (LSA) in the 2 300 MHz–2 400 MHz band, TS 103 235, October 2015
11. ETSI.: System Reference document (SRdoc); Mobile Broadband Systems in the 2300 MHz–2400 MHz band under Licensed Shared Access (LSA), TR 103 113, July 2013
12. ETSI.: System requirements for operation of Mobile Broadband Systems in the 2300 MHz–2400 MHz band under Licensed Shared Access (LSA), TS 103 154, October 2014
13. World Economic Forum.: The Global Information Technology Report 2015: ICTs for Inclusive Growth. Insight report (2015)
14. World Bank Group.: World Development Report 2016: Digital Dividends (2016). https://doi.org/10.1596/978-1-4648-0728-2
15. Gundlach, M., et al.: Recent advances on LSA in standardization, regulation, research and architecture design. In: 2014 1st International Workshop on Cognitive Cellular Systems (CCS), pp. 1–5. IEEE, September 2014. https://doi.org/10.1109/CCS.2014.6933807. ISBN 978-1-4799-4139-1
16. Hermann, M., Pentek, T., Otto, B.: Design principles for industrie 4.0 scenarios. In: 2016 49th Hawaii International Conference on System Sciences, pp. 3928–3937 (2016). https://doi.org/10.1109/HICSS.2016.488
17. Horvitz, R., et al.: TV White Spaces. A Pragmatic Approach. Ed. by Pietrosemoli, E., Zennaro, M. 1st edn. ICTP-The Abdus Salam International Centre for Teoretical Physics, December 2013. ISBN 978-9295003-50-7
18. Ji, H., et al.: Introduction to ultra reliable and low latency communications in 5G. In: Computing Research Repository (CoRR) abs/1704.05565, April 2017. http://arxiv.org/abs/1704.05565

19. Recommendations for implementing the strategic initiative Industrie 4.0. Final report of the Industrie 4.0 Working Group, April 2013
20. Knight, P., Feferman, F., Fodistch, N. (eds.) Broadband in Brazil. past, present and future. Novo Século Editora (2016)
21. Kumar, A., et al.: Toward enabling broadband for a billion plus population with TV white spaces. IEEE Commun. Mag. **54**(7), 28–34 (2016). https://doi.org/10.1109/MCOM.2016.7509375. ISSN 0163-6804
22. Matyjas, J.D., Kumar, S., Hu, F. (eds.) Spectrum Sharing in Wireless Networks. Fairness, Efficiency, and Security. CRC Press, Boca Raton (2017). ISBN 978-1-4987-2635-1
23. Ministério de Minas e Energia.: Plano Nacional de Mineração 2030. Geologia Mineração e Transformação Mineral, April 2011
24. Mueck, M.D., Srikanteswara, S., Badic, B.: White paper: Spectrum Sharing: Licensed Shared Access (LSA) and Spectrum Access System (SAS), White paper. Intel (2015)
25. do Nascimento, M.F.S., et al.: TV white spaces for digital inclusions in Brazil. In: Revista de Tecnologia da Informação e Comunicação, **6**(2), 6–15 (2016). ISSN 2237-5104
26. Noguet, D., Gautier, M., Berg, V.: Advances in opportunistic radio technologies for TVWS. EURASIP J. Wirel. Commun. Netw. **2011**(1), 170 (2011). https://doi.org/10.1186/1687-1499-2011-170. ISSN 1687-1499
27. Ron, C.V.R., de Silva Mello, L.A.R., de Almeida, M.P.C.: A spectrum sharing proposal based on LSA/ASA for the Brazilian regulatory framework. In: 2017 IEEE Wireless Communications and Networking Conference (WCNC), pp. 1–6, March 2017. https://doi.org/10.1109/WCNC.2017.7925440
28. da Silva, R.B.F., da Silva, C.T.R.: Spectrum regulation in Brazil. IEEE Wireless Commun. **23**(3), 2–3 (2016). https://doi.org/10.1109/MWC.2016.7498067. ISSN 1536-1284
29. Empresa de Tecnologia da Informaço do Ceará (ETICE).: Impacto socioeconomico do Cintur ao Digital do Ceará (2016). https://goo.gl/5c2cMJ. Accessed July 2017
30. Agencia Nacional de Telecomunicações.: Portaria No 491, de 10 de Abril de 2017. April 2017

MAC Design for 5G Dense Networks Based on FBMC Modulation

Rida El Chall$^{(\boxtimes)}$, Benoit Miscopein, and Dimitri Kténas

CEA-Leti Minatec, 17 rue des Martyrs, 38054 Grenoble Cedex 9, France
rida.chall@gmail.com , Benoit.MISCOPEIN@cea.fr

Abstract. The fifth generation (5G) of wireless networks is currently under investigation in order to address the well-known challenges of the high capacity demands and traffic volume. The promising solutions to meet these targets can be achieved through ultra-densification, efficient use of spectrum and advanced filtered modulation techniques. In this paper, we present an enhanced MAC protocol for 5G small cells operating at 5 GHz and assuming an FBMC physical layer. The proposed MAC design consists of scheduled-based and contention-based access schemes and involves a listen before talk (LBT) procedure to comply with ETSI regulations. The performance of the proposed FBMC-MAC design is then evaluated in dense deployment scenarios under different PHY/MAC parameter settings. Moreover, we study the performance of FBMC-MAC systems in the context of coexistence with WiFi systems.

Keywords: 5G · FBMC · Multiple access MAC design · LBT · LBE
Dense small cell networks · Contention access · Scheduled access
CSMA/CA

1 Introduction

The ever increasing demand for higher data rate and reliable communications poses significant challenges for the existing wireless networks. Fifth generation (5G) cellular networks are expected to meet these intense demands as well as to support different kinds of applications and quality of service (QoS) requirements. Those included, enhanced mobile broadband, ultra-reliable and low-latency communications, and massive machine-type communications [1].

As far as capacity improvement is concerned, the common approaches are based on ultra-densification, exploitation of heterogeneous resources in available licensed, lightly-licensed and unlicensed spectrum bands; the spectrum resources being possibly used assuming traffic steering or aggregation mechanisms.

Moreover, relying on a modulation technique with higher efficiency than the one used in 4G is another key aspect of 5G network design. Among different possibilities, filter-bank multi-carrier (FBMC) modulation is considered as a candidate for 5G systems [2]. Indeed, FBMC through the use of well-designed prototype filters overcomes the limitations of the widely-used orthogonal frequency division multiplexing (OFDM) technique in terms of tight timing and

© ICST Institute for Computer Sciences, Social Informatics and Telecommunications Engineering 2018
P. Marques et al. (Eds.): CROWNCOM 2017, LNICST 228, pp. 310–321, 2018.
https://doi.org/10.1007/978-3-319-76207-4_26

frequency synchronization requirements. It can provide a very sharp frequency confinement of the signal which translates into a better spectrum utilization.

In this paper, we first present an overview of FBMC modulation and physical layer assumptions considered through our work. Consequently, we propose a medium access control (MAC) protocol for dense small cell networks operating in 5 GHz unlicensed band. This MAC design is based on beacon enabled superframe similar to existing solutions [3,4] with novel extension in order to support broadband traffic, multi-user channel access and to take advantage of FBMC signaling mainly to facilitate the resource allocation and channel access in uplink. In particular, the design is a mix of contention-based and scheduled-based access schemes that enable flexible use of radio resources and spectrum. Since the unlicensed 5 GHz band is considered, the proposed MAC performs listen before talk (LBT) in order to comply with the ETSI regulatory requirements [5] and to ensure fair coexistence with neighboring technologies. In this band, two variants of channel access mechanisms are possible to comply with the regulation: frame-based equipment (FBE) and load-based equipment (LBE). LBE has been recently adopted by 3GPP within the licensed-assisted access (LAA) framework for component carriers in 5 GHz band [6]. Similarly, in the proposed MAC design we rely on LBE as the channel access method used by the small cell to perform clear channel assessment (CCA) before transmitting. Second, we investigate the impact of PHY configuration parameters and MAC-related parameters on the performance of the proposed MAC design in dense deployment scenarios. Additionally, we analyze the fairness of coexistence of FBMC-MAC system when sharing the channel with a WiFi system.

The remainder of the paper is organized as follows. Section 2 describes the main features of FBMC modulation and physical layer assumptions. Section 3 presents the proposed MAC design and describes the frame structure as well as channel access modes. In Sect. 4, the simulation results related to the PHY-MAC designs are shown. Finally, the conclusions are given in Sect. 5.

2   FBMC and PHY Assumptions

FBMC is a multi-carrier modulation considered as a 5G waveform candidate in order to address the OFDM limitations of reduced spectral efficiency and strict synchronization requirements [2]. Indeed, OFDM filters the sub-carriers using a rectangular pulse in the time domain leading to large side-lobes, thus important adjacent channel leakages. It requires the insertion of cyclic prefix (CP) inducing a loss in the spectral efficiency. Moreover, OFDM suffers from high sensitivity to carrier frequency offset and high peak-to-average power ratio (PAPR) that limit uplink multi-user transmissions. In contrast, FBMC modulation uses a set of filters that synthesize and analyze each sub-carrier individually [7]. A proper design of the prototype filter can provide a very sharp spectral localization that allows multiple access and broadband data transmission.

The prototype filter is characterized by its overlapping factor K, which is the number of multi-carrier symbols that overlap in the time domain. The overlapping factor K has an impact on determining the optimum spectrum utilization, the level of adjacent channel leakage (ACL) and the residual inter-symbol interference. In particular, offset quadrature amplitude modulation (OQAM) combined with Nyquist constraints on the prototype filter is considered to guarantee orthogonality between adjacent symbols and adjacent carriers while providing maximum spectral efficiency [2].

Figure 1 shows the power spectral density for OFDM and FBMC for several values of K. As it can be seen in the figure, a larger value of K ($K = 4$) is able to achieve better frequency localization and lower out-of-band emissions on adjacent channel (< -100 dBc). At the contrary, for $K = 2$, the leakage level increases significantly, and is only 10 dB lower than OFDM.

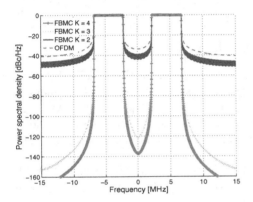

Parameter	20 MHz band
FFT size N	512
Active carriers N_c	330
Sub-carrier spacing Δ_f	60 kHz
overlapping factor K	4
Bandwidth B	19.8 MHz
Resource block (RB)	180 kHz
Sampling Freq. F_s	30.72 MHz

Fig. 1. Power spectral density of OFDM and FBMC with several values of K (left) and FBMC parameters for a 20 MHz carrier (right)

Compared to CP-OFDM, this excellent spectral localization of FBMC signal implies a set of characteristics that can exploited at MAC layer to optimize the medium access:

- Relaxed synchronicity: In CP-OFDM, simultaneous transmissions in contiguous bands have to respect a timing misalignment smaller than the CP length in order to avoid inter-carrier interference. By contrast, FBMC can gracefully tolerate asynchronous uplink communications on contiguous band, because of the very small level of adjacent carrier interference if a guard band of at least one sub-carrier spacing is introduced [8].
- Efficient use of allocated spectrum: In FBMC, the insertion of CP is not required and very low adjacent channel leakage ratio (ACLR) is achieved. Consequently, the MAC layer can manage in an efficient way the allocation of (thin) resource blocks, even if they are fragmented and spread in the band.
- Relaxed uplink power control: Along the same idea of very low ACLR, the uplink signal in contiguous bands can be transmitted without a strict power control. Indeed, provided that ACLR is more than 60 dB, two simultaneous signals on contiguous channels can arrive on a small cell with a very large difference of uplink received power.

In this work, the FBMC physical layer is assumed to rely on a particular implementation of FBMC called frequency spreading FBMC (FS-FBMC) according to the parameters specified in Fig. 1 for 20 MHz channel bandwidth. The total number of sub-carriers is set to 512 with sub-carrier spacing of 60 kHz and overlapping factor of 4. These parameters allow to reach the same level of performance of LTE-PHY with 2048 sub-carries and 15 kHz sub-carrier spacing [8]. We note that the reduction of the number of sub-carriers by a factor of 4 reduces the PAPR which presents another advantage for uplink communication and allows also to reduce the complexity of FFT implementation. More details about the FBMC modulation and the filter coefficients can be found in [2], whereas implementation issues are presented in [9].

3 FBMC-MAC Protocol Design

This section presents the design of MAC protocol for 5G small cells to support broadband traffic operating in 5 GHz unlicensed spectrum. Compared to the state of the art of PHY/MAC systems [3,4], this design supports the use of FBMC physical layer, multiple access operation and incorporate LBT mechanisms to comply with ETSI regulatory requirements in the 5 GHz band [5].

3.1 MAC Superframe Design

The MAC design is based on a beacon-enabled superframe, that specifies a combination of contention-based and scheduled-based access schemes close to the existing systems [3,4]. The basic network operation mode is a master-slave mode, with the small cell (SC) being the master of user equipments (UEs) within the radio range. More specifically, the superframe consists of a beacon period, a contention free period (CFP), a contention access period (CAP) and an idle period as illustrated in Fig. 2. The length of the active superframe part is the channel occupancy time (COT) that is subdivided into multiple time slots, each slot has a duration of 1 ms.

In the beacon period, the SC transmits beacon frames spanning on the whole band during one time slot. The beacon frames provide the basic timing for UEs synchronization and carry the control information for device discovery, network organization and resource allocations.

CFP is the scheduled access period composed of variable time slots that are especially allocated to downlink and uplink data communications. The allocation of resources is generally based on UE priority, QoS requirements and the availability of resources, the allocation being described in the beacon. We note that uplink data traffic is usually initiated by UE through sending an uplink grant request to the SC in a previous superframe, whereas downlink data traffic may be either requested by UE or initiated by the SC.

Meanwhile, the CAP is composed of small number of slots and used by UEs to send control and command frames such as association requests, ACK/NACK, channel quality indicator (CQI) reports and service establishment requests. On the other hand, control information, e.g. CQI, ACK, may be multiplexed with data in an uplink CFP slot when an active UE has both scheduled uplink and downlink traffic, thus allowing more flexibility in resource allocation.

As far as scheduled uplink traffic is concerned, the SC may configure an ACK slot at the end of the CAP in order to send grouped acknowledgments, if any, for the uplink received data in the CFP.

At the end of the superframe, an idle period is considered that can be advantageously used by SCs to sense the channel and feed the spectrum manager with sensing report accordingly.

It is interesting to note that the superframe structure can be dynamically adjusted depending on the traffic type and network load. Indeed, the length of CFP can be tuned to support a given traffic profile like a possible traffic imbalance between uplink and downlink. Alternatively, the CAP duration can also be tuned to provide a better reliability to ACK and CQI updates when the number of active UEs is getting large.

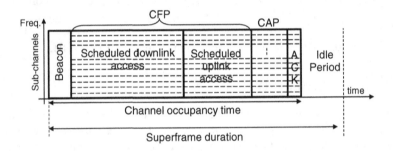

Fig. 2. MAC superframe structure for broadband access in 5 GHz

3.2 Multiple Access

In the proposed FBMC-MAC design, multiple user access is supported both in CFP and CAP to allow efficient and dynamic share of the allocated spectrum.

In the CFP, multiple access is based on OFDMA-like approach for both uplink and downlink channels, using the same concept of resource block (RB) of LTE systems but applied to FBMC modulation. In FBMC-MA, a RB is an allocation of 3 active sub-carriers, i.e. 180 kHz, during a time slot. In this MAC, the scheduler is in charge of allocating both uplink and downlink resource blocks to active UEs, assuming the same kind of schedulers as those used in LTE. Interestingly, as FBMC tolerates asynchronous transmissions with the aforementioned guard interval constraint, uplink resource allocation can be done quite straightforwardly by the small cell using the same modulation scheme for both uplink and downlink communication. Figure 3 depicts the multiple access scheme on the superframe, for the scheduled access parts.

On the other hand, the multiple access in the CAP is based on multi-channel contention scheme. The CAP is therefore subdivided into several sub-channels, where each elementary sub-channel is composed of 17 active sub-carriers and one inactive sub-carrier as a guard band (6 resource blocks). Thus, 9 sub-channels and 18 sub-channels are assumed available for a system bandwidth of 10 MHz and 20 MHz, respectively. UEs attempt to access the channel both in time and frequency domains using a multi-channel carrier sense multiple access with collision avoidance (CSMA/CA) algorithm [10]. Prior to transmission, UE first performs channel sensing to identify the set of idle sub-channels. If all sub-channels are busy, UE defers access until a sub-channel becomes available. Otherwise, UE selects one sub-channel and initiates a random back-off counter. Next, UE should perform CCA using a back-off procedure. If the channel is found busy during a back-off slot, UE may switch to another available sub-channel by maintaining the back-off counter. Otherwise, UE decrements the counter and transmits the frame when this counter reaches zero.

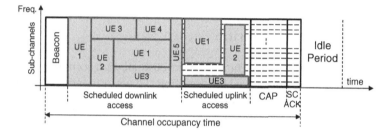

Fig. 3. Multiple access scheme in the scheduled part of the MAC superframe

3.3 Shared Spectrum Utilization Modes

Since the operation in the 5 GHz band is assumed, the SC has to comply with the LBT rule and shall perform a CCA procedure before the transmission of a MAC superframe to avoid interference with others systems. As stated before, the MAC design proposed in this paper can comply with the 2 access options specified by ETSI, which are namely FBE and LBE [5].

FBE defines a fixed timing frame for channel access, where the SC performs CCA in a fixed frame period. This access mode can induce unfair channel access in dense environment since a SC may get a definitive access to the channel and may block the activity of surrounding SCs.

In contrast, LBE relies on a flexible contention scheme prior to triggering the superframe emission that guarantees a better fairness in dense deployments. This channel access scheme has been retained for the LAA procedure in 3GPP specifications [6]. In our design, we have defined a set of parameters for LBE, based on the 3GPP specifications; they are shown in Fig. 4. In this access mode, the SC performs an initial CCA over m_p slot durations of a defer duration T_d. If the channel is found busy during one slot, the SC repeats the initial CCA. Otherwise, the SC shall perform an extended CCA (E-CCA) check over N consecutive time periods of duration T_s. N is randomly selected in the interval $[1, CW]$, where CW is the length of the contention window. If an E-CCA turns out to be negative, i.e. channel is busy, an initial CCA is performed maintaining the current value of N. Otherwise, the SC decrements the counter N and performs transmission of the superframe during COT when N reaches zero. We assume that COT $= 10$ ms and $T_s = 9$ μs. The LBE procedure is shown in Fig. 4 for an example of $N = 3$. More details about access priority of LBE access mode, the contention window size and the duration of the superframe can be found in [6].

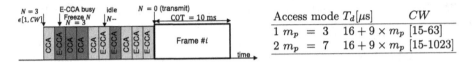

Access mode	$T_d[\mu s]$		CW
1	$m_p = 3$	$16 + 9 \times m_p$	[15-63]
2	$m_p = 7$	$16 + 9 \times m_p$	[15-1023]

Fig. 4. LBE channel access for $N = 3$ and access mode parameters

4   Performance Evaluation

In this section, we first describe the system-level simulation scenarios and various PHY/MAC parameters considered for assessing the performance of the proposed MAC design. Simulation results are presented and analyzed in a second step.

4.1   Simulation Assumptions

We consider an outdoor deployment scenario based on regular hexagonal grid composed of 3 rings of 37 SCs, applying the wrap-around technique [11]. For each SC, we consider 10 UEs with distances to the SC being randomly distributed. The simulations are carried out in non-fading channel, using an extension of the Urban Micro (UMi) model [12], with spatial correlation of the LOS/NLOS and shadowing [11]. Several inter-site distances (ISDs) are considered to evaluate the performance of MAC design in different degrees of network densification and different energy detect (ED) thresholds ranging from -62 dBm to -82 dBm are considered to evaluate the impact of the CCA sensitivity with respect to densification. In terms of traffic, 100% downlink full buffer pattern is considered as a worst case scenario. Adaptive modulation and coding (AMC) scheme is used by the SC similarly to LTE system based on CQI reports sent by UEs. Consequently, the SC assigns a suitable modulation and coding scheme (MCS) for each UE depending on channel conditions, that determines the transport block (TB) size to be transmitted on one slot. The interference between adjacent channels is modeled using out-of-band emissions masks for the considered underlying PHYs, e.g. FBMC and OFDM. For FBMC with $K = 4$, no out-of-band emission is assumed. In case of OFDM and FBMC with $K = 2$, the average of interference level on adjacent channel is assumed equal to -37 dBc and -44 dBc for 20 MHz band, respectively. The main simulation parameters are summarized in Table 1.

In addition, two main coexistence scenarios are considered: non-coexistence and coexistence scenarios. In the non-coexistence scenario, we evaluate the performance of MAC design when it operates without any other interfering system.

In case of the coexistence scenario, we focus on investigation the impact of WiFi system (operator B) on the performance of FBMC-MAC system (operator A) using the same 20 MHz channel. In this case, we assume that WiFi APs are randomly dropped in the area with one AP per SC. WiFi uses standard distributed coordination function (DCF) CSMA/CA (without RTS/CTS signaling) with exponential back-off mechanism and transmission duration of 5 ms are assumed.

The performance metrics used in the evaluation are as follows: per-UE throughput, UE transmission delay, and channel occupancy statistics. Per-UE throughput is defined as the ratio of the number of correctly received bits over the given simulation time. The transmission delay is the averaged time required to successfully deliver a packet once it is at the head of the MAC queue. The mean channel occupancy is defined as the average of the total transmission time of SCs or WiFi APs over the simulation time, which is considered to evaluate the fairness of coexistence between FBMC-MAC and WiFi systems.

Table 1. Simulation parameters

Parameter	Value
Network layout	Hexagonal grid, 1 sector by side
	3 rings / Wrap-around [11]
Inter-site distance (ISD)	30 m, 50 m, 100 m
Carrier frequency	5 GHz
System bandwidth	20 MHz
Frequency reuse	1 and 3
UE density	10 UEs per SC randomly dropped
Path loss model	Extended ITU-R UMi [12]
Shadow fading model	UMi correlated log-normal shadowing [12]
Channel fading model	No fading
SC Tx power	24/12/9 dBm for ISD = 100/50/30 m
UE Tx power	20/12/8 dBm for ISD = 100/50/30 m
SC/UE antenna pattern	2D Omni-directional
SC/UE antenna height	1.5 m/10 m (ISD = 100,50 m) 6 m (ISD = 30 m)
SC/UE antenna Gain	0 dBi/5 dBi
SC/UE noise figure	9 dB/5 dB
Traffic model	Full Buffer 100 % DL (no retransmission)
	Application packet size = 1500 Bytes
Inter-cell interference model	Explicit
Inter-channel interference model	FBMC $K = 4$, no leakage
	FBMC $K = 2$, ACL = -44 dBc/20 MHz
	OFDM-LTE, ACL = -37 dBc/20 MHz
FBMC-MAC parameters	Scheduler: Round Robin
	CCA-ED : -82 dBm, -62 dBm
	COT = 10 ms, $m_p = 3$, CFP/CAP = 6/3 slots

4.2   Simulation Results

Non-coexistence Scenario. In the non-coexistence scenario, the impact of inter-cell interference on the MAC performance is investigated assuming various system parameter settings.

Figure 5 shows CDFs of per-UE throughput and UE delay of FBMC-MAC, given different ISDs and ED thresholds. It is observed that per-UE throughput decreases while transmission delay increases as the network is getting denser. This is due to the increase in UE density which leads to an increase of the offered load per km^2 resulting in higher level of interference. This higher level of interference affects the channel quality leading to reducing the per-UE throughput and increasing the channel access delay. The impact of varying ED threshold is also depicted in Fig. 5. The results show that lowering ED threshold from -62 dBm to -82 dBm improves per-UE throughput performance for dense scenarios (ISD = 30 m and 50 m) due to the reduction of interference level and collision probabilities coming from the overall activity of cells. However, with ISD = 100 m, this increase of ED sensitivity improves the throughput of cell-edge UE, still because of interference level reduction, while degrading the throughput of cell-center UE because more often SCs defer their transmissions. We notice that increasing ED thresholds results in reducing UE transmission delay, due to the increase of channel access opportunities of SCs.

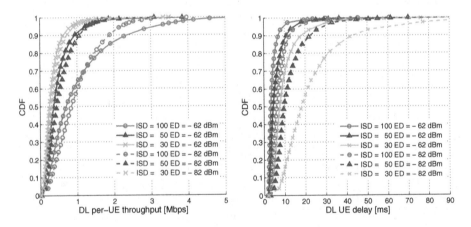

Fig. 5. CDFs of per-UE throughput (left) and transmission delay (right)

Figure 6 depicts per-UE throughput performance of FBMC with $K = 4$, $K = 2$ and ODFM using frequency reuse 3, where adjacent SCs are assigned to different 20 MHz channels. Comparing to the results with single channel in Fig. 5, it is observed that using a frequency reuse 3 significantly improves the performance as the contention for superframes is applied on more resource by the SCs. The increase of UE throughput is approximately 2.5 to 3 times higher compared to a single channel. The mean transmission delay is also significantly reduced as well as better channel access fairness is achieved. The impact of PHY modulation is illustrated in Fig. 6. The results show that using FBMC with $K = 2$ or OFDM reduces the throughput performance compared to FBMC $K = 4$, especially for cell edge UEs. This stems from the adjacent channel interference caused by OFDM and FBMC with $K = 2$, which affects the channel conditions as the level of interference is increased, this is particularly true for dense networks. Consequently, lower MCS will be assigned to UE data resulting in throughput degradation. The average UE throughput improvement of FBMC with $K = 4$ compared to CP-OFDM is about 7.5%, 14% and 13% with ISD = 30, 50 and 100 m, respectively. In case ISD = 100 m, the curves tend to reach a saturation throughput since the majority of UEs experience good channel conditions, and are assigned the higher MCS. It is also observed that there is no significant impact on UE delay since the traffic load in the system has not been changed regardless of adjacent channel leakages.

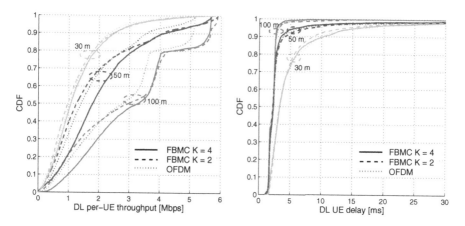

Fig. 6. CDFs of per-UE throughput (left) and transmission delay (right) using different PHYs (FBMC $K = 4$, 2, OFDM), ED $= -62$ dBm, Frequency reuse 3

Coexistence Scenario. Herein we investigate the impact of WiFi system on FBMC-MAC performance and we evaluate the fairness of coexistence by comparing the mean channel occupancy of both systems.

Figure 7 shows the impact of WiFi on the per-UE throughput of FBMC-MAC system and the impact on the channel occupancy of WiFi APs. Due to the shared channel nature and the existence of additional interference caused by WiFi system, we observe significant throughput degradation compared to non-coexistence scenario in Fig. 5. We can see that lowering ED threshold to -82 dBm improves throughput performance and results in reducing the channel occupancy of WiFi system (Fig. 8). Indeed, using an ED threshold of -62 dBm for both systems may result on severe interference and collision and degrade significantly the throughput performance of FBMC-MAC system.

The effect of using similar and asymmetrical ED thresholds of both systems is shown in Fig. 8. The results show that using asymmetrical ED threshold improves

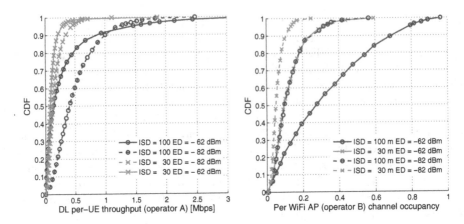

Fig. 7. CDFs of per-UE throughput for FBMC-MAC (operator A - left) and channel occupancy for WiFi APs (operator B - right)

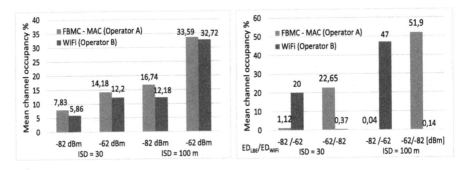

Fig. 8. Mean channel occupancy of FBMC-MAC (operator A) and WiFi (operator B), using similar ED threshold (left) and asymmetrical ED threshold (right)

the performance of one system at the expense of the other system whose activity is almost zero. On the contrary, using same ED threshold allows fair channel occupancy, in which better FBMC-MAC performance is achieved by lowering ED threshold of both systems to −82 dBm as shown in Fig. 7.

Moreover, we have investigated the impact of FBMC-MAC (operator A) on the performance of WiFi (operator B) by considering that both operators deploy WiFi (i.e., FBMC-MAC SCs are replaced by WiFi APs). Although this is not shown in this paper, we have observed that the mean channel occupancy of operator B is similar if operator A deploys either WiFi or FBMC-MAC systems. It indicates that the LBT feature of FBMC-MAC is an efficient mechanism to provide fair coexistence with other systems operating in the same band.

5   Conclusion

In this paper, a MAC protocol for 5G small cells operating in 5 GHz band has been presented. The proposed design exploits the benefit of FBMC modulation and allows asynchronous multi-user communications and efficient use of spectrum. It is based on beacon enabled superframe with scheduled-based and contention-based access schemes, in which superframe transmission is triggered by LBT procedure to coexist with others systems in the 5 GHz band. The performance of the proposed FBMC-MAC design in case of non-coexistence and coexistence scenarios has been investigated for various network densities, physical layer configurations and LBT sensitivities. The results show that FBMC-MAC design using well designed filter outperforms CP-OFDM systems in dense situations. We show also that FBMC-MAC design provides promising features for throughput improvement and fair coexistence with other systems (WiFi) through adjusting LBT thresholds. Future steps include further investigation of the performance of FBMC-MAC design, considering other network layouts (e.g. indoor hotspots), and others traffic models like uplink traffic where FBMC PHY features may provide additional gains compared to CP-OFDM systems.

Acknowledgments. The research leading to these results received funding from the European Commission H2020 program under grant agreement n671705 (SPEED-5G project).

References

1. NGMN: 5G White Paper (2015). http://www.ngmn.org/home.html
2. Bellanger, M., et al.: FBMC physical layer: a primer (2010). http://www.ict-phydyas.org
3. ECMA 392 standard: MAC and PHY for operation in TV white space. 2nd Ed., June 2012
4. IEEE 1900.7-2015 standard: radio interface for white space dynamic spectrum access radio systems supporting fixed and mobile operation, December 2015
5. ETSI EN 301 893 V1.7.2, Broadband Radio Access Networks (BRAN): 5 GHz high performance RLAN; Harmonized EN covering the essential requirements of article 3.2 of the R&TTE Directive, July 2014
6. 3GPP TS 36.213: Evolved Universal Terrestrial Radio Access (E-UTRA), physical layer procedures. Version 14.2.0, March 2017
7. Saltzberg, B.: Performance of an efficient parallel data transmission system. IEEE Trans. Commun. Technol. **15**(6), 805–811 (1967)
8. Gerzaguet, R., et al.: Comparative study of 5G waveform candidates for below 6GHz air interface. In: ETSI Workshop on Future Radio Technologies, Air interfaces, Sophia Antipolis, February 2016
9. Berg, V., et al.: A flexible radio transceiver for TVWS based on FBMC. Microprocess. Microsyst. **38**(8), 743–753 (2014)
10. Kwon, H., Seo, H., Kim, S., Lee, B.G.: Generalized CSMA/CA for OFDMA systems: protocol design, throughput analysis, and implementation issues. IEEE Trans. Wirel. Commun. **8**(8), 4176–4187 (2009)
11. Filo, M., Edgar, R., Vahid, S., Tafazolli, R.: Implications of wrap-around for TGax Scenario 3 and Scenario 4, September 2015
12. 3GPP TS 36.814: Evolved Universal Terrestrial Radio Access (E-UTRA), further advancements for E-UTRA physical layer aspects. Version 9.2.0, March 2017

A Flexible Physical Layer for LPWA Applications

Valérian Mannoni$^{(\boxtimes)}$, Vincent Berg, François Dehmas,
and Dominique Noguet

CEA, LETI, MINATEC Campus, 38054 Grenoble, France
{valerian.mannoni, vincent.berg, francois.dehmas,
dominique.noguet}@cea.fr

Abstract. In the context of Low Power Wide Area (LPWA) networks, terminals are expected to be low cost, to be able to communicate over a long distance,
and to operate on battery power for many years. In order to support a wide range
of LPWA applications, the next generation of LPWA technologies is expected
to provide faster throughput, be more resilient, and guarantee lower levels of
latency for a similar battery lifetime. These contradictory requirements, lead to
consider the design of a flexible physical layer with the aim to be efficient for the
identified operating modes from "low data rate, low power consumption, long
range" to "high data rate". Performance of waveform candidates is assessed in
terms of PER, range and also power consumption in order to obtain the best
compromise between operating modes. A new flexible waveform based on
frequency domain processing is finally proposed to address the large scale of
requirements of new LPWA applications.

Keywords: Low Power Wide Area (LPWA) · Internet of Things
Physical layer · Flexibility

1 Introduction

Machine type communications (M2M) are rapidly expanding: more than twenty five
billion devices are expected to be connected through wireless systems by 2020 [1]. So
far, different wireless technologies have been considered to connect objects to the
Internet of Things (IoT). Before the advent of Low Power Wide Area (LPWA) network
technologies in 2013, short-range radio connectivity (e.g., Bluetooth and ZigBee) was
widely adopted for low power applications but coverage was limited. M2M solutions
based on cellular technology provided large coverage, however excessive power
consumption has limited their adoption. LPWA has provided a low power wireless
connectivity alternative to current generations of cellular systems (2G, 3G and 4G) [2].
Some of these new LPWA systems operate in unlicensed bands, which opened the door
to new market opportunities and new operators. LPWA is a generic term for a group of
technologies that enable wide area communications at low cost and long battery life
(Sigfox, LoRa, RPMA, NB-IoT, Weightless-P, IEEE 802.11ah) [2]. Among them,
LoRa and NB-IoT are two leading emergent technologies [3]. LoRa usually operates in
a non-licensed band below 1 GHz for long-range communication link operation. It uses

© ICST Institute for Computer Sciences, Social Informatics and Telecommunications Engineering 2018
P. Marques et al. (Eds.): CROWNCOM 2017, LNICST 228, pp. 322–333, 2018.
https://doi.org/10.1007/978-3-319-76207-4_27

a proprietary spread spectrum modulation scheme that is derived from chirp spread spectrum modulation (CSS) and trades data rate for sensitivity within a fixed channel bandwidth. CSS, which was developed in the 1940s, was traditionally used in military applications because of its long communication distances and interference robustness [4]. NB-IoT is a new IoT technology set up by 3GPP as a part of Release 13 [5]. It uses the same licensed frequency bands used in Long Term Evolution (LTE) and employs OFDM-based (Orthogonal Frequency Division Multiplexing) modulation together with QPSK (we can also note a mode with only one active sub-carrier). Although it is sometimes regarded as a new air interface, its physical layer is a low power long range derivation of LTE [5]. Many features of LTE, including handover, measurements to monitor the channel quality, carrier aggregation, and dual connectivity have been removed to reduce device costs and minimize battery consumption.

The first generation of LPWA systems has brought coverage for a long battery life, future generations are expected to provide faster data rates and/or lower latency for similar battery lifetime to extend the range of applications the technology can deliver. These new requirements of LPWA have led to reconsider the physical layer for these types of systems. The aim of this paper is to investigate which physical layer should be considered for future generations of LPWA systems by analyzing range, power consumption and throughput performance.

The paper is structured as follows: Sect. 2 introduces the selection of possible waveforms for LPWA systems and presents the propagation hypotheses that have been considered for performance evaluation. Section 3 compares the performance results of the waveform candidates in terms of range, power consumption and throughput. It leads to Sect. 4, where a new waveform candidate for LPWA systems is proposed. Section 5 concludes the paper.

2 Waveform Candidate Selection and Evaluation Models

The authors of [6] identified that turbo processing is highly recommended to provide long-range operation in an energy efficient way. Waveforms adapted to turbo processing have thus been considered for this study. Multicarrier modulation techniques such as Orthogonal Frequency Division Multiplexing (OFDM) have proven to be very effective for mobile wireless communications (WLAN, LTE) and are considered for LPWA systems (NB-IoT). By dividing a frequency selective fading channel into a number of narrow-band flat fading sub-channels, multicarrier systems can easily compensate the channel effects using a simple one-tap frequency domain equalizer. However, the main drawback of OFDM is its high Peak-to-Average Power Ratio (PAPR). Waveforms with high PAPR values increase the linearity requirements imposed on the power amplifier and are therefore less power efficient. Single Carrier Frequency Division Multiplexing (SC-FDM) adds frequency spreading to reduce the PAPR level of OFDM. It combines the benefits of a simple equalization process as performed for OFDM but with a lower PAPR. In the context of LPWA systems, constant envelope waveforms are attractive alternatives as power consumption of the transmitter is contained due to a low PAPR level. Single Carrier with Frequency Domain Equalization (SC-FDE) combines the benefits of single carrier modulations (i.e. very low PAPR levels) with an equalization process in the frequency domain similar to OFDM. Finally, Turbo-FSK is a new waveform introduced in [6] that meets performance close to the Shannon limit for the lower spectral efficiency. It is a constant envelope modulation, and therefore has a PAPR equal to 0 dB. Turbo-FSK combines an orthogonal modulation with a convolutional code.

Therefore, OFDM, SC-FDM, SC-FDE associated with turbo-coding and Turbo-FSK are considered for performance comparison in the context of LPWA. It should be noted that CSS currently used by LoRa systems has not been selected. The scheme, which may be considered as an orthogonal modulation, can be combined with a turbo decoding but this architecture is relatively far from the Shannon limit [6].

In order to compare the performance of the different waveform options in terms of range and throughput, a channel model has to be considered. A simple way to model the channel is to separate two of its main effects into different parts: path loss and impulse response. Path loss model emulates the signal attenuation as a function of its propagation range and central frequency. Impulse response represents the effects of multipath by a discrete number of impulses as follows:

$$w(t) = \sum_{n=1}^{N} \sqrt{p_n} g_n(t) z(t - \tau_n), \tag{1}$$

- where $z(t)$ is the transmit signal
- N is the number of path replica
- τ_n is the delay of the nth replica
- p_n is the relative power strength of the nth replica
- $g_n(t)$ is the weight of the nth replica and vary with time
- $w(t)$ is the received signal

The values of p_n and τ_n are dependent of the environment that is modeled.

Empirical models of path loss are simple and efficient to use: the model provides a first order result for a wide range of locations. One family of empirical models was derived by Okumura from extensive measurements in urban and suburban areas [7]. It was later put into equations by Hata in [8] and is referred to as the COST 231-Hata model [9]. The model provides good path loss estimates for a large range of distance (1 to 20 km), and a wide range of parameters such as carrier frequency, base station height (20 to 200 m), and environment (rural, suburban or dense urban). It is expressed by (2).

$$L_{Hata}(d) = c_0 + c_f \log(f) - b(h_b) - a(h_M) \\ + (44.9 - 6.55 \log(h_b)) \log(d) + C_M, \tag{2}$$

where f is the carrier frequency in MHz, d the distance between the transmitter and the receiver in km, h_b the height of the base station/access point (in m), h_M the height of the mobile (in m), c_0, c_f, b, a and C_M are function of the propagation environment.

In the following of the paper, Open Rural environment has been considered as it provides an upper limit of propagation range for LPWA systems, with the following parameters:

- carrier frequency, $f = 868$ MHz
- height of the base station/access point, $h_b = 15$ m
- height of the mobile, $h_M = 1$ m

This upper limit is of particular interest in less densely populated areas where infrastructure density is much lower and thus range performance is particularly necessary to guarantee connectivity.

For the impulse response of the channel, the power delay profile of the 3GPP extended typical urban (ETU) channel model has been considered. It emulates the impulse response of a signal received in a strong multipath environment with a root-mean square (RMS) delay spread of around 991 ns. Its coherence bandwidth, the frequency bandwidth for which the channel characteristics remain similar, is equal to 160 kHz. Its parameters are given in Table 1.

Table 1. Parameters of the power delay profile for the ETU channel model.

Excess tap delay τ_n (ns)	Relative power p_n (dB)
0	−1.0
50	−1.0
120	−1.0
200	0.0
230	0.0
500	0.0
1600	−3.0
2300	−5.0
5000	−7.0

ETU delay profiles have been used to evaluate the resilience of the candidate waveforms for this LPWA application. The channel models here described are used in Sect. 3 for performance evaluation.

3 Performance Evaluation

3.1 Range Performance Comparison

In this section, the performance (PER, sensitivity) of the waveform candidates under realistic frequency selective channels is studied and evaluated in terms of range and power consumption. These aspects represent critical elements for the LPWA systems. The performance investigation has been performed thanks to a link simulator and the simulation has been operated using the following parameters:

- Tone spacing $\Delta f = 15$ kHz (only for OFDM, SC-FDM and Turbo-FSK)
- $N_{fft} = 128$, cyclic Prefix of size $N_{cp} = 9$ or 4.7 μs
- Packet size: 1008 bits of information
- Perfect synchronization and channel estimation.

Performance in terms of packet error rate (PER) as a function of the E_b/N_0 for the waveform candidates is given in Fig. 1. For these simulations, excepted for the turbo-FSK, the bandwidth and the throughput are equivalent to around 180 kHz and 170 kb/s respectively. This corresponds to 12 active carriers when multicarrier modulations are considered (OFDM, SC-FDM) with QPSK modulation and 1/3 for the coding rate. For the Turbo-FSK, a configuration with a 240 kHz bandwidth or 16 active carriers and throughput of 27 kb/s has been used. This is because the number of carriers has to be a power of 2. Turbo-FSK has been designed as an intrinsically low spectral efficiency waveform. In order to compare these air interfaces operating at different throughput and spectral efficiency, PER curves are provided as a function of E_b/N_0. Figure 1 compares the amount of energy necessary to transmit an information bit for each technology with a limited and controlled amount of transmission errors.

OFDM presents the best performance compared to the other waveforms with a maximum gap of almost 4 dB with SC-FDE modulation for a PER of 10^{-2}. SC-FDM is slightly less performant than OFDM, followed by Turbo-FSK and SC-FDE.

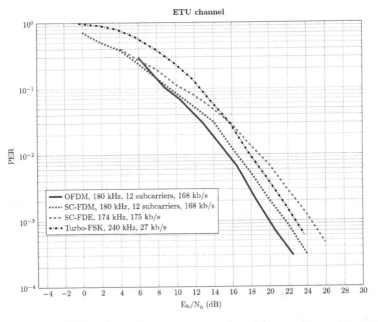

Fig. 1. PER as the function of the E_b/N_0 for OFDM, SC-FDM, SC-FDE and Turbo-FSK.

One key feature of LPWA connectivity is to achieve long-range transmission. Hence performance of Fig. 1 should be revisited in terms of transmission range. We define the transmission range, d, as:

$$d \mid P_{TX}^{dBm} - L_{Hata}(d) = \rho \tag{3}$$

where P_{TX}^{dBm} is the transmit power in dBm, $L_{Hata}(d)$ the path loss for a transmission range of d and ρ the receiver sensitivity which is defined by (4).

$$\rho = \left(\frac{E_b}{N_0}\right)^{dB} + 10\log_{10}(B\eta) + N + NF, \tag{4}$$

where B is the signal bandwidth in Hz, η the spectral efficiency in b/s/Hz, N the power spectral density of the thermal noise ($N = -174$ dBm/Hz), and NF the noise figure of the receiver. A NF equal to 6 dB has been considered in the following of the paper.

Since $L_{Hata}(d)$ is an increasing function of the transmission range, and assuming P_{Tx}^{dBm} is fixed and independent from the selected waveform, the transmission range can only be increased by reducing the receiver sensitivity. Since N and NF are constant, transmission range can be increased by selecting the waveform that exhibits the lowest E_b/N_0 for a targeted level of PER or by reducing the signal bandwidth and/or the spectral efficiency.

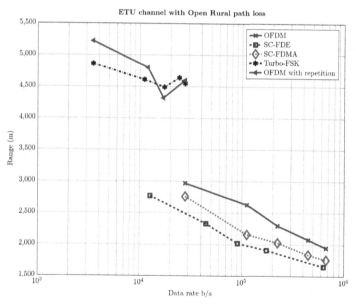

Fig. 2. Range as the function of throughput for communications through ETU channel for the waveform candidates, OFDM, SC-FDE, SC-FDMA and Turbo-FSK.

Transmission range has been evaluated and is given in Fig. 2 using the Open rural Hata model. Simulations have been performed for the proposed waveforms with bandwidths ranging from 45 kHz to 1 MHz and a spectral efficiency of 2/3 b/s/Hz for OFDM, SC-FDM and SC-FDE (QPSK, $R_c = 1/3$). Transmit power of 14dBm and a carrier frequency of 868 MHz has been assumed. Turbo-FSK has also been plotted, but the waveform exhibit a much lower spectral efficiency. In order to provide a fair comparison with Turbo-FSK, the performance of OFDM (i.e. the best performing waveform) has been added with symbol repetitions in such a way that the spectral efficiency is equivalent (8 repetitions have been used i.e. approximately 1/12 b/s/Hz). It can be observed that for the high bit rates, OFDM presents the best performance with the best range for any given data rate with a range of around 2 km at 700 kb/s. Concerning the low bit rates, OFDM and turbo-FSK have similar ranges between 4.5 km and 5 km with a slight advantage for OFDM for the very low throughput. For a given data rate (e.g. 30 kb/s, OFDM with and without repetition), best ranges are obtained for the modes with the wider bandwidth waveforms and with a lower spectral efficiency. This is because theses modes can take advantage of the frequency diversity brought by bandwidths significantly wider than the coherence bandwidth of the channel (160 kHz).

In this section, the performance in terms of PER and range has been assessed for each candidate waveform. OFDM associated with turbo coding seems to give the best performance for LPWA applications. However, the results presented so far did not take the impact of power consumption introduced by the different PAPR of the various waveforms. In the next section, an evaluation of the impact of the selected waveforms can bring on the power consumption is evaluated.

3.2 Power Consumption

Minimizing energy consumption is a very important design consideration for LPWA communication systems and therefore the impact of the physical layer on the power consumption must be investigated. The power consumption at the transmitter is considered as the dominant effect, notably the power consumption necessary to operate the power amplifier (PA) [10]. It has been shown in [11] that the energy consumption per information bit depends on the following parameters: the transmission duration, the PAPR, the drain efficiency of the radiofrequency PA and the circuit power consumption of internal electronic functions. If we denote E the total energy consumption required to send N bits, then the energy consumption per information bit E_a can be expressed by [11]:

$$E_a = \frac{E}{N} \approx \frac{\left(\frac{\varepsilon}{\gamma}\right)E_t + P_c T_{on} + 2P_{syn}T_{tr}}{N}, \tag{5}$$

with P_c the circuit power consumption, P_{syn} the frequency synthesizer power consumption, T_{on} the transmission duration, T_{tr} the transient mode duration, $E_t = P_t T_{on}$ the transmission energy, ε the PAPR and γ the drain efficiency of the radiofrequency PA. P_c, P_{syn} and T_{tr} can be considered as constants defined by the particular transceiver structure in use. From this model, it is necessary to find the best tradeoff between the transmission duration and the PAPR in order to optimize the power consumption. This tradeoff depends on the modulation/constellation scheme. We will assess the evolution of the "estimated power consumption" as a function of the throughput (and/or the waveform used). The following parameters have been applied in order to evaluate E_a:

- $P_c = 100$ mW
- $P_{syn} = Pc/2$
- $T_{tr} = 250$ ms
- $E_t = P_t T_{on}$, $P_t = 14$ dBm (25.12 mW).

The characteristic used for the PAPR and the drain efficiency of the RF PA is given in Fig. 3a [11].

The energy consumption per information bit as a function of the data rate for different waveforms with different configurations is shown in Fig. 3b. For a given waveform exhibiting a constant PAPR, the energy consumption per information bit linearly decreases when the data rate increases. This is because T_{on} is a linear function of the data rate. This can be explained as the transmitted power consumption is mainly dependent on the transmission duration of each data bit. This trend is particularly relevant for SC-FDE and for Turbo-FSK. For multicarrier modulations (OFDM and SC-FDM) the PAPR increases with the number of used sub-carriers and the modulation order (Cf Table 2). The energy consumption saved by the reduction of T_{on} is not fully compensated by the increase of number of carriers necessary to increase the throughput. As a consequence the PAPR increase has a larger impact on power consumption than the transmission duration and the energy per transmitted bit is increased at the same time as the data rate (e.g. for OFDM, a data rate of 40 kb/s gives a E_a of around 2.10^{-2} mJ while a data rate of 200 kb/s gives an energy of 4.10^{-2} mJ per bit). Turbo-FSK provides the most energy efficient option for low bit rates (around 10 kb/s). For the medium and the high bit rates, single carrier (SC-FDE) presents the lowest energy consumption per transmitted information bit as Turbo-FSK does not provide higher spectral efficiency options.

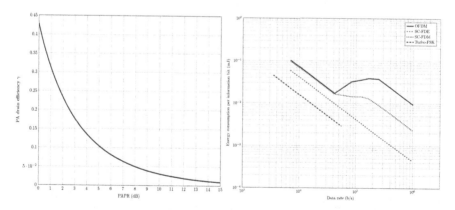

Fig. 3. (a) PA drain efficiency as a function of the PAPR (left). (b) Energy consumption per information bit for the selected waveforms (right).

Table 2. PAPR for OFDM and SC-FDM according to the number of active carriers.

Number of active carriers	PAPR OFDM (dB)	PAPR SC-FDM (dB)
3	4.6	4.5
6	7.6	5.8
9	8.7	6.7
12	9.5	7.1
72	10.4	7.2

In Sect. 3.1, it was concluded that OFDM provided the best range for any given data rate assuming a given transmit RMS power. However, in this section, we concluded that OFDM was the least power efficient of the four selected modulations. This has led to analyze which compromise should be considered in the context of LPWA communications. It seems notably that, for low data rate, constant envelope modulations such as Turbo-FSK are more suitable as performance level is similar while power consumption is much lower than for OFDM. For higher, data rates, OFDM seems to give an unrivalled performance gain.

3.3   Performance for LPWA Applications

Since power consumption, operating range and throughput are key parameters for LPWA operations, it is necessary to further analyze which waveform is most adapted to the LPWA context. Power consumption per information bit as a function of the throughput for a given fixed range of respectively 1 km and 6 km has then been investigated. In this context, instead of considering fixed transmit power (of 14 dBm) and evaluate the associated reachable propagation range for a given selected waveform, power of the transmitter has been increased or reduced to reach the targeted propagation range (of respectively 1 km or 6 km) and a PER = 10^{-2}. Results have been summarized in Fig. 4 ((a) for 1 km range and (b) for 6 km range).

For 1 km range, energy consumption per information bit is dominated by the circuit and frequency synthesizer power consumption (see (5)), transmit power evaluated to be equal to approximately -7 dBm for OFDM, -7.8 dBm for Turbo-FSK and, -2.4 dBm for SC-FDE for 14 kb/s. Hence, the energy consumption per transmitted information bit is for lower data rates almost the same independently of the selected waveform. As the data rate is increased, the PAPR of the waveform is increased notably because the number of active carriers (and the bandwidth) of the multicarrier waveform is also increased. Difference of energy consumption per information bit is increased almost according to the subsequent increase in PAPR between Turbo-FSK and multicarrier modulations when the data rate is increased. For 6 km range, the system energy budget is rather different. Power consumption is dominated by the required transmission energy, E_t. Estimated required transmit power is between 21 dBm and 37 dBm for the highest data rates of OFDM. The required increase of power when data rate is increased is often not compensated by the shorter transmission duration. This is particularly the case for OFDM and SC-FDM.

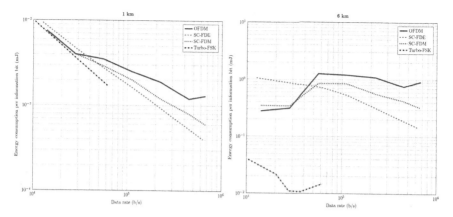

Fig. 4. Energy consumption per information bit as the function of the throughput and for a given range of: (a) 1 km (left), and (b) 6 km (right).

Assuming this scenario, Turbo-FSK provides for data rates lower than 60 kb/s the best energy compromise. OFDM is the least attractive waveform in terms of power consumption. SC-FDM and SC-FDE have intermediate power consumption levels but with level closer to OFDM than Turbo-FSK in particular when the range is larger than 1 km.

The performance results summarized in this section concluded that the most adapted waveform for LPWA operation is therefore highly dependent on the considered propagation scenario. When data throughput is preferred, OFDM should be considered. When range and good energy efficiency should be guaranteed, Turbo-FSK is better (for the low throughputs). Finally, when power consumption is of most importance, but without compromise on data throughput, SC-FDE or SC-FDM should be considered. This imposes some level of flexibility for the choice of the LPWA waveform. We introduce in the next Section an architecture of a physical layer adapted to the four here mentioned modes.

4 A New Physical Layer for LPWA

The level of flexibility and performance required by the LPWA scenarios for the physical layer leads us to exploit different waveforms. The set of selected waveforms are based on frequency domain processing with a prefix cyclic insertion in order to have a simple and robust equalization. These waveforms employ then common elements such as FFT/IFFT, frequency equalization, coder/decoder. Hence, a physical layer with multiple waveforms support using "frequency processing" can be considered as a new physical layer with an extended set of parameters for LPWA applications.

The block diagram of this new waveform is shown in Fig. 5. This block diagram corresponds to the merge of the four selected waveform candidates for LPWA applications: Turbo-FSK, SC-FDE, SC-FDM and OFDM. With a particular parameterization of each block we can provide the targeted waveform with the most adapted

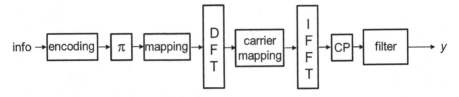

Fig. 5. Block diagram for a flexible physical layer transmitter adapted to LPWA system.

Modulation Coding Scheme. Its transmitter is composed of FEC encoding, interleaving and constellation mapping. A precoding DFT is solely used for SC-FDM and bypassed by the other modes. It is followed by a carrier mapping and IFFT: these modules are only applied to multicarrier modulations (SC-FDM, OFDM and Turbo-FSK). Finally, the insertion of a cyclic prefix and transmit filter common to all schemes complete the transmitter physical layer architecture.

The architecture overview of the receiver is given in Fig. 6. And follows the reverse structure of the receiver. It is interesting to note that in this case, the FFT is not bypassed for receiving any of the selected waveforms. This is because SC-FDE considers equalization in the frequency domain. IDFT is then applied for SC-FDM and SC-FDE modes.

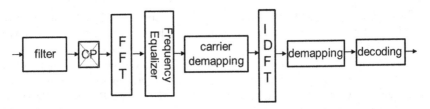

Fig. 6. Block diagram for physical layer the receiver of the LPWA-CB system.

Finally, although this paper does not analyze the overhead in complexity introduced by the support for multiple waveforms, the flexibility introduced should not lead to significant cost overhead in comparison to a less flexible approach. Hardware complexity of a physical layer is often dominated by its receiver. IDFT is the main block that should be bypassed at the receiver when not required (Turbo-FSK, OFDM). Since FFT and IDFT modules are highly optimized for implementation, these blocks have often limited complexity impact on the design [12]. This preliminary analysis should however be confirmed by a more hardware complexity thorough study.

5 Conclusion

The first generation of LPWA systems have brought coverage for a long battery life. Future generations are expected to provide faster data rates and/or lower latency for similar battery lifetime to extend the range of applications the technology can deliver.

These new requirements for LPWA applications have led to reconsider the physical layer for these types of systems. A new flexible approach for LPWA has been introduced and is imposed by the contradictory requirements of long-range, low power consumption and higher throughput. A performance analysis has concluded that OFDM is the most appropriate waveform for throughput performance when the constraints on the power consumption are relaxed, while Turbo-FSK presents the best performance in terms of range and energy efficiency when the throughput is low. Finally, if a compromise between range, throughput and power consumption is desired, either SC-FDE or SC-FDM is more appropriate. A block diagram of transmission and reception for this new approach has been proposed and described.

Future work should further study common approaches of synchronization mechanisms for the different options of the physical layer. This include timing and frequency synchronization and channel estimation. This should be completed and refined before hardware architecture implementation and its associated complexity evaluation of the flexible concept.

References

1. Gartner, Inc.: Gartner Says 4.9 Billion Connected "Things" Will Be in Use in 2015. http://www.gartner.com/newsroom/id/2905717
2. Raza, U., Kulkarni, P., Sooriyabandara, M.: Low power wide area networks: an overview. In: IEEE Commun. Surv. Tutorials, **19**(2) (2017)
3. Berg Insight: Cellular and LPWA IoT Device Ecosystems (2017)
4. Springer, A., Gugler, W., Huemer, M., Reindl, L., Ruppel, C.C.W., Weigel, R.: Spread spectrum communications using chirp signals. In: IEEE Proceeding of Eurocomm, pp. 166–170 (2000)
5. ETSI: LTE; Evolved Universal Terrestrial Radio Access (E-UTRA); Physical Channels and modulation. In: ETSI, 3GPP TS 36.211 version 13.2.0 Release 13 (2016)
6. Roth, Y., Doré, J.-B., Ros, L., Berg, V.: A comparison of physical layers for low power wide area networks. In: Noguet, D., Moessner, K., Palicot, J. (eds.) CrownCom 2016. LNICST, vol. 172, pp. 261–272. Springer, Cham (2016). https://doi.org/10.1007/978-3-319-40352-6_21
7. Okumura, Y., Ohmori, E., Kawano, T., Fukuda, K.: Field strength and its variability in VHF and UHF Land-Mobile radio service. Rev. Electr. Commun. Lab. **16**(9–10), 825–873 (1968)
8. Hata, M.: Empirical formula for propagation loss in land mobile radio services. IEEE Trans. Veh. Technol. **29**(3), 317–325 (1980)
9. European Cooperation in the Field of Scientific and Technical Research, EURO-COST 231: Digital Mobile Radio Towards Future Generation Systems. In: COST 231 Final report. http://www.lx.it.pt/cost231/
10. Raja, M.K., Chen, X., Lei, Y.D., Bin, Z., Yeung, B.C., Xiaojun, Y.: A 18 mW Tx, 22 mW Rx transceiver for 2.45 GHz IEEE 802.15.4 WPAN in 0.18-μm CMOS. In: Solid State Circuits Conference (A-SSCC). IEEE Asian, Beijing (2010)
11. Cui, S., Goldsmith, A.J., Bahai, A.: Energy-constrained modulation optimization. IEEE Trans. Wirel. Commun. **4**(5), 2349–2360 (2005)
12. Berg, V., Dore, J.-B., Noguet, D.: A multiuser FBMC receiver implementation for asynchronous frequency division multiple access. In: 2014 17th Euromicro Conference on Digital System Design, pp. 16–21 (2014)

Late Papers

Knapsack Optimisation for Mobility Load Balancing in Dense Small Cell Deployments

Karim M. Nasr$^{(\boxtimes)}$, Seiamak Vahid, and Klaus Moessner

Institute for Communication Systems, 5G IC,
University of Surrey, Guildford GU2 7XH, UK
{k.nasr, s.vahid, k.moessner}@surrey.ac.uk

Abstract. We present a new approach for mobility load balancing (MLB) and user association in dense small cell scenarios. This Self Organizing Network (SON) approach relies on Knapsack Optimisation (KO) to evenly distribute users across participating cells subject to constraints. It is shown that the new technique referred to as (MLB-KO) achieves substantial improvements (better than three times reduction) in blocking ratios for the studied use cases.

Keywords: Small cells · Self-Organizing Networks (SON)
Mobility Load Balancing (MLB) · Knapsack Optimisation (KO)
Wireless network planning and optimisation
Cognitive networks · 5G

1 Introduction

The ever increasing demands for advanced and bandwidth hungry broadband services as well as enhanced Quality of Experience (QoE) for the end users together with spectrum efficiency and reduced energy consumption, have resulted in several challenges in designing and planning next generation "5G" wireless networks [1, 2]. The use of network densification through the deployment of low power small cells, whether by a mobile network operator or an end user, is recognised as one of the key strategies towards achieving the 5G vision and targets. By densely deploying additional small cell [3–5] nodes within the local area range and bringing the network closer to end users, the performance and capacity are significantly improved. This in turn allows future systems to achieve higher aggregate data rates at lower energy levels, while retaining seamless connectivity and mobility resulting in improved QoE and user satisfaction of the services being delivered by the network.

SESAME (Small cEllS coordination for Multi-tenancy and Edge services) [6] is a project that targets innovations around three central elements in 5G: (i) the placement of network intelligence and applications in the network edge through Network Functions Virtualisation (NFV) and Edge Cloud Computing; (ii) the substantial evolution of the Small Cell concept, already mainstream in 4G but expected to deliver its full potential in the challenging high density 5G scenarios; and (iii) the consolidation of multi-tenancy in communications infrastructures, allowing several operators/service providers to engage in new sharing models of both access capacity and edge computing capabilities resulting in a Small Cell as a Service (SCaaS) concept. Typical examples of

© ICST Institute for Computer Sciences, Social Informatics and Telecommunications Engineering 2018
P. Marques et al. (Eds.): CROWNCOM 2017, LNICST 228, pp. 337–346, 2018.
https://doi.org/10.1007/978-3-319-76207-4_28

use cases include deployment of small cell nodes to serve a busy large business or shopping centre, service provision to a sudden concentration of users in hotspots such as in a stadium, a conference centre, an exhibition or a carnival venue with users generating high data rate real time multimedia content.

With the dense and dynamic deployment of a large number of small cell nodes in a network, there is an essential need to adopt Self Organizing Networks (SON) technologies and advanced radio resource management capabilities [7–9] to facilitate network management and to reduce or ultimately remove the need for human intervention in the planning, deployment, optimisation and maintenance of the network infrastructure. Adoption of SON techniques also known as Self-X (self-planning, self-optimization and self-healing) result in rapid and efficient deployment of network nodes and considerable reduction in capital (CAPEX) and operational (OPEX) costs.

SESAME proposes the Cloud-Enabled Small Cell (CESC) concept, a new multi-operator enabled Small Cell that integrates a virtualised execution platform (the Light DC (Data Center)) for deploying Virtual Network Functions (NVFs), supporting powerful Self-X management and executing novel applications and services within the access network infrastructure.

One of the main self-optimisation strategies in a SON is Mobility Load Balancing (MLB) [10, 11]. MLB addresses the problem of uneven traffic distribution in mobile networks. The main target of MLB and traffic steering algorithms is to enable overloaded cells to re-direct a percentage of their load to neighbouring less loaded cells hence alleviating congestion problems. The expected gains from MLB algorithms are highest when participating cells exhibit different usage patterns with respect to time. The resulting increased network efficiency using MLB, postpones the deployment of additional network capacity hence reducing capital costs (CAPEX). This is traditionally done through Cell Range Expansion (CRE), achieved by either cell coverage and/or mobility parameter adjustments. The CRE based distributed approach may lead to network performance degradation due to the frequency reuse of one adopted in LTE based networks. Re-allocating a user to a base station other than the one offering the highest signal level, as CRE sometimes does, may result in increased interference levels. Suitable self-organizing MLB strategies should automatically react to varying traffic and dynamic mobility patterns and should also take into account multiple tenancy as neighbouring cells can generally belong to any tenant or operator. In multi-tenant Radio Access Network (RAN) deployments, where shared resources are allocated based on static or dynamic Service Level Agreements (SLA), the formulation of the "user-association" problem needs to take full account of multiple (and possibly conflicting) service types and requirements, as additional/new sets of constraints need to be met.

We present in this paper, a new Knapsack Optimisation (KO) approach to MLB and the user association problem for dense small cell deployments. The generality of this KO based centralised approach makes it suitable to answer the several constraints that need to be met in a cluster of small cells densely deployed network wide and also suitable for implementation in a Light DC as proposed by SESAME. The paper is organized as follows: Sect. 1 sets the scene and highlights the need for new optimized MLB techniques specifically targeting small cells. Section 2 presents the mathematical framework of the used MLB-KO approach. Section 3 presents examples of simulation use cases highlighting the effectiveness of the approach. Finally, Sect. 4 concludes the paper.

2 Knapsack Optimisation for MLB in Small Cells

2.1 Background

The main modelling approaches for the user association problem are based on a "utility" cost function maximisation that quantifies the satisfaction that a certain metric is met. Examples of such approaches include game theory, stochastic geometry and combinatorial optimisation.

Combinatorial optimisation has the advantage of being a generalised approach for the utility maximisation problem. Several techniques relying on combinatorial optimisation were previously investigated and reported e.g. [12–21] all tackling the user association problem from different perspectives and with different targets.

Knapsack Optimisation KO [22] is a combinatorial optimisation technique that, to our knowledge has not been reported previously for the target application of this paper (MLB for dense small cell deployments). KO is a natural solution to the problem of associating a number of end users to a number of small cells with the aim of achieving efficient MLB throughout the network under specific constraints as will be described below.

The knapsack problem can be described as follows: Given a knapsack with a fixed capacity and a set of items, each item is associated with an individual profit and a weight. The problem is to select a subset of items such that the total profit of the selected items is maximised without exceeding the capacity. A more generalised form is the Multiple Knapsack Problem (MKP) where a set of knapsacks are considered rather than one.

2.2 System Model

Given N end users and M small cell base stations, then the generalised MKP can be formulated as follows:

Assign each user i with a weight w_i to exactly one small cell base station j such that the total capacity or throughput (i.e. the total profit in the context of MKP) of the network C is maximised and without assigning user weights greater than the individual capacity c_j of any individual small cell base station j.

For LTE networks, the weight of user i if assigned to base station j: w_{ij} is defined as the required Physical Resource Blocks (PRB) by the user to achieve a certain target individual Quality of Service (QoS) while the profit p_{ij} is the achieved individual throughput which is a function of the Signal to Interference plus Noise Ratio (SINR) of user i when connected to base station j. This can be formulated as follows:

$$\max C = \sum_{j=1}^{m} \sum_{i=1}^{n} p_{ij} x_{ij}$$

$$\text{subject to} \quad \sum_{i=1}^{n} w_{ij} x_{ij} \leq c_j, \quad j \in M = \{1, \ldots, m\}$$

$$\sum_{j=1}^{m} x_{ij=1}, \qquad i \in N = \{1, \ldots, n\} \qquad (1)$$

$$\text{with } x_{ij} = \begin{cases} 1 & \text{if user } i \text{ is assigned to small cell base station } j; \\ 0 & \text{otherwise} \end{cases}$$

The SINR of user i associated with small cell base station j can be written as:

$$SINR_{ij} = \frac{P_j|H_{ij}|^2}{\sum\limits_{k=1,k\neq j}^{m} P_k|H_{ik}|^2 + \sigma_i^2} \tag{2}$$

where P is the transmission power of the base station, H is the channel transfer function between the user and the base station and includes the effects of path loss, shadowing, antenna patterns and other losses and σ^2 is the thermal noise power at the user's receiver.

An additional constraint is added to the optimisation problem to ensure that the individual user's SINR is above a certain minimum threshold value to reject users suffering from excessively bad radio channel conditions and/or interference from unnecessarily overloading the target small cell base station.

$$SINR_{ij} \geq SINR_{threshold} \tag{3}$$

When N and M increase, the MKP problem becomes NP-hard [22]. A possible approach to solve the above optimisation problem is to use the Greedy algorithm. This is implemented by sorting all the users in a decreasing order of their profit to weight ratios before associating them to individual small cells. Examples highlighting the effectiveness of the KO approach for MLB in dense small cells are presented in the following section.

3   Simulation Results and Discussion

We first consider a relatively simple case of a two small cell LTE network. Users are randomly located around the centre of each cell with a uniform distribution. The load (weight) of each user is obtained through a uniformly distributed random variable with an average value of 5 PRB. Users' speeds are randomly generated using a uniform distribution with an average speed of 30 km/h. Log normal shadowing with a mean value of 4 dB is considered. The first cell is intentionally made to be heavily over-loaded (>cell maximum capacity) while the second cell has a spare capacity. An illustration of the simulation scenario is shown in Fig. 1 and a summary of the main simulation parameters is shown in Table 1.

The metric used to assess the effectiveness of Mobility Load Balancing using Knapsack Optimisation (MLB-KO) is the Blocking Ratio (BR). BR is defined as the number of blocked (unserved) users U_b divided by the total number of users U_t in the network.

$$BR = \frac{U_b}{U_t} \times 100\% \tag{4}$$

Figure 2(a) shows the load of the two cells before implementing the KO approach. Cell 1 is overloaded and exceeds the maximum allowed capacity. The MLB-KO

Table 1. Main simulation parameters for the two cell scenario

Parameter	Value
Number of cells	2
Cell radius	20 and 10 m
Number and location of users	35 and 10 users uniformly distributed
Cell maximum capacity	100
User load	Variable with uniform distribution Average = 5 PRB
User speed	Variable with uniform distribution Average = 20 km/h
Carrier frequency	2 GHz
Bandwidth	20 MHz
Small cell transmit power	23 dBm
Noise power spectral density (PSD)	−174 dBm/Hz
Path loss (in dB)	140.1 + 36.7 Log10 (distance in km)
Log normal shadowing mean value	4 dB

technique redistribute the users across the two cells subject to the above constraints to balance the loads resulting in a more even distribution as shown in Fig. 2(b). The technique is tested taking into account the effect of the variation of path loss and subsequently the individual SINR value of each user due to shadowing and random user speeds. The blocking ratio is calculated for every simulation time sample. It is concluded that the average blocking ratio drops from 26.06% to 5.89% with MLB-KO resulting in more than four times improvement for the studied network topology as shown in Fig. 2(c).

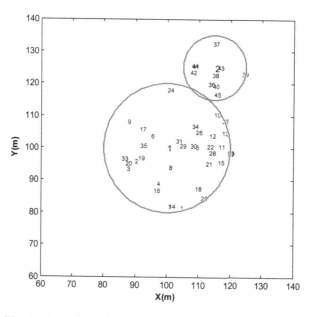

Fig. 1. Network topology example with two cells and 45 users

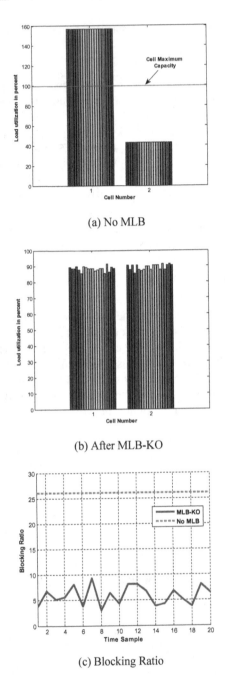

(a) No MLB

(b) After MLB-KO

(c) Blocking Ratio

Fig. 2. Comparison of the blocking ratio before and after MLB-KO for the two cell scenario

Table 2. Main simulation parameters for the seven cell scenario

Parameter	Value
Number of cells	7 (randomly located)
Cell radius	Variable 10 to 20 m
Number and location of users	Variable 5 to 35 users per cell uniformly distributed
Cell maximum capacity	100
User load	Variable with uniform distribution Average = 5 PRB
User speed	Variable with uniform distribution Average = 30 km/h
Carrier frequency	2 GHz
Bandwidth	20 MHz
Small cell transmit power	23 dBm
Noise power spectral density (PSD)	−174 dBm/Hz
Path loss (in dB)	140.1 + 36.7 Log10 (distance in km)
Log normal shadowing mean value	4 dB

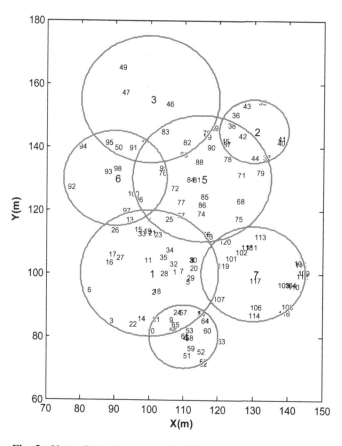

Fig. 3. Network topology example with seven cells and 120 users

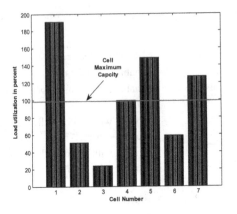

(a) No MLB

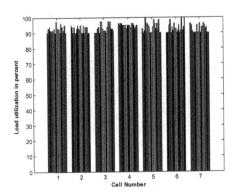

(b) After MLB-KO

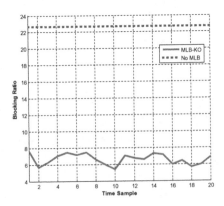

(c) Blocking Ratio

Fig. 4. Comparison of the blocking ratio before and after MLB-KO for the seven cell scenario

A more challenging use case is now considered with a seven small cell scenario and 120 users unevenly distributed as illustrated in Fig. 3. A summary of main simulation parameters is presented in Table 2.

Figure 4 shows the load distribution for each of the seven cells (a) before and after MLB-KO (b). Figure 4(c) shows the variation in BR resulting from path loss dynamics due to shadowing and users' speed with sampling time. It is concluded that the MLB-KO technique achieves approximately 3.5 times improvement in blocking ratio compared to the case where no MLB scheme is implemented for the studied seven cell scenario.

4 Conclusions

A new approach for user association and MLB in dense small cells based on Knapsack Optimisation was presented. Example simulation scenarios targeting dense small cells deployments show that the MLB-KO technique is capable of achieving three to four times improvement in blocking ratios compared with the case where no MLB strategy is deployed in a network or a cluster of small cells. The generality of the technique makes it suitable to support multi-tenancy and the vision for Small Cells as a Service (SCaaS) as advocated by the SESAME project. The future work aims at comparing the performance of MLB-KO with enhanced Inter Cell Interference Cancellation (eICIC) techniques relying on Cell Range Expansion (CRE) and Almost Blank Subframes (ABS) and investigating signaling overheads.

References

1. Hossein, E., Hassan, M.: 5G cellular: key enabling technologies and research challenges. IEEE Instrum. Meas. Mag. **18**, 11–21 (2015)
2. Huawei White Paper: The second phase of LTE-Advanced LTE-B: 30-fold capacity boosting to LTE (2013)
3. Anpalagan, A., Bennis, M., Vnnithamby, R.: Design and Deployment of Small Cell Networks. Cambridge University Press, Cambridge (2016)
4. Fehske, A.J., Viering, I., Voigt, J., Sartori, C., Redana, S., Fettweis, G.P.: Small-cell self-organizing wireless networks. Proc. IEEE **102**(3), 334–350 (2014)
5. Real Wireless Ltd.: An assessment of the value of small cell services to operators. Based on Virgin Media trials, October 2012. http://www.realwireless.biz/small-cells-as-a-service-trials-report/
6. Small cEllS coordinAtion for Multi-tenancy and Edge services (SESAME). http://www.sesame-h2020-5g-ppp.eu/
7. Hamalainen, S., Sanneck, H., Sartori, C.: LTE Self Organizing Networks (SON). Wiley, Hoboken (2012)
8. Ramiro, J., Hamied, K.: Self-organizing Networks: Self-planning, Self-optimization and Self-healing for GSM. UMTS and LTE. Wiley, Hoboken (2012)
9. Gelabert, X., Pérez-Romero, J., Sallent, O., Agustí, R., Casadevall, F.: Radio resource management in heterogeneous networks. In: 3rd International Working Conference on Performance Modelling and Evaluation of Heterogeneous Networks, HET-NETs 2005, July 2005

10. Ruiz-Avilés, J.M., et al.: Analysis of limitations of mobility load balancing in a live LTE system. IEEE Wirel. Commun. Lett. **4**(4), 417–420 (2015)
11. GPP TR 36.839: Mobility Enhancements in HetNets, V11.1.0 (2012)
12. Liu, D., et al.: User association in 5G networks: a survey and an outlook. IEEE Commun. Surv. Tutor. **18**(2), 1018–1044 (2016). Second Quarter
13. Mesodiakaki, A., Adelantado, F., Alonso, L., Verikoukis, C.: Energy efficient context-aware user association for outdoor small cell heterogeneous networks. In: Proceedings of the IEEE International Conference on Communications (ICC), pp. 1614–1619, June 2014
14. Corroy, S., Falconetti, L., Mathar, R.: Dynamic cell association for downlink sum rate maximization in multi-cell heterogeneous networks. In: Proceedings of the IEEE International Conference on Communications (ICC), pp. 2457–2461, June 2012
15. Zhou, H., Mao, S., Agrawal, P.: Approximation algorithms for cell association and scheduling in femtocell networks. IEEE Trans. Emerg. Top. Comput. **3**(3), 432–443 (2015)
16. Madan, R., Borran, J., Sampath, A., Bhushan, N., Khandekar, A., Ji, T.: Cell association and interference coordination in heterogeneous LTE-A cellular networks. IEEE J. Sel. Areas Commun. **28**(9), 1479–1489 (2010)
17. Viering, I., Dottling, M., Lobinger, A.: A mathematical perspective of self-optimizing wireless networks. In: IEEE International Conference on Communications, ICC 2009, pp. 1–6, June 2009
18. Corroy, S., Falconetti, L., Mathar, R.: Dynamic cell association for downlink sum rate maximization in multi-cell heterogeneous networks. In: 2012 IEEE International Conference on Communications (ICC), pp. 2457–2461, June 2012
19. Lopez-Perez, D., Guvenc, I., de la Roche, G., Kountouris, M., Quek, T.Q.S., Zhang, J.: Enhanced intercell interference coordination challenges in heterogeneous networks. IEEE Wirel. Commun. **18**(3), 22–30 (2011)
20. Lobinger, A., Stefanski, S., Jansen, T., Balan, I.: Load balancing in downlink LTE self-optimizing networks. In: 2010 IEEE 71st Vehicular Technology Conference (VTC 2010-Spring), pp. 1–5, May 2010
21. Munoz, P., Barco, R., Laselva, D., Mogensen, P.E.: Mobility-based strategies for traffic steering in heterogeneous networks. IEEE Commun. Mag. **51**(5), 54–62 (2013)
22. Martello, S., Toth, P.: Knapsack Problems: Algorithms and Computer Implementations. Wiley, Hoboken (1990)

Author Index

Printed in the United States
By Bookmasters